DISARMED

AND

DANGEROUS

DISARMED

AND

DANGEROUS

The Radical Lives and Times of Daniel and Philip Berrigan

MURRAY POLNER AND **JIM O'GRADY**

WestviewPress

A Division of HarperCollinsPublishers

Grateful acknowledgment is made for the following sources:

Excerpts from "Homage to Mistress Bradstreet" from *Collected Poems 1937–1971*, by John Berryman. Copyright © 1989 by Kate Berryman. Reprinted by permission of Farrar, Straus & Giroux.

Excerpts from "America" from *Collected Poems 1947–1980* by Allen Ginsberg. Copyright © 1956, 1959 by Allen Ginsburg. Copyright renewed. Reprinted by permission of HarperCollins Publishers, Inc.

Paperback edition copyright © 1998 by Westview Press, A Division of HarperCollins Publishers, Inc.
Hardcover edition copyright © 1997 by Murray Polner and Jim O'Grady. Published by BasicBooks, A Division of HarperCollins Publishers, Inc.

Published in 1997 in the United States of America by Westview Press, 5500 Central Avenue, Boulder, Colorado 80301-2877, and in the United Kingdom by Westview Press, 12 Hid's Copse Road, Cumnor Hill, Oxford OX2 9JJ

Designed by Elliott Beard

Library of Congress Cataloging-in-Publication Data
Polner, Murray.
    Disarmed and dangerous : the radical lives and times of Daniel and Philip Berrigan / by Murray Polner and Jim O'Grady. —1st ed.
        p.   cm.
    Includes bibliographical references and index.
    ISBN 0-465-03084-X (hc).—0-8133-3449-7 (pb)
    1. Berrigan, Daniel.   2. Berrigan, Philip.
3. Catholics—United States—Biography.   I. O'Grady
Jim.   II. Title
BX4705.B3845P65   1998
322.4'4'092273—dc20
[B]   96-25804

The paper used in this publication meets the requirements of the American National Standard for Permanence of Paper for Printed Library Materials Z39.48-1984.

10   9   8   7   6   5   4   3

A friend loveth at all times,
and a brother is born for adversity.

Proverbs 17:17

CONTENTS

ACKNOWLEDGMENTS

WE ARE DEEPLY GRATEFUL FOR THE COURTESIES EXTENDED US by James Tyler and the Daniel and Philip Berrigan Collection, #4602, Division of Rare and Manuscript Collections, Cornell University Library. Thanks, too, to Philip Runkel at the Catholic Worker Collection, Marquette University; Reverend Peter Hogan, S.S.J., and the St. Joseph Society Archive; the Swarthmore College Peace Collection and its curator, Wendy Chmielowski, for the Harrisburg Defense Committee Papers as well as the Anne Morrissett Papers and William Davidon Papers; the Great Neck, New York, Library for its extensive collection and cooperation in obtaining interlibrary loans; the State University of New York at Buffalo, Lockwood Memorial Library; Richard Carbray for the Richard Carbray Collection, University of Washington Library, and Lucy Ostrander, our researcher there; Kent Yates and Lynn Hanson at the University of Illinois Library; Charles Meconis for his mid-1970s interviews with members of the Catholic Left; the State Historical Society of Wisconsin Library for the John Schuchardt Papers; the Lawyers' Committee on Nuclear Policy; the Lyndon Baines Johnson Library for the Ramsey Clark Papers, and our researcher, Diana Claitor; Elmer Maas and the Kairos Community Archive; Bill Roberge and the Federal Bureau of Investigation

Reading Room; the New York Public Library; The Free Library of Philadelphia; St. John's University, Staten Island Campus Library; the Enoch Pratt Library, Baltimore; Robert E. Daggy and the Thomas Merton Center of Bellarmine College; the Merton Archives at Boston College; and St. Aloysius Church and Tricia Sullivan of Pax Christi, both in Washington, D.C.

Thanks also to those who graciously shared their unpublished letters, manuscripts, memoirs, and papers: John Bach; Daniel Berrigan, S.J.; Philip Berrigan; Richard Cusack; Richard Deats; John Deedy; Barbara Dougherty; Douglas Dowd, the Reverend Michael Doyle; David Eberhardt; Jim Forest; John Theodore Glick; Patrick Henry; Robert Blair Kaiser; Dr. George McVey; James Matlack; Dean Pappas; and Jonathan Roberts.

We thank those who granted us interviews or assisted us in other ways with this book: Elliott M. Abramson; Liza Apper; John Bach; Betty Bartelme; Paul Baumann; Zoe L. Belth; James Berrigan; Carol Berrigan; Frida Berrigan; Jerome Berrigan; Rosalie Berrigan; Jason Berry; Greg Boertje-Obed; Jill Boskey; the Reverend Bill Brisotti; Anna Brown; Bishop Charles Buswell; Daniel Callahan; Richard Carbray; Harry James Cargas; Bill Carrington; Barry Cassidy; Esther Cassidy; Gene Chenoweth; Ramsey Clark; the Reverend Frank Cordaro; Tom Cornell; Joe Cosgrove; Patrick Cotter; J. Shane Creamer; Earl Crow; Joseph Cunneen; Sally Cunneen; Richard Cusack; Mary Daly; Bruce Dancis; Ann Morrissett Davidon; William Davidon; the Reverend John Dear, S.J.; Richard Deats; John Deedy; Ellen DeMott; Peter DeMott; Julie Diamond Ahmad; Frank Donovan; Barbara Dougherty; Michael Dougherty; James W. Douglass; Douglas Dowd; the Reverend Michael Doyle; Richard Drinnon; David Eberhardt; Eileen Egan; Daniel Ellsberg; Robert Ellsberg; the Reverend Thomas Farrelly; Pat Farren; Dan Finlay; Linda Finlay; James Finn; James (Jim) Forest; Daniel Freudenberger; John F. Gaffney; Edward Gargan; Charles A. Glackin; John Theodore Glick; Peter Goldberger; John C. Goodwin; John Peter Grady; Bishop Thomas Gumbleton; Richard Haas; Dean Hammer; Reverend John Heidbrink; Patrick Henry; Susannah Heschel; Herman M. Heyn; Philip Hirschkop; John Hogan; Larry Holdfelder; Edward L. Holmgren; Zoia Horn; Robert Hoyt;

Susan Human; Patrick Jordan; Peter Jordan; Donna Poggi Keck; the Reverend Robert Keck, S.J.; Jim Kelly; Lee Kohns; Robert Kristiansen; the Reverend Dexter Lanctot; Terry Lenzner; John Leo; Harold Levy; the Reverend Jack Lewis; the Reverend James Loughran, S.J.; William Lynch; Elmer Maas; Elizabeth (Liz) McAlister; Patrick McCarthy; the Reverend Joseph McCloskey, S.J.; Peter McDonough; Vincent J. McGee; the Reverend William Hart McNichols, S.J.; David McReynolds; the Reverend Richard McSorley, S.J.; George McVey; James Magee; Rabbi Jerome Malino; Daniel Mark; Jack Marth; Douglas Marvy; James Matlack; Paul Mayer; Charles Meconis; the Reverend James Mengel; Bernard E. Meyer; William Michaels; Dennis Moloney; Sister Ann Montgomery; Mary Moylan; Joseph Mulholland; Sister Christine Mulready; James Munves; the Reverend Philip Murnion; the Reverend Edward Murphy, S.J.; Mickey Myers; the Reverend Richard John Neuhaus; the Reverend Earl Newman, S.S.J.; Jim Noonan; the Reverend Fred O'Connor, S.J.; William O'Connor; Bill Offenloch; the Reverend Henry Offer, S.S.J.; James O'Gara; Patrick O'Neill; Joseph O'Rourke; Dean Pappas; Jonathan Parfrey; Joseph Pickle; Vinnie Quayle; Stephen Riley; the Reverend Joseph Roccosalvo, S.J.; Lin M. Romano; Molly Rush; Stephen Sachs; Rabbi David Saperstein; Margaret Saraco; Stewart Schaar; Karen Schiff; John Schuchardt; Bob Schwartz; Monsignor Frank Scollen; Martin Sheen; Edward Skillin; Bob Smith; Samuel F.H. Smith; Fred Solway; Margaret O'Brien Steinfels; Peter Steinfels; the Reverend Alden Stevenson, S.J.; Bishop Walter F. Sullivan; Sue Susman; John Swomley; Marcia Timmel; the Reverend David Toolan, S.J.; Carmen Trotta; Michael True; Arthur Waskow; Sue Wesselkamper; DeAnne Mimms Pappas West; Grenville Whitman; Roger Wilkes; John Williams; the Reverend Charles Winans, S.J.; Bill Wylie-Kellerman; Sister K.C. Young, O.P.; Gordon Zahn; and Howard Zinn. A number of interviewees preferred to remain anonymous.

Thanks, too, to Mark Abrahams for providing a copier and file cabinets; to James and Madeline O'Grady for all their support; and to the Staten Island AIDS Task Force, enlightened employer.

Special mention must be made of Jerry and Carol Berrigan, and Jim and Rosalie Berrigan, for their unsparing hospitality and the loan of family photos (as well as for their patient understanding after a neighbor's dog ate several original prints). We are also indebted to Daniel Berrigan, S.J., and Philip Berrigan for granting permission to use their published and unpublished materials, for never interfering, never trying to influence our interpretations, never asking to see anything we wrote, and for making themselves available for interviews. For this they have our deep respect.

Our warmest thanks to friends who read all or parts of the book in manuscript: Joseph Cunneen; Herman Eberhardt; Jim Forest; Louise Polner; Patrick Jordan; the Reverend Raymond A. Schroth, S.J.; Adam Simms; and Michael True. Obviously, all errors are ours alone. Thanks to our agent Philip Spitzer; and for invaluable guidance provided by our editors, Steve Fraser and Chris Korintus, as well as Richard Fumosa and Chris Goff at HarperCollins. Finally, apologies to any person or institution we may have forgotten to acknowledge.

PROLOGUE

"HOW DO THEY KEEP GOING?"

We taste the spices of Arabia, yet never feel the scorching sun which brings them forth.

—*Sir Dudley North*

TOWARD THE END OF LENT, ON A SPRING DAY UNDER A FALTERING sun, Daniel Berrigan walks a Manhattan sidewalk on a routine errand that will end, as he intends, with his arrest. Actually, he processes. He is one among some 2,000 solemn Catholics performing the Stations of the Cross along the Via Dolorosa of Forty-second Street on Good Friday. Around him, Latin chants lift on a breeze that flutters pennants bearing painted crosses swaying above the marchers' heads, in what looks and sounds like a medieval pilgrimage during rush hour. This "Peace Walk," crossing the city from the United Nations to the offices of a Pentagon defense contractor, is a traditional enactment of the Passion and Death of Christ. But unlike common observances of the rite, each Station is

1

linked to a controversial social justice issue. For example, "Jesus Is Stripped of His Garments," the Ninth Station, is held on a block near Times Square crammed with commercial pornography. It is all very much in the Berrigan style of public demonstration: a fusion of venerated Catholic ritual with acutely modern concerns, with an emphasis on the redemptive power of sacrificial suffering. And, in the Berrigan vein, it is grandly cinematic, concluding with time spent in a precinct with several followers and friends.

It is 1995: forty-three years since Berrigan's ordination, at age thirty-one, as a Jesuit priest; twenty-seven years—including eighteen trying months in federal prison—after his arrest for burning Vietnam War draft files with eight others in Catonsville, Maryland; and fifteen years from the morning that he, his brother Philip, and six others strolled through the front doors of a General Electric plant in King of Prussia, Pennsylvania, hammered and poured human blood on an unarmed nuclear warhead, then prayed aloud while awaiting arrival of the FBI and state and county police.

He wears these credentials lightly, but unmistakably. His weathered face is amply creased and his lips are primly pursed, like a Confucian mulling a paradox, as he leaves the crowd to cross the street with thirteen fellow activists. At seventy-three years old, he has skipped the greater part of the Peace Walk (starting at 8:30 A.M. and lasting four hours, it is something of an endurance test), joining it near the end. He appeared around the time someone mounted a flatbed truck, the procession's portable stage, and recited into a microphone, *"Eloi, Eloi, lama sabachtani?"*—Christ's famous wail to heaven, "My God, my God, why have you forsaken me?"—a signal for the thousands to fall to their knees in a dirty parking lot near the Port Authority Bus Terminal, observing a moment of silence to complete the Twelfth of Fourteen Stations, "Jesus Dies on the Cross."

The crowd has now moved a hundred yards farther west in the direction of Ninth Avenue, and cheers as Berrigan and his group walk into a green granite building at 330 West 42nd Street. They are headed for the ground-floor offices of the Riverside Research Institute, commonly labeled a "Star Wars Think Tank" by people opposed to it. (Riverside claims this may have been true in the past when it did some work for the Strategic Defense Initiative, but not anymore, though it does admit to still conducting systems support for Defense Department weapons programs.[1]) The thirteen cross a dim lobby to the institute's thick glass doors, then sit in a knot on the floor. Berrigan, in the middle of them, looks collected. He's been through this before.

The protesters are immediately surrounded by the New York City police, who have been expecting them, and the building's security officers, walkie-talkies cackling. Either by chance or by tacit agreement between the organizers and the cops, the protesters get a couple of minutes to explain their unlawful presence. Anna Brown, a young instructor at St. Peter's College in Jersey City, stands up next to the centerpiece prop, a podium bearing a brilliant white Easter lily. She reads from "A Devout Meditation in Memory of Adolf Eichmann," an essay by the Trappist monk Thomas Merton, who before his death in 1968 had been one of Berrigan's closest friends. The passage she chooses reiterates Hannah Arendt's observation that the majority of the century's many mass murderers have had much in common with the mental and emotional makeup, even the behavior, of the citizenry that produced them: Dutiful, "sane," and "without anxiety," they win public respect for active devotion to the state-sanctioned cause of the day—which, of course, in Nazi Germany meant assembly-line genocide. Lenny Bruce used to mock the pretensions of blind authoritarianism by reading this same Merton essay in a thick German accent at the end of his nightclub act; Brown means it to reflect similarly on the government research going on behind the glass doors.

> The sanity of Eichmann is disturbing. We equate sanity with a sense of justice, with humaneness, with prudence, with the capacity to love and understand other people. We rely on the sane of the world to preserve it from barbarism, madness, destruction. And now it begins to dawn on us that it is precisely the sane ones who are the most dangerous.

Brown doesn't get very far before the officer-in-charge breaks in with a warning that she and the others are "trespassing at the present time on private property and will be duly arrested if you do not leave the premises." Nobody moves; Brown continues.

> Eichmann was sane. The generals and fighters on both sides, in World War II, the ones who carried out the total destruction of entire cities, these were the sane ones. Those who have invented and developed atomic bombs, thermonuclear bombs, missiles; who have planned the strategy of the next war; who have evaluated the various possibilities of using bacterial and chemical agents: these are not the crazy people, they are the sane people. The ones who coolly estimate how many millions of victims can be considered expendable in a nuclear war, I presume they do all right with Rorschach ink blots too. On the other hand, you will probably find that the pacifists and the ban-the-bomb people are, quite seriously, just as we read in *Time*, a little crazy.[2]

A command is given and the police—who have also been through this before—move in to harvest these ban-the-bomb people in groups of five and four. Berrigan stands and cooperatively places his hands behind his back so his arresting officer can bind him with plastic cuffs. He is led outside to a police wagon where he steps up and in and wedges with the others onto one of two steel benches. Once everyone is loaded, the back doors slam and lock. Two cops enter the driver's cab and discuss the situation, but decide not to close the sliding door that would separate them from their prisoners—there aren't that many of them. During past Good Fridays—in the mid-1980s, say, when President Reagan was joking about nuclear first strikes—more than 120 people would come at the Riverside offices in waves, to be busted and escorted into overflowing wagons, then driven in total darkness through the streets, many standing pressed against other bodies they could feel but couldn't see, singing disjointed hymns, rocking in the claustrophobic space.

Not today. The group sits meekly as the wagon pulls into traffic. For a moment, through a corner of the windshield, one glimpses the crowd across the street as they strain at the blue police barricades, urging on their surrogates being carted off to jail. In seconds the sight is replaced by the weaving, oblivious midtown traffic.

Even contorted in handcuffed posture, Berrigan looks stylish. His fashion theme is basic black: pants, jacket, and rakish cotton cap, with an informal purple stole slung around his neck like an avant-garde flying ace. Protruding from the zipper of his jacket is a daisy. The demonstration organizers had arranged for the group to approach the lab with flowers in their fists. The others have dropped theirs in a pile on Riverside's steps, but Berrigan, with typical flair—or display, depending on one's attitude, and he inspires strong and disparate attitudes—has used one to garnish himself.

He has spent a lot of time in the second half of his life taking rides to precinct houses in dented and graffiti-marred wagons like this one, with blasts of depressing chatter piercing the static on the dashboard's two-way radio: "We've got four shots fired on an anonymous 911." Car horns blare as Berrigan listens politely to one of his comrades, an elderly woman with unruly hair, who addresses him incoherently on a subject that would seem to relate to vegetarianism; at the same time the officer near him waxes rapturously on the kill capacity of his newly issued 9-millimeter handgun. Some days it must take an act of faith just to show up for one of these things. But Berrigan also must see in the several young faces around him a sign that the ranks of the so-called nonviolent Christian resistance that he and his brother Philip have worked so long and hard to build—often in the midst of painful disagreements and defections—will be replenished, if only in trickles. And besides, when it comes to his favorite subject of the proper relation of religion to politics, this is his milieu.

One of the cops pokes his head back into the wagon. Like a steward on a cruise ship, he is expansive. "You all right? You doing OK? Is everybody happy?" he asks the perpetrators of alleged disorderly conduct. Berrigan smiles and answers with emphasis, *"I feel right at home."* The protesters near him indulge the joke with a round of knowing chuckles.

Disgorged into a waiting area of the Midtown South police precinct, the protesters surrender IDs in return for desk appearance tickets, which assign them various court dates for arraignment. The process normally takes a couple of hours and moves smoothly, but for Berrigan there is one hitch: While running a routine check on him, the police have found outstanding warrants. This is serious enough to delay his release while they consider whether to "put him through the system," a fairly dreadful prospect. It means Berrigan will spend a long day and night in Corrections Department custody, including transfer from the precinct to a detention center holding cell while his paperwork is churned through Central Booking. The warrants are for previous acts of civil disobedience in New York. They have probably been attached to his computer file by mistake—the records don't always keep up with the disposal of cases in court, especially for frequent offenders like Daniel Berrigan.

He is calm, though, and sits patiently at an absurdly undersized school desk, one of those oddball furnishings found in the warrens of municipal bureaucracies, before a cardboard American flag tacked to a corkboard. The protesters huddle around to lend support. His daisy has begun to wilt, and he seems to be resigning himself to a possibly rotten fate. Then, after forty minutes, his arresting officer struts across the room to announce that they have kindly decided to drop the warrants—the recidivist reverend can go home.

Berrigan brightens at the news. "My debt's been paid to society," he proclaims, as if to some vast assembled throng. Were this twenty years ago, when his and Phil's portraits made the cover of *Time*, and almost everyone in America had an opinion on the two, there would be a crush of supporters on the steps outside, among them photographers, documentary crews, and reporters straining to capture his every incendiary utterance. Today, he addresses a clutch of beaming allies in a desultory patrol room. "I'm a free man," he declares. Then, cracking an impish grin, he ends with a sly impromptu paradox, delivered on a note of self-conscious bravura: "I'm wearing an Easter smile on Good Friday!"

Four months later, in August, Berrigan and the group, having pleaded not guilty by mail, appear in the New York City Criminal Court on lower Broadway near City Hall. This is Room 158, where

Manhattan's petty offenders come to settle their charges, usually in one of three ways: by pleading guilty and taking their lumps, by claiming "not ready" and postponing their defense, or by asserting their innocence and accepting, after swift trial, something close to summary judgment. It is a narrow room with two rows of scarred blond benches. In faded gold letters on the wall above the judge's seat are the tired words, "In God We Trust," and to the side hangs an American flag on a tilted pike crowned by a brass eagle scowling and flexing its wings. The crowd is mostly poor and nonwhite; there are very few lawyers.

This court is not known for its friendly atmosphere. As the room fills up, the guards shout standard commands at random intervals, "All hats off," and "Take a seat, no standing in the back." When a man approaches a female guard with a question, she interrupts and projects her voice out over his head, "Sit down and listen to the instructions. You'll have your questions answered." When he persists, she loudly addresses the room, "Don't ask us how long it will take. You could be the first in line or the last one in this courtroom." He retreats to a bench, head lowered.

Daniel Berrigan sits bemused, chewing a toothpick. "I hope we get a war veteran. They're always the best," he jokes to a codefendant about the judge they might expect. Just back from vacation on Block Island, Rhode Island, he is tanned and relaxed, his black shirt collar open. Today's proceedings are what he calls "a granola and yogurt appearance," meaning routine—"It might get a little crunchy but it usually goes down smooth," especially compared to the judicial ordeals arising from the civil disobedience his brother continues to commit along the East Coast. Philip Berrigan has recently completed ten months in federal prison, at age seventy, for crawling through the woods with three others onto the Seymour Johnson Air Force Base in North Carolina and covering an empty F15 Strike Eagle fighter plane with blood and hammer blows.

One of the clerks commences a roll call. She reads off several names, then yells, "Daniel Berrigan?"

"Here," he responds.

"Ready for trial?"

"Yes ma'am."

Detecting an unacceptable level of flippancy in his answer, the clerk says, "What?"

"Yes," Berrigan repeats, amending his tone.

At this, a well-dressed man gets up and approaches Berrigan from the other side of the room. As the man, Harold Levy, later explains, "Here I am sitting on the 'Group W bench'—from the Arlo Guthrie song, 'Alice's Restaurant'—with the 'mother rapers' and the 'father rapers.' I'm there with my friend, who wanted someone to be with her for her minor violation (I'm a lawyer in the litigation department for Salomon Brothers). Here I am in my Wall Street blue suit, feeling like I had landed on Mars, and I hear the name, 'Daniel Berrigan' called, and I think, 'There can't be two of them in the world.' "

As a student at Cornell in the late 1960s, Levy had known Berrigan who was then a "religious employee" at United Religious Work, the campus's interfaith chaplaincy. Like many people touched by fame, Daniel Berrigan has made thousands of acquaintances over the years. They reappear, bearing the genial smiles of alumni, at almost any time or place. Levy bends to shake his hand, reminding him of their first meeting at a Cornell building takeover. "Oh yes," Dan remembers, and in response to Levy's query about his subsequent activities, says merrily, "Well, I've gone on to a life of crime."

"I must tell you," Levy later confides, "I felt terribly that I hadn't gone on to do the same." Then he reflects, as others have, on a couple of Berrigan's extraordinary traits: "Daniel Berrigan is a saintly man. It's odd that there isn't more of a place for saintly people in the world. By reputation and by experience, when I knew him at Cornell, he was tremendously difficult to deal with, very uncompromising. Saintliness does not bespeak politesse. It makes life both difficult and simple. When you follow your own moral compass, you're not pushed and pulled by the everyday pressures of life. You set your course hard and fast. You don't have the same complexity in your decisions."

He's right. Dan and Phil Berrigan don't worry themselves with domestic policy prescriptions, or make fine distinctions with regard to foreign affairs. When war breaks out, they decline to examine national causes in the light of the Catholic Church's "just war" theory, or on any pragmatic grounds. Not only that, they declare all government property connected to killing—from draft files to battleships—illegitimate, and therefore worthy of destruction. Work that abets the Pentagon must be exposed, they insist, and indicted for its "high crime" of taking bread from the mouths of the poor.[3] Very simply, they are religious pacifists who condemn every act of violence. "The death of a single human being is too heavy a price to pay for the vindication of any principle, however sacred,"[4] they contend, adding that every person of goodwill should refuse "to take up bombs or guns, aimed at the flesh of brothers and sisters, whom we persist in defining as such," and resist "the enmities pushed on us by war-making state or war-blessing church."[5] Their critics call them tedious scolds; and it is true they are sometimes guilty of a preening moral rectitude. But with a rare devotion to principle and a willingness to stand up to the consequences of their acts, they mean what they say.

Joe Cosgrove, the protesters' lawyer, walks in late. He left his home in Wilkes-Barre, Pennsylvania, more than two hours earlier to get to this courtroom, with which he is familiar. Four days after passing the bar in 1982, he tried his first case here: defending Daniel Berrigan and another group of protesters for an earlier attempt to block the doors of the Riverside Research Institute. He became close to Berrigan in the early 1980s, "completely outside the peace and justice context," when the priest ministered to his family during his mother's terminal illness. They stayed in touch, and Cosgrove wound up working for the defense team during the Berrigan brothers' lengthy "King of Prussia" (or "Plowshares Eight") trial.[6]

Through repeated appearances over thirteen years, Cosgrove is now familiar to the criminal court personnel. As a matter of fact, someone has tipped him that the judge is feeling magnanimous today, and may entertain an offer of adjournment contemplating dismissal, or an ACD—an agreement that the charges will be dropped on condition the protesters don't get arrested during the next six months (a stipulation Berrigan may well skirt, aware that this time the criminal justice computers can be counted on to botch up in his favor).

The group files out to the hall to talk things over. Berrigan stands a little bit back from the circle while his co-defendants parse the prospective deal. Though offered similar assurances in the past, groups of activists have been sent to Rikers Island prison for refusing to pay their court fees, considering them an unfair imposition on the poor, with whom they wished to act in solidarity. This group mulls probable outcomes to responses they might make, while noting that Rikers is an overcrowded and disagreeable place, especially during a rancid August heat wave. Berrigan grows impatient with the details of the discussion. He rolls his eyes and mutters cavalierly, "I think I can raise five bucks if that's what they want." They'll probably want closer to fifty bucks, and anyway, the question is whether to fork over even a penny to the court. But Berrigan's "moral compass" has apparently been set; contingencies have become for him a loathsome complexity. They decide that Jack Marth, another young Berrigan protege, will go before the bench and speak for the rest.

Informing the judge that his clients were engaged in a peaceful exercise of their First Amendment rights, Cosgrove suggests the case be dismissed. The judge wants to know what this protest was about. Marth explains that Riverside Institute is a research arm for Star Wars. The judge shoots back, "But isn't that a defensive weapon? Wouldn't that prevent the missiles from coming in?" Marth replies that no, it would actually be the strategic foundation for a nuclear first-strike attack. Then to the amazement of the courtroom crowd, the two men thrust and parry awhile over subjects such as "resource allocation" and "justifiable self-defense"— the judge getting slightly the better of their debate. Neither the exchange nor any part of this protest will appear in a single news report, but several dozen citizens have just been witness to a discussion on the morality of nuclear weapons. According to the Berrigans' creed of scattering seeds of "truth" and leaving to God the task of nurturing them, such an occurrence, on this day, is enough.

But is it worth the time and effort? This is one of the central questions of the Berrigans' public and, inevitably, because of the painful repercussions, private lives. Their answer rests on stubborn religious and personal conviction, as will be seen.

For them, the "living wine" of authentic existence is poured from "prisons and graves . . . set free by the disappeared and tortured who live at the heart of that darkness we name God."[7] Meaning, for one thing, that the victims of evil do not suffer and die in vain if others go forth resisting violence and oppression. This is, in the Berrigan view, the mandate of Christ's Cross: to overcome nonviolently what Dan calls "death as the social method of society."[8] Really, theirs is the righteous burden of redeeming sin itself—largely the organized kind that spawns "overkill . . . nuclear brinkmanship . . . racism," war, and poverty, among a host of social ills, and requires of those who dare resist it a habitually harsh self-sacrifice.[9] But of course, in the mouths of martyrs, the bitterest gall becomes ambrosia.

Yet even some Berrigan friends and admirers worry they give up too much in pursuit of their moral ideals. (Phil's most recent jailer, who called him "a man I respect" and "not a martyr," nevertheless visited Phil in his cell to plead that he "step aside and let the young lions take up" his vocation of hazardous protest.[10]) Others tell them to accept the role that their age and experience fits them for: radical sages who could inspire and guide a new generation of activists without necessarily going to prison themselves. After all, there is a time for prophetic showdowns, says veteran Catholic activist Tom Cornell (one of the first to burn his Vietnam War draft card), and a time for the painstaking work of "building the political institutions that will make the bomb impossible."[11] It is way too late, however, for the Berrigans to agree with Cornell's analysis.

Everyone gets an ACD with court fee waived. They walk a couple of blocks up Broadway and adjourn to tables at the back of a grease-stained deli. Over coffee and juice, they recount the morning's events and catch up on friendships. Many of them belong to an ecumenical community called Kairos—a Greek word for "a critical moment in time." Since the group was formed in the early 1980s, every moment has seemed critical to its members, partly because of the Berrigans' insistence that as long as the taproot evil of nuclear weapons exists, Christians, first of all, must place themselves bodily in their way.

Which raises a further question about the Berrigans. Since their 1968 burning of draft files in Catonsville, Maryland, during the height of the Vietnam War (not long after Phil had been convicted for pouring blood onto files at a Baltimore draft board), their sense of the times, like their tactics, hasn't changed. This leads Catholic pacifist and historian Gordon Zahn to say that the civil disobedience at the end of the Good Friday Peace Walk—and especially the higher-stakes "Plowshares" actions with their inevitably lengthy prison terms—yield "diminishing," or even self-defeating, returns.[12] Other activists agree, saying there are better approaches to peacemaking than getting locked up for hours to years at a time. The Berrigans counter that "imprisonment could hardly be more to the point."[13] Why? To rephrase Thoreau in Berrigan terms, how could one living under "sane" leaders threatening violence on a grotesque and epic scale do otherwise? And if the jails aren't yet overflowing with prisoners of conscience, as the Berrigans would like, so what? At least they're trying. "We resist because we believe and we believe because we resist,"[14] Dan writes. Their faith depends on their politics, and vice versa, the way their community of family and friends depends on the risks they share, to varying degrees, in trying to bring to bloom an actual paradise of disarmament.

Laughing and chatting, Dan basks in the warmth he feels for the group sitting with him at the pushed-together tables in the deli, several of them longtime friends. It is clear the others have affection for him, too—or, if new to the cause, a touch of awe. This is the kind of place he can go to be nurtured before resuming one or another of his embattled public stances, to be among those "who work hardily for social change," as he tends to glorify them, who "preach and embrace the unpalatable truth," who "overcome death, their lives bathed in the light of the resurrection,"[15] which on this day is a guttering fluorescent. After some personal catching up, he seems gratified as the talk now turns to an upcoming series of demonstrations in Washington, D.C., to mark the fiftieth anniversary of the bombings of Hiroshima and Nagasaki—much of it planned and carried out by Elizabeth McAlister and her husband, Philip Berrigan.

―――

If we are not on the road to heaven,
which is innocence, let us make sure
that we leave not the other road to
heaven, which is penance.
                    —*St. Aloysius Gonzaga, S.J.*

Elizabeth "Liz" McAlister, in the early morning of August 7, 1995, stands outside the south entrance to the Pentagon. She scans the nearby parking lot and looks down at a page on her beat-up clipboard, calculating as she scratches her chin between hurried drags of a cigarette, seemingly satisfied that events are progressing on or close to schedule. Around her lie the still and twisted corpses of Hiroshima, Japan, as portrayed by two dozen demonstrators heaped with ashes. Some have writhed in mortal torment as they joined their fellow casualties in the simulated slaughterhouse tableau; others have crawled before photo enlargements of disfigured Japanese, mingling their wails with the dirge from a kettledrum. "This is theater," McAlister instructed the group the night before at a planning session. "You can have a prolonged dying scene, you can gag and choke and act it out. Moaning, crying—this is good stuff."

McAlister's short white hair is bluntly cut, curling slightly at the edges of her pugilistic face, giving her somewhat the look of an ancient Roman general's sculpted bust, particularly when she surveys the lifeless forms spread out at her feet. Among them is her twenty-one-year-old daughter, Frida, a college student. Moments before, McAlister knelt over Frida and rested a gentle hand on her shoulder. The gesture was by design—other protesters moved among the bodies pretending to check for signs of life—but it was also unaffectedly maternal, as if she had come to that spot to protect her child, which, by leading this protest, she claimed in fact to be doing.

A thickening stream of Pentagon workers converges on the pile of the dead at the entrance plaza. They jam up, milling and wondering what to do, until security guards steer them through a seam in the blockade. A few bold workers with contemptuous strides move over and through the bodies. "People will come and kick you and grind their high-heeled shoes into you—but you have to take it because you're dead," McAlister quipped to the group while previewing "die-in" tactics. "It is also important to remember that these people are not the enemy. The employees of the Pentagon are not the enemy, and the police when they rope you off and drag you away are not the enemy. The violence has its roots deep in our hearts. So we must act in a way consistent with what we want to create: that is, peace."

"Why aren't you getting rid of these people?" one woman employee complains to a guard.

"They have a right to be here," he says.

"And we have a right to walk in!" she shouts. "And who the hell are they?"

They are approximately 200 people from several states and Canada who have gathered over the three previous weeks to demonstrate why nuclear weapons should "Never Again," as their T-shirts say, be dropped. They include a woman who once staffed a U.S. Pershing missile site in Europe; a tie-dyed couple who know Frida from high school (their assessment of her parents: "flaky but cool"); Liz and Phil's thirteen-year-old daughter, Katy, still wearing dental braces; "Spike" from San Antonio, a seventy-ish yellowbeard with a talismanic Alaskan stone that he plans to slip, Princess-and-the-Pea-like, under one of the building's corners; Dan Berrigan and the actor Martin Sheen, who gab while holding a banner reading "Choose Life—Abolish Weapons"; a World War II conscientious objector and former missionary to Nigeria, who describes himself as an "Iowa City Baptist"; a couple of Catholic nuns who have recently joined Phil and Liz's Jonah House in Baltimore; an environmentalist wearing rainbow-striped socks whose only religious affiliation is with the "First Church of the Old Growth Forest" ("I find God in nature," he redundantly observes); a pair of retired grandparents in floppy blue hats who have driven from Kalamazoo to get arrested; several members of past Plowshares actions against military facilities, like Phil's recent infiltration of the Seymour Johnson Air Force Base; and the various dozens loosely connected to the Atlantic Life Community, who travel to these protests when not running a soup kitchen or a homeless shelter, serving on a parish staff, consoling battered women, tending the dying in a hospice, or working at some other charitable, not-for-profit venture.

It is likely that had Phil and Liz gone on from their Vietnam War heyday to die violently, join a Wall Street firm, or overdose on drugs—as many of their high-profile contemporaries did—and failed to organize this most recent series of Pentagon demonstrations, some other event would have bewailed the fiftieth atomic anniversary. But this particular crowd would not be here.

In the 1960s, when picketing priests and ordinary churchgoers raiding draft boards were alarmingly novel, the media shunted people like these to a fringe called the "Catholic Left." Most of those described by the label never really liked it, though it positioned them on the political spectrum with their allies on several issues, including groups that championed civil rights while assailing the ills of "First World consumerist cultures" and the Vietnam War. But the motivation for their activism was, and remains, largely distinct from that of the classic American left. The majority of them, and certainly the Berrigans, were not Marxist, or even liberal. (Phil continues to express contempt for the "uselessness of legitimate dissent," a piece of scorn he heaped in print as early as 1967, as practiced by liberals toying fruitlessly with the civic order's "ineffectual grievance machinery";[16] and the brothers have consistently railed against communism as a system mirroring capitalism in its "gulping down" of consciences "whole and intact."[17]) They are more like abolitionists, in both their methods and their ultimate goals—radicals who break the law on pressing moral grounds. The people in this crowd at the Pentagon, then (with the exception of the tree-lover), that began forming around or in response to leaders like the Berrigans in the 1960s, derive their politics not so much from Jefferson or Mao as from Jesus.

This is far less unusual now than in the mid-1960s, when the Berrigans started to take to the streets, and Phil became the first

American priest to go to jail for giving political offense, back when joining "Catholic" to "Left" struck most as an oxymoron. These days, even the right, with zeal, has become civilly disobedient. But to their credit, the present-day "Catholic Resistance," still led by the Berrigans, continues to act with a disciplined nonviolence— even though they are bound to exchange a sizable chunk of their freedom for deeds leaving little discernible trace on the institutions they would subvert.

Again, so what? The Berrigans refuse to judge their acts on grounds of "worldly" effectiveness. They are more concerned with the mystery of developing and following their consciences, with "a kind of Buddhist truth," Dan writes, that "the good [is] to be done because it [is] good."[18] In the same Zen spirit, Spike sheds indirect light on the subject when asked what he thinks he'll accomplish by placing a pebble underfoot at the headquarters of the most powerful military giant in the history of the world.

"I imagine it will do the same thing a prayer does."

And what is that?

"What do prayers do? Hmmm. They do something, but what? We just don't know . . . Tell me, what do we really know about anything?"[19]

Not everyone is so sanguine about such questions of cause and effect. Take the sailor who responds to the offer of a leaflet from a protester with the following invitation: "Meet me later and I'll kick your ass." Most of his fellow employees, dressed in every shade of military garb—blue, tan, black, green, khaki, white, and fatigue— on their way to respectable, well-paying jobs, would seem to feel roughly the same. Abiding by eons of the commonplace wisdom that holds firm sway today, they, within a vast majority, believe in the use of force in self-defense. And that is the bedrock creed all pacifists hammer at. To do so is to question the definition of "sane" behavior in a world prone to madhouse violence. It means offering by word and example an alternative method of self-defense that works by converting an enemy's heart through what Gandhi and Martin Luther King Jr. exalted as the redemptive power of voluntary suffering.

"When I do serious actions," Phil observes, "they're not going to pat me on the back. They're going to lock me up."[20] He and Liz, with whom he has three children, have spent half of their twenty-four married years separated by prison. They do penance for the sins of the world because it puts them on the road to heaven, they say, to their sorrow and joy. In this they are ambitious in the old-fashioned way of saints, and for this they often appear—in the eyes of both left and right, not to mention the perpetually startled center—both exasperating and bizarre.

Like any set of visionaries, the Berrigans and their movement rely on a primary set of texts: from Deuteronomy, "Thou shalt not kill"; from Isaiah, "Beat swords into Plowshares" (hence the name of their Plowshares movement); and most scandalously, from Matthew's Gospel, "Love your enemies." They call these phrases "injunctions," and profess to fulfill them literally in their protests. They are Catholic to the marrow. Neoconservative Michael Novak, with the vehemence of a former ally, dismisses the Berrigans as "morally flawed" and "men too soon appalled" by a self-styled "politics of guilt."[21] But he allows that in the way they insinuate resonant Christian symbols like blood and fire into their protests, they turn them into religious acts. This is also one reason that, as were the early Christian liturgies, they are so disturbing.

In the plaza outside the Pentagon, the director of a Massachusetts "free meals ministry" named Tom Feagley pulls a plastic jar out of his pocket, unscrews the cap, and dashes dark red blood on the pavement in the spaces between the bodies. It takes only seconds, but he is tackled before he can finish. Two hulking security guards kneel on the square of his back, pressing his chest to the ground as they twist his arms behind his back, cuff him, and drag him across the plaza to a van marked "Defense Protective Service." Then a pair of well-drilled janitors wearing rubber gloves and jumpsuits, with tanks of bleach strapped to their backs, scurry out to disinfect the spill, enacting a metaphor too obvious to resist: dissent as contagion. They squirt frantically at the potentially infectious substance, fanning it out, and in their haste splash bleach on the hair and clothes of the protesters on the ground.

It is alarming to see a pool of human blood. A sense of emergency takes hold, an atavistic quickening at this sight of the violation of some dangerous taboo. One grasps the point being dramatized: Blood shed through violence is a trespass of the fundamental moral prohibition against murder. But that doesn't make it any less disconcerting.

If one of the goals of pouring the blood is to jolt the Pentagon workers into a sudden realization of the humanity of Hiroshima's victims—and, by extension, all civilian casualties of war—it doesn't work. Already inclined to view the demonstrators as a raucous bunch of freaks, those who see the blood spilled merely seem to be repulsed, as they are by the new round of anguished keening some of the women on the ground take up. Had McAlister or the others checked journalist John Hersey's account of the hours immediately following the dropping of the first atomic bomb, they would have been reminded that one of the heartrending peculiarities of Hiroshima was the way the dazed people suffered and died by the thousands in silence. And had it expressed that historical truth, their protest might have gained a bit in impact and dignity.

"Let's face it," Phil replies to such qualms. "You had trouble with us acting at all."[22] If nothing else, he is convinced that objecting courteously to the Pentagon is a futile middle-class gesture with the social impact of a carefully worded letter to the *New York Times*. The point is to shock. Not surprisingly, at the same time the bodies are falling in front of the Pentagon, Phil is elsewhere helping to do just that. Simultaneous Plowshares actions are occurring on each American coast: Two activists—a woman and a Catholic priest—enter the Martin Lockheed Trident manufacturing site in Sunnyvale, California, where they hammer and throw blood on parts and plans for a nuclear missile; and in Newport News, Virginia, four others cut a hole in a fence and show similar disrespect for the USS *Greeneville*, a nuclear submarine.

Phil does not risk arrest himself, but he has spent many days over the past ten months in shepherding both groups to the brink of their acts, which will probably earn their members serious jail time. Later that evening, Phil calls Liz to share the details, which she relays to the fifty-seven people who, after their Pentagon witness, have gathered in a Washington chapel with a group of supporters. *"Good news!"* she announces, alluding to the Greek root of the word "gospel," a reference her listeners appreciate. "In a pair of Plowshares actions today, two groups used hammers and the symbol of blood against weapons of mass destruction." The faithful whoop and cheer. The next day, as is customary, neither action is mentioned in a single national news story.

"The beauty of Dan and Phil for me is their anger," says a Jesuit priest with watery eyes, a recovering alcoholic, while vesting for early Mass the following morning in the basement of an inner-city Washington, D.C., church. He brings the white stole to his priestly lips and imparts a thoughtful kiss. "They have lived with that anger, whether or not it's consumed them," he goes on, after a pause in which he seems to compare a few notes with his past. Then he looks off into the middle distance and asks with genuine wonder, "How do they keep going?" Contending with that question entails, for one thing, exploring the Berrigan anger, its quality and its roots— and the brothers' rare accomplishments as a result of and despite it. And that leads to their childhood.

1

PATER UNFAMILIAS

. . . tireless I phrase
anything past, dead, far,
sacred, for a barbarous place.
—To please your wintry father?
                    —*John Berryman*

IN HIS 1987 AUTOBIOGRAPHY, *TO DWELL IN PEACE*, DANIEL Berrigan suggests that the curtain rise of a play about his life would reveal this stage set: the weathered porch of a tar-paper shack under a blinding winter sky, decorated with an old tin washtub hanging from a nail. At the edge of the porch, a four-year-old boy dangles damaged, sticklike legs down the steps of a stoop. Immobile, and with little to do, the boy squints into the void of a too-bright light. This is his introduction to the world, and the world's to him. He is a "midge . . . in a frozen landscape," a figure dabbed on a Japanese painting to lend meaning and scale through its insignificance. Static, spare, and mute, it's a curiously drab beginning for a drama. Or a life.[1]

21

Enter the father. His long strides carry him squarely to center stage. To a boy's eyes, he is a sinewy giant who drives steam-engine locomotives across the snow-choked wastes of northern Minnesota, which takes him away for weeks at a time. Returned from another extended run, he is wearing his railroad uniform: overalls and black steel-buttoned high-top boots, a striped cap, and a cinder-singed kerchief knotted at the throat. He pulls from the pocket of his blue cambric shirt a gold watch on a chain—a seventeen-jewel Hamilton that looks almost dainty in his workman's hands—and checks the time. There is work to do.

Tom Berrigan knows no Sabbath, so there is always work to do. He has grown up the oldest boy in a family of ten on a fatherless farm, has dropped out after a year of college to drift from job to job, and now has a wife and six young sons to feed. The Berrigan family's company shack in the isolated town of Winton is perched near the bottom of Basswood Lake, which spills across the border into Canada. Winter approaches. To cut the wind and keep foraging bears at bay, Tom will need to encircle the house with a two-foot mound of packed leaves held in place by a wood-plank barricade. The boy has seen his father work cunning wonders from simple materials before—he is ingenious with tools and radiates force and physical competence, confirming him in the family's undisputed leading role, despite his lengthy absences.

Tom looks around the yard to see what needs fixing. His deep-set eyes have the sour look of a scratch farmer scanning unpromising skies. He turns to Daniel, the fifth of six boys, and the only one not brimmingly robust, whose ankles fold when he tries to walk, requiring him to strap on gawky prescription shoes and undergo various rites of specialized care, like the spoonful of mint-flavored cod liver oil his mother insists on feeding him every day. He is a skinny kid with a button nose pinched by awkward metal glasses, who looks up shyly at his father.

"Mama's boy," the father spits, disgusted, "little four-eyes!"

"Leave 'im alone—he's fine!" his wife, Freda, shouts as she enters the yard with their two-year-old, Philip, balanced on her hip.[2]

Freda releases Philip to play with the windup train he has pulled from its secret hiding place in an old gray steamer trunk. She already knows this youngest child will be all right. He is healthy, untroubled, and big for his age—like the four oldest Berrigan sons—and for the most part should be pleasing to his father. Daniel, on the other hand, needs protection. Freda and her mother, Grandmother Fromhart, try to defend the boy from Tom's periodic fits against his frailty: his church-mouse eyesight and house-pale arms and the enfeebled will, according to Tom, that actually cripples him. Freda tries to reason with her husband. Her mother wastes no words with appeals to decency.

"Taam, you do a *sindt*!" she scolds in a thick German accent on rounding the house.[3]

To the devoutly Catholic Tom, this is more than a casual charge. As a self-styled bringer of Christian civilization to the dark woods of the frontier, he feels that his authority rests on a record of spotless virtue. And this is precisely what Grandmother Fromhart attacks in accusing him—as a woman, no less, an affront in itself—of *doing a sin*. All of which temporarily shuts him up.

Now Grandmother Fromhart picks up Daniel and carries him to a blanket spread over a sunny patch of grass. She gently removes the expensive shoes she has bought him with her savings. They are exotic-looking contraptions made of whalebone struts encased in heavy leather—one of the few store-bought items on the Berrigan's modest homestead. They might as well be opera glasses at the bottom of a coal mine, for all the impracticality they represent to Tom. Unlike a scythe, a hammer, or a washtub, they accomplish no immediate task related, in the strictest sense, to survival. They are superfluous to the harsh setting of the 1925 Minnesota frontier, a place unkind to any but the strong. If his childhood and work life have taught Tom any creed, it is that the world makes few allowances for infirmity. In fact, it looks for weakness to exploit. One either keeps pace or is left behind—as with the migrating herds that pass through the northern range each year, which the Berrigans sometimes resemble during Tom's long searches for work. It's never too soon to learn that in the unforgiving world of "the whistle's shriek and the clang of steel," only "the rude harsh strains of honest toil" are to be "honored as a power to make boys men,"[4] as Tom extols at length in his unpublished poetry. Anything less is womanly pampering.

Away with maudlin kindness, then,

he has written in another poem, in which he venerates the father's task of personifying the heartless world to his sons.

And more the kindness of the rod,
For duty owed our fellowmen
Is often stern as that owed God.[5]

Freda doesn't share her husband's urgency for toughening up their offspring. For the rest of his life, Dan would recall that "illness, physical incapacity of any kind, always brought my mother swiftly on the scene and kept her there. With my father, it was exactly the opposite. He wanted nothing short of perfection"—a clearly impossible standard to which Dan and Phil, in subtle ways, still cling. Freda and her mother, however, have worked out the tactics of what Dan describes as a tentative "slave rebellion." They stand against Tom during key disputes, especially over childrearing, a subject about which women have some say. And, defiantly, they converse in his presence in German.[6]

His father would turn what Daniel remembers as "Superman's frosty eye" on him as Grandmother Fromhart gathered one of his bare feet in her hands. She could sympathize with the wobble in his ankles. She had a limp herself from breaking her leg once while stepping from a streetcar into a ditch. She is also an experienced frontier nurse. By several family accounts, she protected the older boys from the worldwide influenza epidemic when it swept through the region seven years earlier. Lately she sits with Daniel for an hour or more each day, singing in German while massaging his feet and legs. Her program of healing is to fix him in a sunbeam while working his limbs with her "big-boned and vigorous" hands. And gradually it works. Daniel grows stronger. With love and will and uncommon persistence she knits his tissue and muscle and bones together. Soon, at about the age of five, he'll be taking his first shaky steps. Then he'll start to walk, and not long after, he'll be running and playing with brothers Phil and Jerry. In time, he'll join the cheerleading squad for his high school basketball team, mainly to root for its captain, the multisport star, Phil.

But these developments are years and several family moves away. For now, Tom leaves to change from one set of workclothes to another. Freda, seeing Daniel content and Philip lost in play, walks deliberately to the porch and lifts the washtub from its nail. She has a typical day of chores ahead: washing and scrubbing, drying, ironing, and folding the family wash; canning quarts of homegrown food (like pickled chicken); and sewing heavy clothes for the boys— Tom Jr., John, Jim, Jerry, Dan, Phil—herself, and Tom. Money is tight, jobs are perpetually scarce, and winter approaches.

2

———

BLOODLINE

There are no boundaries dividing
reality from unreality. Workers descend
into the mine, weavers spin branches
of ivy, explorers take paths that end at
a wall, ironworkers smelt the sun into
an improbable dawn.
    —*Adriana Bianco, "Immigrants*
        in the Land of Imagination"

IN THE 1890S, WHEN FREDA WAS A GIRL GROWING UP IN THE thickly forested hill country north of Lake Superior, the snow at times would pile in drifts up to the eaves of the family cabin. Then bears would come and walk on the roof. On nights when the temperature fell to 30 or 40 degrees below zero, travelers and Indians came in to sleep by the stove on the kitchen floor. Across the lake, wolves howled, waiting for the waters to freeze. One night, Freda's bored Aunt Alice sang counterpoint to the baying wolves with an intrepid rendition of "Danny Boy." It's hard to imagine a more baleful two-part harmony.

The Fromharts clung to forty acres they'd staked out under the federal Homestead Act. Freda's parents, Wilhelm and Louise, were among the first in their families to emigrate from Germany to America. Freda lived on the family "claim" from the age of five until roughly a year after the day she met Tom Berrigan, a "handsome bucko" she was probably introduced to at a dance. In a photo, Freda wears a dark dress with a white lace collar and a plain metal cross on a chain. She smiles, but her eyes are serious, bearing the "level look she casts on life," in Dan's later words, "weighing her chances against the world."[1] A reader of novels, she was also fond of opera, and familiar with the names of the divas on the concert and stage show circuits. She attended the theater after her day shift as a telephone operator, decked out in full-length gowns and extravagant hats of her own design. Her youth was for the most part sunny (though clouded now and then by the deaths of relatives) until the day a voluble railroad man, in his own words, "puffed through" town.[2]

Tom and Freda Berrigan were married on June 21, 1911, by a Slovenian missioner named Joseph Buh, the formidable pastor of Ely, Minnesota—population, "1,900 souls." The monsignor, who sported a forked white beard that made him look like Moses, was known to the local iron-ore miners as "Apostle of the Red-Gold Diggers," and to the area's Chippewa Indians, whose language he spoke and whose lodges he slept in, as a Catholic priest of uncommon tolerance.[3] Freda thought him a holy man, and took his presence at her wedding as a favorable omen. The service would have taken place at St. Anthony's Church—a monument to Buh's and the church's ambitious evangelization of the region. Before Ely had a paved main road, it had St. Anthony's Church, boasting stained glass windows, thousand-pound bells, and a 125-foot steeple inlaid with a chiming clock from Buh's Balkan homeland.[4] The groom, age thirty-two, had a couple of railroad friends on his side of the aisle; the bride, age twenty-five, had many close family members attending. The difference lay in the disparate roads they had traveled to that altar.

Freda Fromhertz (the family's pre-immigration name) was born and baptized in the southern Black Forest in 1886. The name of her village is forgotten, though when Dan paid it a visit in the spring of 1953, he reported that "in the churchyard there were memorials to family members of times immemorial; I remember the names Stoll, Fromhertz, Gottstein."[5] She was the first child of the former Louise Stoll—later known to Dan and Phil as Grandmother Fromhart—and her husband, Wilhelm.

In 1888, the family began to immigrate to America in stages, when four of Louise's brothers made the trek to Minnesota. They settled themselves on 160 acres, courtesy of the Homestead Act, near Ely. At their beckoning, Wilhelm followed two years later. Either in a burst of Anglophilia or at the whim of a customs agent, Wilhelm's surname changed en route from Fromhertz, meaning "gentle heart," to Fromhart. The Berrigans find this loss of meaning significant. They say Wilhelm possessed a martial or "Prussian" mentality—though the charge may be tinged with guilt by association, since his father was a musician in the band of Kaiser Wilhelm, for whom he named his son. Photos of Wilhelm (never referred to in family accounts by the familiar Grandfather Fromhart) show a dapper, mustachioed man in linen suit, starched white collar, and plaid bow tie. There is the slightest tilt of arrogance to his jaw. In one, he stands before a giant tree trunk shaggy with wrinkled pine bark and set as part of a row of pillars at the entrance of what looks like a public building. His hat is crisp, his black shoes gleam, and his arms are tightly folded. His left leg, bent at the knee, suggests a dancer's first position—evidence, maybe, of a physical grace to temper his reported Teutonic severity.

He took a mining job with the Stoll brothers' backing, along with the forty-acre spread of Freda's childhood. With frequent help from his brothers-in-law, he spent his first year clearing the land for a garden and hay crop, sinking a well, and raising rudimentary versions of a log cabin, barn, and privy. Then, the claim secured with required improvements, he sent for his wife and children. And so it was that at five years old—the same age at which Tom Berrigan suffered the upheaval of his father's death—Freda found herself passing through Castle Garden at the Battery in lower Manhattan, the entry point for immigrants before Ellis Island opened one year later. She, her two brothers, sister, and mother, then crossed another 5,500 miles by rail and boat before reuniting with Wilhelm in an obscure but booming outpost of a rapidly mechanizing America.[6]

The place was beautiful, and dangerous. When Freda was nineteen, her twelve-year-old brother, Charles, died by stumbling into an abandoned mine shaft; and eight years later her sister Angela, seventeen, was crushed between two streetcars on a visit into Winton. (Jim Berrigan, Dan and Phil's older brother and the family genealogist, takes care to record that the car was run by "strikebreakers.") Grandmother Fromhart, as noted, broke her leg after taking a misstep off a streetcar. And Freda's uncle Reinhart died "at a tender age" in a knife fight with a drunk.[7] So Freda knew loss by the time she met Tom Berrigan. It was the summer of 1910, the year not only when she and her sister Bertha got engaged but when their father deserted the family.

"Somebody said his daughters were getting married so it was time for him to leave," remembers Rosalie, Jim Berrigan's wife, of Wilhelm's odd abandonment. "The boys had all left home because of poverty," Jim adds. "They had to get jobs in the logging camps at very young ages."[8] Over the course of twenty years, Wilhelm had toiled to become supervisor of a mine, own property, and all but raise his family. Then one day he laced up his boots and walked out of town, leaving behind a wife and eight children and the cabin he had built by hand. His descendants believe he wound up homesteading in Alberta, Canada, after once again changing his name. The site of his grave is lost to his American descendants.

When it came time for Freda to choose a husband, she, too, picked a man who, like Wilhelm, apparently chafed throughout his life at family bonds, finding them constraints against self-perceived greatness. Jerry Berrigan argues that considering the burden of his many responsibilities, Tom retained a surprising degree of "humanness and humor."[9] But Dan calls his father a "free agent" who did exactly what he pleased around their home, whose behavior toward his family could hardly have been worse.[10] Both are right. According to their brother Jim, paradox defines the man with whom Freda fell in love: resentful of his siblings, yet obsessively drawn to them; politically autonomous, yet swayed by the Depression-era "radio priest" and populist seducer Father Charles Coughlin; intellectually curious, yet slavishly beholden to church authority. "The last thing you'd expect from him was consistency," says Phil.[11] Dan considers it possible that his mother was naive as she strode the aisle of St. Anthony's Church on her wedding day. As a late bride at age twenty-five, she could have been betting that the goodness she glimpsed in Tom Berrigan would, with help, overcome the ominous. Had Freda fully known of his difficult past, she might have refigured.

To the Irishman, there are only two
final realities: Hell and the United
States.
          —*Evelyn Waugh*

Around 1860, a lone figure tramped a Canadian country road. He had separated from his three brothers after embarking with them a few years before on a sea journey from their home in rural Ireland to the port of Charlottetown, Prince Edward Island, where today there's a Berrigan River. One can imagine the brothers remarking on the irony of their landing in a British province named for the Duke of Kent, father of Victoria, England and Ireland's reigning queen and among the exacerbators of the recent Great Potato Famine of 1845–49, that epic Malthusian disaster and spur to a quarter-century exodus of some 3 million Irish emigrants, mostly the dislocated poor, including four young Berrigan brothers from County Tipperary.[12] The traveler was Dan and Phil's paternal grandfather—call him Thomas I. His destination was America.

Having made his way west from Charlottetown, he walked across the border into New York State. If there was some kind of road sign to inform Thomas I of his passage into a wholly new country and future, he couldn't read it. He was an illiterate, nineteen-year-old laborer without claim or possessions. He would have read the landscape, though, seen cattle and corn and tawny cuts of wheat, and perceived that, unlike Ireland, this countryside was wide and in places remained to be firmly settled. Arriving on foot in the Finger Lakes region of northwest New York in 1860, a man might dream of living independently on the land, instead of waiting for Old Da to die and bequeath the family heirloom, an overworked and rented square of sod. With this simple central prospect, he might rouse himself from the Irishman's wounded morbidity as one of modern history's celebrated victims, and attempt to make a mark on his particular time and place.

Well, to a certain degree. First-generation immigrants are not often radicals, especially after quitting tumultuous homelands. Along with the distractions of surviving and modestly thriving, the nineteenth-century immigrant's new political lords routinely treat his franchise, among other assets, as tradeable stock. (One Berrigan forebear would be "taken to vote" in Syracuse by a helpful "volunteer" who made sure he cast his ballot straight Republican.[13]) This in turn would aggravate your average Irish Catholic's inbred cynicism and political passivity. Thomas I was probably no different. As a boy, he lived through the doomed Young Irelander uprising, a nationalistic movement ultimately crushed by the British army in a Tipperary cabbage patch in 1848. If he were like many of his countryfolk, witnessing such a remorseless rout would have disposed him to viewing politics as both dangerous and ultimately futile—an attitude that persisted in immigrant culture even as the Irish worked themselves up the rungs of government. Thomas I belonged to the first major wave of Irish immigrants, whose main goal was to capitalize on America's economic opportunity. Ethnic and religious discrimination still needed to be faced here, but they could be, and were, effectively thwarted by the Catholic talent for communal conformity. Call it a wily assimilation or the habit of obedience, it is a defining Irish-American trait that has flowed through what Phil calls "the bloodline"—his ambivalent nod to one's valuable family heritage and the competing obligation, as he and Dan began to assert at the height of the Vietnam War, to transcend family ties in the cause of social justice.[14]

By 1862, Thomas I had worked his way to Onondaga County,

New York, near the city of Syracuse, where he met and married Bridget Doherty, a dark-haired twenty-one-year-old. She had gentle eyes and an overbearing farmer-father, Edmund. Equally willful, Thomas I didn't warm to his new and wealthier relation, though common sense and custom would recommend he give it a serious try. Instead he rejected a stake in the Doherty spread and took his bride to Iowa. As one family chronicle primly sums up, "the relationship between Thomas [I] and Edmund was not cordial or lasting."[15]

The couple joined a colony of Irish Catholics who had followed a band of Cistercian monks from County Waterford, Ireland, to establish the New Melleray Abbey—an interdependent community between the cloistered priests of the monastery and the farming families clustered about its walls. Normally tranquil and self-reliant in a quiet corner of eastern Iowa, New Melleray was increasingly embroiled in the widening Civil War, most bitterly in the clashes over slavery racking nearby "Bloody Kansas" and Nebraska. (On this subject, abolitionist William Lloyd Garrison had shocked the nation a decade before by publicly burning a copy of the U.S. Constitution, a theatrical agitation that Dan and Phil will reprise.) For $300—a hefty sum mysteriously raised—Thomas I bought his way out of soldiering in the Union army. From the sidelines, as he broke ground on his homestead in a Union state, he cheered the Confederacy. Aside from a native contrariness, or an ingrained partiality to rebellion, it is hard to know why.

Preserved from great events and safe from battle, Thomas I and Bridget, Dan and Phil's paternal grandparents, built up farm and family over the next four years. They had two daughters, and seemed settled in, when a letter from Edmund arrived in the winter of 1867. His health was failing and with it the farm in South Onondaga, New York; would Thomas I and Bridget consider coming back to help him? In retrospect, the request seems strange. Edmund would live for another fifteen years, and his adult sons John and William were still on the farm. It is possible that around this time the central women in Edmund's life—his mother, wife, and daughter Mary, "whom he idolized"—died by fire, a calamity that could have shattered his health. Or it could have been that Edmund, who was "exacting, close, tyrannical, and more or less a hard customer," wanted every last family member under his thumb.[16]

Edmund Doherty's immigration had prefigured Wilhelm's in a couple of ways—he had also changed his name (from "Daugherty") while traveling ahead of his wife and children to America, where he'd been told "the sugar would be heaped in the street free to all comers."[17] But his departure from Ireland in the late 1840s suggests that, unlike Thomas I and his brothers—young, unmarried men who could have been following an established route toward seasonal work in the Newfoundland fisheries, besides escaping the famine's lingering repercussions—Edmund and his family had been fleeing starvation.[18] They had hung on and followed Edmund as soon as he raised their passage. A Doherty narrative recounts a six-week sea voyage racked by a violent storm, during which Edmund's wife clutched her children beneath a cloak and prepared to perish. (The waters were stilled, the story goes, when the captain threw a dead man to the sharks.) As the family later ferried in a small boat toward Manhattan, ten-year-old Bridget had removed her shoes and tossed them into New York harbor, a kind of symbolic submerging of her family's desperate past.

The family moved through the Mohawk Valley in upstate New York as Edmund took jobs with the Black River Railroad, a lumber mill, and as a blast furnace operator in a Syracuse factory. He was a hardworking "immigrant empire builder—one of the famed hewers of wood and drawers of water," the family history states, who knew how to save his money. Nicknamed "Wild Ned" back in Ireland for his strange habit of kicking his hat down the road as he walked, he became, "like others of his kind, when transplanted to America, a sterling citizen and the backbone of his community." Eventually, he purchased the hillside farm from which he now petitioned Bridget and Thomas I to return to his side.[19]

The couple responded by moving from Iowa to New York. But Bridget's father and husband couldn't fashion a peace that would allow them to farm in partnership. After several months, Thomas I moved his family to a farm near Lafayette, a crossroads town on the far side of Syracuse. They lived on Sentinel Heights Road in an area called Vinegar Hill, a name that echoes to a celebrated piece of high ground one county over from Tipperary in Ireland, where British forces had rifled down the Wexford rebels seventy years earlier—another in a long line of hallowed defeats for Irish Catholics.[20]

Thomas I and Bridget took their places as part of an Irish-American minority within an entrenched Anglo-Saxon, or Yankee, ascendancy. Not unlike conditions in segregated Ireland, the Protestant Yankees farmed the rich bottom land, went to market over passable roads, and banked among themselves. From the vantage of their spare, impeccable homes and modes of worship, the Yankees regarded the local Catholics, with their panoply of stained glass–cast and incense-shrouded saints, as mawkish rustics. The disdain was mutual. When harvest arrived and the farmers "traded works," exchanging labor, each group stayed within its kind, a sour arrangement lending Vinegar Hill its second, pointed, meaning.

The Berrigans were subsistence farmers on a medium-sized tract of 120 acres, including woodlot. Their fields covered part of a sinuous slope that rolled from the road to the crook of a shallow valley, then climbed to a distant line of low blue hills. The land was creased by subtle folds and tree breaks, patterned in summer by high cloud and dotted at harvest with yellow haystacks. They lived in a whitewashed two-story clapboard wrapped halfway around by a narrow porch. Their most sophisticated piece of household equipment was a hand pump at the kitchen sink that drew water from a cistern. Dan says his grandparents drove themselves to keep up appearances, explaining that "there is a memory in Ireland of always having to live on a ramshackle, broken-down farm. If you improved your house or barn the English landlord raised the rent. Now surrounded by 'the English,' they probably wanted to show they could run a respectable operation."[21] The six-mile route to Syracuse—steep, winding, and rutted—took a full day to cover by horse and buggy. When winter landed, snow drifts clogged the roads for months, and the only way to St. Joseph's Church (one still had the obligation of attending Sunday Mass, whatever the weather) was by horse-drawn sleigh in a snaking line over pitched and blanketed fields.

The soil was poor compared to the neighboring Warwick and

Tully valleys where the more prosperous operations lay. Thomas I carted the occasional load of hay to sell in downtown Syracuse, but didn't have a team of horses for bringing cash crops to market. It had been largely Irish immigrants who dug the 360-mile Erie Canal from 1817 to 1825, but forty years later, only Yankee farmers owned the means to reach Port Syracuse, which allowed them to ship many tons of expensive produce to New York City. The Irish were left to raise less profitable crops, such as cheap grain for pig feed and whiskey mash, as had long been the lot of the area's poorest farmers.[22]

Though indigent, Bridget and Thomas I had no intention of completing their brood at six. Their mandate was not only to multiply for the church's sake but to increase the number of hands around the farm. Besides, they needed a boy. In those days Irish parents would dress up newborn boys in petticoats to lead kidnapping fairies into thinking they'd found a girl—which the fairies, naturally sharing the prevailing cultural biases, were expected to leave in the crib as inferior goods. A more pragmatic reason for wanting a son was contemporary Irish laws that made inheritance of property difficult for women, a vestigial worry to the immigrant father of a half-dozen daughters.

The son arrived in 1879: Thomas (II), Dan and Phil's father. He was favored with the quintessential Berrigan first name—the only one that will pass through five American generations—and in time he will display the prototypical Berrigan temperament: fiery, bright, articulate, charming, grandiose, and charismatically muleheaded. As soon as she could, Bridget started teaching Tom to read, as she'd done with her husband and daughters during their long nights on the prairie. Education, beginning with literacy, was at that time an immigrant's best rebuttal to the popular notion of the Irish as merry simpletons or criminal primitives. Much was expected of the oldest son, including, in the Irish style, a facile literacy. Bridget proved an exceptional tutor. Four of her daughters went on to be teachers, and Tom developed a deep and lasting love of literature, making her legacy doubly critical in the lives of Dan and Phil.

Tom was four years old when his father contracted tuberculosis, or "immigrant's lung," named for the rampant infection rates in the cramped holds of many oceangoing ships—though Thomas I probably caught the germ from a neighbor or his cattle. Once ill, there was little to do but die very slowly. Increasingly, shuddering coughs would fold him in half, and there were days when instead of working his fields, all he could do was stare at them out the window from his bed. Vinegar Hill was remote from a doctor, but that didn't matter much. Once, when Thomas I's gums started bleeding spontaneously, the attending doctor told one of the girls to break a chunk of ice from a rain barrel and bring it inside. By way of medical remedy, Thomas I got to suck on it. On the morning of his death, Bridget retrieved the family Bible—a ten-pound, gold-leaf Douay edition with translation from the French, the Catholics' answer to the King James version—and in a stunned hand penciled onto the frontispiece under a list of family names and dates: "Thomas Berrigan . . . died 1884." They had been married for twenty-two years. It was Christmas Day.

Tom, now five, slept in the arms of a neighboring farm woman. After his father's funeral service, he trudged with the small, bent band of family and neighbors "up scoured December hills," as Dan later wrote, behind a wagon with the body, the wheels as high as his head.[23]

Four of his five surviving sons, including Dan and Phil, agree that Tom suffered a permanent wound from his father's terrible death. He seems never to have trusted the capricious world again. In a poem, he remembers standing as a boy by the window during a February sleet storm, listening to the "melancholy dirge of bewildered sparrows and famished crows." Betrayed by nature, the weakened animals are abandoned to pathetic ends beneath a darkened sky unmoved by "the broken arms of the prayerful trees." In the last line, this child of "Mother earth"—Tom himself, grandiloquently rendered—even ponders a dire new posture toward God: "Shall her young prodigy curse you now?"[24]

In fact, he did the opposite. He clearly couldn't fight God, so Tom yielded to the notion of a demanding and all-powerful God whose favor could be strenuously won. Toward that end, he created a chivalrous alter-ego named Sir Spot (an oddly diminutive title for a titan of righteousness), who leads his knights against the "God of

Storms"—a usurping, devilish destroyer who "howls and hammers, bellows and wheezes" as he rains "oblivious death beneath conquering feet."

> When the elements rage as if jealous of man
> Conspiring to ravage God's orderly plan,

he wrote of his newfound enemy,

> good is my challenge, "Come forth if you dare
> We'll fight in the open by foul means and fair."[25]

Maybe Tom, having failed to save his father from "great Nature's law of death," could set things right by restoring the world "to its quaint fairy state" of pre-death innocence.[26] The task, as he sees it, will require two things: that he remain pure—"NOTHING DEFILED WILL EVER ENTER HERE," he reads emblazoned on the gates of heaven in one particularly hallucinatory epic—and that he always be ready to fight.[27]

When not battling cosmic chaos, Tom faced the much more ambiguous struggle for his place within the family, which also may have fed the troubled allegory of his poems. It is hard to overemphasize the turbulence ensuing from the early death of an Irish Catholic patriarch. Alive, Thomas I would have functioned as a kind of Hobbesian Leviathan, a sovereign authority binding each family member to the whole; on his death, the household's power needed redistributing, or, in the case of the oldest daughters, seizing.

At this pivotal moment, the ten surviving Berrigans consisted of Bridget, forty-four, a widow with nine children, including a baby, on a dirt-poor farm; Molly, twenty-one, a teacher; Margaret, twenty, a registered nurse; Bridget, sixteen, a student at Onondaga Valley High School; Johanna, Agnes, and Elizabeth—respectively, twelve, nine, and seven years old—all attending the one-room grade school down the road; Tom, at five years old expected to shoulder a premature share of a man's responsibility, even as his sisters, later known to Dan and Phil as the "Matson Avenue aunts," boss him around; John, three; and Edmund, or "Ned," a sickly baby unable to nurse. (One doctor counseled Bridget to tie a necklace of string and salt pork around baby Ned's neck, so he might suckle the boneless chunk of meat for nourishment. Not only did it pull him through, it instilled in Tom, who loved his younger brother, a nearly sacred devotion to the healing power of salt pork.)[28]

Initially, they scraped by on Margaret and Molly's salaries and by growing much of their food. They may also have rented out their fields. But as with any small farm, the margin of survival obtained from unrelenting labor. Jerry Berrigan pictures his father at "ten years old—and he's stuck behind the plow out there behind a team of horses, following a single furrow, sweating, anguishing, hurting, in the grip of forces hard to understand." He believes this precocious slaving developed in Tom a sort of negative "pioneer spirit," in the sense of "I against nature. Nature is earth, and earth has to be turned over so seeds can be sown, and out of that growth, livelihood. And here I am a young boy and it's hard sometimes. The rains come down, the ground freezes. It looks as though nature is against me."[29]

Winter could be eight months long. Trees needed felling and hauling and cutting, animals needed constant tending, and anything that broke got repaired by hand. Jerry says that these would have been his father's jobs. The work was demanding, but worse for Tom was his low spot in the siblings' rancorous pecking order. Jim Berrigan says that Tom's "sisters really bore down on him. They were quite bossy and domineering. My father had the life of a dog. 'Tom did you milk that cow? Why didn't you? Did you have the horse shod? Why not?' " And Tom, looking down the family ladder, saw weaker, younger brothers to exploit—not so much Ned, whom he cared for as the baby, but John, whom he never much liked. (The older brothers squabbled and competed for most of their lives, but for a brief, miraculous respite when an elderly John, with Ned's help, recovered from decades of alcoholism.)

No wonder Tom was prone to slip into detailed heroic daydreams. While trudging through his mundane chores—fixing fences, feeding livestock—he simultaneously defends the Queen of Virgins in an imaginary war against the forces of disorder; and slogging buckets of feed through ankle-deep mud, he is sustained by visions of a paradise filled with perfume, lute-song, "gems of divers hues," and (what else?) "maidens clothed in white." In Tom's mind, the world was divided against itself. There was nature's feminine side, divinely ordered and revealed by all things beautiful. And there was her nemesis, the malevolent elements, poised like "a barbaric despot laying siege at the gates of heaven." He resolved this conflict by casting himself as a Christ-inspired Parsifal, bounding "with a pure and gladsome heart" to nature's defense.[30]

In fairness, one grants that risible fantasies are common in young men. They certainly didn't deter Tom from effective, disciplined work around the farm. But sadly, he never outgrew them. Even after he'd left home and entered the adult world of complexity and compromise, he still held overblown views on the ineffable virtue of womanhood, the fixity of moral laws, and the magnitude of his unique abilities. He was a cross-eyed romantic who raged at life's inevitable frustrations—a trait that will later envelop those close to him.

The exception was his mother, whom he regarded from the foot of an exalted Victorian pedestal. To Tom, Bridget was "the acme of earth's loveliness."[31] In reality, she was wizened by her early middle age. She was heart-worn from the death of her husband, Thomas I, the pair of stillborn children she had delivered in Iowa, her memories of famine, and the recent passing of her parents. Still ailing from some poorly healed broken ribs, she ceded oversight of the household to her daughters, who had aligned themselves in factions in the struggle for control. One day the house would ring with shouts, on another it would smother in accusatory silence. Tom remembered how near evening he would sometimes find his mother sitting alone on the back porch steps, "with the sun in her lap about to die," as it slipped behind the hills. Her eyes would be gone to memory, and tears would be streaming down her cheeks.

With the 1882 death of their father, Edmund Doherty, Bridget's two brothers had both left home. John had "declared his free-dom" and enrolled in a Syracuse business school. William had entered the Seminary of Our Lady of Angels in Niagara Falls and become a Roman Catholic priest. For years, he'd been sending money to help the Berrigan sisters complete their educations. With each letter came an admonishment that Bridget and the family quit the "slavery" of the farm.[32] If the Irish were going to rise in Amer-ican life, they needed to shuck their landed peasantry and enter the professions. The sisters, thanks to their smarts and their Uncle William's thoughtful subsidies, had begun to do just that. Mar-garet was a practicing nurse, while Molly, Bridget, Johanna, and Agnes had all become teachers—which left the fate of the farm in the hands of the Berrigan sons, now young men. The family could remain on Vinegar Hill if one of them wanted to stay and make his life there. None did.

Tom, twenty-one, lit out westward with his brothers John and Ned to look for work. They landed jobs at the Niagara Falls pen stocks, massive tubes feeding water into turbine generators at the region's first power plant. Shortly thereafter, as men with new standing in the world must do, the brothers spent part of a free day posing for portraits at a photographer's studio. In the surviving faded prints, they sit on chairs before a majestic panorama of the New York falls reproduced on wrinkled canvas, their feet propped up on rocks arranged with artful randomness. Their poses are stiff and their muscled limbs bulge inside dark, tight-fitting suits. Tom, clearly young and strong and free to be his own man for the first time in his life, looks grim.

Niagara Falls was a railroad hub, with several tracks leading sug-gestively west. Tom was ready to move again. He had heard about plentiful work to be had in the copper and iron-ore smelting plants then opening in the upper Midwest. By hiring on as a railroad engine fireman, he'd get to stoke a locomotive furnace for sixteen-hour stretches while traveling the length of four Great Lakes. The idea appealed to him. When he got the job, he packed his scant belongings and said goodbye to John and Ned, marking the occa-sion with a fulsome set of verse—"Unless God rule your heart, the Devil must/For virile is our animated dust"—titled, "Au Revoir."[33]

Reaching Minnesota, he joined a workforce of some 41,000 immigrants from twenty-five countries enticed by New World tales of cornucopia. Norwegians, Frenchmen, Slovenes, Poles, Ukrainians, Lithuanians, Croats, Finns, Italians, Greeks, and Serbs, among others, read sepia handbills crying, "3,000 Laborers Wanted!" over engravings of three-masted clipper ships pledging to bear them "Direkte Till America." Another claimed "Constant Employment Will Be Given—Wage Ranges from $3 to $4 Per Day." And several hailed Minnesota's northeastern tier as "The New Eldorado," whose mineral riches were "The Most Extraordinary Feat of Nature in All the Continent." Early settlers had named it the Mesabi Iron Range, after a Native American word for "Sleeping Giant," an apt description of the huge deposits that, once yanked from their underground beds, rose into four generations of skyscrapers, bridges, factories, cars, and armaments.[34]

Tom landed a fireman's job on a Mesabi Iron Ore Company train, carrying red ore from distant mine sites to the Lake Superior barges, for ferrying to Chicago or Detroit. The work was fierce and grueling and suited him fine. He hand-fired the engine's boiler, which meant thrusting a heavy scoop shovel into the tender's pile of coal and heaving a load of it into a furnace that in summer felt like hell itself. In winter, Tom and an engineer sometimes found themselves pounding their locomotive through a zero-visibility blizzard on a –60°F night. The flanges on the engine sprayed a constant geyser of snow that hit the superheated boilerhead and drove steam clouds thick as a "London Fog" into the driver's cabin, Tom remembered, extinguishing the gas lights on the gauges, and drenching him and his partner down to their flannels. "He was a good and smart workman," says Jerry Berrigan of his father; "Oh yes, he had a tough body," Jim concurs. Wiry, tough, and tireless, with an aptitude for mechanics, Tom had reached the height of his power. You'd think he would revel in his youthful prowess, relax and enjoy the liberties of his unencumbered life.

Not if you knew him. Toiling across the interminable range, he saw little to alter his view of the world as a hostile pitch on which good and evil waged apocalyptic war. In one remarkable passage from his memoirs, he describes a 1909 fire in the muskeg swamps along the railroad's right-of-way:

> Imagine if you will, thousands of acres tenanted by Norway pines, each tree a symbol of grace and beauty, straight and resilient, much like whale bone buggy whips, which were common in those days, even to the tassel of the foliage on top . . . [Then] this flashing, crashing, roaring holocaust—this monster of madness that was unleashed in the form of a demonic inferno of insatiable hate for natural beauty—[burned nearly every tree] in a fifty mile radius . . . until this giant affront to decency gradually sank into the ashes of its own ruin.

For months after the fire, Tom rode through the resinous pall of a devastated landscape. "The sun no longer shone," he claimed. "The stars were not. Some advanced interpreters of Holy Scripture declared the end of the world imminent." For a while deer starved in numbers that seemed to threaten their extinction, until at last the plentiful autumn rains—Tom called them "lovely, pure"—extinguished the smoldering wreckage. The ordeal had passed, or so he thought, until he heard a strange hum from the side of the tracks: millions of yellow-brown timber worms had infested the fallen tree trunks and were gnawing the unburned flesh beneath the blackened outer skins. What nature couldn't consume from without, it would finish from within. The sound unnerved him.[35]

Tom belonged to the "Brotherhood of Boomers," railroaders named for the notoriously fickle nature of their industry, busted as often as booming. He and his co-workers suffered the continuous adversity of an orchestrated labor glut. When the iron-ore industry fell into one of its regular slumps, he, and thousands of others, would be laid off without thank you or goodbye. Like tramps, they'd have to hit the road, as Tom did repeatedly, scrounging fieldwork during the wheat harvest in Saskatchewan, Canada or some equally exploitative, far, and fleeting alternative. If they protested work conditions, management would train in hundreds of half-starved Montenegrans—or whoever were the latest and most desperate immigrants—and use them to replace the fired dissenters.

This was capitalism red in tooth and claw, its injustices so routinely blatant that it actually prompted Tom to question authority.

Dan credits both his father and his mother with a healthy skepticism, which he says rubbed off on him and Phil, much to their benefit. Considering this, Tom's unionism would appear to be in character. Nearly every profiler of the Berrigans seems to think so, and credits Tom with teaching his sons concern for social justice by example. But Dan and Phil themselves, in interviews and voluminous ruminations, don't mention their father's labor activity as an influence on their moral development. If it played a role, it was probably a small one. In fact, the story the brothers tell is of Tom's impulsive train trip from Syracuse to New York City for the purpose of personally breaking the 1949 Catholic gravediggers' strike. "I've come to support the Cardinal!" he is said to have bellowed in Grand Central Station, brandishing a homemade shovel at Dan, who'd come to meet and talk him out of it. (Then aged seventy, he spent a few days haunting the chancery in baggy overalls, until sent home with a letter of warmest thanks from Cardinal Spellman. "They should have cut his pension, too," his son Jim says, referring to the International Brotherhood of Electrical Workers, which shortly thereafter fired Tom, their turncoat business agent.[36])

In the early 1900s, he joined the Brotherhood of Locomotive Firemen not as much from conviction to abstract principles of justice, or to be consistent with any strongly felt political philosophy, as out of affection for his fellow workingmen. Brute, broke, ornery, scrofulous, talented, and proud, like Bret Harte characters sprung to life, turn-of-the-century railroaders were "romantic types" whose honor and camaraderie he craved. If he ever made fiery speeches in their cause, as some writers claim, it was probably to impress his friends with classy Scripture quotes, and aphorisms from Shakespeare and Thomas Carlyle.

He never became an organizer. And the one time he did take a stand for workers' rights, he wound up agreeing with the company judge. Socked with the "appalling penalty" of ten days' suspension for refusing an illegal call to work, he slipped into his best suit, "and of course my ever faithful self-confidence," and trekked to Lackawanna to make his case before a court of appeal. In the proceeding's climactic exchange, Tom recalled the judge leaning forward and angrily lecturing him: " 'Young man, you are too smart. What do you think is the object of discipline?' I was unready. He supplied: 'Discipline is to eliminate the need of discipline.' So be it." He concludes that the company's style of "discipline, somewhat like the hope and spirit of any wise law—The Ten Commandments for example—realized many of its aims by its mere existence, and our close acquaintance with, and respect for, its mandates."[37] (In their own climactic courtroom exchanges, his sons will later respond with a radically different notion of what makes a law wise, though with equal self-confidence.)

Tom's loyalty was to order, which prompted his deference to authority—a version of the soldier's practice of respecting rank by saluting not the man but the uniform. He was also a conservative who held every man responsible for improving his situation. He distrusted mass movements for social change—worrying, for example, that union leader Eugene V. Debs "could fire the passions of men but lacked the rare facility to control them when aroused." He opposed the 1916 railroad strike, led by Debs, an engine fireman from Tom's union, who was jailed for his trouble. And in written reflections on collective action, Tom turns to metaphors of nature gone amok: "the original, beautiful crystal snow flake soon surrenders its identity to the anger of the storm, whipped, rubbed and buffeted into powder form."[38] His model for bringing purposeful change, however eccentric, remained the knight errant—the singular man who turns people toward the holy truth through a sacrificial commitment to uncompromised moral standards in debased times. Of course, this is Dan and Phil's model, too.

Dan writes that in photos from this era, his father can be picked out by finding "a head of burnished locks, a high brow/a cynic's sidelong look . . . [with a] mouth [that] reminds me of a whip/sensual and punishing."[39] To be sure, there was allure to his bottled intensity. Freda recalled many women being attracted to Tom Berrigan. "I'll have you boys know your father was considered *a great catch*," she vouched in standard reply when her sons would taunt her years later about the cuss she'd brought to the altar: "Tom, Tom the farmer's son, why did you ever marry that one?" Once when they pleaded, "Come on Mom, level with us," she mulled the question, then answered, "You know, someone should have kicked me in the head!"[40]

Tom's vocal unionism led him away from religion awhile, because of the Catholic Church's opposition to labor's often communist and socialist leadership, and the reactionary ire it tended to level at threats to the status quo. Freda won him back to the faith by the gentle expression of her "practical German piety, unselfconscious, a matter of yea and nay, intellectual only in the sense of being firmly held and consequential"—traits her fiancée genuinely admired, according to Dan.[41] She almost did too good a job. Tom recommended his stream of rococo paeans to the deity ("Great Godhead eternal, Great Nature fraternal . . . "[42]) and only days before their wedding at St. Anthony's Church in Ely, Minnesota, he confided to Freda his vocation to the priesthood. "Oh no you don't!" she roared, her fear of impending scandal preempting feelings of furtive relief.[43]

"Well, she certainly saved the priesthood from something," Dan tartly remarks on his father's brush with religious life, then on further reflection rolls his eyes, "Oh God!"[44] In an essay on his mother, he also describes—with chilling detachment, since his existence will depend on its positive outcome—this same confrontation as Freda's "lost chance, the bad luck she put on with her wedding ring."[45]

Daniel Berrigan entered the world on May 9, 1921. Ahead of him were the first four of Tom and Freda's six children, "unaccountably" all male, says Dan: Thomas Jr., John, James, and Jerome (Jerry). Two years later, on October 5, 1923, Philip arrived. Enrico Caruso heralded Phil by filling the Berrigan home with crackling arias—Tom had splurged on a hand-cranked phonograph and a stack of records to celebrate the birth—which may have been when Dan began to perceive his brother as an otherworldly grace note. "For many years I remember him, and I think the others did, too, as the kid who had no mean streak in him," Dan says, "He was very peaceable, lovable, beautiful. Blond, blue-eyed."[46] It

was also fitting that his life began with an operatic flourish, in light
of the tumult in the family growing up, and later as he courted the
wrath of America's most powerful institutions and their leaders, like
the Wagnerian J. Edgar Hoover, a sort of vindictive King of the
Nibelungs to Phil's Siegfried.

Dan was born in the only house his parents would ever own,
bought with a loan from Grandmother Fromhart, in the town of
Virginia, Minnesota. Soon after, when Tom lost and found another
railroad job, the Berrigans sold and moved to roughhewn Babbitt
(ironically, at the same time Minnesotan Sinclair Lewis was using
"Babbitt" as a namesake for all things vapid and bourgeois) in the
windy Vermilion Range, squeezing into an abandoned miners' bar-
racks with another family. In descending degree of likelihood, the
reasons for Tom's vagabond career were his union membership, the
volatile mining industry, fights with other workers over their anti-
German slurs before and during the First World War, and his practice of spouting huge chunks of Shelley and Keats aloud when he
should have been on the job. The first two seem quite credible, and
the last is untrue (not that he didn't do it, but he didn't let it interfere with his work), while his combativeness in defense of Freda's
ancestry, which he normally looked down on, is typically incongru-
ous. There is a story that he refused to blow the whistle on a troop
train he was driving, objecting to popular war hysteria and the celebration of young men being sent to their possible deaths. At age
thirty-six in 1917 when America entered the war, he was too old for
the draft. He probably hated the Hun as much as the next patriotic
American, but he considered his sons "half-German," an ethnicity
worth defending when disparaged by Scandinavians, though inher-
ently inferior to the Irish.

In 1923, Tom and Freda packed the family into a cloth-top
Model T touring car and moved upstream to a tar-paper shack in
swampy, forlorn Winton. The town was on the downward slide of a
short-lived boom as a lumber milling center. All the virgin timber
had been clear-cut, leaving a dreary terrain of scrub pine and bog.
The summers, brief and grudging, spawned opportunistic mosqui-
toes that flocked like birds and were almost as big. Tom's job was
to move entire houses by railroad flatbed over to Ely, the latest

town to amass demographic gravity from the region's revolving economy.

Money was scarce and existence primitive. In winter, Freda paid a local man 50 cents to dip the family wash through a hole cut into the lake ice, then return the clothing in a frozen pile on a "stone boat," a low-slung sled used by farmers to clear their fields. Freda would place the clothes in a copper wash boiler on her stove, add snow, and, with Dan helping, cook them clean. As it did during Freda's early years, rural Minnesota still produced bumper crops of comical, freak, and tragic accidents. A bear once chased Tom Jr. in the middle of his paper route; a shod horse reared and clipped John in the head, inflicting a minor wound; one of the brothers got hurt, not to mention critically embarrassed, while blowing up a manure pile with firecrackers on the Fourth of July; and Jim remembers coming across a dead man in a ditch not far from the cottage. He had been shot the night before in a poker dispute.

Dan wishes they'd lived there longer. Despite his wobbly ankles and his father's meanness, he remembers the rugged countryside with pleasure. "There was pride, and life on the land," he says, "and food, homegrown and sensibly prepared."[47] The Berrigans bartered with the Chippewa for wild rice grown in the Birch Lake fens and dried on animal skins, and in season Freda led the boys on back-woods blueberrying expeditions (one time crossing paths with an oblivious mama black bear). What berries they didn't eat off the bush, they finished at home with fresh milk from the pail. Grand-mother Fromhart heaped their table with vegetables from her gar-den, and wild game was a lunch and dinner staple, served to "put a bone" in the growing boys.[48]

Dan recounts in his autobiography how he and his brothers played a game called Fox and Geese in the snow-covered fields near home. One brother, the fox, stood at the hub of a circle etched by foot to resemble a wheel with spokes. The rest of them stood on the rim like wary geese, waiting for the fox to strike, rotating in escape. He remembers laughter and shrieks and falls and collisions and brother pulling brother off the ground, "and our breaths wreathing about and marrying in the frosty air." They often stopped to argue the rules, until a roving band of Finnish boys, "blue-eyed demons, with tousled blonde pelts," would mount a surprise attack, at which point the brothers, in early precedent, quit their fighting to unify for mutual defense.[49]

One time John decided to have some fun with Dan. He hoisted him on his shoulders and raced out into the dazzling winter sunlight, then burst inside a pitch-dark shed, where he thrust his little brother's face against a stiffened, bristling pelt. Dan, half-blinded, blinked furiously till he realized he was looking into the dead green eyes of a wolf's head hanging openmouthed from a rafter. The shock of it rendered the desired effect—he screamed in holy terror. Dan makes much of the incident, rehashing it in poems and prose, claiming it as one source of the recurring theme of death throughout his literary work. But it could just as well be the other way around, that it's his fondness for the theme that has him dwelling on particular memories. Whichever the case, his first five years in the northern Minnesota woods gave him a feel for life's precariousness, for the hard facts of the hunt, and for the fixed stares of both predator and prey.

As the neighbors around them quit town one by one, Tom began to contemplate reversing his migration. After twenty-five years, northern Minnesota seemed no more hospitable than when he'd arrived. The winters lingered longer in his bones, and jobs were still like cat tails he could chase but never hold, through no fault of his own. And he missed the clan. Tom's mother, Bridget, had died in Syracuse two years earlier, in 1924. Too poor to afford the trip back home, Tom had had to mourn the loss from a thousand miles away.

Freda also grieved. She had met Bridget on a get-to-know-the-in-laws trip made with Tom Jr. and John, then a baby, to Syracuse in 1915. "The visit was less than fulfilling," says Jim Berrigan in one family history. "The maiden Berrigan sisters were inhospitable to Freda and intolerant with my brothers." Bridget had tried to protect Freda from the animus of her spinster daughters—Margaret, Johanna, and Agnes, the co-owners of a house in the city on Matson Avenue, bought with proceeds from the sale of the farm on Vinegar Hill—who regarded their brother's wife as an emotional interloper. "Freda always spoke well and gratefully of her," writes

Jim of Bridget, who in one photo stands in a thicket of irises crowded around the hem of her dress like tame geese waiting for bread (she had planted what looks like acres of them in a thick row by the side of the house), and who, though she "had experienced a full measure of austerity and sadness, was serene, thoughtful and kind."[50] Bridget's friendship proved Freda's only solace during her stay in the high-strung Berrigan sisters' home, lengthened by her husband's months-long delay in sending the train fare home.

Given this unhappy rehearsal, Freda could not have been pleased with Tom's announcement that the family would pull up stakes and move to Syracuse, New York. Essentially, it meant giving up her relations for his. She had sisters and brothers still living in Minnesota, as well as Stoll family uncles, cousins, nieces, and nephews. Every summer the families would gather at Wilhelm's claim site for fishing and visiting, swimming and play. Since the age of five, she'd lived on the Iron Range. She was forty now. But Tom had decided it was time to replant his family on the rolling farmland he'd known as a boy, to be back among the Irish—specifically his three unmarried sisters, who, sensing an early rift in his marriage, had already sided with him. Freda must have envisioned a dismal life for herself should the family move, and balked. Resolving the impasse was simple: They did what Tom wanted. Freda had the power occasionally to resist, but Tom had final say on important decisions. Such was his traditional male prerogative, which he believed in and exercised freely.

Freda had seen this principle at work a number of times, no more definitively than the day her husband took her for a spin in the Model T Ford. Tom sat behind the wheel with Tom Jr., a teenager in his father's brazen image, on the passenger side. Freda slumped in the backseat, looking trapped. This was the first car Tom had driven, and it wasn't as simple to steer as a train on a track. Unconcerned, he bucked the car forward and gathered speed, causing Freda to straighten up and grip the door. Then, jolting down a county lane, Tom started swerving the car. Suddenly they bounced off the road and were zigzagging through a field of boulders, barely missing one before they rushed toward and narrowly missed another. Tom shouted, "Stop me, stop me!" as Tom Jr. roared hilariously. With another near miss, Freda had seen enough—she stood, kicked open the door, and leaped into space. She rolled to a stop in a cloud of dust, scared half out of her wits, as the car charged on erratically with Tom in the driver's seat, the sound of his derisive laughter fading. Freda got to her feet and took stock of the situation. Her wounding was exterior, and tomorrow she'd be black and blue, but basically she was whole. She turned and walked back home, where she was needed.[51]

3

FIGHTING IRISH

It is lurid and melodramatic, but it is
true.

—*D. H. Lawrence*

FREDA TRIED TO DELAY THE INEVITABLE BY STOPPING OFF ON
the way from Minnesota to New York in 1926 for a visit with one
of her brothers and Grandmother Fromhart in Detroit. There Dan,
Phil, Jerry, and Jim were reunited with their older brother John,
who earlier had been dropped off by Tom—now known to his sons
by the informal Irish nickname "Dado"—before he and Tom Jr.
had continued on to Syracuse. Dado had found a job as a licensed
steam boiler operator and handyman at St. Mary's Maternity Hospital, which included a rent-free house on ten clay acres to the
northwest of the city in Liverpool township. Now there was nothing to prevent the family's reunion. Freda lingered in the Midwest
anyway, until one day in a grocery store she turned to Dan, now
five, to give him the melancholy news that they would be taking the
train to New York because "we're wearing out our welcome."[1]

The gray stucco house in Liverpool had once been a summer home for orphans run by the Syracuse archdiocese. It sat on a hill overlooking the number six stop on a trolley car line that swayed "like dromedaries," Dan remembered, as they crackled electrically on the two-lane macadam out front. Paralleling the road farther down the slope were the New York Central tracks, and in the distance, Onondaga Lake. The three-story house had a low porch and yawning angular windows and was topped by a four-sided glassed-in cupola. The Berrigans arrived to find the wooden floors refinished and the spacious rooms painted and plastered, but there was no interior plumbing or central heat. Their furnishings, which had filled the home in Winton, looked disjointed and forlorn in the big empty spaces. Dan wrote that "along with my mother and brothers, I grew in time to hate the house; its creaking discomfort, its spiritless, immense rooms. And then, with more time, I came to love it, or at least am reconciled to it, as a captive long inured to his keep."[2] Dan and Phil would spend the bulk of their youth and adolescence here, until war and religion would take them away.

Out back there was a vast weathered barn. Dado spruced it up by handing each brother a can filled with used motor oil and red ocher powder, his homemade version of paint, then told them not to come back inside till they'd smeared the sticky concoction over the walls. When the paint eventually dried (it took a while), the boys would play handball against the barn or go inside and swing out from the hay mow, clinging Tarzan-like to ropes. Dan would escape to the barn's upper reaches, "agleam with dusty shafts of autumn light," to read, or, when Dado was on a rampage and ready to lash out at whoever came in sight, to "be off his retina." One day, while investigating a faint mewling under the straw, Dan uncovered a clutch of newborn kittens clinging blindly to their mother. He proposed to his parents to keep them as pets, but in a rare moment of agreement, Dado and Freda decreed that on a hardscrabble farm as theirs was, hearts must be hardened. The kittens were tied in a sack and drowned in a watering trough, then buried in the yard.[3]

For the most part, death on the farm came seasonally. Phil recalled how every fall his father would choose a hog for butchering. The animal would be forced by several farmhands into a rope harness, "screaming, terrified for its life," then thrown on its writhing back and pinned to the ground. Then Dado maneuvered in and with a fierce stroke cut its throat. At the end of the ordeal, Phil said, the men would raise the hog by its short back legs to let the blood drain into the grass. Dan remembered vats of scalding water and "an array of gleaming knives" on the great occasion, which "was terrible for a child to behold . . . when an innocent orchard of plum and cherry rang with the screams of an abattoir. And until snow fell, and even through the snow, the grasses flourished, wild and green for the blood that drenched their roots."[4]

On this morbid subject, the story all the brothers tell is of the day their plow horse, Old Maj, had to be put down. A few years earlier Dado had paid $5 for a gelding he'd then placed in care of the boys. Though the previous owner had broken the horse through overwork, the brothers climbed all over their prized possession and let the neighborhood kids ride him in circles around the yard, until Old Maj would get to be "wheezing like a person with emphysema," said Phil, who also confessed that "we weren't too competent in taking care of animals." One day the horse caught a leg on some barbed wire, or someone let a noose slip down his neck and almost choked him. The causes given differ, but pinched nerves were the result for Old Maj, which led to his disabled legs and difficulty swallowing. Soon after, he couldn't take grain and seemed likely to starve. Dan says it was then his father ordered "a mercy killing."[5]

Dado directed Tom Jr. and Jim to lead Old Maj to the edge of an open grave out by the plum orchard, shoot him, and tip him in. Tom Jr. borrowed a neighbor's shotgun and purchased a birdshot shell. The next day, he and Jim coaxed the horse from the barn to the lip of a freshly dug hole. Out of sentiment for Old Maj, and to keep things neat, they covered his head with a burlap sack. Then Jim stood back as Tom Jr. raised and cocked the gun, aiming the barrel at a spot above the eyes. And *bang!* The brothers crouched and watched for Old Maj to buckle.

Nothing happened.

"He shot the horse and the horse continued to stand there," Jim recalls. Either Tom was a very poor shot or, more likely, he had used too little firepower. And he'd only bought one shell.

"So Tom stood there with this finger in his ear and didn't know what the hell to do," Jim says. "I took off on a dead run and I got the sledge hammer. And I came back and I took a healthy swing and I hit the horse dead in the forehead. The horse fell like a ton of bricks." Jim ends the story there. But as the brutal facts of the ending start to sink in for the listener, he adds, "Somebody had to do something, even if it was wrong."[6]

Now Dan picks up the story. He says his older brothers, out of laziness or inexperience, had dug the hole too shallow for the corpse, so that "after they buried him, there was a huge mound of loose dirt" visible by a laundry post behind the house. "My father was angry this was done so badly. Anyway, a week later, my mother was hanging clothes out there by the orchard when a huge fart erupted from the soil and one of Old Maj's legs shot straight up in the air. The poor horse had gassed out and given up the ghost. My mother dropped everything and ran screaming back to the house."[7]

"I can just imagine Dan adding something like that," says Jim, a little annoyed. (Endowed with his father's bent for precision, Jim prefers his memories somewhat factual.) When asked what happened to the leg, Dan ventures, "I guess they roped it down and put a rock of ages on it." Jerry is now so used to Dan's droll ending that he vaguely remembers having taken an axe and hacking the offending leg from the rest of the horse, then reburying it separately. (Of course, the plausibility of Jerry's detail is reduced by his not having been there. Which doesn't bother Dan; informed of Jerry's postscript, he doesn't hesitate to confirm it.) When Phil talks about Old Maj, he places the emphasis, with characteristic empathy, on the poor horse's suffering, and how those who should have looked after him let him down. One can also imagine Phil's approval of his brother Jim's decisiveness with the hammer, as well as his explanation for being bold in a moment of crisis: "Somebody had to do something, even if it was wrong."

Not to make too much of a family legend, and speaking metaphorically, Old Maj the undead horse can be seen as the comic and miraculous incarnation of a constant motif in Dan's writing: the need to stand one's ground, to come to a moral decision and stand by it, to stake out a place opposed to injustice and stand there—

he has dozens of ways of saying it—come what may. (Years later, Thomas Merton would eerily echo the image in a letter to Dan describing his spiritual state as a type of death-in-life experience, "I just continue to stand there where I was hit by the bullet . . . And when I fall over it will be a big laugh because I wasn't there at all."[8]) Of course, Dan might insist on an analogy with a more self-aware protagonist than Old Maj. But the big laugh is not on the horse but on the bumbling boys with guns, and on the woman at the gravesite unprepared for the sudden advent of the flatulent resurrection. In other words, it is the human pretensions of normalcy and control that are the joke, especially in Dan's retelling. And finally, it's worth noting that in the three versions of the Old Maj story, Dan's is the only one that stops the narrative to observe, "my father was angry."

Dado was often angry, but he aimed a special bitterness at Dan. It wasn't just that Dan was "a species of house boy," as he writes in his autobiography, staying inside to help his mother while his brothers worked outside around the farm. It was more that Dado saw his absence as an intolerable exception to his perfect scheme of absolute obedience. One recalls Tom's epiphany after his run-in with the railroad company judge in Lackawanna: his acceptance of the judge's view that discipline should achieve its aims by "the mere fact of its existence," making contrary claims, even just ones, irrelevant. Jerry Berrigan confirms that when his father took the judgment seat as the patriarch of the family, he sought to instill in his sons the same reflexive obedience: "We were brought up to totally accept church rules and school rules and, most of all, his rules. To us, from Pop, it was, 'You do as I say'—that makes you like me and it is right to be like me."

As "an undersized myopic tacker," Dan just couldn't measure up, so he stuck by his mother's side. Freda, opposed to Dado, appreciated and encouraged her son's love of reading and tried to stimulate his precocious religiosity. She installed a life-sized plaster statue of the Virgin Mary (with a few chipped fingers) in the house, then frequently plunked him in front of it and started him on a rosary. But deeply insecure as Dado was, he tried to undermine Dan's devotion to his mother, calling him names like "Sweet Sonny Boy" while attempting to shame him into performing more "manly" chores. "He stays in the house and helps with me!" Freda would call out to her husband, forcing him to relent but stoking the source of future conflicts, Dado's anger.[9]

No longer away on the railroad for weeks at a time, Dado would hover like bad weather over the family. Dan said the house would fill with "dread at the father's return home from the day's work, his face unsoftened and his temper unmediated"; Phil concurred: "There was a terrible gnawing fear, when he got home, there was no telling what would come down"; and Jim remembered the air being charged with threat, "He wouldn't hesitate to crack you on the rear, or he'd say, 'I'll give you a damn good warming,' which meant he'd spank your hind end hard."

In the very fact of their maturing, Dado discerned an implicit threat from his sons. "He gloried in prowess," Dan says, "but only in his own. In others he saw only adversaries, challengers."[10] While Dan took the brunt of Dado's verbal abuse, it was John, the second oldest, who battled him physically. John was husky and strong, though racked with a chronic asthma that kept him awake at night and slowed him during work. In addition to this weakness, he was shy to the point of brooding, except when he would intervene during Dado's sarcastic attacks on Freda. It was John who had the gall to contradict the natural order, so to speak, by telling his father to pipe down and back off.

Dado's response was to jeer John's manhood constantly. It got to the point that rather than endure his father's pique, John would fill his dinner plate and eat upstairs by himself. One evening, Dado arrived at the table and objected to John's empty chair. He demanded to know the reason for this absence; nobody answered. Angrier by the minute, Dado stormed upstairs and commanded his son come down and eat with everyone else. John obeyed. But as the two of them entered the kitchen, Dado exploded with an inexplicable rage and turned and swung at John, who had finally had enough. Like bare-knuckled boxers, they pummeled each other in front of the seated family. Phil scored the fight clinically: "John knew how to box and he marked him up." Dan said the brawl made him desolate: "I wanted to hide, get out of there"—an anxiety his brothers also say they felt. "I mean, there's nothing worse than vio-

lence going on in front of children," Dan said. "It's enough to
make you nonviolent, or very violent I guess."[11] In a poem, Dan
later described living with a father who could erupt at any moment,
how he and his brothers

> . . . sat on our perches blinking like six marmosets
> There were scenes worthy of Conrad,
> the decks shuddering;
> the world coming to an end![12]

"I don't want to come on like a shrink," Jerry offers, "but as I
see it, he had an overwhelming sense of his own importance, his
own talents, energies, intelligence, and just had concluded as a sop
to his own vanity that the world would never come to appreciate his
greatness. The world never gave him credit, put it that way, for who
and what he was. And so a lot of what you might call the interper-
sonal in his life—dealings with his sons and with his wife—were
kind of dire reflections of his own disappointment. Acting out, as
they say in the books."

For his part, Dado found the fights with John cathartic. Normally stymied in his low-wage work and essentially loveless marriage, his poems rejected by even the most obscure Catholic publications, he released his frustrations by turning his sons into verbal
and physical punching bags—even as Freda screamed at him to
stop. Dan and Phil remembered staring at their father across the
breakfast table some mornings, his smiling face all welted up, his
bearing, for once, content.

Jerry continues, "He felt he wasn't appreciated and had kind of
a tremendous, undisciplined ego. He thought he was the world's
best poet, farmer, locomotive engineer. He had an intensely competitive spirit with anybody in those areas. He wanted all of us in his
image: strong, good with our hands, with tools, inclined toward
the land and farming, devout with the faith, a good Irish Catholic
who goes to Mass every week, a lover of literature."[13] When Dado
nicked himself shaving he would sometimes look in the mirror and
mutter, "The blood of Irish Kings!" while Freda stood at the stove
and rolled her eyes.

Considering the later effect of Dan and Phil's resistance to violence and illegitimate authority, it is tempting to find a simple cause
in the outbursts of their father. For example, in their book *The FBI
and the Berrigans*, Jack Nelson and Ronald Ostrow declare in a
chapter titled, "What Manner of Men," that "a novelist sketching
the early life of a pair of revolutionary priests would have to look no
farther than the actual experiences of the Berrigans." The authors
then describe the brothers' frenzied life with Dado. "Well, that's
interesting," Dan says, when reminded of the quote, "but I think
it's a lot of bullshit myself"—rightly concerned that his life's work
not be reduced to a form of psychological compensation. On the
other hand, there can be no doubt that witnessing Dado's bouts of
rage was a formative experience for the brothers. It instilled in
them, if nothing else, a keen appreciation for the indivisibility of
suffering. When one is besieged, then so is the whole. And enduring such scenes at an age when they were powerless to act has
helped make them productively uncomfortable with what most of
the world accepts as the unfortunate reality of force used to
threaten or tyrannize the weak.

Part of their father's problem was his emotionally stifling relationship with his sisters. Dan observes that, "As in many tardy Irish
marriages, my father's loyalties were divided from the start,"
adding, "His primary affection and bent was toward [his sisters],
not toward his wife and children. Domination is a twisted form of
affection."[14]

Five out of seven of Tom Berrigan's sisters, as well as his
brother John, never married. His brother Ned wed, but his wife
died giving birth to their only child. So Ned arranged for others
to raise his baby, then joined the priesthood. Their rural Irish
roots had imparted to Tom, John, Ned, and their sisters a severely
repressed sexuality that sprung from the memory of poverty and
famine (the land will falter if everyone in the family reproduces),
and from the medieval Catholic Church's loathing of the body (an
idea with legs in Ireland and beyond). As a result, it was expected
that one devote one's heart to the clan, and have the heart's needs
met by the clan in return. This meant that most of Tom's siblings
chose professions over marriage (an either/or proposition for

many women), while treating Tom's marriage as property of the clan.

"They were all screwed up," Jim summarizes helpfully. "I mean, look at how many old maids there were in that family. And that was a very common situation among Irish families. We knew of any number of Irish families where either the men or women weren't married . . . They were very frustrated and unhappy, and had very unhappy lives."[15]

Almost every Sunday after Mass, Tom crossed town to visit the family on Matson Avenue. Dan and Phil were regularly dragged along for the tedious streetcar ride to their aunts' and uncles' drab house of "damp celibates and bachelor souls" (in Daniel's phrase), where the boys would be dumped in a gleaming wax parlor with an "ageless, evil parrot" named Patrick who bit if you came too close, while their father repaired to the kitchen to be with his siblings. There they would all eat pumpkin pie and talk about the good old days on Vinegar Hill and the world's ongoing ruin. Meanwhile, Dan sat bored as Phil lolled around on the floor reading "Prince Valiant" in the comics. Occasionally Uncle John, trailing a sweet bouquet of alcohol fumes, would straggle in and make a production of passing the boys a nickel each. Aunt Maggie would offer Lofts Hard Candies or, as a special treat, some harder-than-molars molasses cookies that Dan and Phil would jam beneath the couch cushions after she'd left. At a certain hour, the occupants of the two rooms switched: Dan and Phil would be sent to the kitchen for dry peanut butter sandwiches, while Dado and his sisters adjourned to tune in Father Charles Coughlin's weekly radio program, to which they clucked their populist approval. In the Great Depression's darkest years, Tom even formed a cell of Coughlin's national third party. It was made up of local factory men, small farmers, and day laborers—all frustrated, among other things, that anti-Catholicism had played a part in blocking former New York State governor Al Smith's recent bid for the White House. But the project unraveled when Coughlin went crazy and the New Deal started up.

Freda was seldom invited to these Berrigan convocations. When summoned for major holidays, she'd spend most of her time in silence as her husband's family rudely talked around her. Why? She was German (not Irish) American; an immigrant (not a second-generation) citizen; and high school (not college or professionally) educated. In short, because of snobbery. Phil writes in his auto-biography that his aunts thought his father had "married 'down'; that Freda is beneath him. Nothing could be farther from the truth. She is far superior to him. She is balanced, has more common sense, better judgment, and is emotionally stronger." Phil also reveals that at one point Freda consulted Ned, her brother-in-law priest, about separating from her husband. Predictably, he discouraged it. Later she got so desperate that she thought about fleeing Tom with the children—but had no place to go.[16]

"They stuck together—that's all that could be said," Jim concludes of his parents' fifty-eight years together. Beset by a querulous spouse and hostile in-laws, Freda focused on raising the boys. She sewed their clothes and filled them with good food: potatoes and salt pork and steaming piles of sauerkraut, and homegrown plums and pears from chilled glass jars. And she spoke for her boys when Dado lashed out at them. "She was quite a spirited woman, she was no milquetoast," says Jim.[17] When Freda caught tuberculosis and was hospitalized for a year in the early thirties, it was the thought of her boys being raised by one of the miserly Maston Avenue aunts that spurred her astounding recovery.

Freda also found relief in religious devotion. Dan remembers, "During the day, we would find her praying there by herself in the cold room [with the Virgin Mary statue]. When we went shopping downtown, we never left without stopping at the Cathedral, where we would kneel for quite a long time." Yet her religion was more than piety. In the late thirties, Tom's sister Agnes was diagnosed with cancer. Freda overcame her resentment and made it a point to take her sons to visit the hospital regularly. Agnes, moved by the kindness of the sister-in-law she had snubbed, said, "When I'm recovered and through this, Freda, things between you and me will be different."[18]

Her sons recall with gratitude how she lugged "tons" of the Victorians—Dickens, Hardy, Trollope, and Scott (with an occasional *Rover Boys* thrown in)—each week on the trolley to and from the downtown public library. "Like lion cubs waiting for the kill, we devour[ed] those books, then call[ed] for more," says Phil. And she was generous to those Depression nomads who occasionally made their way up from the tracks. She offered them leftovers and invited them to take their ease on the backyard cistern stone, then ladled out cherry preserves for dessert. Jerry once spied a ragged man eating a meal near where his mother was hanging the wash—an occurrence he would have forgotten had not the police showed up soon after the man had left. It turned out Freda had just served supper to a freshly escaped prison convict. Freda wasn't fazed; the man had needed help. Phil claims that Freda even misled the law on occasion, "giving the authorities false information, deliberately leading them away from their prey."[19]

Dan declares, "Whatever substance has accrued to our lives, whatever goodness, must be laid at our mother's feet."[20] But against his father he wields an almost infinite vocabulary of revulsion: "a flaring Turk, absurd, byronic"; "Caller of Tunes"; "old pirate, old mocker and weeper"; "descending cyclone . . . forensic tongue . . . stalemated, powerless"; "the original Olympian," and more. (Indeed, several reviewers criticized Dan's harping on his father's faults in his autobiography.) Phil is almost equally hard on Dado, but believes that Dan, in his writing, has gotten obsessive about the subject. He has "felt like saying on a number of occasions to Dan, 'Back off. It isn't going anywhere, this crap about Pop.' "[21]

Dan does try at times to paint a more complex portrait of his father. In an essay from *Lights On in the House of the Dead*, he writes of how Dado "walked with us to Sunday Mass, some two miles of open road, in the days when we were too poor to own a car or to take a streetcar or bus. At Mass, he prayed, as far as I can remember, with all his heart. He was capable of a sense of mystery. He was honest and generous and hardworking; for many years he slaved as a common workman for a Depression pittance; when he was laid off from work in the early thirties, he was not ashamed to apply for a public relief job, and to work for even less than before. Perhaps just his irascible, stubborn, anger will keep us afloat."[22]

Family acquaintances remark, as Dan has written, that the influence of Dado on "his sons, was enormous, penetrating, enduring, there can be no doubt. He shadows us, who knew him best; we advert to his ways, mannerisms, attitudes; sometimes we laugh, at times a wave of melancholy washes over. Others note how he lives in us; it is not invariably a compliment."[23] In her wisdom, Freda foresaw that her sons would later reflect on Dado's legacy, and be tempted to feel self-pity. Freda said, don't. "She told us not to use him as an excuse to be mediocre," Dan vividly recalls. "She used to lecture us sternly, 'You boys have had enough good family. Don't use it as an excuse to do nothing.' Oh, it was something! I never forgot it."[24]

Philip tries to find perverse virtue in having grown up in such a volatile household. "All those rhubarbs helped us control our fear later on," he contends, before paraphrasing from the Gospel of Matthew, "Faith and fear are opposite things. You can control fear in so far as you believe—believe that God is in charge and with the nonviolent."[25]

Dado's ill-temper was aggravated by his life of hard manual labor. Working as a groundman in a line crew for the Syracuse Lighting Company, he dug hundreds of holes for telephone poles, the skin on his fingers cracking from the cold. In 1929, he made $18 a week, enough to keep the Berrigans at what is now known as the poverty line. After the company laid him off, he eventually found a job at the Franklin Auto Plant polishing car bodies. The plant soon closed. In 1933, he joined a WPA work project at Onondaga Lake, where he helped drain swampland, build highways, and install a public swimming pool with a bathhouse. He also cut stone and worked on bridges. After a while he rose to foreman's pay at $21 a week.

Phil now thinks material scarcity brought some benefit to the family. It taught them to value the things they had: "If you owned a baseball glove or a bike, you took good care of it. You got schooled in the necessities of life: What's necessary—and what isn't—to survive. Knowing what you can do without. . . . It's the old distinction between needs and wants."[26]

Most importantly, the brothers had each other. Up on the house's slick tin roof, Dan, Phil, and Jerry—the three youngest, who had banded together—would sometimes run around like "hellcats,"

Jerry says. "We used to go to be under the sky, feel free, escape and be boys." Phil zoomed back and forth like a circus daredevil, nearly plummeting off the edge and into the bushes a couple of times. Jerry also remembers that Dan and Phil formed "a strike," an easy bond, at an early age. Dan agrees, saying he and Phil "used to tool around and do everything together. We had the same friends in the neighborhood. I just loved him and I guess he loved me. . . . We'd just wander around trying to get away with what little work we could. We would swim in forbidden waters or build fires in the culvert under the road. (We got severely treated for that—someone saw the smoke pouring out.) We would pick berries and tomatoes and go around selling them door to door."[27] Their rounds complete, the brothers would then take turns bouncing down a steep hill in their wagon. Dan remembers hanging on "like the Buddha in an earthquake."

When not with Phil or Jerry, Dan would climb up to the cupola to be alone or escape from Dado, to read, or to stare at the sky and think of his future. His view of Onondaga Lake and the green pleated hills beyond would have been entirely idyllic if not for the charcoal-colored clouds belched by the smokestack of the Solvay Processing Plant as it manufactured gun powder on the far shore, and the dark yellow slick on the lake that came from a spill-pipe running to Will & Baumer's Candle Factory, supplier of candles to the area's churches and self-advertised "Purveyors to the Pope."[28] Sometimes, in the middle of these reveries—part Wordsworth, part Blake's dark satanic mills—Dan would hear Dado hollering out his name.

It seems his father would occasionally be seized by his youthful muse. At such times, he would hide himself in a room with a wooden pencil and stab out great florid reams of poetry. Now and then he would burst into the living room to recite an especially inspired passage to Freda, who knew enough to judge it all great art. When an abundance of timeless verse had been thus produced, Dado would call for Dan, the family typist. Then Dan would be seated at a "wacko old typewriter" and be made to transcribe his father's latest contribution to the pantheon of world literature. (He remembers there being a lot of "Brother Christ" and "earth repar-

adised" involved.) When Dan was done, the work would be submitted to a magazine or newspaper. In this way, over the years, a
large trunk of unpublished manuscripts accrued.

Now and then Freda dispatched the boys on a mercy mission to
the neighborhood's poorer precincts. They carted fresh milk and
homegrown produce to old loners in broken-down swamp shacks
(including a shell-shocked Civil War vet), and Depression-socked
families with yards full of skinny kids and rusted farm tools. It made
the brothers realize that in an era of the forgotten and foreclosed,
their condition was far from the worst. They may be poor, their
mother was teaching them by example, but there was always a little
extra they could give.

It was years before the Berrigans could afford to buy a car again.
So it was up to the boys to cover the long two miles from home to
church and school. They spent hours trudging Old Liverpool Road's
dirt shoulder. They passed a farmers' market and an auto plant before
crossing over Leg Creek bridge, then the hedged-in estate of salt
magnate Thomas Gale, walked by wood-frame houses and grocers,
through pastureland and up a long rise, then crossed a green square
to St. John the Baptist elementary and high schools on Park Avenue,
run by the Sisters of St. Joseph of Carondelet. There they fell into line
with the other boys wearing pressed pants, shirts, and ties. The girls,
in their uniform collars and long-sleeved blouses, did their learning,
undistracted and undistracting, in a separate building.[29]

The usual Catholic grade-school horror stories apply. One nun
made her misbehaving students stand in a corner holding a stack of
heavy textbooks till their arms gave out and the books clattered to
the floor. Another would shriek, when particularly upset, but apro-
pos of nothing, "And to think they shot Lincoln!" Dan summed up
the school's pedagogy this way: "Dun, dun, and it was done." Phil
adds, "I learn[ed] by rote, swallowing propaganda, and in exami-
nations regurgitat[ed] nonsense and half-truths."[30] Out in the
schoolyard, as might be expected, Dan was the runt of the scuffling
litter. "With my granny spectacles, spindly form, and general air of
hebetude, I fairly invited insolence," he says.[31] Fortunately, Phil and
Jerry were large in body and reputation as home-hardened brawlers.

Part of every student's school obligation was attending the Sunday 9 A.M. children's Mass. Phil remembers the church crammed with nuns and priests, putting a coin on the gold collection plate, and having his attendance recorded by a teacher stationed for that purpose in his pew. "No-shows had hell to pay. They called your parents. You just endured it. It was all in mumbled Latin. It had meaning to receive the sacraments, to be in a state of grace and the presence of God. You went to confession the day before, Saturday. Half the time we walked in the good weather. In my junior and senior years, I used to ride a big red balloon-tire bike. I kept it shined up and running well."[32]

Unlike most of his schoolmates, Dan went to Mass on his own; he had a feeling it might have something to do with his future. It was this same obscure impulse that prompted him during lunchtime to slip away to a basement grotto, light a votive candle, and pray to Jesus. He prayed about his father, and about his growing conviction—it had come to him all of a sudden during a movie matinee—that he had been blessed with a vocation to the priesthood. One of his best friends, Jack St. George, felt similarly. So they sent away to dozens of Catholic orders for brochures.

Though Dan liked to insist in the 1960s on having been lured into the Jesuits by the aloofness of their sales pitch—they had a stark brochure with "just a couple of tight little quotes from St. Ignatius. . . . We thought that cool scene was revolutionary. We applied immediately"—the explanation is almost certainly flippant. The Jesuits, after all, were the virtual founders of Syracuse, brave men who faced violent death to spread their Gospel faith. Every Catholic child in the area learned of how in 1656, a French Jesuit mission, one of the first in the Americas, was built on the shores of Onondaga Lake, the future site of Syracuse. It was abandoned but later reestablished as Fort Ste.-Marie de Gannentaha by Father Simon LeMoyne. The area was rich in salt deposits, which had made it a crossroads since the time of the League of Five Nations Iroquois Indian Council. With typical Jesuit acumen, LeMoyne had realized the commercial value of the salt springs , and begun an industry that would last 200 years. Thus he was successful in the realms of both God and Mammon (not unusual for a Jesuit), and held up as an example to the young.

But school was not where Dan first learned the history of the church in upstate New York. It was during one of Dado's home education sessions, in which he read aloud from the great books while his family sat and listened. This usually meant recitations from Lord Byron and W. B. Yeats. But one night he pulled from the bookshelf the first in a set of five "livid green volumes" entitled *Pioneer Priests of North America*—the story of the continent's Jesuit martyrs. This time, as Dado conveyed the lurid tales of righteous sacrifice, fat tears striped his cheeks. Duly impressed, Dan read further on his own, and by the time those plain brown pamphlets arrived from the Jesuits, he was hooked. Both he and Jack St. George applied in 1938. They traveled by train to Auriesville, New York, where a trio of senior Jesuits took their measure. Then letters arrived that set the course for the rest of the two boys' lives, and filled Dan with a feeling as strong as any he had known: acceptance.

Entering adulthood, Dan and Phil were now set to move apart. Dan and Jack St. George prepared to join the most rigorous order of priests in the Catholic Church. They'd be leaving their families and the world for almost a decade. In isolated seminaries, they would immerse themselves in laborious and arcane scholarly pursuits: Latin, Thomistic theology, systematic philosophy, and sixteenth-century Jesuit history. Their days would revolve around disciplined study, lectures, liturgies, prayer, and demanding exams. Dan longed for such a life.

Phil, on the other hand, was evidently bound for worldly success. A barrel-chested natural athlete, he was the star of the St. John's basketball team and in his senior year made the Parochial League all-star team in baseball. Jerry remembers admiring Phil's play at first base from the stands: "He was a good, rangy, brainy, competitor. He played with his heart and was very skilled." Everyone assumed Phil would go to college, where his smarts and charisma would carry him into whatever career he chose. And this may have been the case had not World War II intervened, and, in the way of wars, changed everything.[33]

4

FORMATIONS

I select this case because it shows how
in these inner alterations one may find
one unsuspected depth below another,
as if the possibilities of character lay
disposed in a series of layers or shells,
of whose existence we have no
premonitory knowledge.
> —*William James*
> The Varieties of
> Religious Experience

Jesus striking . . .
a playful beckoning; why not come?
> —*Daniel Berrigan*

ON ENTERING THE CATHOLIC SEMINARY AT AGE EIGHTEEN,
Dan traded one overweening paternity for another. But where his
father was given to violent rage, maudlin self-pity, and confusing
bursts of affection, the church was as stately and collected as an
oceangoing ship—formidable and bejeweled by tradition, surviving stormy weather through the clever application of inertia. To

understand Dan's displacement, one must imagine a pious country boy sitting down to the table for the first time in a dining room filled with the suave, black-cassocked ranks of *la compagnia*—a six-teenth-century nickname, suggesting a synchronized elite, for the Society of Jesus. Occupying the front benches are the faculty and administration of St. Andrew-on-Hudson's Seminary in Pough-keepsie, New York (Dan describes them in tremulous letters home as "giant men with whom one short visit is a benediction and a joy."[1]) The meal proceeds in silence but for the drone of a young man reading aloud from a learned text: the life of a saint, the rules of the order, a history of the Jesuits in China, or some meandering speculation in ancient Greek. The light of dusk as it sifts through the fifteen-foot windows gives the scene its gilded feeling of an early church mosaic. Like a Cambridge University freshman who walks the streets and hears the echo of Sir Isaac Newton's footsteps, Dan is overwhelmed by the place's lineage. And the incredible good luck of his enrollment.

Freda, on the other hand, was probably torn by her boy's leaving home. She was unquestionably proud of Dan, and believed in the value and meaning of his vocation. But his departure for the seminary was, to a mother, like having a child pass into adulthood in a single afternoon—or, given the Jesuits' nickname as the "Light Cavalry of Christ," seeing a son march off to war. A fully-trained Jesuit priest was prepared to accept immediate and indefinite assignment to "un-Christianized" lands at any time. The direction of Dan's future was now not only beyond his mother's will, but his own—which lent the endeavor its unmistakable mystique.

"In those days," says former priest Vinnie Quayle, "if you joined the Jesuits, your mother went straight to heaven."[2] Freda savored the reflected glory due the woman who raised her son to Holy Orders. She joined the Syracuse Jesuit Mothers Club, a group whose "chests were really puffed up" with maternal pride—though Freda, with true Midwestern reserve, kept her excitement decently circum-scribed. "She adored Dan, but was sensible about it," remembers Jim Berrigan. Dado, too, admired Daniel's decision to join the priesthood, and from then on "treated him differently from when he was a kid . . . [and] with a greater regard."[3] Dan is less sure about this, detecting a continual ambivalence in his father toward his son's religious and, later literary achievements, fields in which Dado continued to consider himself an undiscovered genius.

Finally free of failing to live up to Dado's mania for Herculean labor, Dan could at last work to his strengths. He had always been a talented student with a love of books and poetry. He had also been tending his faith like a private garden. "He spent much time by himself," says Jerry of Dan's adolescence, "read a great deal and did a lot of praying. He developed a whole secret side right there in front of us."[4] In the Jesuits he could cultivate and reconcile these interests.

Both streams of the Berrigan immigrant background supported Dan's choice. German-American Catholics organized their political and social lives around the church; and the Irish, as they adored their mothers, also adored their priests. Generally, it was a cultural moment in the American Catholic Church during which the center not only still held but exerted a strong transformative pull. And the Jesuits, their reputation for serious achievement widely known within Catholic circles, assumed that ambitious men would learn of their history, aspire to join it, and seek them out. In the case of Daniel Berrigan, they were right.

In 1939, there were 6,000 Jesuits in the United States, comprising more than 20 percent of their worldwide total. Over the next fifteen years, when Dan was "in formation," as Jesuit training is called, both these numbers rose impressively.[5] So he was entering a select order at a time when both the Jesuits and the Catholic priesthood were held in high regard, and were poised for a golden age.

It was also the traditional way out of his predicament. For a working-class kid growing up on a farm, professional choices were few; "the only alternative we saw to the priesthood were the lives of our fathers, lives of drudgery," says Jim Kelly, a former seminarian.[6] Unlike his brothers, Dan had no prospects in a physical trade. There was no precedent or money for his attending a college that would satisfy his intellectual gifts. Voluntary outlets for altruism, like the Peace Corps, were more than a generation away. The priesthood, with its rigorous education and the possibility of dispatch to foreign missions, beckoned with a relative glamour. For centuries in Ireland, it had been the sole path to higher learning for many, accounting for its prestige among Irish immigrants. Another attraction was practical, as Peter McDonough (one of Daniel's former Brooklyn Prep High School students) explains in his history of the Jesuits in America: "Famine, land hunger, and rules of inheritance that favored one son to the exclusion of other male offspring combined with a legacy of sexual asceticism to generate large numbers of applicants to the priesthood among Irish men and boys."[7] So, like his grandfather, Thomas I from Tipperary, Dan was embarking on an established immigrant's route—from *lumpen* obscurity to the far shores of the Catholic Church's spiritual elite.

The Jesuit path was straight and well-marked. Since 1591, when the order was founded by Ignatius Loyola, a converted Basque courtier and crippled military officer, many thousands of men had walked its length. When Dan entered in 1939 with his best friend Jack St. George, they were, as he describes it, "great innocents, with the dreadful, uncharted future lying out there . . . thinking our lives would go straight as the arrow of God's (purported) will: safe, sound, bell, book, candle, cassock, rule, long black line, classroom, rec room, womb-to-tomb security."[8]

When Dan entered St. Andrew's Seminary, he passed down a birch and pine-hemmed road, leaving behind the traces of human habitation for a rolling manor on a bluff overlooking the Hudson River. He has often compared the experience to a birth—deliverance into an utterly new form of being. If it was a birth, it was out of this world. A Jesuit's lengthy training was designed first for the "disposing . . . of all disordered affections," as is stated in the opening paragraph of Loyola's *Spiritual Exercises*, then, "after their removal, of seeking and finding God's will in the ordering of our life for the salvation of our soul."[9] It was felt at the time that to do this properly, Dan and his fellow seminarians must be separated from the compromised and compromising world. Thus freed from all mundane temptations, they could concentrate on the order's course of spiritual development. "On the altar of obedience," went the cheery Jesuit motto, "we make our lives a holocaust to God."[10]

St. Andrew's was a self-supporting system. "Brother Cook" supervised the making of meals, and "Brother Barber" cut everyone's hair. The seminarians themselves maintained the 700 acres interspersed with life-sized, full-color statues of the saints. They cleared the brush, painted the buildings, and raked the gravel pathways. (Occasionally hobos would wander up from the train tracks by the river, offering labor in exchange for a meal, an arrangement familiar to Dan.) All learning and the sacraments were conducted on the grounds, as it had been since 1902. There was no hot water. Comportment was strict, Rome dictated the reading list, and "liturgy was inflexible," according to the Jesuit writer John L'Heureux. "Theology had nothing whatsoever to do with society, or, for that matter, with the living."[11] In his autobiography, Dan fondly remembers his teachers as uniformly "caustic and curmudgeonly."[12]

Yet this austere and demanding life was profoundly satisfying. "I fell in love immediately and incurably with the Jesuit style," he writes. "I found in the talents and youth and drive around me a constant spur to make my own life count."[13] Like his fellow aspirants, Dan considered it an honor to dedicate his life to religious service. He wrote to Freda that "Tomorrow is the Feastday of our Holy Father St. Ignatius. I always thank him in profound humility for singling me out from all the more fit ones to be part of his great family."[14]

The sacrifice was heroic, but then, the enterprise was sublime. The priesthood, especially the Jesuits through their schools, held together the sprawling mid-century American Catholic Church. The Jesuits' moral and intellectual influence ran deep among the laity, who generally revered them. And a critical part of the order's aura arose from the long, arcane submersion of formation, when the "chariot swung low and swept one up"[15] into a baroque and cloistered universe of secret penances, midnight prayers, murals of martyred or conquering saints, litanies and Latin chants, lilies at Easter and bells to call out Christmas Day, splinters from the One True Cross, ash-smudged foreheads, silence at meals, averting one's eyes when a woman passed, Aquinas and Aristotle.

The Jesuit-in-training climbs a fifteen-year ladder with six distinct rungs: (1) a novitiate of two years, after which he takes perpetual vows of poverty, chastity, and obedience; (2) juniorate, two years, classical studies and work toward a bachelor of arts degree; (3) philosophate for three years, similar to a master's degree in philosophy, with an oral exam in Latin; (4) regency, three years' work in a high school or foreign mission; (5) theologate, a four-year program in theology—after the third year, he is ordained a priest; and (6) tertianship, an introspective final year of prayer and preparation before full-time work in the world.[16]

Some fifty years later, Dan still loves being a Jesuit but has little good to say about his training. He complains about St. Andrew's semimonastic dreariness and its military regimen—a smug retreat, as he now regards it, from the order's dynamic founding by the controversial Loyola, who was jailed for a time by the Inquisition on grounds of too great evangelical zeal. By contrast, Dan describes his novitiate as more in the spirit of the persecutors of Loyola than of the innovative man himself: an inculcation in sacred irrelevancies and corporate conformity. "Everyone was in the same lockstep," he declares. "Out there was the world, a remote object of curiosity and some longing. You would be rusticated."[17]

There was also the pressure of constant testing. Academic exams were frequent and exhaustively comprehensive, but they paled against the constant judgments superiors applied to the novices, mostly having to do with their adherence to the institution's complicated rules. Standards were high and rigorously upheld; there were plenty of customers to take the place of men who didn't measure up. Almost nightly, Dan walked down a long hall to confront the "seignorial gaze"[18] of the Father Master, the priest directly over him, whose private habit was to seek the greater glory of God by binding himself in heavy iron chains.

One night, Dan recalls, the Father Master challenged him: "I don't think you have this vocation, but go to the chapel and pray over it and come back and tell me what you've learned."

Reflecting on this assignment decades later, Dan, in a forgiving mood, explains, "I think this tactic was to give one a boot, to get one over a hump. Father Master had the uncanny sense when something was being held back, when one was riding easy, on a plateau."[19] But to Dan, the young seminarian, the task was nearly devastating. He left the room in shock and spent an agonizing session on his knees, suddenly forced to contemplate a life apart from the Jesuits—his new but hard-won home. Though the learning could be dry and some of the spiritual chores quite tedious, Dan reveled in his chosen order's commitment to excellence. No one back home, save Freda, had ever expected much from him. To be turned away from this chance to make good would confirm these low opinions. And where would he go? This first of many suggestions, official and otherwise, that he think about leaving the priesthood set the precedent for his reaction to the idea: He hated it.

After a while, he returned to face the Father Master, determined to hold his place in the seminary. Near tears, he blurted, "I won't go, I'm staying." And the Father Master, having gotten what he was after, deigned to agree.

Dan writes that because of these and other manipulations, "there crept into our souls a kind of siege mentality,"[20] in which one conducted feats of contrition and rote academics and marathon observances just to impress and ensure one's survival in the order. As a result, Dan became what he calls "a Good Young Pharisee . . . a wooden Indian Jesuit," who "kept the rule woodenly, was difficult to live with, all elbows and opinions . . . and much wanting in the quality of mercy, whether toward myself or others."[21] Sometimes acts of great self-sacrifice can leave traces of impatience and imperiousness. This seems to have been the case with Dan. Along with the better angels of his wit and warm-heartedness, he developed a habit of harshly judging anyone who failed, in his view, to match his commitment to a moral cause, to the later annoyance of some of his friends and allies in the peace movement. It can fairly be said that the Jesuits, with their fabulously arrogant practice of not only counseling but demanding perfection, contributed to this aspect of his formation.

Still, in his letters home at the time, he laments not being able to give adequate description to his overwhelming happiness. Repeatedly, he writes that however steep the climb, he is convinced there is no better road for him. He and his seventy co-novices entered the seminary "hardly hatched,"[22] yet for incubation they had "friendship, community, the promise of support for one another, a vision of great work to be done, which those before you had done so well."[23] Within their red-brick and white-pilaster cocoon, the novices shaped their identities as Jesuits, absorbing through constant religious devotions, dry theoretics, yearly retreats, and good and bad examples, those habits of the heart and mind that would govern them wherever they should travel.

This made for an intense camaraderie. One former seminarian likened the bonding to that of soldiers in the same army platoon, brought together to train for a vital cause. He recalls being nineteen and eating ice cream on Sunday night with his fellow novices—the social and gustatory highlight of the week—and thinking of his childhood friends, probably pub-crawling in Manhattan at that moment, and not envying them at all. He and his "brothers" were preparing to be priests, "the protectors of the Catholic people . . . we were really doing something with our lives."[24] And in return, his life gained a purpose, coherence, and clarity it would not otherwise have known.

Judging from his letters home, Dan seems to have found a sense of belonging in the Jesuits that he had sought in vain while growing up. In one passage, he describes a party touching in its innocence: "I was just getting a bit homesick when the Archangel [the name for an older Jesuit seminarian] announced that we would now go down to meet those Novices who have just finished their first (and a few their second) year. We proceeded down to one of the parlors, lined up, and the Brother Novices suddenly shouted the Jesuit greeting, '*Laudetus Iesus Christus*,' Praised be Jesus Christ, to which we shouted back, '*In saecula saeculorum*,' Forever and ever! Then came the rush for us. I never in my life shook so many hands or saw so many genuinely happy faces. After a half hour exchange of riotous greetings we started a songfest which lasted about an hour, with Father Master of Novices at the piano. Many of the older Brother Novices gave sparkling imitations and parodies. What a night!"[25] After a bitterly fractured home life endured as a bright, bespectacled boy within a muscular immigrant enclave, how could this be anything less than paradise?

Presume not that I am the thing I was;
For God doth know, so shall the world
     perceive,
That I have turned away from my
     former self;
So will I those that kept me company.
     —*Shakespeare*, Henry IV, Part 2

While Dan was at St. Andrews, Phil was finishing high school at St. John the Baptist. Some of his teachers, when asked to recall his performance, rated it roughly as follows: B-minus in academics (he toiled in Dan's lingering shadow, the oft-invoked star pupil); A for demeanor (one nun called him "heavenly," possibly commenting on his straw-blond hair and strapping good looks); and an A-plus for faith and morals (he stopped in a church to recite the rosary before picking up his dates). The scouting report on his baseball skills described him as a slow-footed, power-hitting first baseman; in basketball, he was a husky center with the finesse moves of a wrecking ball.

Despite the several teachers and clergy in the Berrigan family, Phil set out, on graduating, to be the first to complete four years of college. (Years before, Dado had briefly attended Valparaiso College, but became dissatisfied with academia and dropped out.[26])

Tom Jr. had left home as soon as he could for itinerant farm work; John and Jim had joined the Civilian Conservation Corps in 1941 and were sending home portions of their meager paychecks; Jerry was doing the same from his job with the nearby Niagara Mohawk Power Company. But Phil lived at home while working so he could save for his college tuition. Like Dado, he got a job with the railroad, doing the least romantic work there was: scraping the sooty skin off steam-powered locomotive trains in the New York Central yards. With his extra energy, and for pocket change, he played first base for a local semiprofessional ball team. During that year, a priest from the little-known Order of St. Basil came through the area recruiting students for the small Catholic college of St. Michael's in Toronto, Canada. Phil liked what he heard and enrolled a year later. He completed the fall semester and became captain of the freshman basketball team, before being drafted into the army in early 1943. He was "nineteen years old, and excited to be following my brothers into battle, anxious to slaughter infidels and to return home bearing the standard of peace and justice," he now mournfully recalls.[27]

Phil, Tom Jr., and Jerry entered the military a few months apart. Each of them would eventually serve in Europe, while John enlisted in Hawaii and shipped off for the Pacific war. Jim stayed home with the lingering effects of a broken back, suffered when he sleep-walked out a second-story window. (In the year before entering the seminary, Dan had studied Latin and helped his mother nurse Jim back to health.) Earnestly conventional in his thinking about religion and politics, Dan now wrote a poem to honor his four enlisted brothers, called, "You Vested Us This Morning," portraying their military service as akin to holy anointing. In it, he described the raising of a "cross-hilt sword" that brings "white-dolmatic peace"—exactly the mix of devotional and military imagery he would later come to loathe. His second published poem, it appeared in the Jesuit journal *America*.[28]

Dan invited Phil to pause before going to war by taking a four-day retreat at St. Andrew's Seminary. Phil says that as he prayed the Ignatian *Exercises* and walked the wooded acres he considered filing for a military exemption to become a priest. But in the end he decided he would rather "charge pillboxes, blow up machine gun nests, and fight hand-to-hand with my country's enemies." Action beat contemplation. And besides, "War was an abstraction" to him: "Pictures in a book. Words on the radio. Flourishes good to hear, and good to feel running up and down my spine." So he embraced his brother and hopped the next train south.[29]

Phil took his basic training at Fort Gordon, Georgia, with mostly Polish-American recruits from western New York State: "steel mill people, a tough bunch," he says. They shot Enfield rifles at cutouts of German and Japanese soldiers and learned to fire howitzers and long-range eight-inch guns, to obey orders without a second thought, and to march in tight formations. In a year of training, Phil moved through Fort Blanding in Jacksonville, Florida, and Fort Bragg in North Carolina—and up the ranks to sergeant. In July 1944 he landed in Great Britain and was assigned the task of combing several bombed-out urban neighborhoods for salvageable equipment. His searches took him through London, Coventry, Birmingham, Sheffield, and other skeletal English cities. The bombed-out devastation he saw— "Children suffocated in the rubble. Old people burned to death in the firestorms. Survivors . . . crippled for life."—both horrified and steeled him for worse to come on the continent.[30]

After the Allied D-Day invasion had secured a foothold in northern France, Phil's artillery unit took a position near the town of Brest, overlooking a fortified German submarine pen. He and his men prepared to launch a "vertical control operation," which meant firing an incessant barrage of 200-pound shells down on the Germans. Phil flew over the U-boats in a Piper Cub, then performed calculations that fixed the target positions. He sent them to the gunners, and the shooting began. Today he describes himself as being "complicit" in this operation, which went on for months. But at the time he had no doubts about his task. "I was a gung-ho young jerk, an eager warrior," he says of himself at twenty-two, a typical soldier from the American working class without an inkling of the pacifism that would later guide his life, "a very good killer who knew no history or morality. Just an Irish Catholic kid."[31]

Phil's unit also opened their guns on the city of Lorient, France, before moving through the Netherlands to the Ruhr coal districts near Baeswiler, Germany. Then the Battle of the Bulge began before Christmas 1944. Phil and his men fired on part of the dug-in army of General Von Runstedt—avoiding a direct engagement, but coming under mortar and anti-tank gun fire. The Twenty-ninth Infantry, which included Captain Tom Berrigan (Tom Jr.) of the Maryland National Guard, moved up near Phil's position. Tom Jr. and his men had landed on D-Day and pushed through France while taking enormous casualties. The oldest Berrigan brother was now an infantry leader with heavy combat experience. He sought out Phil, who had been killing from a distance.

While they were visiting each other, a formation of Luftwaffe planes flew in and began to drop their load of hundred-pound bombs. Tom Jr. yelled, "Hit the deck!" and dove for cover in a cellar. But Phil stayed upright for several moments, exhilarated by the fierce explosions less than a block away. Finally, he crouched on the floor and flashed his brother a satisfied grin. Tom Jr. called him a fool.

Not long after, Phil moved to a barbed-wire Allied camp near the Elbe River in Germany, where he pulled guard duty on German POWs. His orders were to keep a round in the chamber of his rifle with the safety on; he was to shoot to kill if a prisoner made the slightest questionable move. Pacing back and forth, he studied the elite troopers of the German Africa Corps. "They were arrogant and proud," he says, and looked down on their American captors. "They were Nazis to the core. I decided to go to OCS [Officer's Candidate School] simply to fight against those bastards."[32]

He volunteered for the OCS in Fontainebleau, south of Paris. He became a "90-day wonder" second lieutenant, and was appointed to the Eighth Infantry Division in Westphalia, outside of Münster, Germany. He wrote later that he was looking forward to plunging into battle. But the end of the European war thwarted his ambition— luckily, since a platoon leader's combat life expectancy was, by army calculation, about two minutes.

After V-E Day in May 1945, Phil and his men spent ten days in Münster. He wrote later that there was a "sweet stench hanging over the city . . . a vast, accidental cemetery, with people rotting where the explosives had caught them—in homes, offices, even churches." One afternoon, a GI from his unit returned from patrol and shared a leering description of an abandoned, bombed-out hospital with "some of them fetuses in bottles, and a bunch of naked women lying around in vats. Just like a museum, only better." Phil and some other GIs, "being red-blooded American boys," went out to investigate. They tramped to the hospital and made their way down to a fetid basement where they found what they were looking for—an offhand display of human grotesquerie. According to Phil, the Germans, "with characteristic economy," had stockpiled bombing casualties to supply the hospital with spare body parts. In the dimly lit room, the blast-mutilated corpses floated naked in rectangular vats of formaldehyde. Most were headless, yet there was "a strange, collective dignity about them," wrote Phil. A few of the vats had leaked, leaving the bodies inside exposed to ravenous swarms of bluebottle flies. The flies and the stench and the casual horror combined to drive the soldiers back to daylight.

Returning to camp, Phil and his men spoke little of what they'd seen—it was just another brutality in the life of a World War II infantryman. Phil says, "We could not comprehend then, or even now, what all that meant: the ravaged city, its dead and refugee population, its embalmed victims in the stinking cellar." But he adds that such experiences took an insidious psychic toll, on himself as well as others.[33]

Shipped back to Camp Leonard Wood, Missouri, Phil trained to invade Japan. Then in early August 1945, America dropped atomic bombs on Hiroshima and Nagasaki. The bombs' exponential degree of destructive power was hard to grasp from news reports, even after years of journalistic descriptions of mechanized slaughter on a global scale. All most people cared about, including Phil, was that World War II was over.

Phil, though, found he'd been scarred by the war in paradoxical ways: He was emotionally coarsened by the killing, yet extremely sensitized to the racism suffered by black Americans. While shuttling through the Deep South during training, he got a close look at the poverty and "sheer exclusiveness"[34] inflicted on blacks who were trapped in the massively unjust sharecropper system.

"Week after week we maneuvered through that strange, time-warped Georgia landscape," Phil wrote of his first exposure to the world of Jim Crow. "Marching past little tarpaper shacks, flapping in the wind, smoke coughing out of metal chimneys sprouting from their roofs. The blacks . . . didn't own their shacks, and they didn't own the land they worked from sunup to sundown. They rented these plots from white men, bought seed and other necessities from white men, borrowed money at usurious rates from white men. Seventy-five years after their emancipation from slavery, southern blacks were still living in brutal poverty, kept down by . . . racist violence, working like mules, and dying without hope."[35] Many southerners he met derided even casual contact between whites and blacks as suspect and unnatural. After one exhausting all-day march, Phil and some other men bought barbecued chicken for one dollar apiece from a black man's roadside stand. A local white man saw this and made it his business to approach the recruits and mock them for eating "buzzard." Too busy chomping their roasted meat, Phil and the others waved off the man and his bitter non sequitur. But the fierceness of the stranger's racial animosity stayed with Phil.[36]

Other disturbing racial incidents had dogged Phil throughout his military service. During a stormy North Atlantic crossing on the *Queen Mary*, black troops were forced to sleep on an outside deck. While they shivered miserably in the bitter weather, Phil and four white soldiers shared a stateroom. In Paris, most French citizens would tolerate a black soldier taking a white woman out to a night-club or cafe. But, says Phil, if a group of white American soldiers came across them, "this guy was suddenly risking his life." More than once, he saw black soldiers verbally and physically attacked by whites. One day a column of trucks in which Phil was riding came upon a black GI and a white woman walking together by the side of the road in northern France. Immediately, white soldiers on the back of Phil's truck dug out K-ration tins from their packs and, drawing even with the couple, threw them as hard as they could at the black GI, shouting insults to round out their pleasure. "Those cans were heavy and they hurt," remembers Phil. Between such brutal behavior and his own troubled feelings, he "realized military life was not for me. There was too much drinking and womanizing. I was drinking far too much."[37]

Later profiles would describe Phil as an exceptional warrior—a latter-day Loyola or Martin of Tours who went through a convulsive religious conversion after surviving the terrors of war. It's a good story, but it isn't true. From all evidence, his religious faith seems to have been meaningful and constant throughout his life. If anything, his conversion was political, not religious.[38] And his awakening came in stages. The first involved reading Dado's copies of the *Catholic Worker* as a young man growing up. The next was his experience of the unyielding intolerance directed at blacks. Part of his sensitivity on the issue may have come from Dado, who started the first Catholic Interracial Council in Syracuse; the rest derived, initially, from the moral offense he took at seeing black men who were risking their lives in the service of their country treated by other Americans like the enemy.

Meanwhile, in the Hudson Valley, Dan toiled in splendid isolation up the rungs of the Jesuit ladder. All he knew of his brothers came from sketchy dispatches sent by his parents. Except for a two-day-old front page from the *New York Times* tacked to a bulletin board, he and his fellow seminarians had little news of the war, or much else. After taking vows and completing his classical studies, Dan moved to Woodstock College in Maryland, where he would further imbibe from the Jesuit springs of theological conservatism. As a member of an elite corps, he was being intellectually outfitted to defend the American Catholic Church which nativist movements had attacked for its largely immigrant base, alleged control by the papacy, and, to some, mysterious rituals. One approach to this problem was to cultivate a traditionalist in-house culture around which clergy and laity could rally—such as Dan was being taught to embody; the other was to be out front on every patriotic issue—like the four Berrigan boys who went to war and their brother seminarian who blessed them for it.

The Berrigan veterans returned home intact in 1945. Tom Jr. arrived with Honor, his English war bride, and settled in Syracuse. John hit the road to pursue a string of jobs that would keep him moving—from newspaperman to stevedore on a Great Lakes barge—and sometimes out of touch with the rest of the family for years at a time. Jerry enrolled in Holy Cross College, a hundred year-old Jesuit school in Worcester, Massachusetts. Jim married Rosalie and moved to Walla Walla, Washington, and started a family. And despite Dado's threats of lethal resistance against any attempt to move him, the Sisters of Charity had recently sold the house on Liverpool Road out from under him. He and Freda now lived in the house on Matson Avenue—the aunts had either died or were living elsewhere.

Phil, discharged, spent the next year doing construction work in Syracuse, contemplating marriage to a woman he was dating, and drinking to excess. Life was pleasant but pointless. "The sun rose, the sun set. Days turned into weeks," he says of this strangely listless time. "Weeks turned into months. My friends and I seemed to be waiting for something, but we didn't know what it might be." He broke up with his girlfriend and fell deeper into his "postwar torpor" until at last his brothers and Freda convinced him to follow Jerry to Holy Cross on the GI Bill.[39] Phil arrived at the school in the fall of 1946. He liked the way the Mount St. James campus spilled pleasantly down the upper folds of a leafy hill that overlooked the city, and he was relieved to find that half the freshman class consisted of older vets like himself. Students living in dorms, like Phil, followed a set of rules peculiar to the age—notably, bedchecks at 10:45 P.M. to ensure the alertness of the all-male student body during the next day's mandatory 7 A.M. chapel service. Phil kept the rules and studied enough to get by. His European service helped him earn A's in freshman French, he squeaked through math, and he almost failed Catholic theology. He got the hang of English, his major, as time went by and settled into B's.

Jim Berrigan came east to visit him regularly over the next few years, and from his perspective, Phil lived the life of a campus golden boy. He remembers Phil's fine set of golf clubs and sweet swing off the tee, and that Phil, older than the average student, carried himself with a worldly dash that made "everybody like him." Jim added that Phil was "handsome," "personable," "fun to be around," and "very cool"—and that when Phil once wanted to dress up sharp, he borrowed Jim's tweed jacket and became "an instant hit with the ladies."[40]

Phil remembers that he still wrestled inner demons. Returning home on breaks and holidays, he would spend "a lot of time in bars, and going out with women. With my buddies in Syracuse I'd go cruising around." Like his other physical abilities, Phil's drinking was prodigious. But there was no satisfaction attached to it, and he would often reel home feeling empty. "It's purposeless, the drinking. The whole thing's egotistical. My mother knew something about putting her son to bed drunk and sick. . . . Four or five times, I would get up with an enormous hangover. Freda would fix tea and poached eggs to settle my gut."[41] Dan only learned of this difficult period years later when his brother, testifying at trial, spoke of the experiences that had turned him into a pacifist. Both Phil and Jerry "were very hard hit by the war, no doubt about it," Dan says now. "They were kind of crazy. Oh, they had seen a lot of awful—. . . Anyway, they were a long time simmering down."[42]

Phil began questioning the direction of his life. His roommate of four years, Richard Cusack, recalls that unlike the average callow undergraduate, Phil "had a more refined sense of what he was about, what he wanted to do, which he had gotten from Dan and Jerry. He thought life could be more." As he went to parties and drank on Saturday nights and attended proms and football games,

Phil also searched for a meaningful expression of his talents. One of them was an "extraordinary commitment to other people that I think is inborn, inbred in him,"[43] says Cusack, telling the story of Phil waiting tables for extra money in the campus dining hall.

"There was this man named Mooney," Cusack recalls, "who was a real Napoleonic type. He bossed around the waiters, and he just didn't like Phil's uppity nature. One night Mooney thought Phil was giving extra rolls or something to one table, so he blocked Phil's way as he came out the swinging doors. Mooney had his hand up like a traffic cop, telling him to stop. Phil had a tray of food in his hand but without breaking pace he gently nudged him aside saying, 'One side Mooney, these men gotta be fed.' He sailed right through him. It was pure Phil . . . fighting Goliath." Cusack adds that it's easy to read too much into the incident in the light of Phil's later battles with stubborn authorities, but it illustrates his drive to serve, and a certain fearlessness backing it up.

Along these lines, some of Phil's courses were beginning to engage him with questions of conscience and divided allegiance. He says it was "devastating" to his respect for the status quo to find a professor who taught Shakespeare not solely as dissected literature, but "from a moral and political standpoint—*Henry IV, Julius Caesar* . . . It was the first time anyone in higher education had spoken that way to me."[44] Until then, for Phil, most classroom discussion had occurred at an abstract remove from the world. Now, as in another class taught by a Jesuit professor that included scrutiny of the Catholic "just war" doctrine, Phil began to consider moral action as more than one's obligation to follow orders handed down by authority. Holy Cross exposed him to unsettling ideas, such as the statement from his religious ethics textbook that "men must be taught that it is not 'sweet and becoming to die for one's country' if one's country is fighting for that which is unjust."[45] How did he react to this more challenging and ambiguous moral reasoning? "I absorbed it like a plant absorbs water," he says.[46]

He shared his concerns with Dan, who was now studying theology a short drive away in the Massachusetts town of Weston. He also paid overnight visits to Jerry, who had entered the Newburgh, New York seminary of the Society of St. Joseph, an order of priests more commonly known as the Josephites. The two brothers, with whom he had always been close, were models for him now. He compared their poise in pursuit of exalted endeavors to his own mundane activities, "which didn't amount to a piss hole in the snow." He resolved to do something "serious." Phil says, "My experience in the service showed me there was nothing better I could do with my life than devote myself to helping blacks."[47] So, shortly after graduating in 1950, he again followed Jerry—this time into the seminary. He liked the Josephites' abbreviated training, at least compared to that of the Jesuits: a one-year novitiate and four years of theology. But more importantly, the Josephites had been founded at the turn of the century as the only American order of priests dedicated to serving black Catholics. Phil would be spending his talents on behalf of a largely poor group of people whose claims on justice he had begun to understand personally.

The move stunned many of his friends and classmates who had come to expect big things from Phil based on his popularity and charisma. "If Phil didn't enter the priesthood, the world would have been his oyster. He could have chosen from many women, many business pursuits,"[48] says Jim. But, like Dan, to whom he'd grown exceptionally close, he wanted to make his life count through religious service. He says he and Jerry revered their brother for his intellectual sophistication, the poetry he was beginning to publish in Catholic periodicals such as *Commonweal* and the *Catholic Worker*, and his halting but significant probing of the church's role in the modern world. Phil says of Dan that "in many ways—tangible and intangible—he was a decided influence on our decisions about our own lives."[49]

Dan had gotten a first taste of life outside the seminary during his three-year regency as a teacher at St. Peter's Prep in Jersey City, New Jersey. During insomniac strolls through the city, he began thinking about the relevance of the priesthood to the lives of the poor, like the students who lined up every morning in the school's glass-strewn parking lot. He was reading in the French the collected works of Teilhard de Chardin, with his emphasis on incarnational theology—God would be found in this world or not at all. It increasingly troubled Dan that the majority of the European church had not responded to the challenge of fascism, but had mainly been docile during Hitler's reign of foreign war and domestic atrocity. And he had been learning about the French worker-priest movement spearheaded by the progressive French Cardinal Emmanuel Suhard—clerics who wore civilian clothing and toiled in factories alongside the workers while preaching a nascent form of liberation theology. Dan was enthralled by the possibility of a priesthood engaged with social issues, but this did not as yet effect rapid change in the way he lived his life—it would take more seasoning and challenges from Phil to accomplish that.

On June 21, 1952, in what Jerry calls an "ecclesiastically riotous event,"[50] Dan lay prostrate with his face pressed against a marble floor in the Weston chapel. It was the scene of his ordination as a priest in the Society of Jesus. The formidable Richard Cardinal Cushing intoned the words of the service with a voice that came from on high, it seemed to Dan, who was caught up in the moment's awesome solemnity. There were scores of friends and family and former teachers to greet him as, bedecked in black robes and biretta, he strode from the church as a newly ordained Jesuit priest, and, as he confessed some nine years later, "a most unfinished man."[51]

Among those waiting to greet him were Freda and Dado. A poem Dan later composed about a Mass celebrating his first decade as a priest expresses the similarly bittersweet gratitude he felt as he greeted his parents on the day of his ordination:

> I summon my parents, a jubilee morning.
> When in gold vestments I came down
> to kiss them where they stood, their tears and mine
>
> were a clear pressing of the eighty-year vine.
> I touched their faces, a gentle unweathered grain
> the blind might visualize, as of green leaves
> up from exposed ground.
>   What winter fury
> that moment tempered, they and I know.[52]

The whole clan gathered for a party back at 123 West Matson Avenue in Syracuse. At one point, Dado and Freda posed on the couch for a photo with Dan, Phil, and Jerry—the brothers who had prompted one admiring neighbor to compliment Dado on the local church steps one recent Sunday: "Three sons in the priesthood, Mr. Berrigan, that's being a quality parent."[53] In the array of smiling faces beneath a devotional portrait of Christ praying in the Garden of Gethsemane, one could read a family's fulfillment: happy parents, content that their sons have started down the road toward wholesome and predictable lives. When Dan is shown the photo forty-three years later, he greets his youthful image with a gust of laughter. "That was the apogee," he interprets, pointing to himself. "Things were still holding close together then. I mean look at that guy there—untried by the world."[54]

Within three years, Jerry will have abandoned his priestly studies and married; Phil will be stirring up trouble in Washington, D.C., as the first American Catholic priest to speak out forcefully on civil rights; and Dan will gain national recognition by winning the Lamont Prize for his first published volume of poetry, *Time Without Number*. After that, their trying by the world would really begin.

5

AWAKENINGS

> To care for the quarrels of the past, to
> identify so passionately with a cause
> that became, politically speaking, a
> losing cause with the birth of the
> modern world, is to experience a kind
> of straining against reality, a rebellious
> nonconformity that, again, is rare in
> America, where children are instructed
> in the virtues of the system they live
> under, as though history had achieved
> a happy ending in American civics.
> —*Mary McCarthy*
> Memoirs of a Catholic Girlhood

FOR CENTURIES, "THE CAUSE" HAD BEEN THE MEDIEVAL
Catholic Church's religious, philosophical, and cultural supremacy
throughout the Western world, with its resultant ties to monar-
chy—and nowhere had its loss been more resounding, politically
speaking, than in 1789 with the French Revolution. Through generations of labyrinthine church involvement in French state affairs,

often for no greater apparent good than the spiritual solace derived from amassing wealth and power, a feeling of anticlericalism had been bred in your average Gallic sensibility, and had recently been aggravated by the church's poor performance in World War II. And now, in the autumn of 1953, with the most pressing popular issues being labor rights and decent wages, the French church had decided to oppose an emerging union movement in the name of anticommunism. All of which contributed to the greeting given Dan and his fellow Jesuit seminarians as they flocked down the cobblestone streets of the provincial town of Paray le Monial, near Lyons, their long black cassocks flapping in the wind: The people leaned from their windows, cawing like crows.

Having come of age in an energetic and optimistic American Catholic Church, Dan was, to say the least, unprepared for this reaction. But then, the American Church, unlike the French, was not dealing with the hangover of a frequently pitiful, occasionally heroic, and disappointingly ambiguous response to Nazi occupation. There was a feeling in France that the church, along with other key institutions, had failed to confront the moral shame and violence of the Vichy era. It is true that several heroic bishops and isolated lay Catholics had conscientiously defied their government's collaborationist policies and had paid severely. But these were exceptions. And despite mounting evidence of mass Jewish deportations and murders, the Vatican, after all, had been virtually silent on Europe's fascist and Nazi governments, as Albert Camus and others have pointed out.[1] Finally, while a significant number of ordinary people risked their lives in the French Resistance, few church officials took similar chances in their roles as moral leaders.

Among those who did were a group of French "worker-priests" who underwent voluntary deportation to Germany so they might minister to their captive compatriots. But even these priests, when they tried to raise spiritual issues with their fellow prisoners of war, often found themselves treated like salesmen pitching obsolete merchandise. "I am a stranger," said one of how working-class men regarded him, "I belong to another culture. My Latin, my liturgy, my theology, my mass, my prayers, my vestments, all help to make me an

object of curiosity, something set apart, like a strange lingering survivor of an archaic cult."[2]

Now in 1954, France's miserable postwar wages and labor conditions were leading droves of working-class Catholics to defy their
church and join the socialist and communist parties. This split had
even reached Paray, Dan's seminary outpost far from Paris. In portraying the divided town, Dan also describes the country: "On the
one hand the families of the poor, their squalor and contempt. On
the other, the religious and their holy indifference and secure liv-
ings and noses on high. I [have] never seen the like: two planets
whizzing by, different orbits, muttering. Incompatibilities, injustice. Two walls set one against the other."[3]

All this for the first time made him fear for the church's future.
Commonly, when Dan said Mass at a local chapel, the place would
be nearly empty—just a handful of women and nuns and a few old
men. Then he would return to the seminary, pick up the paper, and
read something like this not untypical roasting of the Catholic
Church by a national French commentator:

> You served the Roman Emperors; you served the feudal Lords;
> you served the absolute monarchs; you served the triumphant
> *bourgeoisie.* You have always (though not without subtle maneu-
> vers to show your independence and superiority) been on the
> side of the strongest, and you have made yourselves even
> stronger than they by your pretense of defending the weak.[4]

Clearly, if the church could be so despised in France, the same
could happen elsewhere. The question, for those who considered
it, was how should the Catholic Church address the material concerns of ordinary people? Traditionalists said it shouldn't, that its
sole task was the cultivation of souls. But the worker-priests, by
now a vivid presence in French society, had a different idea.

They were led by men like the Jesuit Henri Perrin, who had
served as an underground chaplain among the thousands of
Frenchmen deported to work in Germany during the occupation,
and who now agitated for the rights of labor; and by Abbe Pierre, a

former Resistance leader who was goading the French bureaucracy into building affordable housing for the poor. Dan took them as models in many ways: in their disdain for the traditional trappings of the priestly life, their support of strikes and their presence at demonstrations, their communal life of shared sacrifice, the intellectual rigor of their journals, their wide and varied circle of friends, their energy and sheer ambition.

For their efforts, they made powerful enemies. The worker-priests faced the same accusations that opponents of Dan and Phil's confrontational tactics would later use against them. Their critics said they neglected the pastoral care of the people and lost sight of the spiritual side of their faith in a single-minded pursuit of worldly justice. Traditionalists claimed the worker-priests had been seduced by communism, had scant respect for authority, and preached revolution. The priests had rankled conservatives with their protests against the atom bomb and "American imperialism." The French establishment was already on the defensive from the collapse of its hold on Indochina. It was losing a bloody colonial war, and it was on the eve of total defeat with the disaster at Dien Bien Phu. And the country's ecclesiastical powers were alarmed at the sight of rank-and-file priests and lay people taking initiative on religious and social issues; for at least the preceding four hundred years, popular reform movements had displeased most bishops in the Roman church. As writer Adam Gopnik puts it: "In France, the Catholic Church has a strong feeling that there is a place for the individual conscience offering Christian witness on the issues of the day, and that this place is called Protestantism."[5]

In 1954, Pius XII, whom Dan called "our icebox Pope" pointedly warned against the "spirit of innovation" embodied by the worker priests as being "more dangerous than it was useful."[6] Dan, among others, was stunned. It was a telling indication that the priests had lost favor with Rome, where they had barely been tolerated all along. Within months the Vatican officially ordered the movement be suppressed. French church authorities told the worker-priests to quit factory, mine, and fishing boat, and report to their parishes. Many refused. For several months, the controversy raged like "another Dreyfus Affair," in which the underdog inevitably lost.

But the worker-priest movement, which had conceived itself in part as a campaign to raise the social-justice consciousness of Catholics, had succeeded with Dan. A few years before, he and Phil had been quietly discussing and exchanging hard-to-get scholarly texts by "new theologians" like Yves Congar (a preacher against Nazism and minister to French deportees) and Henri de Lubac (a worker-priest theoretician and eloquent critic of anti-Semitism). Now Dan had seen some of Congar's ideas in action, and had met de Lubac when the priest was shoved into a kind of internal exile in a house near Dan's seminary.

The effect on Dan was exhilaration—"like Cognac for breakfast," he later said—and some of the first steps taken on the long road of his radical education. Shortly after ordination, Dan had written an essay in which he tentatively answered the questions, "What [does] it mean to be Catholic?" and "Who [will] be my teacher?" with, "the world we breathe in [and] . . . the men and women who toil in it, sin in it, suffer and die in it. Apart from them . . . the priesthood is a pallid, vacuumatic enclosure, a sheepfold for sheep." The worker-priests and France—which had "stamped him inside and out," said a friend—had now shown him the institutional costs of an alienated flock, and that sometimes shepherds must follow the lead of their sheep if they would be good.[7]

Dan's stay in France was interrupted by a forty-day Lenten assignment to a military chaplaincy in West Germany. There he ministered to American soldiers on several bases, including the first nuclear installation in Western Europe—an experience that amazes him now for the piercing moral anxiety so many doomsday weapons failed to induce in him. Instead, he spent the season fulfilling his sacramental duties, enjoying his time with the soldiers, many of them as young and idealistic as himself.

Only two things bothered him. The size and expense of the American military operation in West Germany ominously reminded him, he wrote in a letter home, of the advance of the Roman Empire. He was also made uncomfortable by his "commanding" chaplain, a lieutenant colonel and Jesuit from New York, who went everywhere with a pistol in a holster on his belt. Dan admired the man's dedication and noted that many servicemen liked and respected him. But he worried that his fellow Jesuit had subsumed his priestly identity in a commission from the state. For his part, Dan chose not to wear a uniform.

Yet for all the fruitful provocations of this seminal trip to Europe, Dan says he had yet to develop the "acuity of conscience"[8] that would eventually lead to his "questioning Cold War lunacies, well underway." He and the other American seminarians remained patriotic Catholics somewhat in thrall to their pre-modernist faith in the rightful collusion between Christian hierarchs and secular authorities. After all, the French may have been compromised by recent history, but there was no reason (yet) to question American power. "We were, after all, favored by being 'on the right side,'" Dan later wrote: "Cardinal Spellman at home, the Army in Germany. Who would question so mighty a fortress, the conjunction of holy church and mother state . . . ?"[9]

Dan ended his tertianship and returned to a teaching assignment at Brooklyn Prep, a Jesuit high school in Flatbush. In 1954, the school was enjoying what one former student refered to as its "Periclean Age"—as much for the Hellenic flavor of its studies as for the school's high standards. Dan taught in the honors program, in which students were required to read *The Odyssey* in ancient Greek, Dante's *Divina Commedia* in Italian, *Cicero* in Latin, various works of French literature, and fifteen to twenty Shakespeare plays per semester.

Dan quickly established himself as a creative and highly motivated teacher with a sharp eye for spotting and encouraging gifted students. Several of his former pupils also recall his impatience with shoddy work and his infectious love of language. One student insists, "Dan's [Latin] translations weren't very precise, the other teachers paid much more attention to parsing. [But] Berrigan encouraged a much more free translation that appreciated the literature . . . he liked the sound of the Latin itself, the poetry." Sometimes poetic fervor outstripped comprehensible content, though, remembers James Loughran—"He had a monotone. He didn't always know exactly what he was saying. He would blabber."[10]— blending lyrical incoherence with flashes of brilliant insight, an enduring trait of his public speaking style.

In the competitive, cutting mode of all-boys schools, Dan some-times wielded a wounding sarcasm. Larry Holfelder recalls, "Father Berrigan always came across as a pompous person, a little intolerant of persons not up to par." But then "all the Jesuits walked around like they were gods, and in those days they were. They were our dis-ciplinarians. We were in awe and fear of them to a degree."[11]

For reasons unremembered by Bill Carrington, Dan singled him out to serve as his "Brother Beadle," a lowly office named and modeled after the functionary at a medieval university. Dan had Carrington erase the blackboards, kick the pipes when the heat was weak, and even mow the lawn outside his classroom. And to strike some fear in the rest of the class, he would sometimes upbraid Car-rington for not doing as well as he might have on a paper or a test. Then Carrington made the mistake in his senior year of telling a female student he had met on a train trip to write him from her home in Chicago in care of Brooklyn Prep. That is how Dan became the mailman for Carrington's very first love letter. He held it up in front of the class, paused dramatically, and announced, "Brother Beadle has received amorous correspondence from the Midwest," setting off a riot of taunts and laughter at Carrington's expense. Of that distant trauma, Carrington now says, "Of course, it embarrassed me to tears but it was done in a spirit of fun . . . I think."[12]

Outside class, Dan was somber and reserved, a crew-cutted "portly poet" with a continental *gravitas*, one student recalls. Loughran says that unlike Brooklyn Prep's other teaching star, the six-foot, six-inch John Culkin, who could often be found throwing elbows and crashing the backboards during after-school basketball games, Dan "didn't come out to the schoolyard and play with us."[13] One was more likely to glimpse him gliding, monklike, down the corridor to his room.

Culkin and Dan worked together, however, in challenging their second-generation immigrant students to strive for more than the professional lives for which they were being groomed. At the end of each school year, Culkin would address the seniors in a world-weary voice, describing their predictable futures—college, a job on Wall Street, marriage, kids, retirement—as all very pleasant, "but at the end of it, you'll wonder what you did with your lives."[14] Then he would hit them with his pitch for joining the Jesuits. He was prompted by the paradox that schools like Brooklyn Prep were actually undermining the American church's traditional structure. Throughout the fifties, as its upwardly mobile graduates left Flatbush and other immigrant enclaves for the suburbs, those graduates were becoming, in general, less oriented toward their parish community and more toward their families and homes, less inclined to find comfort in religious practice than consumerist gratification.

Dan called it "hopping on the first car to nowhere." He bristled when he sensed his students falling for the seductions of an unexamined and unexalted life. "The best way to goad Dan," Loughran remembers, "was to pretend to swoon for the American Dream." When Dan was nearby, Loughran would sometimes launch into a Babbitt-like soliloquy: "When I grow up, I'm really looking forward to living in the suburbs with a nice car. Make that two nice cars. And a big family." But as he waxed materialistic, Loughran would also make sure to avoid loosing Dan's forensic wrath by "watching his slow burn out of the corner of my eye," being "careful not to rouse the beast too much. I had to watch out, or he would go for my balls."[15]

To his credit, Dan did more than hector his middle-class students about serving more than themselves. He challenged their insularity by sending them out as volunteers to poor parts of New York City. Vinnie Quayle says when he grew up in Rockaway Beach, Queens, "we had the world by the seat of our pants." He and his friends belonged to stable families in a neighborhood both ethnically and economically homogeneous. But because Dan dispatched him on the subway one day to "play pool with the Puerto Rican kids" on the Lower East Side, he awoke to the realities and satisfactions of inner-city service—a vocation he continues to this day. Peter McDonough remembers that while Dan was by then a daring poet, he "wasn't all that radicalized" in his political thinking yet. But Dan knew Dorothy Day at the Catholic Worker, and arranged for McDonough and other students to volunteer at her Lower East Side soup kitchen, after playing basketball with the poor kids around the corner in Nativity parish.[16]

Dan also led by example. Joe Roccosalvo remembers attending a Mass conducted by Dan at an ornate Manhattan church—"when he preached, his poetic language held me spellbound"—then afterwards hopping a bus with him and heading to the Gold Street Mission, where they mingled with a group of children, playing games or simply talking. Roccosalvo says that on that day, "One kid named Winston was being absolutely obstreperous. He wouldn't calm down. I looked at Father Berrigan and shrugged my shoulders. He said, 'Let me see what I can do.' Next thing you know, there's no noise. He was in the corner with the boy. He had bought Coca-Colas. Now he was holding Winston spellbound with the story of the genie in the Coke bottle. Here we have this accomplished poet, managing to hold the interest of this little black kid. It was very beautiful to watch. I never forgot it."[17]

In his spare time, Dan served as chaplain to the Young Christian Workers, an extraparochial group of lay Catholics that met over a grocery store on Flatbush Avenue to study scripture before venturing out to do social justice work in poor neighborhoods. He also took part in Walter Ferrell Guild meetings, in which clergy and mostly liberal laymen met in a church basement and shared cocktails and heavy discussions on modern literature. Though routine-sounding now, informal gatherings of priests and laypeople was a highly innovative—and controversial—practice in the late 1950s. In keeping with the formalized times, most clergy kept their distance in relations with lay Catholics, which incidentally buttressed their monopoly on church leadership. But in France Dan had seen an entire church rocked by a schism between these constituencies. So to serve his vocation and because it would be silly, he felt, to do otherwise, he made friends among the laity.

After five "highly ascetic" years in the Josephite seminary, Phil was ordained a priest in a class "of about twelve serious young men" in the late spring of 1955. The ceremony was held at the Shrine of the Immaculate Conception in Washington, D.C. Phil stayed in the city afterward to begin his first assignment as assistant pastor at Our Lady of Perpetual Help parish in the Anacostia district, working with indigent blacks residing in dismal public housing.

Phil later wrote, "During the twelve months I lived and worked in . . . Anacostia, my parishioners were educating me. I taught them catechism and scripture; they taught me the real meaning of hate, fear, and discrimination. Postwar Washington resembled (and still resembles) a huge plantation. Blacks lived in battered neighborhoods, went to rundown schools, and worked at rotten jobs. They were expected to be thankful for small favors, to grin and shuffle before their masters. Whites sat in Congress and the Senate; blacks collected their garbage. Whites owned the banks and businesses; blacks mopped the floors. It was the systematic oppression of African-Americans, not the collective failure of a people."[18]

In his correspondence with Dan in France and after, both agreed that the measure of their priesthoods would be how they addressed social issues, such as racism in America, in the light of Catholic morals. Phil immediately started raising vexing questions. He asked in an unpublished essay from the time, "What the Negro Needs Most," whether the Josephites should pitch a gradualist message on civil rights so as not to alienate a majority of white Americans, or should they forcefully assail the denial of voting rights and the lack of jobs and decent housing for blacks? [19]

Having decided on the latter, he began to lecture the all-white members of Catholic Sodality and Legion of Mary groups that it was their moral indifference that propped up social injustice toward blacks, and that it was the Church's silence on the matter that provided the theological underpinnings of racism. Phil's audiences were, to say the least, infuriated. But as outraged white Catholics turned away, he began receiving speaking invitations from the NAACP and the Urban League. Soon word spread in nearby parishes, seminaries, and convents that a white priest in Washington was saying the right things about race relations.

He spoke everywhere he was invited—from dank church basements to university halls—and showed up at many sparsely attended rallies and meetings, lending an air of respectability in his starched Roman collar and crisp black suit. After a while he became a personality on Washington's burgeoning civil rights scene, as much for his "personal charm, his integrity, the fire of his eloquence," by Dan's adoring testimony, as for the bravery of his rhetoric.

And this was precisely what got him transferred, in 1956, to St. Augustine's, an all-black, all-male, Josephite high school in New Orleans' French Quarter. The school provided a rigorous education from an excellent faculty to some six hundred children of the city's black professional class. Many of the graduates later moved on to prestigious universities in and outside the South, as well as serving as pioneers in integrating Tulane University and the Catholic Loyola University in New Orleans.

By all accounts, Phil was an exacting, admired and stimulating teacher of English and religion, often kindling spirited debates among his students. His colleagues spoke of his charismatic personality, his ability to persuade people to work for the common good, as well as his single-minded pursuit of causes he deemed vital. "I've never lived with a more industrious man," said Father O'Rourke, then the school's principal. "There was not a lazy—or selfish bone in his body."

Rising at 6 A.M., he would pray and reflect for thirty minutes, dress indifferently, attend Mass, eat rapidly, and then immerse himself in an 18-hour day, seven days a week. After classes he would change into work clothes and voluntarily help maintain the school grounds and building, never put off by hard labor in the blistering summer heat. He had little patience with small talk at the dinner table, preferring instead to ignite heated conversations about the issues of the day—especially race relations in the South. Evenings, he read prodigiously from a mountain of magazines and newspapers, many of them black publications from the high school's well-stocked library. He clipped stories and took copious notes while listening to classical music. (When Phil had been a boy he'd sometimes come across Dado asleep at night in the living room with his big hands resting on the volume of poems he'd been reading. Now a fellow priest remarked of Phil, "We'd find him there after midnight, wearing a green eye shade, sound asleep in his chair with a book or magazine open on his lap.")

His outgoing personality made him the school's most effective fundraiser and publicist. He was praised for his work with his students and for organizing his most faithful and socially concerned parishioners into adult and student sodality groups—associations of practicing Catholics who did voluntary charity work. But despite his burning anger at the racism all around him, by his own account he was initially reluctant to challenge publicly New Orleans' status quo. Until, that is, an attack that affected personally.

In 1957, Archbishop Romell mandated the integration of the Catholic institutions of the Archdiocese of New Orleans. Not surprisingly, the process met with determined resistance from the local white community. This led some of Phil's students to speak up in theology class one day. A few boys, football players from the neighboring town of Algiers, asked their priest and teacher what they might do to help Romell's program. Phil said simply, "Next Sunday go to the nearest Catholic Church—that's where you belong." The following Sunday the students attended an all-white church, only to be cursed and threatened. Undeterred, they returned the following week. But on their way home after the service, they were jumped and beaten by whites with tire irons. One of the boys took forty stitches to close his scalp. When they heard about it, Phil and Father O'Rourke rushed to the hospital. O'Rourke was so angry that he stormed over to Bishop Romell's residence and convinced him to slap an interdict on the offending parish. Romell told the parishioners, "You'll get Mass and the sacraments when you stop this barbarism. Only when you accept that you've done something gravely wrong can there be healing." Four months later, the church reopened. But this time it was integrated.

Phil grieved for the violence done to the boys, whom he "loved … unconditionally," and briefly felt responsible for contributing to the circumstances that led to the attack. "The whole thing shook me," says Phil, "and left me deeply troubled."[20]

While Phil was grappling with race issues in the south, Dan felt like he was stagnating at Brooklyn Prep. After three years, he wasn't satisfied anymore as a high school teacher. "The big line from the other Jesuit teachers was that he should be teaching college," says Loughran. Many nights he read or studied restlessly until 2 A.M., then "sleepless as a bat" he would toss in his bed for a couple of hours before rising and stealing out to say Mass alone.[21] He was beginning to be known among Catholics for his monthly radio ser-

mons on a national show called "The Sacred Heart Hour." In them
he stressed that since Christ had been a poor worker himself, his
church should show special concern for working people and the
dispossessed. Then in 1957, his collection of poems, *Time Without
Number*, won the prestigious Lamont Prize for a first book of
poetry, and was nominated for a National Book Award. Now he
longed more than ever for greater challenges. "He had very, very,
very big dreams," McDonough recalls. "He was different from the
run of the mill . . . I remember once hearing Dan Berrigan say
about Culkin, 'That guy is really going places,' as if he wanted to go
places, too."[22]

Later in 1957 he finally jumped to the college level when Le
Moyne College in Syracuse hired him as an Associate Professor of
Dogmatic Theology. After establishing himself as an intense and
engaging teacher with the longest required reading list of anyone
on the faculty, he conceived the idea of rallying students to investigate slum housing conditions in Syracuse. Much to his new
employer's chagrin, he and the students discovered and publicized
the fact that some of the guilty landlords were benefactors of Le
Moyne. Picketing and disparate calls for his resignation ensued.
Next he helped set up Karl Meyer, a new friend, in a Catholic
Worker-style house in downtown Syracuse to serve the homeless
and hungry. When the local bishop heard of the plan, and worse,
that Meyer was a pacifist and tax resister fresh out of jail, he phoned
Dan and thundered objections. No work by a "known pacifist"
would ever be sanctioned in his diocese, he warned, and threatened
to expel him if it continued. But Dan's new Le Moyne colleagues
rallied around him ("It was, in my experience, one of the few times
when professors stood by a colleague in trouble," he says.[23]) and
threatened to quit if Berrigan were fired. The bishop needed faculty
for his new college more than he needed to make an example of
Dan, so he backed down.

Newly confident, Dan tackled teaching and several large projects
with burst of optimistic energy. "Time . . . is a perpetual spring-
time," he wrote in the manuscript he was working on that would
later become *The Bride*, a collection of essays on the church, "with
unlimited opportunity for the planting."[24]

After a couple of years, he founded International House—an off-campus gathering place for students interested in iconoclastic moral discussions, inner-city activism, social work tours-of-duty in developing nations, and non-traditional liturgies, led by Dan. Dan and a core group lived in the house, fixing their lives around a routine of group prayer and Masses said in English, with the altar facing the congregants, a scandalous reform before Vatican II. International House members organized a series of protests at financial institutions they held responsible for some of Syracuse's crumbling, segregated neighborhoods, and once they joined with Jerry Berrigan and his new wife, Carol, in a demonstration against the Niagara-Mohawk electric plant at which Jerry had once worked, charging it with discrimination in hiring.

One of the joys for Dan at this time in his life were frequent visits to Jerry and Carol, who'd recently bought a home in a nearby neighborhood, and to Freda at the house on Matson Avenue. He also tried to affect some sort of reconciliation with his father. Many Sundays he sat on the porch or in the living room with Dado, whose health and attention span were steadily fading, just trying to "be present" to the man who'd caused him so much childhood pain.[25] Phil, on the other hand, had decided by now that his father didn't have it in him to engage his sons in healthy relationships. He'd resolved to maintain only minimal contact and banished Dado as much as he could from his thoughts. Dado never broke through his crusty persona to speak with Dan about their relationship, but in indirect ways he let him know he was proud of how his son had turned out. The centerpiece of International House was a basement chapel with a beautiful wooden altar handmade by Dado. In offering it as a gift to Dan's community, the father had shown approval of the son and his work on behalf of racial and economic justice.

From 1960 to 1963, Dan sent his students to Phil in New Orleans to work on Congress of Racial Equality (CORE) campaigns; while Phil encouraged bright black students to attend Le Moyne on scholarship, an arrangement Dan helped facilitate. He and Phil tried to join a Freedom Ride in 1961 but both were forbidden by their superiors to take part. In 1963, the brothers were invited to join with other clergy in attempting to integrate the facilities at the Jackson, Mississippi, airport. Again Dan's superior flatly turned him down. But Phil gained permission, and after meeting in New York with CORE Director James Farmer, he and another Josephite, Father Richard Wagner, got on a plane for Jackson. Farmer had warned the two men that they faced a probable beating and jail time once they got there, despite their priests' collars. But the bishop of Jackson learned of the action and flew into a rage, partly over fear of white retribution against his churches and clergy if he didn't stop the airport demonstration. He placed a furious call to Rev. George O'Dea, the Josephite Superior General who'd approved the trip, threatening to throw a dozen Josephite houses out of his bailiwick unless O'Dea recalled Phil and Wagner. When the two priests landed in Atlanta, O'Dea reached them by phone and told them to return right away to his office in Baltimore, which they did.[26]

Dan was sickened by the airport affair when he heard, and still furious at being rejected for the second time in his quest to work for civil rights down south. Fifteen years ago, in 1948, he had written a letter to the Trappist monk Thomas Merton to praise his spiritual autobiography, *The Seven Storey Mountain*. Acclaim for the book had deluged Merton with mail, and his abbot had forbidden him to respond to many letters, including Dan's. But in 1962 the pair had renewed their correspondence. Now Dan wrote to Merton for advice. He was so upset, he said, he might leave the Jesuits. Without much trouble, Merton talked him out of it, arguing that "if you allow this to happen, you may turn adrift those who have begun to follow you and profit by your leadership."[27] Dan stuck by his vocation, but the cumulative stress of his groundbreaking work at Le Moyne got him sent back to France for most of 1964. Throughout his sabbatical, he would undergo a transformation from "well-scrubbed, secure American" priest, in the words of his friend, Jim Forest, to a "blizzard-worn" and self-possessed "man of experience."

Phil returned to New Orleans where he openly confronted racial laws, even supporting a white Catholic's effort to challenge a blacks-only golf course on the grounds that it maintained racial segregation. He and several other priests recruited hundreds of students to collect and distribute food and clothing to the poorest of the poor throughout the city. They began marching with blacks for civil rights, organizing voter registration drives, and recruiting high school students to picket whites-only restaurants.

His sodality groups were the heart of his efforts to relieve the pain of the poor, and he continued gathering students and encouraging them to attend Mass in churches where priests and congregants would not let them in. He entered into the struggle to improve the Desire Homes, a public housing complex erected alongside a onetime city garbage dump, where crime and afflictions of many sorts were common.

He visited the "colored and white" poor in their wretched homes, where "privation, delinquency, and dull forlorn misery" flourished, where fathers had long since vanished and their children roamed the streets. The Josephites did what they could, offering "food, clothing, medicine, counselling, referrals to welfare agencies." Phil still considered these efforts admirable and absolutely necessary, but was troubled that good works such as these were no more than Band-Aids—then and now. There had to be a redefinition and reworking of the Josephites' and the church's role. Drawing upon Emmanuel Cardinal Suhard's words that priest and layperson are "the indispensable pair of the apostolate, the complete evangelist," he advised his students, "A church which remains aloof from this world [of the desperately poor] loses its reason for existence."[28]

Certainly, the Josephites understood his capacity for leadership, though clearly he wanted to take them where they dared not go— toward challenging state and government laws, toward organizing black and white supporters, and toward embracing the impoverished in the name of God and humanity, and challenging the church to do the same. Father Michael Coffey had never met anyone with Phil's ethical intensity: "You could leave a conversation with the impression you'd just talked to the fourth member of the Holy Trinity," he said. And Virginia Welch, another teacher, added, "Once Father Phil decided a thing was right—or wrong— that was it. There were no pastel shades to it." Elliot Willard, a black man who later became principal of St. Augustine's High School, remembered that Phil "would say, 'Those people down in Desire [housing project] shouldn't suffer like that. If Christ were here, he'd be the first man down there. You have to take care of our stray sheep. You'll be blessed one hundred times for it. Your life will be better.' "[29]

In a key passage in his book *No More Strangers*, Phil described how a young priest in the South—obviously himself—was sent to a white church to offer Mass, at which a congregant angrily objected to his sermon on the "injustice of segregation," and another shouted as he stormed out of the church, "If I miss Mass today, you're responsible." The lesson, he wrote, was that white Southerners were undergoing a "crisis of conscience" but that the church had to stand decisively and clearly on the side of racial justice: There was no alternative. Clearly, what he had seen with his own eyes led him to profess that evil was evil and no compromise with the devil was possible.[30]

When he expressed this conviction to the delegates at a National Catholic Social Action Conference, he added a note tinged with arrogance and righteousness, but also with a strong sense that morality, justice, and a right reading of the Gospels were on his side. The bigotry of white Americans, he proclaimed to people already involved in doing what they could in the name of social justice, "eclipsed Hitler's slaughter of the Jews in ingenuity, in longtime ruthlessness, in the number of people affected."[31] His audience was stunned. To modify his language or to soften his blazing admonitions on racial issues was by now out of the question. For him, the overall treatment of blacks was nothing less than satanic, and its consequences for the future devastating. He was disillusioned by the church and the powerful elite that ran New Orleans. He now saw his church much as did the convert Richard Gilman years later: "obdurate, ungenerous, the castle of belief with its wide moat and every parapet bristling with defenses." Figuratively and in fact, Phil had become the church's first "Freedom Rider."[32]

Something else happened to Phil in New Orleans that forever transformed his life and the lives of everyone who fell within his sphere of influence: the threat of nuclear war. "My turning point,"

Phil explained, "occurred . . . during the Cuban missile crisis in 1962," when he witnessed the fear gripping local Catholics as nuclear war suddenly seemed a real possibility.

"I was called to Xavier University any number of times to hear confessions. Sometimes it went on all day—students and faculty. [The crisis] convinced me that nothing had ended with World War II. We simply used the bombing of Japan to move directly to the Cold War. I was thirty-seven years old, a veteran, a priest. I knew nothing. I was ill-prepared. Meanwhile, other people were deciding whether I would live or die. I felt betrayed, and not just about the urban crisis but for all that was behind the threat."[33]

By 1963, Phil's Josephite superiors felt he needed to be moved out of New Orleans, so they offered him a posh assignment in New York City. He arrived there on June 25, 1963, and moved into a Josephite residence in the Bronx, an impeccably scrubbed rectory with many painted portraits of popes on the walls. There he wrote a little, ate well, and commuted to Harlem, where he helped found community houses for recreation and education. His fund-raising efforts were mediocre—his heart just wasn't in it anymore.

Without consulting anyone, he dreamed up a study group to examine the entire Josephite operation and then report its findings to the superior general. Naive to be sure, Phil thought that an independent commission could recommend ways to serve and evangelize the black community. His group suggested a $2 million project that the order's governing council promptly turned down. Once again, Phil had stretched the Josephites' institutional patience—which snapped when he spoke at Cornell University and called the Southern Catholic bishops a bunch of racists.

Again he was shifted, this time to the lower seminary of the Josephites' Epiphany Apostolic College, an imposing Georgian brick mansion in Newburgh, New York, some sixty miles north of Manhattan, high above the Hudson, where, decades before, the Ku Klux Klan had burned crosses. Phil had served his novitiate at Epiphany; now would teach English in a provincial city with a potent John Birch Society chapter and conservative politicians. His superiors deluded themselves that this setting would somehow keep Phil in check.

But there was no way Phil's forceful personality could be contained in a backwater classroom. Newburgh was beginning its thirty-year decline: Many of its businesses were fleeing, its downtown was showing signs of deterioration, and its growing black neighborhoods were beset by poverty and miserable slums owned by absentee landlords. He quickly managed to outrage Newburgh's conservative Catholics and hard-right citizens by decrying the city's shamefully neglected housing stock. As Dan had done in Le Moyne College, and as he had done in New Orleans, Phil drew together blacks and whites and set them up in a shop to give out clothing and food and provide free legal assistance. His passion for winning fair treatment for the poor had made him a prominent Josephite; and his calls for racial and economic justice had made him the most disliked priest in the Hudson River valley. He kept up his spirits by carrying out a rewarding sacramental life. He said daily Mass and heard weekly confessions. And gradually he attracted a following of Catholics from the area who were hungry "for good liturgy and a good homily, or they'd be peace people looking for a more serious orientation for their own lives, and wanting to discuss issues."[34]

In March 1965 Phil trekked down to Manhattan and joined an eclectic group of Protestants, Jews, and Catholic clergy in a silent vigil against the war in Southeast Asia. It was the first such gathering on the issue. Phil stood with Father Peter Riga, the Buffalo diocesan director of the Catholic Council on Civil Liberties and director of the Buffalo Catholic Interracial Council; Father Thomas Crowley, a British Dominican priest; three nuns; the Catholic theologian James Douglass; Edward Keating, publisher of the new religious and countercultural magazine *Ramparts*; Martin Corbin of the Catholic Worker; and Elizabeth Bartelme, a book editor.[35] The group prayed for peace, and its speakers denounced the sanctioning of war by religion. Though barely visible to the wider public, the gathering was a sign of things to come.

Phil carried the message back to Newburgh and began attacking U.S. policy in Southeast Asia. This, plus his formation of a local peace group, were too extreme not only for Newburgh but even for some of his own more liberal colleagues, shocked that a fellow priest would assail the United States government in wartime. By what right, they wanted to know, did a priest dedicated to a life of the spirit embark on such an unprecedented cause? Word spread through Newburgh that a communist was teaching at Epiphany High School. Protests inundated the school principal, filled the letters column and editorials in the local conservative newspaper, and soon reached the Josephite motherhouse in Baltimore. Father O'Dea directed Phil to stop commenting publicly about the war. The next week, though, he was at it again, and was once more denounced in the newspapers. The Josephites abruptly moved him to Baltimore, warning him again to hold his tongue. A few of his fellow clerics at Epiphany rationalized the transfer by saying that constant harassment prevented him from doing his teaching job properly. Yet Barry Cassidy, one of his former students, remembered him as a stimulating and rigorous instructor, much admired by the boys.[36] All the same, he was out once more, and Newburgh was free to decompose, atrophy, and stumble toward economic paralysis.

As progressive Catholics were contemplating strategies for opposing the Vietnam War, they naturally turned to Thomas Merton for guidance. Merton's opinions on war, peace, and faith were extremely influential among the growing number of priests, nuns, seminarians, and other Catholics uneasy with the church's role in society and the moral timidity of its hierarchy. When he first knew Dan, Merton advised him that "the great problem is the blindness and passivity of Christians, and the way they let themselves be used by crypto-fascist elements who get stronger and stronger every day. I have just realized that, as Catholics, we are almost in the same position as the Catholics before the last war in Hitler's Germany."[37]

Thomas Merton thought highly of the Berrigan brothers, so much so that as early as the autumn of 1962, he portrayed Dan as "a man full of fire, the right kind, and a real Jesuit, of which there are not too many. . . . He is alive and full of spirit and truth. I think he will do much for the Church in America and so will his brother Phil." He was also remarkably prophetic about their future: "They will have a hard time, though, and will have to pay for every step forward with their blood."[38]

Merton and Dan developed a friendship beyond the ordinary. Merton had complimented Dan's poetry in 1962, and Dan had written approvingly about Merton's book *Seeds of Contemplation for America* in the Jesuit journal *America*, calling him "the New Merton who is involved and more human." Merton's biographer, Michael Mott, dates their first face-to-face meeting as August 21, 1962. Merton was clearly won over by Dan, saying later that he possessed an "altogether winning and warm intelligence, with a perfect zeal, compassion and understanding. This, certainly, is the spirit of the church. This is a hope I can believe in, at least in its validity and spirit."[39]

Merton was, by 1962, along with Dorothy Day, the most prominent voice for peace in the Catholic Church. "Violence today," he wrote, "is white collar violence, the systemically organized bureaucratic and technological destruction of man . . . abstract, corporate, businesslike, cool, free of guilt-feelings and therefore a thousand times more deadly than the eruption of violence out of individual hate." He was equally admired and condemned for saying, as far back as 1962, in his book *Breakthrough to Peace*, that nuclear war "in attack or retaliation" was a violation of "Christian morality."[40]

In November 1964 he invited the Berrigans and a small group of fellow peacemakers to Gethsemani Abbey in Kentucky for a three-day retreat on the "Spiritual Roots of Protest." Attending were the veteran pacifist A.J. Muste; W.H. "Ping" Ferry of the Center for the Study of Democratic Institutions and the Fellowship of Reconciliation (FOR); Anthony Walsh of the Montreal Catholic Worker House; the Mennonite theologian John H. Yoder; John Oliver Nelson, onetime national chair of the FOR and professor at Yale Divinity School; and Catholic activists Robert Cunnane, John Peter Grady, Tom Cornell, and Jim Forest. And Dan and Phil Berrigan.

The retreat was held in March 1965. Merton began by laying out what he thought should be done in the years ahead, and worried out loud that protest would reach a swift dead end unless it contained a significant measure of, as Forest put it, "spiritual maturity." Merton then rose, looking directly at his visitors, and posed these questions: "By what right do we protest? Against whom or what? For what? Why?"

It was raining, Merton noted in his journal, but the ensuing conversation was "remarkably lively and fruitful." Merton went on at length about Franz Jagerstatter, since he had just read Gordon Zahn's biography *In Solitary Witness*, about a mundane Austrian farmer and father of three who refused to serve the Nazis in their army, a unique act of moral defiance, for which he was beheaded on August 9, 1943. Zahn wrote that Jagerstatter's bishop had advised him to "do his duty like all the rest." Was Jagerstatter the only one to uphold the Gospels' dictum of nonviolence? asked an aroused, intense Merton. And why should others like him ever again have to stand alone? Dan agreed, telling the others that "the Church's fearfulness is our confession of convertedness," another indication of his emerging priestly reputation and a reflection of Merton's dictum: "the root of war is fear."[41]

American pacifists, though, were impotent, ignored, and without much influence. Catholic pacifists were limited to Catholic Worker houses, endured by the hierarchy as long as they fed the hungry and avoided offending church doctrine. Jim Forest has suggested that Paul Hanley Furfey's "A Debate Between Christ and Caesar," which was published in the *Catholic Worker* in 1934, gave impetus to the American Catholic peace movement, such as it was. When the Catholic Worker had been founded the year before, it was centered on Dorothy Day and the French-born Peter Maurin, and had been equally devoted to creating "Houses of Hospitality" for men, women, and children abandoned by society.[42] The Catholic Worker, which drew inspiration from a "Christian perfectionist tradition" grounded on the Works of Mercy and the Sermon on the Mount, identified closely with labor unions during the Great Depression. By 1936, at the outset of the Spanish Civil War, it remained neutral (along with *Commonweal*) despite the church's support for the Spanish fascist rebels under General Francisco Franco. Opposed to entry into the Second World War, it sided with Catholic conscientious objectors. In the fifties it refused to seek cover during New York City's mandatory civil defense drills.

In addition, the theologian Justus George Lawler and his *Continuum* magazine pointed out time and again that any reliance on nuclear arms, even against a military force, was "immoral because once these weapons have been brought into play, the proximity of the total war is heightened immeasurably." Gordon Zahn argued that the church's "just war" theory was obsolete, given the existence of nuclear weapons, though the judgment was disputed by many Catholics, even those willing to apply its principles to the Second World War and Vietnam.[43]

"The problem of Catholic opinion before the Vietnam War was not its militant anti-communism, so often simplistically interpreted as merely the emotional reflex of an uncritical nationalism, but rather the pervasive parochialism of the American Church," hypothesized David J. O'Brien of Holy Cross College. But it was precisely that "parochialism" and the hierarchy's imperviousness to consider seriously the limits of its "just war" theory that drove Catholic pacifists and near-pacifists wild.

Galvanized by the Merton retreat, many of those in attendance began to organize faith-based groups to resist the Vietnam War. Forest was hired as the full-time staffer for a new group, the Catholic Peace Fellowship (CPF), and Cornell later became co-secretary. The idea for the group had first been broached in 1961 over lunch in Ratner's Jewish Dairy Restaurant on New York's Lower East Side. Presbyterian minister John Heidbrink, church work secretary of the Fellowship of Reconciliation, had suggested to Forest that a more aggressive Catholic group be formed. Nothing happened until 1964, while the two of them and other FOR members—Cornell, Hermene Evans, Jim Douglass, and Dan— were in Czechoslovakia for the Prague Peace Conference, a meeting dreamed up by Czech Protestant theologians interested in exchanging ideas with Eastern Bloc communists. There they reached a decision to start a far more militant, nonviolent Catholic Peace Fellowship, which Phil, Merton, Zahn, and Tom Cornell immediately joined. Dan was enthusiastic and gave Cornell and Forest his address book from which to solicit funds and members.

Another antiwar religious group came together in 1965, the Clergy and Laymen Concerned About the War in Vietnam—CALCAV— ultimately the largest religious peace group in the country. It was organized by Rabbi Abraham Joshua Heschel of Conservative Judaism, Lutheran Pastor Richard John Neuhaus from Brooklyn, and Dan Berrigan (co-chairs) to lend a spiritual tone to the wave of antiwar protests. Many prominent Protestant leaders eventually joined, including Martin Luther King Jr., Robert McAfee Brown, Harvey Cox, William Sloane Coffin, and Reinhold Niebuhr. In the beginning, Dan's name stuck out conspicuously as the only Catholic priest in the organization. Soon the group was organizing rallies in front of the White House and sending hundreds of thousands of direct-mail appeals for contributions, one of which pictured a young civilian alongside an illustration of a combat trooper, with the headline: "I sent them a good boy—and they made a murderer!" Reinhold Niebuhr, the eminent and highly regarded Protestant theologian, was just as outspoken and outraged, portraying the war as "a fantastic adventure of U.S. imperialism in an Asian civil war."[44]

6

EXILE AND SHUNNING

what clean young figure, innocent of
  blood,
dares with his cape the avalanche . . . ?
  —*Daniel Berrigan, on Phil*

UNLIKE WASHINGTON, D.C.—A COLD WAR CAPITAL RADIANT
with power—Baltimore in 1965 was on the decline, aging ungrace-
fully as its southern neighbor matured into a city of the world. Baltimore, however, retained much of its character. The red-brick row-
house neighborhoods still held sizable blue-collar enclaves, with
their eclectic politics of union-based progressivism and social conservatism, working-class solidarity and middle-class aspirations. An
Old South elite ruled city hall, more or less blessed by the churches,
while a large black population simmered unnoticed in the slums. A
community of old-left loyalists endured, as their political heirs but
temperamental opposites in the countercultural new left grew to
strength. These younger radicals tended to congregate in a relatively integrated neighborhood near Johns Hopkins University—

"one hundred to one hundred and fifty activists living along Guilford and Abell Avenues awaiting the Revolution," one school official recalled.[1] This was the scene of what was supposed to be Phil Berrigan's quiet exile.

After attending a Manhattan party celebrating the publication of Phil's book on race in America, *No More Strangers*, the brothers drove down the East Coast together in a steady April rain. Dan brooded darkly throughout the long ride on Phil's recent banishment—the first heavy blow that either of them had absorbed from the Catholic Church. "My heart was raw with bitterness," he remembered years later with undiminished pique. "I saw a rare Christian whom I loved, plucked summarily, in midyear, from his work." Phil's forced transfer at the behest of his conservative adversaries offended Dan. And it bothered him that his brother's community initiatives would be dropped by the Newburgh church, that the ecclesiastical powers would rather suppress any social agenda than brave the narrow-minded backlash, "among Catholics and others," provoked by a single enterprising priest.[2]

On matters of church and conscience, Dan wrote soon after in his fourth book, *They Call Us Dead Men*, that mid-century "fires" of rapid political and technological change had led to a "connivance of human pride with the powers of darkness in war, in racism, in the neglect of the poor, in the vicious uses of power," and in a sad retreat from urgent human issues by "religious structures that serve the well-being of an ingroup, that concentrate on possession and control, that are indifferent to suffering and obsessed with pride of place."[3] Even so, he felt the church was evolving new forms of vocation—not surprisingly, on the models he and Phil were pioneering.

After all, this was the era of Vatican II. The historic three-year council in Rome of Catholic clergy, religious, theologians, and laypeople, as well as observers from Protestant and Orthodox Eastern churches, was nearing conclusion. Among its reforms was a relaxation of the rules of eucharistic celebration, including worship in the vernacular and priests facing congregations—liturgical innovations Dan had practiced for years. It also called for a greater collaboration between clergy and laity, a mission whose cutting edge Phil had been defining in his community work. In opening remarks to the council, Pope John XXIII had pointedly criticized in-house "prophets of doom" and their revanchist domination of Catholic doctrine, especially the habit of sniffing a heresy in every new theological or pastoral technique. He had also rehabilitated the worker-priest theoretician Yves Congar, appointing him an expert to later council sessions. Even Henri de Lubac had been exhumed from professional burial in Dan's old Burgundy seminary and been made a cardinal. *Aggiornamento*, or church renewal, was in the air. It had been less than a century earlier that the church had called Vatican I, mainly to consolidate curial power by encoding the doctrine of the pope's infallibility. But now Pope Pius XII's antimodernist clampdowns were being reversed, and the once-banned French theologians whom Dan and Phil had furtively studied, and still admired, were among the leaders of an unprecedented opening in the church.[4]

In this spirit, Phil had written in *No More Strangers* (dedicated to "my brother, Father Dan, S.J., without whom neither my priesthood nor this book would be possible," with an introduction by Thomas Merton and imprimatur from Francis Cardinal Spellman of New York) against a clergy afraid to act without Rome's approval and a laity obsessed with personal piety at the expense of social action—"strangers to the world they are expected to redeem." He had also echoed Dan's call for a Christianity of "personal and social heroism" in the struggles for civil rights and nuclear disarmament. And seconding Dan again, Phil hoped in print that the church was now embarked on a constructive "return to the world."[5] Maybe Vatican II's clear emphasis on the equal importance of humanity's social and spiritual states would filter down to the parish level, making Phil's political activism less upsetting to places like Newburgh, New York. Such was the glimmer of optimism the brothers still maintained. "We had much to learn," Dan later wrote.[6]

"Something is afoot in the universe, some issue is at stake, which cannot be better described than a process of gestation and birth,"[7] Phil had quoted the Jesuit philosopher Teilhard de Chardin, in *No More Strangers*, as had Dan in *They Call Us Dead Men*. (The brothers tried originally to co-author a single volume, but found that Dan's metaphoric density did not jive with Phil's straightforward rhetorical bursts. So they ended up writing separate books, drawing similar conclusions from many of the same intellectual sources.) Generally speaking, Teilhard de Chardin's observation applied as well to American culture circa 1965. The issue was one of legitimate authority. Like progressive forces in the church, American life had long been artificially constrained: first, by wartime imperatives, then afterward, in the fifties, by a rush to prosperity. Now Johns Hopkins University, and schools all over the country, were filling up with the alienated daughters and sons of the middle class, restless products of a highly individualized mass culture.

Dan and Phil themselves embodied the sixties' early movement from fifties conformism to direct questioning of the purpose and premise of essential institutions. They knew by now that challenging power, like birth itself, was painful. But the times being charged with what felt like an irresistible urge toward change, the brothers still believed they could help reform both church and country from within. They might have felt differently had they paused to consider the fate of Pierre Teilhard de Chardin. For his groundbreaking attempt to reconcile faith with contemporary science, the church had quashed the French priest's writings and banished him to China. Now, however, his insights had been published and were gaining popularity—a decade after his death.

Driving through Baltimore, Dan looked around at this next stop in Phil's moveable school of continuing education. He saw a segregated city of 1 million, sustained by a combination of overt racism and malign neglect. Phil's next assignment was to St. Peter Claver Church on North Fremont Avenue, in the heart of one of the city's several black ghettos. He pulled up the car not far away, on North Calvert, at the entrance to the sprawling early twentieth-century red-stone motherhouse of the Society of St. Joseph, where he would be living in a tiny third-floor bedroom facing the street. After carrying Phil's few belongings inside, they shared a couple of drinks. Then the brothers said goodbye. Dan told Phil not to worry, reassuring himself as much as his younger brother, "You always wind up on your seat but then end up standing."[8]

Phil did not stand for long, but was off and running. He threw himself into every kind of apostolic work. He taught school, said Mass, heard confession, and counseled premarital couples. He arranged for six student interns from Marymount College to move in with local black families, the better to get to know them and learn about racial discrimination. He began a program helping needy parishioners to negotiate the bureaucratic maze of social services and defend themselves in housing court. He organized block clubs, a community center, and the inner city's first chapter of Alcoholics Anonymous. He recruited an instructor from Saul Alinsky's school in Chicago to teach the fundamentals of neighborhood organizing to diocesan priests, Jesuit seminarians brought in from Woodstock College in Maryland, and inner-city residents. And when he learned of a luxury hotel with no black workers, he promptly formed these same groups into a vocal picket line, compelling management to integrate its staff. "You could wake him up in the middle of the night and he'd get up smiling saying, 'What do you want me to do?' And he'd do it, cheerfully," said Father Henry Offer, his approving new pastor.[9]

His commitment and drive electrified Baltimore's Josephite community. The order, founded in 1866 in England, had been organized as a "Negro apostolate," intended to serve the needs of black Catholics. It had reached the United States in 1871 when four priests arrived to spread the faith among groups of freed slaves. In 1965 the Josephites numbered 250 priests and brothers.[10] Phil Berrigan was their rising star.

His friend Jim Forest described him then as "huge, striding . . . a verbal linebacker when the occasion required . . . with piercing blue eyes, [and] a Gary Cooper grin."[11] This description became a staple of the scores of press features filed on Phil in the next few years. It seems to have been a shorthand way of depicting him as the lone man of integrity willing to take on sinister forces without mussing up his down-to-earth good looks (think of the sheriff in *High Noon*), connecting him to an American myth that in no way hurt his growing reputation. And there was truth to it, too—at least in the minds of Phil's friends and supporters, and probably in his own. More substantively, Phil's concern for his congregants, friends, and fellow priests was manifestly real, and his analysis of race relations was as powerful and acute as anything written or said at the time by a white American. He was, in fact, one of the few Catholic priests who argued for nothing less than full and immediate racial integration.

For these and other statements he earned the trust of St. Peter Claver's black parishioners, one of whom confided to him, "Everywhere I go in this city, I am reminded that I am something less than a man and a full American. My neighborhood is segregated, and I know I could not buy out even if I had the money. I can't compete with white men of my education, because they're white and I'm colored. I don't have the political voice that I should have, though I vote regularly. I can't spend my money as I would like to, in fact, my dollar is worth less. I turn around and look and everywhere the fences are up."[12] Phil was determined to spend himself at the service of this man and his community. And in a time of creeping tension between black militants and white civil rights workers, Black Power spokesman Stokeley Carmichael said there was one priest in America who could be trusted. "Phil Berrigan," he declared, "is the only white man who knows where it's at."[13]

Before Phil had moved to Baltimore, his Josephite provincial, Father George O'Dea, had gotten him to agree again to keep public silence on Vietnam. But as Phil yanked at the weeds of systemic racism, he more often than not found the roots of war in his hands. Bizarre as it may seem, Berrigan regularly came across racists who would justify segregation by claiming that 350 years of the "brutal sport" of white supremacy had not been harmful to black Americans. Such stunning, self-serving amnesia, Phil believed, helped explain the glib acceptance by the majority of the American public, in 1965, of the war in Vietnam. He contended that the horrors of slavery and segregation had created a moral vacuum in the national character, as Americans over the centuries had learned to "turn away, with undisguised aversion from the misery of our own citizens, with a feeling of querulous injury that their sufferings should pierce the inviolability of our sensual and dreamlike existence"—which now made it equally hard to imagine the human disaster beginning to occur in Indochina. This left many Americans "trapped in a web of impregnability," Phil concluded, which inclined them to support a war driven by "the same psychosis as the one employed so widely and effectively at home." He was by now convinced that racism, Vietnam, and the nuclear arms race were the linked symptoms of a "gravely sick" and "schizophrenic" American culture.[14]

Of course, a nation's cultural and moral life, and its citizens' understanding of it, are seldom so simple. Though he fulminated from the pulpit on the interconnected themes of war and racism, few of his black parishioners joined the peace movement, as he would have liked. To some of them, fighting in Vietnam was simply their patriotic duty, while others were loath to antagonize the military, which, for all the patronizing injustice of the arrangement, still offered one of the few escapes from the ghetto. But most saw opposing the war as a secondary issue to surviving poverty and racism in America. "Phil baby, I know what you mean," a young black man said to him on the steps of the church after Mass, "but I can't bother, I don't know where my next meal is coming from." Frustrated, Phil felt his community work and preaching were inadequate to the times, "given the critical nature of the world." He wanted to help build a broad antiwar coalition of blacks and whites, liberals and radicals, believers and nonbelievers. "I feel in conscience that I can not remain quiet," he wrote to a friend, explaining his decision to break the pledge he had made to O'Dea.[15]

Barely three months after his arrival in the city, Phil helped organize the Baltimore Interfaith Peace Mission, a group of Protestant, Jewish, and Catholic clergy who had been active in SANE, CORE, and other civil rights and pacifist organizations. Their first task was visiting area colleges to speak against U.S. military intervention in Southeast Asia—first showing students where Vietnam could be located on a map. By all accounts, Phil was unusually persuasive. In late-night reading binges, he continued to digest prodigious amounts of politically oriented reportage and analysis—from the *I.F. Stone Weekly* to the *Wall Street Journal* to Simone Weil and the latest church encyclical—which he would then unleash from the podium in a gale of passionate argument, "battering mercilessly at his audience." Such was his charisma, and so compelling was the sound of a priest saying things like, "The American Church, in regard to Vietnam, has already reached the measure of default of the German Church under Hitler," that those who weren't appalled asked to join the cause.[16]

Soon Phil was making links between faith-based activists like himself and some of those secular "revolutionaries" on Guilford and Abell avenues. One Josephite priest remembered how Phil often let broke or homeless activists sleep the night on a floor in the North Calvert motherhouse. Thanks to Phil, the Josephites' formal breakfasts now enjoyed long-haired antiwar agitators as guests.[17]

As such strange social mixing showed, secular and religious circles were overlapping as never before. The civil rights movement had greatly sped the process, as the Reverend Martin Luther King Jr. and other black Christian ministers radically broadened their roles from dispensers of spiritual balm to outspoken leaders of a national coalition of religious and secular groups pressing for passage of legislation. (In fact, King would stand over President Johnson's shoulder later that year as the Voting Rights Act was signed into law.) And though the Catholic Church was finally updating its medieval concept of authority—power flowing from the divine down corresponding chains of church and state command—the idea of, say, a Catholic priest leveraging change from the federal government at the head of a popular movement was just unthinkable. (The redoubtable Father Coughlin, who had briefly achieved something close to that kind of influence, had had to be yanked offstage by the Vatican after spiraling into an ugly, anti-Semitic incoherence.) In the American Catholic political tradition, as opposed to the more activist and decentralized Protestant ethic, the hierarchy preferred to deal discreetly with the state, negotiating and accommodating out of view.

No one relished this exchange between church and state power, or practiced it more skillfully, than Francis Cardinal Spellman of New York. After building his reputation in the Vatican's secretariat of state, Spellman had ascended to the New York see in 1932, appointed by Pope Pius XII. With the bishop's seat he automatically served as vicar to Catholics in the United States armed forces, a job he fulfilled with an overflow of patriotic zeal. Short, stout, and easily provoked, Spellman was a staunch assimilationist with a taste for the trappings of military might, who believed that service in war would continue as a key means of Catholic advancement in America. Needless to say, he choked on the very concept of Catholic pacifism, and failed to be edified by the views of Dan and Phil Berrigan.

Spellman had backed Ngo Dinh Diem for the presidency of Vietnam as far back as the early 1950s, when the Catholic Diem had served a two-year exile in a New Jersey seminary. Diem took power in 1954, but his regime soon faced a threat from the Vietcong, forces sponsored by his longtime rival, Ho Chi Minh. The cardinal—alarmed by the sight of Catholic refugees fleeing the communist North, and by the danger to Saigon, his foothold for increasing religious market share in the region—had thrown his support behind American intervention to prop up Diem (of whom an underwhelmed Lyndon Johnson, when asked why the U.S. State Department was sinking so much money and prestige into such an isolated autocrat, once said, "Shit, [he's] the only boy we got out there"[18]). Likewise, Diem had been Spellman's boy until his troops mowed down Buddhist demonstrators in 1963, a critical blunder that led to his assassination before the year was out. The death of Diem redoubled Spellman's backing of a forceful American presence in Vietnam, which he would have supported on principle anyway. As James O'Gara, former *Commonweal* editor, remarked with a rueful laugh, "Spellman never saw a war he didn't like—if America was in it."[19]

Phil Berrigan, on the other hand, didn't see anything at all to like when it came to the war in Vietnam. He began meeting with members of Baltimore's countercultural left, frequently in the brownstone home of Bill O'Connor, a college professor of literature and sociology. "Phil brought a sense of urgency that was almost Faustian," said O'Connor, who had been hoping his grim foreboding about American involvement in Vietnam would turn out to be wrong. But as the fighting spread, and the White House grew more belligerent, O'Connor felt confrontation between the government and its citizenry was inevitable, and that in Baltimore it would be led by Philip Berrigan, a religious man rallying deeply secular radicals, a seemingly fearless iconoclast whose Roman collar lent him tremendous mystique. "I knew he was going to sustain a drive to bring the war in Vietnam home to people here and end it," O'Connor said, describing a distant resolution that would take more suffering, death, and wasted years than his worst fears let him imagine.[20]

The catalyst came in August 1965, when President Johnson used confused reports of a skirmish between communist patrol boats and the American destroyer *Maddox* in the South China Sea's Gulf of Tonkin as a pretext for presenting a congressional resolution granting the White House power to "take all necessary measures" against North Vietnam to "prevent further aggression"— though evidence since has shown that the "attack" had been an overreaction by an inexperienced American crew to the faulty detection of enemy craft. The president even remarked at the time to an aide, "Hell, those dumb stupid sailors were just shooting at some flying fish." Fish or fowl, formally declared or not, the war was on. Johnson's resolution passed in a day, and by his order, jets from U.S. aircraft carriers stepped up the bombing of North Vietnamese targets.[21]

The peace movement, still mobilizing, responded with a student demonstration in Washington, D.C. At the time, there was no real precedent for mass domestic opposition to the American government's decision to engage in (or start) a war. Polls showed that most of the country believed in an unsubstantiated "domino theory" of the communist drive for world hegemony; and based on America's record of supporting the "good side" in previous wars, a majority were willing to extend a presumption of virtue to their leaders' foreign aims. But as the year wore on, the Vietnam bombing and ground campaigns began racking up steady body counts— with American casualties tabulated on the nightly TV news— prompting some moderates to move toward dissent. For one example, realpolitik theorist Hans Morgenthau from the University of Chicago and Professor Robert S. Brown of Fairleigh Dickinson University carried 6,000 names of respected academics on an antiwar petition to the doors of the U.S. State Department in late 1965, where they were summarily rejected. Foreign policy architects could still brush off such protests, as long as the public, for the most part, remained indifferent.

As their antiwar reputations grew, Dan, and especially Phil, were denounced in some Catholic newspapers for their insufficient deference to the wisdom of federal authorities. Phil defended himself in a letter to Martin Corbin of the Catholic Worker: "If it is questionable that the Gospel ever allowed Christians to participate in war, it is more questionable today, when war can either be nuclear or total, both morally condemned . . . I for one am rather tired with being forced to subscribe to the fears and ignorance of those in authority." Ever the scrupulous documentarian, he referred Corbin to the writings of Vatican II: "I suggest you read Chap. 5 of Schema 13 from the Council."[22]

Dan later wrote that Phil did not share the fervor of liberal Catholics for the Vatican Council's reforms, a skepticism that eventually proved correct, contended Dan, because "those who were acting on the assumption of instant change from Rome were bound someday, and soon, to be put down hard."[23] Yet Phil, who had already been "put down hard" by his church, continued to buttress his antiwar statements with precise citations from official Catholic doctrine. It would not be long, however, before he abandoned those justifications altogether, and started searching for a way to shock the president and the Pentagon, the State Department, Cardinal Spellman, and the entire political system of what he called "this magnificent, frantic, insane, nation-empire to which God has hinged so much of the future of mankind."[24] The time was coming when Phil would consider reform of church or country to be passé—the timid tinkering of those he viewed as gutless middle-class liberals.

Simultaneously the civil rights movement, which Phil still followed closely, had arrived at a similar crossroads. Malcolm X had been shot down in February 1965, aborting his nascent attempts at moving from a strict black separatism to searching out common ground with liberal whites. And many civil rights rank-and-filers had traded their New Testament, with its exhortations to forgiveness and universal love, for Franz Fanon's manifesto on armed revolution and Che Guevara's diaries, tilting power away from Martin

Luther King Jr. and other movement moderates. In an explosion of frustration at the agonizing pace of racial reform, the Watts neighborhood in South Central Los Angeles had burst into summer riot (Dan would have been in the city had the Archbishop of Los Angeles not barred him from leading a seminar for an order of Catholic nuns), leading many black Americans to despair of measured change and to call for "Black Power"—in part a defiant expression of independent identity, and in part a surrender, says historian Robert Weisbrot, to "an alternative utopianism for embittered idealists."[25]

These same conflicts, also bitter, would eventually emerge in the peace movement as the Vietnam War ground endlessly on. As usual, Phil had come to his personal turning point a little ahead of the game. He "pondered long and hard" about what more he and others could do to oppose the war, while continuing to lecture and attend demonstrations (dropping a note to his superior after he was already on the way to his latest protest).[26] As he searched for new forms of civil resistance, some others who shared his views gave in to despair. Misguided utopians and disillusioned idealists, they chose to be heard above the din on the question of Vietnam by committing acts that went beyond the power of words to comprehend.

When eighty-two-year-old Quaker Alice Herz, a German-born *mischling*—part-Jewish, part-Christian—set fire to herself in March 1965 on a street in Detroit to protest the escalating war in Southeast Asia, she said, as she lay dying, "I wanted to burn myself like the monks in Vietnam did."

Eight months later, Defense Secretary Robert McNamara, one of the war's prime movers, looked out his Pentagon window to observe the curious sight of a young man holding a one-year-old girl, sitting in the parking lot not forty feet away. The man was Norman Morrison, secretary of the Stony Run Quaker Meeting near Baltimore, a married father of three, and the girl was his daughter. Morrison's profound and corrosive loathing for the Vietnam War and the Pentagon's part in it had brought him to the point that he poured kerosene on his body and immolated himself. Horrified bystanders shrieked, "Save the child!" and snatched the girl from his arms. Morrison himself was consumed by flames, under the appalled gaze of the Secretary of Defense. Unknown to anyone at the time, McNamara had been nursing doubts about his aggressive public promotion of the war. Three decades later he would confess that as he stood frozen, watching the young man burn, "I believed I understood and shared some of his thoughts." But instead of changing course, McNamara said, "I bottl[ed] up my emotions and avoided talking about them with anyone."[27]

A few days later, Phil accompanied David Eberhardt, a poet and local journalist, and several other Baltimore activists to visit the site where Morrison died and mourn him as a martyr. The group stood in reverent silence, and Phil said in the moment he found a certain "power in [Morrison's] rage and sorrow."[28]

The American public did not.

Unprepared for a rash of martyrdoms in an Eastern religious context, most people viewed the suicides as an inexplicable waste. Morrison and Herz had been following the example of the Buddhist monks in South Vietnam who had burned themselves in protest over crackdowns on their religion. While suicide is not sanctioned in Buddhist culture, monk immolations were understood in many parts of that country as a serious call for national change through an act of self-purification. Sixty-six-year-old Quang Duc, the first monk to die by fire in the streets of Saigon in 1963 (and whose last moments hit front pages around the world in a grisly photo), had left a "respectful" note asking civil authorities to show "charity and compassion."[29] No such rational plea was gleaned from the ashes of America's homegrown martyrs. Their gruesome deaths were merely another sign that the decade's domestic politics were shaping up to be unlike any other in recent memory.

"It was fall," Eberhardt remembered about the day spent grieving for Morrison, in all its surreality: "The chrysanthemums stood out with their pungent, spiky heads, the Capitol dome in the far distance behind them. They were bright as frost, bright as fire, bright as the fires of burning martyrs!"[30]

A week later, twenty-one-year-old Roger LaPorte burned himself alive in front of the United Nations building in New York City. As word of his immolation spread from the Catholic Worker on the Lower East Side to Cardinal Spellman's Madison Avenue chancery, the latent tension between Catholic critics and defenders of Vietnam—and deeper, between the promoters and detractors of a flexible church authority—found an issue around which to gather and explode, ending in Daniel Berrigan himself being "put down" for a time.

LaPorte had been the well-built, six-foot son of a lumberjack, who had distinguished himself as a student throughout Catholic high school and college. After graduation he had drifted a bit, studying at St. John Vianney Seminary (named after a French army deserter) in Connecticut, and later experimenting with the Trappists in Wisconsin. In the autumn of 1963, he had appeared at the Catholic Worker House of Hospitality on Chrystie Street in Manhattan, close by the Bowery, to help with the soup line. He had also enrolled at Columbia University, then transferred to Hunter College, before dropping out to live with a couple of other volunteers in one of the Lower East Side's shabby nineteenth-century tenements, doing the Catholic Worker's good work of serving the poor.

Around the Worker, Jim Forest knew him as well as anyone. He described LaPorte's last day on earth: "Eating his hot dog, he spoke of draft cards, pacifism and Christ. There was no reference, however, to immolation, no sense of desperation." Nicolle D'Etremont, another Catholic Worker, also talked with LaPorte only hours before his death. Forest says he gave neither of them any sense of what he was planning.

At 5:20 in the morning of November 9, 1965, LaPorte sat down across the street from the United Nations near a granite wall chiseled with a quote from the Book of Isaiah—"They shall beat their swords into plowshares, and their spears into pruning hooks; nation shall not lift up sword against nation, neither shall they learn war any more." First Avenue was quiet, with only a few people present to witness what happened when he doused himself with kerosene and set himself ablaze. In the ambulance that rushed him, dying, to Bellevue Hospital, and just before he fell into a coma, he told an attendant: "I am a Catholic Worker. I am against all wars. I did this as a religious action. I picked the hour so no one could stop me."[31]

LaPorte had been fairly new to the Worker, and Dorothy Day hadn't known him. But her enemies wasted no time in trying to tar her with his act. A writer in the *National Catholic Reporter* criticized her and the Worker for having "never been well-grounded intellectually," and functioning with a "sort of built-in rejection of complexity"[32] (a charge that would become familiar to the Berrigans). And a small group of New York University students who blamed her for the death tried to attack her physically when she spoke at the school's Catholic Center. For her part, Day sorrowed over LaPorte and his terrible error. She wrote that the church had always taught that "suicide is a sin," but in this case, "mercy and loving-kindness dictate another judgment." She compared the young man's sacrifice to the mounting deaths in Southeast Asia and mocked a *Wall Street Journal* story that trumpeted the war as a boon to the economy, saying, "There is something satanic about this kind of writing."[33]

Meanwhile, in distant, bucolic Kentucky, news of the suicide reached Merton, to his horror. His first inclination was to blame the growing stridency of the antiwar movement for creating a climate that had made LaPorte's act possible. He fired off a telegram to the Catholic Peace Fellowship:

> Just heard about suicide of Roger LaPorte. While I do not hold Catholic Peace Fellowship responsible for this tragedy current developments in peace movement make it impossible for me to continue as sponsor of Fellowship. Please remove my name from list of sponsors. Letter follows.

Searching his memory, Dan recalled the shy LaPorte "only as an innocent face on the edge of the Worker community," with whom he "had scarcely even spoken, apart from greeting one another on occasion." To the best of Dan's or anyone else's knowledge, LaPorte had acted alone. So Dan, Day, Cornell, and Forest all wrote letters to Merton informing him of this fact, explaining further that the war had pressured some to act in unpredictable ways, despite the efforts of many to channel the need for protest into productive, nonviolent behavior.

Temporarily mollified, the monk withdrew his resignation, adding that because his abbey had finally allowed him to become a hermit, he really didn't want to get immersed in "external problems." But soon he was writing the Fellowship again, this time worrying whether the LaPorte and Morrison suicides might not bring out copycats; and more, he feared that an atmosphere of madness was overwhelming the contribution of religious peace activists, which, as he saw it, was to offer "patient, constructive and pastoral work rather than acts of defiance which antagonize the average person without enlightening him [or her]"—acts like immolation.[34] Merton concluded by summing up the United States at the end of 1965: "The whole atmosphere is crazy, [marked by] an air of absurdity and moral void, even where conscience and morality is invoked. The joint is going into a slow frenzy. The country is nuts."[35]

Merton was already edgy from another recent innovation in the peace movement led by Catholics: draft card burning. Catholic Workers had been among the first to torch their Selective Service cards to protest the Vietnam War. Tom Cornell had been especially incendiary, burning his first card in 1960, then every replacement sent to him up through 1965, for an impressive total of nine. His latest had been during a late summer rally at Union Square Park in New York City. Jim Forest, who had helped the elderly Day to the stage so she could speak in support of Cornell and his fellow dissenters, recalled two essential details about the event. First, that Roger LaPorte had been present; and second, that counterdemonstrators had yelled from across the street, "Burn yourselves, not your draft cards!"[36]

Responding to such sentiments, Congress had shortly thereafter passed a law that made burning a draft card a crime punishable by a $10,000 fine and five years in prison. Then, fatefully, a Catholic Worker and former student of Dan's was the first to defy it. While participating in the hyperbolically named "International Day of Protest Against the War in Vietnam" on October 15, 1965, David Miller had decided that if Congress wanted to raise the stakes, he'd call. The next day, he appeared in a dark suit and tie, his short hair neatly combed, before a crowd of 500 at the Whitehall Street Induction Center in Lower Manhattan. "I'm not much at giving speeches, so I'll let this speak for me," he said before holding his draft card in the flame from a cigarette lighter. Reporter Gabe Pressman, noting Miller's apparent serenity, commented on live television, "I seem more nervous than you are." Miller smiled as the FBI swooped in to snatch up bits of unburned draft card (later to be used as evidence at his trial; he was convicted and sentenced to two years in federal prison), and the crowd burst into cheers mixed with curses and shouted insults to his manhood and patriotism.[37]

Miller was a former altar boy and graduate of a Christian Brothers high school. He had sought out the Worker after reading about the movement in *The Other America*, ex–Catholic Worker Michael Harrington's influential book on the country's millions of disregarded poor. But to Cardinal Spellman—who fumed against the spectacle of a Catholic burning his draft card, branding Miller "a simple-minded fool"—the most grievous item on Miller's alarming résumé was his involvement as a student at Le Moyne with Daniel Berrigan's International House.[38] When asked about the now-notorious Miller by the press, Dan replied that he knew him and had taught him and was proud of it. Phil, too, deepened the cardinal's ire by telling the *Baltimore Evening Sun* that in his opinion, Miller's rebellion had been "the highest expression of loyalty," and a demonstration that "dissent is a cherished part of the democratic process." (Afterward, Phil bragged in a letter to Forest that his intimidated superior now feared to stop him from making provocative public statements.[39]) But harmful allegations—"atrocious rumors," an incensed Dan later called them—were also reaching Spellman, in Rome for the closing sessions of Vatican II, that Daniel Berrigan had somehow goaded Roger LaPorte into committing his final act. The claim was false, and there is no proof Spellman believed it. But here is where the cardinal drew the line.

The New York Jesuits were ostensibly independent from the archdiocese, but over the years the generous and politically skillful Spellman had become a key financial patron to the order. ("After all, we do have to get along with the Cardinal," one Jesuit later said to Dan about supporting a single priest as it compared to the cost of displeasing His Eminence.) Now the cardinal called in his chips. He contacted the Jesuits in New York, who in turn had Dan's superior phone him. Dan was ordered to make no public statement about LaPorte's self-immolation; only the cardinal would comment, officially, which he did. Roger LaPorte had sinned by committing suicide, said Spellman, adding that he had ignored the law of Christ's compassion for the family he left behind. That was all. There was no mention made of context, or the mitigating circumstance of a young man's disturbed sensibility. The chancery had spoken.

Dan found himself pinched by a pair of formidable wills. On the one hand there was Merton, his friend and mentor, preaching a strict nonviolence of hand and heart, citing LaPorte's death as the kind of disaster that occurs when front-line activists make a fetish of winning and quick results. (At the same time, many activists grumbled that only a monk sealed in a hermitage could set such impossible standards in times of crisis.) On the other hand was Spellman, calling LaPorte's deed pure self-destruction. But, Dan wondered, what if the death had been more of a "self-offering attuned (however naively or mistakenly) to the sacrifice of Christ? Would not such a presumption show mercy toward the dead, as well as honoring the grief of the living?" Killing oneself, said Dan, arose from hopelessness. And he failed to see how LaPorte had acted in that spirit. Or as Dan's close friend, the Vietnamese Buddhist monk Thich Nhat Hanh, explained to him, immolation was sometimes an act of creation, "the willingness to take suffering on yourself, to make yourself suffer for the sake of purification, for the sake of communication." When Dan was invited to say a few words during a memorial Mass for LaPorte at the Catholic Worker a few days later, he spoke in this vein, concluding that the young man's "death was offered so that others may live."[40]

Perhaps he was not attempting to address this difficult issue in a comprehensive way. But Ross Labrie, professor of American literature at the University of British Columbia, points out, "Berrigan did not, in fact, deal squarely with the issue of the violence of

LaPorte's act; nor did he, in comparing LaPorte's action to Christ's, point out that Christ was slain by the violence of others."[41] Classic moral theology teaches that true martyrdom is the chief act of the virtue of fortitude.[42] And clearly, for all his guilt-racked identification with the victims of war, LaPorte had failed to show fortitude. But if Dan had missed a chance to tackle the question of violence and its place within moral protest, he would have many more chances to do so. From the LaPorte debate to the present day—through draft board raids to Plowshares actions—violence, at least against property, has been one of the chief objections to the Berrigans' brand of civil disobedience.

Dan felt, and still feels, that in speaking briefly at a religious service, as opposed to delivering a statement on LaPorte to the media, he had honored Cardinal Spellman's prohibition. But he must have known he would not be allowed the last word.

Spellman was furious when he heard of Dan's remarks. He dispatched Bishop John McGuire from Rome to a meeting with the Reverend John J. McGinty, Jesuit provincial of New York, to talk about getting rid of the vexsome priest. After the summit with McGuire, McGinty summoned Father James Patrick Cotter, Dan's boss at *Jesuit Missions*, to his office. McGinty told Cotter that Dan was to be expelled from the Archdiocese of New York for "a multitude of reasons," including his peace work. Sometime later, according to Cotter, McGinty revealed that McGuire had claimed the decision to banish Dan was also based on a letter LaPorte had allegedly written to his girlfriend on "the day before [the suicide, telling] her that she probably would not be able to understand what he was about to do. However, if she wanted to understand it further she should talk to Father Berrigan because he would understand." Such a letter has never been produced. And even if it had existed, its testimony to a connection between Dan's beliefs and LaPorte's real motivation is specious. But it would seem it was enough at the time for McGinty to order Cotter to boot Dan out of New York.

Cotter was stunned. Later he spoke to McGinty, asking if he might send Dan to Latin America on an extended reporting trip, since "I had planned to go there anyway with [photographer]

Father Alden Stevenson and I could just send Father Stevenson with Dan. Father McGinty said that was fine." The assignment became the cover story for Dan's entire exile.

On November 16, a downcast Cotter visited Dan, whose spirit and his opinions he admired, in his apartment. Francine du Plessix Gray, in *Divine Disobedience*, writes that "the following conversation, or something very similar to it, took place:

" 'The fat's in the fire,' Father Cotter said.

" 'I haven't got much fat, and where's the fire?' Daniel said.

" 'You have to go on a trip,' Father Cotter repeated.

" 'What if I don't want to?' Daniel asked.

" 'Be sensible,' Father Cotter pleaded. 'I've fought for you. It's infinitely better than what they originally planned for you.'

" 'What was that?' Daniel asked.

" 'I can't tell you,' Father Cotter said darkly.

" 'The meat cleaver, huh?' Daniel quipped."[43]

This snappy piece of dialogue has been reproduced many times, and, exact words or not, it conveys the sense of the actual exchange, while revealing two truths about Dan: that there is no greater threat to him than his removal from the priesthood and the Jesuits, as was contemplated in Spellman's "original plan"; that the keener the menace, the more likely he is to keep it at bay with banter, buying time while preparing a forceful intellectual counterpunch. (Whereas Phil, say friends and acquaintances, tends to shrink from personal confrontation, though he's glad to argue for hours over moral and political questions.)

Forest recalled, "Dan called me at the CPF office, voice choked, and asked me to come up immediately. He seemed to be crying." As Forest explained, Dan was faced with a difficult choice: Defy the command and risk his own defrocking in a fight against church authority (which he would probably lose in the court of mainstream American Catholic opinion), or "take the one-way ticket" with the hope that "there might even be some providence in going south for a while." As is his habit, Dan called many people for advice. Most told him not to cloud his peace stance with a scandalous act of priestly disobedience at this time—no matter how justified.[44] Dan had announced with arrogance, while recently complying with the order to conduct a more traditional liturgy, that should he need to take a stand against the church, it would be by his own initiative on an issue of his choosing. A nice idea, but Cardinal Spellman had proved him wrong. The initiative was his, and Dan would obey.

He sought an appeal, but the Jesuits denied a hearing. He also tried, but failed, to penetrate the wall of secrecy between Cotter's intimations of official animosity and the reason for his punishment. As he later explained to John Deedy, former managing editor of *Commonweal*: "I had no access to any superior, no voice in decisions. And to cook my Xmas goose, all Jesuit houses refused to house me while I waited for visas—including Le Moyne College where I had given the word for six years. I was also not allowed to visit my parents who were quite aged—and quite bewildered."[45]

First exile, then shunning. Finally, the Maryland Province and the Jesuit Georgetown University found an empty Quonset hut at the edge of campus—Dan could stay there till his paperwork came through. Cotter, feeling badly, called the journalist John Leo (Dan called him, too), who promptly broke the story in the Catholic press. Dan was at this point widely admired in progressive Catholic circles, especially among Jesuit seminarians, for his poetry and probing critiques of the church and society. These groups reacted with outrage when they read about his impending departure. Cardinal Spellman had probably anticipated a clamor from that quarter and expected to weather it with ease. But he could not have predicted the manner in which Dan's banishment struck a deep and angry chord among ordinary Catholics, many of whom, while occasionally chafing at the Berrigan style and substance, felt they were seeing their hopes for an open church undercut by an old-fashioned silencing.

Commonweal called it "a shame and a scandal, a disgustingly blind totalitarian act, a travesty on Vatican II."[46] Based on those characteristics, Dan personally placed the blame on Spellman and his advisers, whose use of the tactic had precedent, after all. In 1956, the cardinal had bounced a priest from the Catholic chaplaincy of Columbia University to an obscure rural parish for daring to publish a positive review of Lionel Trilling's work on Sigmund Freud—an exile that endured until the more tolerant Terence Cardinal Cooke succeeded Spellman after his death in 1967. And the day Dan left the country, less than two weeks after being told he'd be taking a trip of indefinite length, two other young Jesuits were forced to resign from CALCAV.

McGinty very quickly came to rue his response to McGuire, and deeply regretted his acquiescence to archdiocesan pressure. He was "very unhappy and quite a bit mystified about the whole thing," and wrote Dan an apologetic note, says Cotter, and even wanted to visit him in Latin America, though he never did. Cotter, too, lamented that he should have "resisted very, very strongly this sending away of Dan." Not long after Berrigan's departure, he sat down and composed a long memorandum to himself.

> I am dictating this now so that if sometime in the future the question comes up in connection with Dan I wanted to be clearly understood, as best I can remember it just now, that Dan was never told really why he was being sent away and I'm not sure that there was any one reason. I think, moreover, that a great mistake in justice was made at the time; whether Dan was out of line or not, he deserved more than he got in terms of treatment. I think this is what ultimately bothered Fr. McGinty very much.[47]

As the cardinal was overreacting, Merton, partly in response, was softening his stance. After reflecting on further letters from Dan, including a description of LaPorte's memorial Mass, he apologized to his friends for the rush to judgment. He also wrote to Cornell and Forest at the CPF and told them that "the more I think about draft card burning, the more I think that you, Tom, are utterly right before God."[48] When the news reached Dan months later in Chile, he wrote to his allies, "It was good to hear that Tom Merton was back with us. I had the feeling his first reaction was not up to his usual thoughtfulness and that we would see his face again."[49]

Dan's four months in Latin America, crucial as they were to the development of his theology and politics, were downright miserable. A few days before Thanksgiving 1965, he landed in Cuernavaca, Mexico, at "Centro de Investigaciones Culturales," a commune of progressive lay and religious run by the former Jesuit and caustic social critic Ivan Illich. Dan liked what he saw of the commune's collective rural life and program of free intellectual inquiry, but his heart and mind remained in New York, as chatty letters home attest. Writing Forest and Cornell, he asked after Tom's condition, having heard from Phil that Cornell had been beaten at a march in Washington; named and sent his love to a variety of activists; asked to be included by mail in discussions about the direction of the CPF; encouraged the idea that a group should start a fast in a church to protest his "demise"; inquired after Merton; and mused that "we have in a sense been through a lot since Roger's death, but what a time of strength and joy too!"[50]

Asked years later why he chose to conceal from his friends the bleak depression closing in on him, he said, "That epoch was so painful for everyone on all sides, including my family. I didn't want to add to the grief. Writing a letter is different than talking with a close friend—that's when I can do some of that stuff. But mostly I just swallow with a big lump in my throat and hope for the best." His father had also taught him to conceal his vulnerability, even from people close to him, lest he be attacked or considered a burden. "It's probably a Berrigan trait: You keep an even keel, at least in public. It's an Irish stoicism, not wanting to add to the trouble of others."[51] In a letter to Freda on her eightieth birthday—begun "Dear Mama"—Dan wrote blithely about "the human comedy," and joked that for her ninetieth, "even if I am in *Siberia* I will fly in for the event!"[52] And as one would expect, Dado, too, was shielded from Dan's distress; he beamed at the hubbub surrounding his son, who seemed at last to be showing some mettle. "Dear boy," he wrote to Dan, "I slept on thoughts of you and the true dimensions of your Greatness."[53]

But no encouragement could relieve the sting of injustice and defeat, and the ache of separation from the people he wanted to be with and the work he wanted to do. Dan hoped his acceptance of ecclesiastical discipline might work out over time to his advantage, as his friends were beginning to plead his case in the liberal Catholic press, but he also feared that "the outcome [would be] merely to place the lid more firmly in place and to vindicate the old order; with certain sighs of relief that the delinquent at least had the minimal sense to obey."[54]

At the inaugural meeting of CALCAV held a few days after his leaving, Rabbi Abraham Joshua Heschel and Lutheran Pastor Richard John Neuhaus sat on either side of an empty chair with a large sign bearing the name of their absent co-chair: "Daniel Berrigan, S.J." And Phil filled in for his brother by giving the meeting's opening speech—a cracking attack on the Vietnam War. But Dan, wandering at the outer reaches of the unreliable mails, took no comfort in such gestures. Feeling persecuted, he brooded on "the mystery of the Cross," comparing it to "the mystery of this war, which has destroyed so many lives, including the moral lives of those who destroy. A war that has now reached perilously into my own life and destroyed its former shape, deflected its energies, disrupted its friendships, made of my life an occasion of division instead of the sign of unity I had hoped for."[55]

He flew to Caracas, Venezuela, where he teamed up with a translator and his *Jesuit Missions* colleague, Father Alden Stevenson, a gifted photographer with experience as a journalist in the Middle East, Asia, and Africa. Stevenson found Dan to be "incredibly sensitive," a priest out of sorts who was "hurt and kept asking 'why?' they had expelled him." They traveled through ten South American countries visiting Catholic officials and Jesuit houses and American Peace Corps volunteers, and for their magazine assignment, they toured the teeming tin and cardboard slums at the fringes of the cities. Dan would be briefly cheered by meeting the saintly Dom Helder Camara, the justice-seeking bishop of Recife, Brazil, and a community of São Paulo worker-priests, modeled after the French movement that had remade his own philosophy of the church. But then he would sink back into "unutterable loneliness, dread, even despair."[56] His Lenten meditations centered on gloomy texts from a few of his favorite thinkers: Camus, Weil, and Isaiah. He took voluminous, almost obsessive, notes on the predicament of his exile, comparing himself to "an animal taught to survive in water, never loving the water," and at one point looked with an envious twinge on a wizened priest passing slowly through a Sunday crowd, the unruffled product of a bygone era of somnambulant church order. "[I am] without mail delivery," he moaned to his journal, "having to imagine my friends' lives, looking at a watch to help imagine what they are doing at this time of Christmas."[57]

They were doing a great deal, actually. Students at Notre Dame University were fasting to protest Dan's removal, and a pacifist in New Hampshire had begun a hunger strike in a Catholic church. And on December 4, 1965, about fifty seminarians, priests, and Fordham University students had demonstrated on the sidewalk outside Cardinal Spellman's Madison Avenue office. "Merry Christmas, Dan, Wherever You Are," read one of their signs. A passerby stopped to gaze uncomprehendingly on the scene. She turned to a reporter and asked, "Are they picketing the church?" Yes they were, as several breathless news reports confirmed the following day. Then adding to the astonishment over Catholics publicly questioning the leaders of their church, a remarkable full-page ad appeared in the December 12 issue of the *New York Times*.[58]

Titled "Open Letter to the Authorities of the Archdiocese of New York and the Jesuit Community in New York City," it began: "The issue here is simply freedom of conscience."

The statement openly challenged the cardinal to deny that he had exiled Daniel Berrigan, and asked whether any priest could

> speak out on Vietnam only if he supports the American action there? . . . [and] if a priest is controversial [and] takes a position different from that of conventional wisdom . . . [is he] as a result dangerous to the Church? The Roman Catholic manner of dealing with such a priest is not to debate him, not to offer alternative arguments, but simply to silence him and send him to another country where his attempt to give Christian witness will not offend . . . Such a meaning is intolerable in the Roman Catholic Church [and] . . . denies what the Church has achieved. It must be eradicated.[59]

The ad was the work of the "Committee for Daniel Berrigan," which had formed quickly on announcement of his expulsion. Prior to publication, the group had sent the letter to many churches and seminaries, and to the subscription list of the influential Catholic quarterly *Cross Currents*. Considering Cardinal Spellman's reach and the well-known price to be paid for incurring his wrath, the request to sign implied some risk for many of the Catholics asked. Organizer Joseph Mulholland of Queens College remembered receiving a phone call at 11:30 one night, requesting his immediate presence at Fordham University in the Bronx. On arrival, he found a worried bunch of Jesuits in a room with the lights turned low. What was this all about? they wanted to know. He reassured them by insisting that the thousands of other signers would lend a certain amount of protection to any one person's name. This, it happened, was the right thing to say. Everyone signed the ad, and some donated money. (Mulholland also said he approached Phil for his signature, but, curiously, Phil declined, claiming he was already in enough trouble with the Josephites and Baltimore's conservatives.) In another instance, a Woodstock seminarian said the statement's arrival split the ranks of the Jesuits-in-formation. Admonished by their superior not to sign the ad, seven seminarians lent their names to it anyway. (A dozen others, in a classic display of self-preserving Jesuit discretion, disapproved of the Berrigan exile in a stern but private letter to their superior.) In the end, the ad carried nearly a thousand signatures, more than seventy-five of them belonging to priests.

For many Catholics, signing the open letter was a radicalizing act. This was especially true for those priests and nuns who had begun examining the implications of Vatican II on their vocations. They had read or heard of the council's "Pastoral Constitution on the Church in the Modern World," which had drawn on Pope John XXIII's historic encyclical, *Pacem in Terris*, in supporting Catholic pacifism and conscientious objection to service in the military, while pointedly denouncing "any act of war aimed indiscriminately at the destruction of entire cities or of extensive areas along with their population." And they understood that the church had now commissioned them to give flesh to these principles. But when one among them tried it, a prince of the church had slapped him down and shipped him off the continent. So Dan's cause became a rallying point for an energized block of Catholics (some of whom later graduated to the militant antiwar "Catholic Left" or "ultra-resistance") fed up with a brusque and impervious hierarchy, and various others upset by the muffling of an important antiwar voice. In a strange way, Roger LaPorte's tragic immolation had led to the creation of a more palatable public martyrdom in the form of Daniel Berrigan, exiled priest.

What did Cardinal Spellman do? On Christmas Day 1965, he flew to Vietnam in a U.S. air force plane to minister to the troops. Sporting a military uniform, he celebrated Mass, proclaiming in his homily that "this war in Vietnam . . . is, I believe, a war for civilization!" Before his trip, he had had to weigh the competing claims of a pair of recent events: Pope Paul VI's October 15 address to the United Nations General Assembly, at which he had pleaded passionately to the gathering of diplomats, and the world, "No more war. War never again!"; and a proposal in the U.S. Congress to mine the Haiphong harbor and extend the American bombing campaign to the North Vietnamese capital of Hanoi, based on the rise in Chinese and Soviet aid to that country. After the Mass, when questioned by reporters about America's growing role in the war, Spellman said, "[M]y country, right or wrong." Having chosen, and having bestowed his blessing, he expected his flock to fall in line.

"Let there be no romanticizing about the enchantment lent by distance," Dan was writing in his journal. "Exile is a terrible burden, a terrible weight . . . deprived of the faces of those I love, of their voices, of the unexplainable beauty and terror of wartime, of evening gatherings, of the Eucharist celebrated with those I love. . . . Now I am fastened down. To an obedience as hard as it is inhuman; to injustice."[60]

"I've got a wounded deer with me," Stevenson said.

Finally, a letter from Merton caught up with Dan in Ecuador. The monk's exuberance and common sense were exactly what he needed. "I have never managed to get awful sorry for you going to Latin America: it is where everything is going to happen [which is] why it is so important for someone like you . . . Man, you are one of the most popular priests in the U.S. You are all over the front page of *The Critic*, you have a fine piece in *Jubilee* [two Catholic journals], you are teamed up well with that wild great nun Sr. Corita [Kent—a graphic artist who illustrated his poetry] . . . you got all the cats eating out of your hand. And you ask why you were shipped out? Nothing but good can come to you from it."[61]

Merton also expressed his regret in a later letter that he wasn't permitted by his abbey's "rock-bound establishment" to join him. He knew Dan's crisis had caused him to think of resigning from the priesthood before church authorities forced him out, as seemed very possible. But Merton advised him to cling to the Jesuits, which Dan says "helped me . . . many times." Merton himself had previously struggled with quitting the Trappists during censorship battles, and Dan in turn had encouraged him to endure. Now Merton told his fellow priest: "We must stay where we are. We must stay with our community, even though it's absurd, makes no sense, and causes great suffering." [62]

These strong words in mind, Dan seemed able to focus more on the realities around him. He walked through Lima's Monton slum and got "sick at the stomach, eyes smarting from the smoke of spontaneous combustion arising here and settling in a pall upon the whole area"; flying over Argentina, he looked down on farmlands stretched "like endless gardens from the Andes to the sea," interspersed with the semifeudal arrangement of "a miserable clutch of huts, and then a vast park and a mansion"; and in Rio de Janeiro, he toured the aftermath of a horrific flood in January 1966 that had crashed through the city's hillside *favellas*, churning animals, shacks, and hundreds of people in "a stew of death."[63]

As Stevenson worked his camera, Dan fell mute before the squalid calamity. He refused to insult the people he met—the homeless, community organizers, and families of the victims—with platitudes seeking to justify the ways of God to man. Instead he wondered plaintively in his journal, "What happens to people who are condemned to live and die in the places we have seen? And, more to the point, what happens to the chiefs of society, who allow such conditions to prevail; indeed, whose power of place depends exactly on the existence of such places?"[64]

The answer, as he came to understand it, is that the chiefs grew rich off their CIA and American corporate sponsors—the backers of their militaries—while the poor led their brutish and brief lives on what margins they could find. Sometimes the Catholic Church tried to speak about justice, as did twenty-seven Brazilian priests while Dan was in their country, writing a letter to their bishops that begged for an end to religion by and for the rich, that asked that "the good name of Christ and the sacred realities we are privileged to serve be not misused to serve personal interests."[65] But most of the time, the Catholic Church aligned itself through silence with the reigning oligarchs.

All of which raised the question, what to do? Dan talked with countless Latin Americans, in and out of the church, about fostering radical change in their part of the world. Could organized nonviolence on the Gandhian model work? The legendary son-of-wealth-turned-Catholic-priest Camilio Torres had thought so, and had recently waged a campaign in Colombia for land reform, academic freedom, and state ownership of leading industries. Then the Archbishop of Bogotá had denounced his efforts in early 1965 as "erroneous and pernicious." So Torres had left the priesthood, convinced that the yawning gap between Colombia's rich and poor could be bridged by revolutionary violence. He had ultimately chosen to take to the hills with a Cuban-backed guerrilla force. While in Lima, Dan and Stevenson, with the rest of Latin America, learned Camilio Torres's fate: He had been shot and killed in a battle with Colombian government troops.[66]

Dan was later quoted in *Jesuit Missions* magazine, speaking in reference to issues raised by Torres: "I think the responsible people we met were speaking of responsible revolution," while the ruling class "were using it as a scare word, perhaps because any notion of change frightened them. . . . Of course, one hopes that the revolution would be non-violent. But I came back from Latin America much more tentative about the possibility of forging the needed changes apart from violence. This was true in countries where all the forces of Church and society seemed to be united against change."[67]

The statement was significant for its hedge against an absolute nonviolence. Even Gandhi had said that if limited to a choice between forceful defiance or passive submission to injustice, he would have to fight. Yet he'd hastened to add that there is always another option: *Satyagraha*, the "spirit-force" of active nonviolent resistance to oppression. But Dan, having witnessed the suffering of millions in country after country, and having explored its causes, had concluded that Latin America was quite possibly the exception to Gandhi's rule. Ross Labrie has written that "the note of violence here, paradoxically cradled within a philosophy of pacifism, became more pronounced in Berrigan's writing late in the 1960s and early 1970s, generating a tense and complex emotional torque that would become the hallmark of his writing style."[68] It will also generate for its author, his brother Phil, and others, an opening to consider that in the struggle with "illegitimate" authority, damage done to property can be properly said to exist within the spirit of nonviolence.[69]

Meanwhile back in the United States, picketers were trudging in circles on Jesuit college campuses, angrily chanting for Dan's return. And hundreds of seminarians were threatening their superiors with desertion if Daniel Berrigan was not hastily reinstated. After ten weeks the pressure reached critical mass, and negotiations opened between the chancery and the Jesuit's New York province, which eventually led to Cardinal Spellman's concession of defeat, and the letter Dan received from Father McGinty in the middle of February 1966: "Come back. All is forgiven. You can continue with your peace work."[70]

Dan says in his autobiography that he made sure to impose the condition that no further limits be placed on his peace activities (and he still bristles at the notion that he needed to be forgiven; forgiven for what? he wants to know). He arrived home on March 8, 1966, at Kennedy Airport, a certified *cause célèbre* to his allies and an *enfant terrible* to his critics. He partied that night in the *Jesuit Missions* office with jubilant friends. The next day, he dropped in on Father McGinty to pick up his apology in person. (Several years later, as McGinty lay dying, the two priests reconciled at Dan's initiative.)

Then on March 11 he presided at a press conference in New York's Biltmore Hotel, surrounded by lay and clerical supporters. Dan thanked his defenders and announced to the crowd of reporters that he was back to oppose the Vietnam War. "Our presence in Southeast Asia represents a contempt for the rights of innocent individuals and constitutes a continuing divergence, for the purposes of destruction, of resources that are badly needed in other parts of the world," he said, thinking of the Latin American destitute and dead.[71]

From Merton came a pep talk and welcome-home letter. "Very happy to have you back! Glad things have cleared. I thought they might. Go to it, man! Maybe with this dirty war the nation will learn a few things about itself and grow up."[72]

Unchastened and plunged back into nonstop peace work, he was "worse than ever," Dan liked to say; and any official hopes that a little banishment to the wilderness might have taught him to hold his tongue were dispelled by publication within the month of *They Call Us Dead Men*, and *No One Walks Waters*, a volume of poetry. Three weeks later he headed a peace march of interfaith clergy through the streets of Manhattan, past synagogues and churches, stopping to pray on Fifth Avenue under the frowning facade of St. Patrick's Cathedral, where Cardinal Spellman presided.[73] He resumed co-chairmanship of CALCAV and began a CPF campaign against Catholic priests serving as military chaplains. Reviewing a draft of a Fellowship appeal for funds, he urged it be recast to make it tougher. "The letter sounds a bit as though we were keeping house in normal times," he wrote in a note. "Can't you give . . . some hint of the suffering the war is bringing home to our doorstep . . . Give us a bit of anguish, or why talk about hope?"[74]

7

KENNEDY AND CORNELL

> The highest flights of charity, devotion, trust, patience, bravery to which the wings of human nature have spread themselves have been flown for religious ideals.
>
> —*William James*

> Dan, do you really believe in all that God stuff?
>
> —*Antiwar activist Bruce Dancis*

ONE OF THE FIRST ALTERATIONS DAN MADE TO HIS APARTMENT on returning home from exile was to paste a newspaper photo of Cardinal Spellman in full military regalia to the underside of the top lid of his toilet. Pleased with his work, but finding the juxtaposition insufficiently didactic, he added the beatitude "Blessed are the Peacemakers" to the inside of the bottom lid, which then ringed the cardinal's head when raised.

Now, with that kind of attitude, Dan had pretty well thrown

away any chance for advancement in the Jesuits or the church at large. More to the point, his well-known clash with Spellman amid his outspoken calls for an activist, ecumenical, and antiwar church, drawn from "a more authentic universality . . . [with] a sense of the world's poor, amid the spoilation of the arms race,"[1] had placed him in roughly the same relationship to the Vatican as the French worker-priests more than a decade earlier: a rabble-rousing force to be monitored closely, bluntly discouraged, and possibly quashed. But whatever his regrets, they were more than offset by the fun he was having. He reveled in taunting authority—"Now remember to look southeast at the corner and smile for the FBI cameras," he announced with trademark cool to fellow protesters during a march—and was shrewd enough to lace his critiques with sharp japes and elegant wit. "I would whitewash the whole," he declared in a poem called, "Sistine Chapel," in which he proposed to repaint the famous church ceiling with a copy of *The Card Players* by Cezanne—the better to make "Divine things . . . look [more] human."[2]

In his writing and public action, as he repeatedly argued for a more prophetic and less distant Catholic Church, he was trying to make divine things look more human. "To draw the mysteries of God away from their human soil," he wrote, "is to kill the mysteries as far as true understanding goes."[3] He had grown stubbornly confident in his vision of a radical Christianity confronting concrete political issues, and in his own life as an emblem of the modern priest's vocation, despite the fact that his conventional church career was moribund. (When asked about never having climbed a single academic or religious institutional rung, and what regrets that might have caused, he replied, "How boring.")

Dan's books were selling well in early 1966, and his articles and poems were gaining attention among the politically engaged. One of his readers, Sargent Shriver, the director of the Peace Corps, had called him in the last year and invited him to say Mass for the Kennedys. Dan accepted and began visiting the family regularly. "I enjoyed them," he says of his three years spent as a member of the Kennedys' Hyannisport salon, "it was copacetic. They were collecting talented people . . . they always did, the more priests the better.

They were after an *élan vital*." Moving within the cocoon of Kennedy glamour, Dan must have felt as if he'd stumbled across a looking-glass version of his own family growing up. He had once described his ideal version of the church as "a secure community of sons . . . reflecting and radiating the intelligence of the Father"—a poignant revision of his insecure life with Dado. But now he'd been welcomed into a rich and flourishing Irish Catholic family—"excellent world servants," he called them—a little of whose golden glow was rubbing off on him. "There was a stroking of my ego," he recalls, "[when] it got to be known that I was one of the Kennedy priests."

In the late spring of 1966, Shriver threw Dan a welcome-back-from-exile party at his home on Cape Cod. The gathering was small, Dan says, "Bobby Kennedy and his wife, the Shrivers, an ambassador, and Robert McNamara. At the end of dinner, Shriver got up and said, 'We would like to hear from the Secretary [of Defense] and Father Berrigan on the subject of Vietnam.' We went into another room and had drinks. I said, 'The war is only about killing people, why not stop it now? End it tonight.' McNamara was cool: 'In response to Daniel Berrigan I would say this: I think of Vietnam as Mississippi. When the law is not obeyed, we send in the troops.' I was stunned by the analogy, and didn't say anything beyond it. But when I got home I wrote it all down in my diary. I thought, in a week I won't believe this. I've remembered it thirty years."[4]

Dan immersed himself in efforts to thwart the war. In the fall, he traveled to Paris on a three-pronged peace mission: to recruit ordinary Vietnamese Catholics for an American-speaking tour to rebut Cardinal Spellman's contention that the Vietnam conflict was a kind of rerun of the Spanish Civil War, requiring Catholics to defend their faith by defeating the "atheistic" North Vietnamese government; to meet with the global head of the Jesuits, Father General Pedro Arrupe, and convince him to officially urge all Jesuit priests to speak and lead "on the moral import of the war"[5]—based on a three-page, single-spaced analysis Dan would hand him; to obtain a visa to North Vietnam, where he wanted to travel to be "under the bombs," so he could comment on the war from firsthand experience. None of these plans worked out. The Vietnamese tour fell through, Arrupe listened carefully but declined to follow up, and the American embassy denied him a visa. Dan traveled on to Italy for a conference of International Pax Christi, a Catholic peace and justice group.

Phil was also working hard to shame the U.S. government into shutting down the war. Early in his priesthood, Phil had looked to his older brother to be "a big, strong leader to him." When it had come to their vocations, he was the neophyte to Dan's suave man of accomplishment. "I helped him get started on some things because his own community really wasn't offering him the kind of outlets that would urge him on," Dan said. "But his talents and understanding grew so quickly once he got a little bit of foothold. I remember quite vividly saying to myself by the time I came back from Europe in '64 that this business of Phil following my lead is all over. It was quite clear that he was setting his own pace and going on in his own direction."[6] The change had been natural, and had deepened the brothers' mutual respect.

Phil was leader by consensus of the newly renamed Baltimore Interfaith Peace Mission of Clergy and Laymen. Throughout the second half of 1966, he led prayer vigils and leafleting campaigns at street corners and in shopping centers. He also met with U.S. congressmen and senators, imploring them to halt the bombing and open negotiations with North Vietnam, as recently called for by United Nations Secretary General U Thant. Phil put a good-faith effort into these meetings with national leaders, but in the end felt sweet-talked and placated. His Maryland senators would not look him in the eye, he said, which to him meant more than all their pledges to bear in mind the Sermon on the Mount when constructing American foreign policy.

Phil and the group decided to speak to the public directly. So the Peace Mission ran an ad in the *Baltimore Sun* that cited the war's toll of dead and wounded—many at the hands of U.S. high-tech weapons of destruction—and that called attention to the group's short-lived *Vietnam Journal.* But when the group tried to run a second ad, the *Sun* rejected it. (Baltimore antiwar folks blamed the action on Lyndon Johnson, a daily *Sun* reader.) When the group tried again with another ad on the war's campaign of "genocide," the newspaper told them bluntly, no more ads. They adjusted by taking space in the *Baltimore Afro-American*, asking "Why Are the Colored People of America Sent 10,000 Miles Away to Kill the Colored People of Vietnam?" and claiming, "It Costs About $30,000,000,000 a Year to Fight This War . . . That Would Give Every Negro Family in the U.S. $6,000 Every Year." But without the *Sun*'s wide circulation, their inflammatory words had little impact.

Phil still liked the idea of bringing the war's moral issues to the highest officials in Washington—but on his terms. On December 29, 1966, he and nineteen others visited the suburban homes of Robert McNamara and Secretary of State Dean Rusk. The group picketed and prayed on the men's snowy lawns, holding signs painted by Thomas Lewis, an artist and devoted Catholic who would be one of Phil's staunchest allies for years to come. The event received broad media coverage, including a photo in *Time*. The next day Rusk phoned the motherhouse at St. Peter Claver's and invited Phil and Peace Mission members to an audience at the State Department. The impromptu delegation—consisting of Phil, Lewis, Unitarian Bob Alpern, and Jon Higginbotham (later a draft board raider with the "Milwaukee Fourteen")—debated Rusk for two hours in his office, with the same disappointing results as their previous meetings with politicians. "I leave all morality up to you clergymen," Rusk had patronized them. Even the National Council of Catholic Bishops, in its overall timid statement on the war a few months earlier, had asserted that "no one is free to evade his [or her] personal responsibility by leaving it entirely to others to make moral judgments."[7] So if Rusk's equivocation would have displeased even the National Council of Catholic Bishops, how could it help but incite Phil Berrigan?

In late January 1967 Phil and the Georgetown Jesuit Father Richard McSorley led a group of fifty activists in picketing the homes of the chiefs of staff in Fort Myer, Virginia. They had written a statement condemning their support by force of an undemocratic South Vietnamese government, and when the base's provost approached them anxiously, they asked him to deliver it. The

"BLOODLINE"

The Berrigan brood, "unaccountably all male." *First row, left to right:* Philip, snarling like a bulldog; Daniel, toes together, knickers pressed; Jerry, typically good-natured. *Back row:* Jim, John, Tom Jr.

Courtesy of James Berrigan

IRELAND

Daughter of
Edmund and
Bridget
Daugherty
(surname
changed to
"Doherty"
when they
moved to
America)

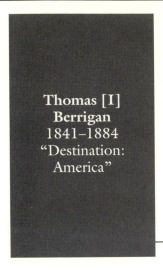

**Thomas [I]
Berrigan**
1841–1884
"Destination:
America"

Grandmother Berrigan
(Bridget Doherty)
1840–1924, "serene,
thoughtful, and kind."

Courtesy of James Berrigan

Tom Berrigan, 1879–1969, "handsome
bucko," circa 1900, Niagara Falls

Courtesy of James Berrigan

Daniel Berrigan, S.J., b.1921.

Bob Fitch Photo

GERMANY

Grandfather Fromhart (Wilhelm Fromhertz) 1861–?, "restless and Teutonic."

Courtesy of James Berrigan

Grandmother Fromhart (Louise Stoll), 1862–1941, "Taam, you do a *sindt!*" in Minnesota with grandchildren. *Clockwise from bottom left:* Dan, Jerry, Jim, Phil

Courtesy of James Berrigan

Freda Fromhart, 1886–1976, "weighing her chances against the world," with John and Tom Jr.   *Courtesy of James Berrigan*

Family portrait, *left to right:* **Philip Berrigan** (b. 1923), **Elizabeth McAlister** (b. 1939), and their children, **Jerry, Kate,** and **Frida** (*not pictured:* the family's addled orange cat, **Pope John Paul Pumpkin**)   *Courtesy of Liz McAlister*

The soldier and the
seminarian: Phil, a World
War II vet just returned
from Europe, visits Dan in
1943 at his Jesuit seminary,
St. Andrew-on-Hudson,
New York.

Courtesy of Jerry Berrigan

In the Matson Avenue living room on the day of Dan's first Mass as a priest in
1952. *Left to right:* Jerry, then a Josephite seminarian; Dado, proud but still
competitive with Dan; Dan, freshly minted "foot soldier for Christ"; Freda,
member of the Syracuse Jesuit Mothers Club; Phil, big man on the Holy Cross
College campus before following Jerry into the Josephites.

Courtesy of James Berrigan

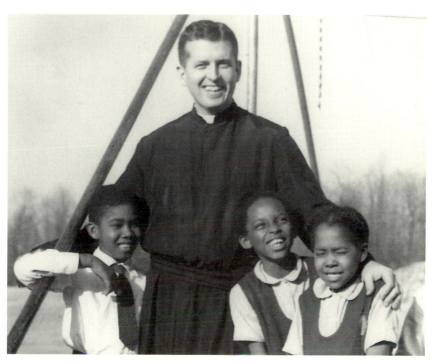

Phil, an early and vocal civil rights activist, as a priest in Washington, D.C., 1956. "You could wake him up in the middle of the night and he'd get up smiling saying, 'What do you want me to do?'"   *Peter J. Kenney, S.S.J.*

THE SIXTIES AND BEYOND

Dan with Dorothy Day—forerunner, friend, and Catholic Worker co-founder.

Courtesy of the Division of Rare and Manuscript Collections, Cornell University Library

Thomas Merton,
Trappist monk and
critical influence on both
Berrigan brothers.

Courtesy of Burns Library,
Boston College

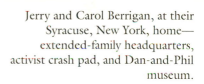

Jerry and Carol Berrigan, at their
Syracuse, New York, home—
extended-family headquarters,
activist crash pad, and Dan-and-Phil
museum.

Courtesy of the Division of Rare and
Manuscript Collections,
Cornell University Library

Latin American exile, 1966:
Dan looks glum even while
posing as one of two "saps"
in a joke photo with fellow
Jesuit, Alden Stevenson.

Alden Stevenson, S.J.

Photo of Phil from a 1966 *Life* magazine profile that called him, "a vociferous critic of U.S. policies in Vietnam," and, along with Dan, a "vehement critic of his Church." *Ted Polumbaum, Life Magazine © Time Inc.*

A pioneering member of the Social-Commentary-through-Collage School of interior decoration, Dan ponders in his office at United Religious Work, Cornell University's interfaith chaplaincy.

Courtesy of the Division of Rare and Manuscript Collections, Cornell University Library

Backstage at the Town Hall "Poets for Peace" reading. *Left to right:* Vietnamese Buddhist monk, Thich Nhat Hahn; Dan, bemused, takes in fellow performer, Anaïs Nin.

Photo © John Goodwin/Courtesy of Fellowship Publications

Dan, with Boston University history professor, Howard Zinn (*far right*), negotiates with North Vietnamese officials for the release of two American Air Force pilots in 1968.   *Courtesy of Howard Zinn*

Defining moment: Phil and Dan burn Vietnam War draft files in the parking lot of a Selective Service office in Catonsville, Maryland, May 17, 1968.

UPI/CORBIS-Bettmann

Dan addresses the huge "America Is Hard to Find" rally at Barton Hall, Cornell University, in 1969. Though the event was crawling with FBI, Berrigan slipped out a side door inside a larger-than-life apostle puppet. Three months in the underground followed, galling J. Edgar Hoover, the already dyspeptic FBI Director. *Bob Fitch Photo*

Dan is hauled off Block Island, Rhode Island, by a pair of FBI "bird watchers." The photo was later made into a poster captioned, "Which One Is Free?"

UPI/CORBIS-Bettmann

Daniel Berrigan:
Sixties icon.

*Drawing by David Levine.
Reprinted with permission
from The New York
Review of Books.
© 1970 Nyrev, Inc.*

Freda visits Dan and Phil at Danbury Prison in 1972. When asked what she thought of the law her sons had broken, she said, "It isn't God's law."

Courtesy of Howard Zinn

Boyd Douglas: part-time peacenik, full-time FBI informant. Douglas, an ex-con, was the main prosecution witness at the trial of the "Harrisburg Seven" in 1972, at which the U.S. government tried Phil, Liz, and five others on conspiracy charges.

Courtesy of the LBJ Library Collection

Left to right: Bill Davidon, Jim Forest, Liz McAlister, Sr. Jogues Egan during the Harrisburg Trial.

The Philadelphia Inquirer/*Courtesy of the Division of Rare and Manuscript Collections, Cornell University Library*

Supporters hold a sign with a quote from Dan's biting Catonsville statement, outside Danbury Prison on the day of his release in 1972.　　　*Photo © John Goodwin*

The "Plowshares Eight." *Left to right:* Carl Kabat, Elmer Maas, Phil, Molly Rush, Dan, Anne Montgomery, John Schuchardt, and Dean Hammer on their first day of trial during Easter Week, 1981.

The secular meets the religious left: Abbie Hoffman kibbitzes with Dan at a "U.S. Out of El Salvador" rally outside the United Nations in 1981.

Jonah House in Baltimore's Reservoir Hill neighborhood: longtime home to a continuously changing "resistance community," as well as to Phil, Liz, and their children; ground zero for the international antinuclear Plowshares movement; and site of at least one FBI raid.

Jim O'Grady

Brothers

Courtesy of the Division of Rare and Manuscript Collections, Cornell University Library

provost was unwilling, and threw them out. When the group returned three weeks later—Phil swerving his car past an M.P. road-block—the provost yelled, "The next time you return, you'll get three years!" after yanking Phil, Lewis, Eberhardt, activists Dean and DeAnne Pappas, United Church of Christ minister James Mengel, and seven others up from their knees (they'd been praying around a flagpole), and driving them off base on a military bus. One of the trespassers later described Phil's face as they departed: "He looked illuminated, like Moses receiving the command-ments." On the drive back to Baltimore, wrote Francine du Plessix Gray, he told the group, "Kids, we've got them by the balls. If they don't arrest us next time, we give a mandate to all peace groups to enter government property. If they jail us, that'll be just the kind of witness I want to offer."

"Get *this* son of a bitch," the provost ordered his camera-toting aide, pointing to Phil, when a group of twelve Peace Mission pro-testers appeared for a third and last demonstration in June. Phil smiled broadly for the camera, then he and the others fell limp into postures of passive resistance they had learned in the civil rights movement. They were hauled off base and reunited with their towed-out cars, at which point they said goodbye, seeming to indi-cate that their work for the day was done. But ten minutes later they came barreling onto base again, hopped from their cars, and resumed their prayerful positions around the flagpole across from the joint chiefs' picturesque homes. Phil was reciting the Twenty-third Psalm—" . . . Thou preparest a table before me in the pres-ence of my enemies . . . "—when armed guards encircled them. This time, they were driven to the base's M.P. headquarters.

They waited on a stifling bus for over an hour while the provost consulted by phone with the Pentagon. It seemed sure that the authorities would be forced to arrest the group, and Phil and the others would gain what they had sought: the platform of a court trial from which to denounce the Vietnam War. But rather than play along, the provost regained his composure and again drove Phil and the radical nucleus of the Baltimore Peace Mission outside the Fort Myers gate and dumped them onto a forlorn patch of grass. As the bus drove back onto base, Reverend Mengel jumped from a hiding spot in the back, stuck his head out the window, and belted out the opening verse to "We Shall Overcome." He was tossed out the door and landed in a heap.[8]

Mengel was all right, and his extra bit of defiance had given the group a small moral victory and some badly needed comic relief, but Phil's mood during the drive home was obviously grim. The proceedings had struck him as too much of a game. More than anything, he wanted (and wants) to be taken seriously. Consequently, he has come to judge an action as much for the severity of the government's response to it as for its content and sincerity, which, of course, remain important to him. To this day, his favorite word to describe the antinuclear Plowshares movement, which he admits might not exist without his leadership, is "serious." He declares that this is the quality that distinguishes Plowshares actions from every other form of protest. "You ask [people] to do serious work for peace," he says of his attempts to recruit for the actions, "and you find out how their fear controls them."[9] And when it comes to facing and rooting out fear, Phil was, and still is, ruthless. By June 1967, he felt he had reached a dead end with the many traditional protests he had tried, and wanted to attempt a more "serious" brand of civil disobedience. But he didn't know what.

The Baltimore Peace Mission commenced a series of all-night planning sessions. Rumor had it that the Green Berets were using dilapidated huts in an overgrown corner of Fort Howard to train in conditions meant to simulate rural Vietnam. Someone proposed destroying the huts. Lewis and Eberhardt were dispatched to the base to check it out, but couldn't find the huts or any sign of the military exercises, so the Peace Mission dropped the idea. Instead, they settled for brandishing skull-and-crossbones signs while marching outside the Charles Village, Maryland, draft board, alarming the female clerks. Meanwhile Phil started searching for a nonviolent means of confronting the government that would force it to arrest him and try him for a crime.

While Phil was intruding on Fort Myer, Dan was conducting a retreat at a Benedictine Monastery in New Jersey, for an order of

Catholic nuns called the Religious of the Sacred Heart of Mary. Its provincial was Sister Jogues Egan, a friend of Dan's, and one of its members was the twenty-eight-year-old Elizabeth "Liz" McAlister—both soon to become main figures in the brothers' lives. The retreat culminated with Dan's conducting a Baptism in a nearby lake, attended by the nuns and several members of the Catholic Worker and the Catholic Peace Fellowship who had driven out from Manhattan for the occasion. The gathering sipped beer on a wooden deck as Dan stood in knee-high water and gave a sermon in his bathing suit about the deceptive power of water and its ability to foil such "principalities and powers" as pharaoh's army, then casually mentioned that he'd recently decided not to allow his celibacy to interfere with his becoming a parent and that he was going to adopt a child—and wouldn't that throw the cardinal into a panic? (Nothing ever came of this, except for the idea being leaked to the press, which no doubt rankled Spellman one last time before he died, as Dan may have intended all along.) He completed the Baptism to a group "Amen!" just as the heavens parted and poured down rain, drenching everyone equally.[10]

Afterward Dan asked Jim Forest if he could catch a ride with him back to Manhattan. He was facing a decision and needed a confidante. Dan had thought that for the fall he would teach at a black Southern college, but another attractive offer had come along: to become an associate director for service at Cornell University's United Religious Work—the "subversive God Box," as it was known around the Ithaca campus in upstate New York, not far from Syracuse.

Jack Lewis, a tall, bearded Texan and Presbyterian minister, and the Reverend John Lee Smith had visited Dan at *Jesuit Missions* and invited him to join them in their ministry at Cornell's Annabel Taylor Hall. His salary would be $11,000 a year, and his duties would include teaching, counseling, offering the Catholic sacraments, and "promoting student activism on campus." Dan had been to Cornell the year before while visiting former students from Le Moyne, and had felt drawn to the campus improbably perched among the cataracts and limestone gorges high above Lake Cayuga, with its sharp air of Ivy League learning. But instead of moving north or south, Dan fretted that maybe he should stay in New York, a place he'd fought so hard to get back to, and help with the new and struggling Clergy and Laymen Concerned About the War in Vietnam (co-chair Heschel joked that if CALCAV wanted a hundredfold boost in membership, it should change its name to Clergy Unconcerned). Forest recommended Dan take the job at Cornell, where he might affect the minds and consciences of America's future white elite. After agonizing, Dan agreed, insisting it was not a sell-out but an "experiment."[11]

At Sargent Shriver's suggestion, Dan spent the rest of the summer of 1967 teaching poor Hispanic students in the Upward Bound program in Pueblo, Colorado. By the end of it, he had had his fill of ameliorative social programs. He'd decided that "an issue is genuine only when it is organically in relation to every other issue; in this case to the impact of militarized consumer-technology on the fate of man." In other words, with 500,000 U.S. troops waging war in Vietnam at a cost of $2 billion a month, any work not directly related to opposing such a fundamental wrong was beside the point. He wrote as much to Shriver, and later repeated the thought in *No Bars to Manhood*: "It seemed to me spiritually absurd and suicidal to be pretending to help the poor at home while we bombed the poor abroad."[12]

When Dan arrived on campus in August 1967, Cornell was already a northeastern hub of the student antiwar movement. From the earliest days of American intervention in Vietnam, many of its students had defied the draft, then later worked for the Eugene McCarthy and Robert Kennedy presidential campaigns, marched on Washington, sat-in at the Syracuse draft center, and criticized universities, including their own, for selling their souls to the Defense Department in exchange for classified research contracts. Cornell also boasted the country's largest chapter of Students for a Democratic Society (SDS). Many of its members had attended a "We Won't Go" conference in Chicago the previous year to discuss the historical precedents for draft resistance and military desertion during wars of "imperialist aggression," such as the colonial French's lengthy engagement with the Algerian independence movement. The Cornell SDS had then published a summons to a massive draft card burning that had occurred the previous April at Central Park's Sheep Meadow. More than 200 draft cards were burned that day, part of the 3,500 that were put to the torch during the ten-year Vietnam era. The event's manifesto, written by Cornell students, had proclaimed: "The armies of the United States have, through conscription, already oppressed or destroyed the lives and consciences of millions of Americans and Vietnamese. Powerful resistance is now demanded: radical, illegal, unpleasant, sustained."[13]

Cornell professor Walter Berns, who viewed radical students as among "the more selfishly disposed young men," would later lament in a *National Review* article that Dan's presence on campus gave an immediate boost to Ithaca's coalition of antiwar groups. Dan was "no ordinary opponent of the war and no ordinary priest," Berns wrote.[14] Father David Connor—the United Religious Work's Catholic chaplain and Dan's friend, who, with Reverend Paul Gibbons, Cornell's Unitarian minister, would soon risk prosecution by returning his ministerial deferment card to the government also recognized the effect that Berns observed. "I don't think [the administration] realized really who [Dan] was or what he represented," Connor said, "and certainly didn't realize how much of a focus he would be for the antiwar movement."[15]

On arrival, Dan wrote a letter to Cornell's president, James A. Perkins, announcing that he looked forward to being part of the traditionally liberal student body's "explosive awakening." That was fine with the amenable Perkins, who replied that Dan should also know that the president's office had received a letter signed by 300 faculty demanding that he crack down on student agitators. (Among the signers was philosophy professor Allan Bloom, who later found his faculty opponents guilty of academic heresy for "expressing their willingness to change the university's goals and the content of what they taught."[16]) But Dan had little sympathy for Perkins's tenuous position, dismissing the other letterwriters as having been drawn from the "reactionary" schools of "law, engineering, history, government, and agriculture."[17]

Shortly thereafter, a group of alumni who objected to the hiring of the mildly notorious Berrigan pressured Perkins to rescind his position at the Cornell United Religious Work. Perkins called Dan to his office and requested his help in drafting a nonthreatening statement of "objectives" that could be used to soothe alumni fears. Dan listed two: teaching and building an on-and-off-campus community of activist objectors to the despicable Vietnam War. The president fidgeted. Then realizing there could be no more fruitless task than asking a radical priest to make reassuring noises for a collection of authorities, he gave Dan a copy of his latest book and showed him to the door. Dan read the book. He found it to be a blueprint for conducting government and military research using university resources, and pronounced it, and the gesture, "bizarre."

Dan pursued his first objective by teaching a noncredit course on nonviolence with John Lee Smith at the Commons Coffee House for more than 200 students and mostly younger faculty. He held another popular class titled The Imagination of God, on the Gospel of John. He led discussions on Pirandello and organized play-reading groups and poetry readings on religious and secular topics, always addressing questions of social conscience. Sacrifice and purification were among his themes in a lecture on *Lear*, whose plight he called an "indication that man creates himself under terrible pressures of history and choice."[18]

James Matlack, a Quaker and assistant professor of American literature who had been active in the civil rights movement, attended some of the classes because he liked the way Dan was constantly "discovering and rediscovering, posing such questions as, what does this say to you? How does this text connect to your life?" Matlack also respected Dan's penchant for publicly raising unsettling questions about Cornell's operations: How did the agricultural school treat the seasonal migrant laborers it hired to bring in the apple harvest? Shouldn't the school ask its mostly well-off students to get involved with Tompkins County's rural poor, to volunteer their time at local soup kitchens, prisons, and mental hospitals?; and speaking of the board of trustees, those "robber barons of the twentieth century, who ... control university decisions," what about Cornell's holdings in Chase Manhattan Bank, investor in apartheid South Africa?; and didn't the school's economic clout oblige it to desist from its absentee landlordism and become a builder of low-income housing?; and his favorite: What were the moral consequences of the university's scrounging for lucrative research grants from a military-industrial complex waging a cruel war in Southeast Asia?[19]

This gadfly stuff did not go down well with many faculty and alumni at Cornell. Dan was accused of "undermining academic freedom" by criticizing the income-generating research of the science departments, and for aggravating, even orchestrating, campus tensions—particularly because, as Francine du Plessix Gray reported, he "accompanied war objectors to their draft boards, inductions refusals, and court hearings, attended their press conferences, appeared as a character witness, raised money for their defense, comforted them in time of anguish, [and] suffered that he was above draft age, too old to share in their action." And based on his guru status with the SDS ("We're still anti-Church, but we're pro-clerical. That guy is *useful*!") and the daily stream of serious-minded students to his Taylor Hall office, the most popular way of disparaging him was to say, as did an employee with the office of public relations, that "he doesn't have friends. He has disciples."[20]

When it comes to Daniel Berrigan's friendships, especially with young men and women, the distinction isn't always useful. Like any appealing public figure with a strong personality, he also serves as a mentor to some of his friends. Dan Finlay, for example, a young assistant professor of English at Cornell in the sixties, and his wife, Linda, say that with Dan's devoted company comes the pull of his influence. Dan frequently visited the couple's home for dinner, often bearing flowers or little gifts, and very quickly, Dan Finlay says, "infused in us very deeply a concern about peace and justice." Still, though their friendship may have been prompted by common values, affection sustained it (and they remain friends to this day). But the relationship helped lead Finlay to return his draft card in 1966. And after speaking with Dan at a teach-in, James Matlack did the same—even though he'd been classified as a conscientious objector. (The draft board punitively reclassified Matlack and ordered him to report to a mental hospital for two years of alternative service.) Matlack and the Finlays are not at all Berrigan "disciples"; they are intelligent and independent, and each of them was working for antiwar causes before meeting Dan. But their friendship with him unquestionably moved them toward risks they might not have otherwise taken.

It is worth noting that Dan's friendships do not rest on "ideology," says Dan Finlay, who has known Dan almost thirty years. "His friendships are broader than any movement . . . the variety of people who were and are close to him is remarkable—men and women, artists and activists, the young and the old, believers and atheists, those who are committed, who are questioning, or even uninvolved."[21] At Cornell he moved in a wide social circle, attracting the devout and disillusioned. Connor remembered that both Catholic and Protestant students were taken "with the idea of a rebel priest who was a poet and who was kind of hip, and who wore beads, and you know, was on the streets and willing to go to jail."[22] And some of them, though they observed no other religious rites, would attend his liturgies.

He also influenced Jewish students—not by proselytizing but by challenging them to learn and fulfill the mandates of their faith. David Saperstein recalled that "the power of his message opened up for me the concept of being called into a partnership with God in creating a better world," and later wrote of Dan that "with his gentle voice and potent poetry, he sliced through political complexities and reduced the test of the ethical person to a kind of biblical simplicity: What we *do* for the least of us; what we *do* to bring peace into the world; what we *do* to arouse ourselves—and others—from our moral slumber. He introduced me to the work and thinking of Martin Buber, Rabbi Abraham Joshua Heschel, Dorothy Day, Thomas Merton and others who fleshed out my understanding of the broad range of options one has in responding to G-d's call to partnership."[23] Some of Dan's Jewish students even journeyed on their own down to Manhattan and volunteered with the Catholic Worker.

One of Dan's closest friends at Cornell was the Bronx-born and Jewish Bruce Dancis. As chair of the Cornell SDS, Dancis had helped organize the Central Park draft card burning. Then when he turned eighteen, Dancis became the first Cornell student to tear up his draft card publicly, at which point he dropped out of school to work full-time in the Ithaca peace movement. With Dan, he started

Year One, a campus journal devoted to examining Cornell's institutional ties to the "military-industrial network." And before long, he and Dan joined economics professor Douglas Dowd in a traveling antiwar speakers' bureau that visited other colleges on weekends and holidays. After chugging onto campus in Dowd's ancient automobile, Dan would open the trio's usually crowded "public forum" with one of his patented calls to resistance—not so much a logically crafted argument as a highly charged string of poetic associations. Dowd, like many in the audience, listened "mesmerized"; but Dancis, like others, was more often than not confused. Dowd followed Dan's emotional plea with a sober academic appraisal of the war and why it should be abandoned. Then Dancis would mount the rostrum and deliver an organizing pep talk.

After one such appearance in New York City, the three men paid a secret visit to H. Rap Brown in a Brooklyn convent. At the time Brown was on the run from federal agents—his supporters called him "a fugitive from injustice." The meeting was intended to "enhance cooperation between black power and antiwar groups," remembered Dowd, but it ended with little accomplished, leaving the three men tired and frustrated during their five-hour trip to Ithaca. It was then that Dancis asked Dan if he believed "in all that God stuff." Exhausted and similarly discouraged, and familiar enough with the question to effectively deflect it, Dan replied, "Sort of." Then a few days later Dan convinced Dancis to do a Bible reading at an ecumenical service—letting the ritual, and what Dancis chose to make of it, take the place of any possible harangue.[24]

Eventually Dancis was tried for draft card destruction in a Syracuse federal court. Dan and Dowd testified as character witnesses, but Dancis was convicted and served nineteen months in the Federal Youth Center in Kentucky. After the riots at the Democratic Convention in Chicago, Dancis felt, "I could no longer call myself a pacifist. It no longer worked for me." He returned to Cornell and joined the campaign to evict military recruiters from campus. He also found that "conscience was more important to Dan and the Catholic radicals than movement building"—as it had been before he left. But this now became a point of contention between Dan and the SDS, many of whom "had moved to the point where we were going to take active actions and we didn't care whether they were nonviolent or not," Dancis said.[25]

For his part, Dan was still committed to a Catholic Worker–style "personalist" approach to social change: "working through small groups and personal contacts" rather than movements, as he wrote to Merton, who in reply faulted mass actions for their "totalitarian compulsions . . . [which] destroy true Christian quality, or pervert it."[26] So when chided by the SDS for being "romantic" and "inefficient" in his pacifist convictions, Dan countered that "The New Left suffers from American pragmatism. It fights violence with the tools of violence, I fight it with the Gandhian and Christian dimensions of non-violence. They measure effectiveness by pragmatic results, I see it as immeasurable, as the impact of symbolic activity, I would like to be more classical and Greek, I am like Socrates choosing jail, choosing the *ideal*."[27] Having seen so many students with whom he had formerly shared "an assumption of trust and rejection of violence" move in despair over the seemingly endless war toward domestic revolution by any means, with some joining groups like the Weathermen, Dan thought it better to lose a few friends than to "play . . . an old game in fresh costume" by endorsing "just wars of the left."[28]

Merton, too, had warned in a letter that the violent methods of Regis Debray and Che Guevara, while they might make some sense in Latin America, would be disastrous for this country. Then for good measure, he rebuked what he saw as opportunistic antiwar elements presenting themselves as nonviolent one day and "burn baby" and "hellfire" the next. "Is radicalism *asking* to be put down," he wondered to Dan, by inviting a "fascist totalism or police state? Are we getting involved in a fake revolution of badly mixed-up disaster? . . . How nuts is the whole damn business? Cornell sounds good. Keep in there slugging. Pray!!"[29]

Even in an era of exotically plumed public figures, Daniel Berrigan was to many a curious bird. Describing him then is an exercise in compiling contradictions: political priest, radical Catholic, whimsical ascetic, dashing celibate, lawbreaking intellectual, and cryptic sloganeer. He began self-consciously to cultivate a style—a kind of a mendicant Beat-poet look based on black berets and turtlenecks, a peace pendant or ancient Christian "fish" symbol on a chain, and what one journalist called a "Joan of Arc haircut" for its bowl shape and jagged black bangs. For many, it was hard to know what to make of this dazzling hybrid, particularly in the school's conventional academic quarters, where he was sometimes condescended to as "a minor/humorously welcomed/species in the great think tank," as he griped years later in his autobiography.[30]

He had never lived as an adult outside a community of priests, so his biggest adjustment was learning to function as a private citizen. Jack Lewis took him "step-by-step" through the opening of a bank account, hooking up a telephone, and renting his own apartment. He lived off-campus on Dryden Road near a leafy railroad right-of-way that made him "one of very few mortals who walked to work of mornings, through a woodland, the sound of birds and released waters gushing in the early sunshine." He papered his apartment walls with photos and protest posters, including a half-page photo of the My Lai massacre clipped from the *New York Times*, on which he had superimposed a quote about mercy from the Psalms. And he decorated his office wall with a found-object sculpture of his own devising: a wood-and-rope venetian blind set twisted in the shape of a giant whale and inscribed with an original poem about Jonah. This was all part of an outpouring of "creativity and exuberance" in response to his new surroundings, remembered Dan Finlay, which occasionally inspired extravagant gestures in return from admirers, like the young black poet who for a while left a daily rose on his office desk. And in a grand gesture of his own, Dan never locked his apartment door. When a visiting student asked why, he drawled, "In case I'm not here and someone needs to get in." "But what if someone steals?" the student wondered. "Well, that just means he needs it," Dan said, paraphrasing Gandhi on a similar question.[31]

Many were surprised that such a militant antiwar activist could be gracious in person, even shy. "We had expected a firebrand," someone wrote in an unsigned memoir from the time, "and instead found a slight, soft-spoken man who never drives a car, always wears a beret and was a thoroughly delightful and charming human being. As gentle a man as I have met, his power comes not from the flaming rhetoric of his brother but from a quietly powerful use of the English language."

Linda Finlay recalled that "in person, Dan was different than most priests. He didn't deaden down his emotions." He had long ago dropped the solemn aura that many priests still projected. One of his favorite visitors to the office was student Fred Solway, who would launch into a wicked imitation as he came through the door: "Hi! I'm Father Dan. C'mon in. Have you seen my whale? Well, my brother Phil and I have just . . . ," tying Dan up in a fit of laughter as he fruitlessly begged him to "Stop, stop!" only spurring on Solway in his parody of the Groovy Sixties Rebel Priest and Hero to the Young. On other occasions, Dan would respond to a student's need with instinctive generosity, as when a draft resister from a Southern state dropped in one day to ask for moral and financial support. Dan took out his paycheck and signed it over to the man.[32]

Had he wanted to, he could have slept with a lot of women. The times were Dionysian, and Jerry Berrigan recalled that there were any number of women willing to "throw themselves" at his brother. Dan was widely admired for his politics and published works, and for a while in the early seventies, while FBI director J. Edgar Hoover hounded him, he entered the realm of American pop celebrity, under the category of Anti-Establishment Icon. He was also vibrant, witty, and physically attractive. All this fed what Jerry calls "the whole syndrome of the camp follower—[women and men who] attach themselves to a luminary and fantasize." Accordingly, women approached Dan with "sexual overtones," he says, though he couldn't say how many. Not only did their offers make Dan uncomfortable, but he found the idea of casual sex, and what he saw of it at Cornell, immoral and demeaning.

Even so, no doubt there were women with whom he could have carried on a substantial romantic relationship—and who would have liked nothing better. Phil, in fact, would later form such a partnership with Liz McAlister, and Merton, toward the end of his life, seriously considered doing the same with a female companion ("One thing that kept [Merton] on an even keel was friendships like mine," Dan said of the monk's decision not to leave the Trappists to be with the woman with whom he had fallen in love. "The other was he had good, sensible guidance from the abbot . . . [who was] tender and compassionate and helped him." Phil, on the other hand, kept secret from Dan his relationship with Liz.) But in Dan's case, all evidence points to the fact that he has been true to his vow of celibacy.[33]

When you think about it, what could possibly be more counter-cultural, especially in the hedonistic hothouse of the sixties? "Sometimes it was a struggle," Jerry's wife, Carol, recalled of Dan's unhappiness at having to reject repeated sexual advances. "But he always had such dignity that they knew they wouldn't get past first base."[34] Why not? There is no great mystery: because of the mutual reinforcement of his principles and personality.

The idea behind a Catholic priest's vow of celibacy is to make him uniquely available to his church and community and, in its most catholic application, to the world—a sort of sublimation of *eros* (love of one) for the benefit of *agape* (love of all). To men like Dan and Phil, who from an early age yearned to lead useful and extraordinary lives, "the appeal of celibacy depended not only on its status as a sacrifice for personal salvation but also on a view of the priesthood as a heroic instrument of meaningful service that might not be performed otherwise," as Peter McDonough explains in *Men Astutely Trained*, his tome on American Jesuits in the twentieth century. But McDonough goes on to say that "by the 1960s the credibility of both these views had declined."[35] Before then, the vow of celibacy was a virtually unquestioned part of an American priest's vocation. But this was no longer true by the time Dan landed at Cornell. As the liberal reforms of Vatican II began filtering down to the clergy amid the time's ongoing breakdown of social and sexual conventions, each Catholic priest, more than ever before, had to personally commit to his celibacy. Which was also true for nuns. And many concluded, as did Phil and Liz, that they could better work for *agape* by allowing *eros* into their lives.

Dan did not. "I had come of age in a church that, for all its shortcomings, honored vows and promises," he relates in his autobiography. "In important matters (always excepting the vexed question of war)—in matters that touched on life and death and innocence and marriage and the vindication of the poor . . . Christians were blessed with moral guidance."[36] Simply put, honoring his priestly vows remained the best way to attain what was most important to him: a coherent and consistent moral life. In 1967 he was forty-six years old. From the day he had entered the Jesuits at age nineteen, he had worked to reach his current station as a seriously regarded moral critic, in the manner of his early French heroes: Georges Bernanos, Yves Congar, Henri de Lubac, Charles Peguy, Jacques Maritain, François Mauriac, Emmanuel Mournier, and the worker-priests. And he had succeeded to the extent that he was frequently quoted as a leading voice of faith-based opposition to the war, and conservative intellectuals were often required to refute him when discussing Vietnam. So why, when his arguments rested on a rigorous approach to biblical ethics, should he sleep around and allow himself to be dismissed on grounds of hypocrisy?

He could have tried to get away with it anyway, as many well-known men have done, from John F. Kennedy to Martin Luther King Jr. But his convictions on the advantages of chastity ran too deep. In *The Discipline of the Mountain*, he asserts that "social innovators, those who bring about nonviolent change, tend to be sexually conservative. They are experimental, they improvise, they imagine or enact (both) profitable human arrangements in widely diverse areas of life. But in one area they tend to draw back, even to be strait-laced: the sexual. And the same strait bounds are usually laid out for their followers." It is hard to figure to whom he refers here (not even Gandhi fits the bill), but the passage, if nothing else, describes himself.[37]

This led to another of his conflicts with the Cornell SDS, which he supported for "hav[ing] the right social goals," but took to task for "trampl[ing] people too much, some of them are so messed up in their sex life, their friendships . . . I say to them: 'Have some charity in your relationships, don't be so pragmatic, don't use others as steps in your own self-exploration.'"[38] But Dan's exhortations toward nonviolence and sexual abstinence struck most of his students as pertinent to precisely the same degree: not at all. "You mean you actually don't go with *anyone*?" he said people would ask him time and again. "Well," he said, sighing at the memory, "actually I didn't."

Had he done so even once, it is likely Hoover's FBI would have aired the indiscretion publicly, as it did to Phil and Liz. Dan says, and some of his Cornell friends confirm, that soon after he went underground in 1970, FBI agents visited campus "to try to get something sexual on me. It was so malodorous." They failed. "It's very much to his credit and sense of himself and of his mission that this never became an issue," says Carol Berrigan, who, while Dan was on the lam, watched FBI agents drive by her house, binoculars in hand.[39]

So, given these principles, how does his personality affect his celibacy? "Dan is the most asexual man I have ever met," says a female activist who has known him several years, who also noted that most of his closest friends are men. One of them, a fellow Jesuit, describes Dan as "a loner. He's very lonely. Every celibate person is, frankly. We're meant to be with others, or another." He isn't gay—though some assume so, if only because he's a Catholic priest—but he is a friend to the gay community. While he was at Cornell, the student Homophile Society asked him and a number of faculty to sign their petition requesting university recognition. Endorsing it was controversial not only because the proposal was completely unprecedented, but also, friends cautioned, because many would read it to mean that Dan himself was gay—making him the object of not a little discrimination. Several faculty resolved this quandary by ignoring the group's request. Dan signed. Among gay and some straight students, this burnished his reputation as much as any stand he took in his time at Cornell (as has, in more recent years, his support of ousted Jesuit John McNeil, author of *The Church and the Homosexual* and founder of the gay Catholic group Dignity, and his commitment to offering pastoral care to people living with AIDS, many of them gay).

Yet, despite Dan's favorable blend of temperament and resolve, living as a celibate priest is difficult. "But by no means so difficult as commonly assumed (The assumption being that responsible sexual conduct is so nearly impossible that it could engage no one in fact)," he writes. The trick, he says, is not to treat it as "a noose of principle," but to compensate for a lack of *eros* with an abundance of *philia*, as it were—the joy of friendship.[40]

"Celibacy is such a strange and difficult thing," said John Dear, a Jesuit priest in his thirties who counts Dan his best friend. "Friendship is all we've got. Friendship is the only way to get through it." And Dan would seem to have cultivated, at least since his early priesthood, a gift for friendship. "It's almost a moral law with him," said Jesuit Joe Roccosalvo, Dan's former student at Brooklyn Prep and his friend for many years. "It is a kind of marriage, in a way. If you are engaged to him, it is a steady thing. I've always thought of Dan's friends as his conglomerate lover."[41]

As with a lover, friendship with Daniel Berrigan is more than the occasional or sentimental commitment—it is demanding, like marriage. His many friends will rhapsodize freely on the bounty that comes their way: the fond letters signed with a red crayon heart and a picaresque P.S. (as in his description of a "dreadnought nun" who once rose up in public to denounce him for his ill-advised politics and heretical theology, concluding with the ultimate and irrefutable charge: "and just look at you, your socks don't even match!"); the fresh-baked loaf or blown-glass angel left for no particular reason at the door; the fine wine and home-cooked gourmet supper served to a creatively mismatched five or six guests (Dear calls these parties a gathering of "the sinners and the tax collectors and the Publicans and the Pharisees" in the egalitarian manner of Jesus, and in "the Jewish tradition of upholding meals as a sacred time . . . a spiritual act, a time of blessing"); and the solicitous care during periods of illness, even unto death. But they also mention that Dan expects—insists—that his friends reciprocate.

Longtime Jesuit Fred O'Connor compares his friendship with Dan to the back-and-forth crossing of a bridge, and says that each time Dan ventures over, he expects O'Connor to do the same, or "at least shout back" his gratitude. The image depicts, as well as any, Dan's essential solitude, and his labors to relieve it. ("I'm a loner by nature, and communal by discipline," he says.) O'Connor gives a small and a large example: Sometimes Dan will lean a serendipitous bouquet against his door, then drop by later and gravitate toward the vase by the window to comment on his gift: "Oh these flowers are holding up well aren't they?" Then O'Connor, cued, will thank him. And when Dan returned from exile and saw the *New York Times* ad in his support, he combed the lengthy list of names, and finding O'Connor absent, inquired through Roccosalvo about the failure of his friend to sign (O'Connor says he had not been approached).[42] The point, O'Connor and others contend, is that Daniel Berrigan is a man who takes his friendships seriously—which is probably both wise and unavoidable on his part, because his priestly celibacy, and really his entire emotional life, depend on them.

As Dan became a national figure, beginning with the Cornell years, his primary friendships intensified. He leaned more and more on friends for support, especially his brothers Jerry and Phil (the three have corresponded weekly for more than thirty years), and Merton (he carried in his wallet a well-creased photo of Merton affixed with a construction-paper heart). And as his life became increasingly embattled, he turned to a nun he had met at a Kennedy gathering, and with whom he shared a crucial friendship: Sister Mary Corita Kent.

Both of them artists, Dan and Kent seemed to suffer the world in similar ways. She was intelligent and sensitive in the extreme, and though known for her colorful word-paintings and exuberant collages (several of which graced the covers of Dan's books), she often wrote Dan of struggles with censorious superiors and her agonizing effort to reconcile art with a life of the spirit. Clearly, they had much in common. Their intimacy was built mainly on letters, as well as Dan's yearly visits to Los Angeles to conduct a long retreat (when he wasn't banned, that is, by the conservative local cardinal) for Kent's progressive order of nuns at Immaculate Heart College.

Dan says he and Kent were profoundly "*simpatico*"—"almost like [me and] Merton. That doesn't happen twice." He illustrates his point with the story of a "New York shrink" who came to speak to Kent's community while Dan was there. While most of the nuns in attendance listened closely, some straining forward on their floor cushions, Dan squirmed in acute discomfort (he is philosophically opposed to psychological analysis of just about every sort) and took advantage of a pause in the lecture to slip out a side door. "I went to the beach to clear my head," he said. "And who is coming my way but Corita. She'd gotten out at the same time." Almost instinctively, the two knew how to cheer each other up, whether by simultaneous escapes to the beach or by an exchange of risqué letter-collages in which they encouraged each other to dance, drink whiskey, not take life so seriously, enjoy a movie, and relax.

Of course, there were rumors of an affair. Dan didn't help matters much by taping a photo of Kent to his shower wall at Cornell. "It was a happy picture, showing Corita laughing heartily," reported Francine du Plessix Gray in a widely read piece in the *New York Review of Books*, "and on her shoulder Daniel had pinned a button, bought in an East Village psychedelic shop, which said, SAVE WATER, SHOWER WITH A FRIEND."[43] By all accounts but one, however, this was the work of Dan the provocateur, not the expression of a lovesick middle-aged man. The dissenting claim is implied by a participant in a later documentary on Kent's life, who said Kent was in love with an unnamed priest whom she had asked to leave religious life, as Corita herself had done, to get married. Many viewers acquainted with Kent assumed the priest in question was Dan. But Mickey Myers—who knew Kent from the age of nine and had studied with her at Immaculate Heart College, and with whom she had "shared everything" on a daily basis until Kent's death in 1986—flatly denied that any romantic relationship existed between the two. "I knew what Corita's fantasies were; they weren't Dan," said Myers, now Kent's art executor. "What Dan did for her was convince her she could remain a nun and still be an artist. He did this by encouraging her to dig deeper into their faith."[44]

Of the woman who may have been suggesting the contrary in the documentary, Dan says, "I disbelieve her utterly. Two things: If Corita had felt that way or been in love with me, I feel very sure she would have talked with me and we would have talked about it. I had that much respect for her. So it was a fabrication, partly out of jealousy. It's wounding to her community to have that stuff on tape. I was recently on retreat there, and here we are twenty-five years later and the women are very pained about it. Corita was loved and mourned; the ties are not broken. And here's this woman nosing in with a kind of snide, offhand remark." In Dan's remarks for the documentary, he mentions Kent's insomnia and how because of it he thought of her as vigilant guardian angel to the world. The description is loving, and, as was Dan and Kent's relationship, sweetly platonic.[45]

8

VIETNAM

In peace the sons
> bury their fathers
and in war the fathers
> bury their sons
>
> —*Francis Bacon*

PHIL WAS FEELING OPPRESSED BY THE JOSEPHITES. AFTER YET another phone conversation with the Josephite superior general, Father George O'Dea, in which Phil felt he'd been told again to shrink from civic quarrels and, worse, constrain his conscience on the question of Vietnam, he whipped off a letter.

"Controversy is indispensable to our work," he wrote in frustration to O'Dea, while contrasting the order's timidity on the war to some of the risky stands it had taken at the height of the civil rights movement. (This was probably Phil's way of motivating his superior with a bit of revisionist flattery, since he had often criticized the order for pursuing charity at the expense of justice when it came to civil rights, as when it handed out food to both blacks and the National Guard during riots.) And it burned him up, he wrote, that merely questioning America's actions in Vietnam meant facing accusations of patriotic and religious disloyalty. He demanded to know why "General Curtis LeMay [commanding general of the Strategic Air Command] can talk of a wider war, can advocate the bombing of the Chinese, and can be held to be supremely patriotic—whereas if a priest will speak for the 'folly' of peace, he immediately is pilloried, or handled as a leftist, or treated as someone strange or demented. Or investigated by the FBI, as I have been. . . . I left Newburgh branded a Communist—there has never been an official denial of that charge, which came from Catholics predominantly."

This was vintage Phil: profoundly affronted and unwilling to back down. He was now on the verge of taking the first step toward the primary thrust of his life—an ongoing series of prophetic confrontation with the U.S. government, no matter the cost to his family or himself. He told O'Dea he would try to remain obedient and "fight to remain a Josephite," but if that wasn't possible, he could always "serve elsewhere." And then: "I have been driven to think what is wrong with a Church whose great leaders have always been against war, yet, who in a national situation, are never against this war. Do we honestly think there are no alternatives against war?" Then, indulging himself in a bit of self-mythification, he closed with a retort that could not but offend: "I happen to be the only man in the Society speaking and acting on the question of war and peace."[1]

Outside the confines of the church, the war was now impinging on the lives of millions of eighteen-, nineteen-, and twenty-year-olds and their families, especially men ineligible for student exemptions. The choices were stark: military service, which more than likely meant a tour in Vietnam, or, not accepting that, a prison term or flight from the country.

Despising this intractable situation, Phil was no longer a liberal. By 1967 he had formulated a radical analysis of American economic and political life that led to his newfound working tautology: The church and the country he had loyally served in the Second World War were not, in fact, global liberators but partners in an imperialist endeavor against the poor at home and abroad; such imperialism was an evil and an injustice; a citizen can either oppose such evil with the entirety of his or her being or, by default, lend injustice credibility and support. Calling Lyndon Johnson, Dean Rusk, and Walt Rostow—among the war's primary architects—"no dopes," he bitterly contended that they had mastered the art of cloaking power politics with the language of morality. "Such an exercise in morality—or power—imposes its own limits upon both policymaker and policy," he wrote in *A Punishment for Peace*, a book he worked on through the summer of 1967, "making frequent liars of the first and moral disasters of the second."[2]

After his Newburgh ousting, Phil had written that "if the priest is to be the man of reconciliation of the altar and in the pulpit, then his action there demands a consistency of life in what he does and what he says. Otherwise, the Eucharist becomes less than a new relationship to all men, and the Word of God less than light to all men." And what if that entailed, he asked, "attack[ing] governments when they are abusing power or doing nothing?" "Yes, if necessary," he answered, preparing the ground for his ideological break with legal and gradualistic politics, and concluding that "submissive acceptance might be more damaging to the Church today than protest."[3]

As the Vietnam War dragged on through 1967—the year of "America's nervous breakdown," wrote newspaper columnist Murray Kempton—many Catholics started to turn against it. *Commonweal* was the first Catholic intellectual journal to sharply decry the war, which led a conservative priest to thunder to its editor, James O'Gara, "I will never forgive the editors of *Commonweal*, in this world or the next." But the conservative priest's list of unredeemable publications was soon swelled by *Jubilee*, *Ave Maria*, and *The Critic*. And the liberal *National Catholic Reporter* filled its pages with debates and investigative reports of corruption and repression in South Vietnam, while providing detailed and mostly sympathetic coverage of Dan and Phil's activities. Then it took a firm position by editorializing that the Vietnam War was "clearly immoral," and quoted Tacitus in describing American involvement there: "You make a desert and call it peace."[4]

Pope Paul VI condemned the war, as did noted Catholic American academics such as Notre Dame Scripture scholar John McKenzie and Boston College Law School dean Robert Drinan. Bishop James Shannon of St. Paul, Minnesota, lent his name to an antiwar petition drawn up by the Catholic Committee on Vietnam at Fordham University, which eleven Catholic college presidents also signed, joined by prominent Catholics Thomas Merton, John Leo, Daniel Callahan, James O'Gara, Michael Novak, and Gordon Zahn. Some parishes, citing Vatican II's recognition of the rights of conscientious objectors in its edict, "The Constitution of the Church in the Modern World," were even opening in-house draft counseling programs. Jim Forest was counseling 200 Catholic conscientious objectors a month in his work with the CPF. And while still a minority, the number of activist Catholic dissenters was growing, inspired mainly by the words and work of the Berrigans.

But the overall Catholic tendency to identify with and support government policies was not to be so easily overthrown. Many bishops and pastors, and millions of ordinary Catholics, still supported the war. And their natural conservatism was repulsed by the mainstream American peace movement, which they widely viewed as a hotbed of cultural and political anarchy. When they thought about the Berrigans at all, most American Catholics tended to lump them in with secular forces of civic disruption and were disapproving.

Yet the Berrigans, like the pacifist Catholic Worker, were in many respects in wary coalition with the broader antiwar movement. They recognized they were heirs to the mostly nonreligious American radical movements of the past—abolitionists, suffragists, unionists, and early twentieth-century socialists—from which the current peace movement drew much strength (its quarrels with the old left aside). And Phil was especially knowledgeable and respectful of the country's activist history, in the same way Dorothy Day and her Catholic Worker cohort, the tireless agitator Ammon Hennacy, had once looked to labor's Elizabeth Gurley Flynn and Eugene Victor Debs as political models. But the

Berrigans' inspiration was drawn largely from their reading of Christian Scripture—"do not repay evil with evil; love your ene-mies"—not the justice-seeking humanism of most legitimate mass movements. Dan particularly looked to religious sources to find precedents for his faith-based opposition to the state, such as the handful of martyred German Jesuits who had actively resisted the Nazi regime.

So the brothers saw themselves, wrote John Deedy, a former managing editor of *Commonweal,* "as part of an old Catholic story—people of conscience daring to stand against the state in a witness for life and truth." He also compared Dan and Phil, and what would come to be known as the antiwar "Catholic Left," to such religious figures as Joan of Arc and Thomas More: "People [who] gave their lives," just as the Berrigans and their allies "would give, if not life itself, then years of life behind bars."[5]

Phil was by now Baltimore's most prominent antiwar leader, and one of the peace movement's prime catalysts. Before an audi-ence, his magnetism was unmistakable. "He was so handsome, so strong," said a woman who heard him speak; another young woman who would later join the Catholic Left said that the first time she and a friend heard Phil on the war, it was as if they were in the presence of "a saint." And a New York activist observed a subway ad for Johnnie Walker Red, which asked, "If this were the only bottle left in the world and you had it, who would you share it with?" on which someone had scrawled the reply: "Phil Berrigan."

Yoked to Phil's fierce drive, the members of the Baltimore Peace Mission performed more novel and confrontational operations. They entered buses taking new conscripts to Fort Holabird and lec-tured their occupants on the evil of the war. On another occasion, they ripped a huge sheet of brown paper on which an American flag had been drawn, arousing the fury of several congressional repre-sentatives who condemned them for dishonoring a sacred symbol, and even from some of their antiwar allies who worried that such a strident act would alienate the uncertain political center.

But Phil was fed up with spooning out discreet appeals to reason, and past caring about whom he offended. Earlier, he had sent an extended antiwar analysis to Secretary of Defense Robert McNamara, and received what can now be seen as a strange reply. By 1967, McNamara already knew the Vietnam War was a lost cause and a ghastly error. On May 19 McNamara had even sent President Johnson a warning: "Most Americans do not know how we got where we are, and most, without knowing why, but taking advantage of hindsight, are convinced that somehow we should not have gotten this deeply in. All want the war ended and expect their President to end it. Successfully. Or else." Even so, in reply to Phil, he glossed over all the war's failings and downplayed his conflict with Phil as a difference of opinion. One wouldn't expect the secretary of defense to confide his feelings to an antiwar priest, but why did McNamara continue to supply the same misdirectional rhetoric? Why did he not keep silent, or if not that, then resign and speak out on his convictions? At least Phil had the courage to follow his mind and conscience.[6]

Led by Phil, the Baltimore Peace Mission now held protracted planning sessions, raising and discarding many reasonable and often unreasonable protest strategies. Phil was opposed to programmatic violence. He had condemned "romantic 'revolutionaries' who preached that 'only violence works,'" for seeking "to advance their own glory at the expense of the lives and welfare of their people." He had also denounced as terrorists Palestinians, Quebeçois, white racists, Minutemen, and the Weathermen, and had even judged Yippies and Black Panthers "obstacles to social and political change and 'basically reactionary.'" And he'd concluded with the good Catholic credo: "We believe the means determines the end."

But despite such relative restraint, Phil was now in a full-blown rage against the war. His anger about the killing affected his every waking moment. He had come to detest electoral politics and scoffed at working with grassroots organizations. He had resigned from the CPF and CALCAV, whose legal protests he now criticized as safe, even fashionable—"another liberal bag"—to concentrate on radical actions with a small band of antiwar diehards. "The amazing thing about the Berrigans," said one who worked with them, was that they "believed they can work with few people and yet change the world." Phil believed that if a dedicated group pulled off the right symbolic protest, then maybe individual consciences would ignite across the country, forcing peace. Thinking along these lines, he became intrigued by the notion of immobilizing the government by filling up the courts and jails. But someone would have to take the first step and offer himself or herself up.

Phil arranged a meeting between members of the Baltimore Peace Mission and Philip Hirschkop, a lawyer in Alexandria, Virginia, who had frequently worked with civil rights organizations and was the principal attorney for the peace movement in the Washington, D.C., area. (Hirschkop had first met the Berrigans at the Pentagon demonstration made famous by Norman Mailer's *Armies of the Night*, and later defended them many times in court.)

Bill O'Connor, who was at the meeting, says Phil opened the discussion by informing Hirschkop that the group had been considering a plan to blow up the U.S. Customs House in Baltimore, where thousands of military draft files were stored, but wanted to keep the action "nonviolent" by ensuring that no one would be anywhere near the building. Hirschkop said, "My God, don't do that," then jumped out of his chair and ran from the office. O'Connor says he and the others had to search up and down the halls before finding the shaken lawyer and guiding him back behind closed doors. Hirschkop told the group, "OK, I didn't know we were going to talk about this." Phil adjusted to Hirschkop's alarm by disclosing the group's Plan B: entering the draft board and jamming up its door locks with a jellylike substance. What, he wanted to know, was the legality of such a protest? Hirschkop thought it over, then suggested instead that the group do something less serious, like pouring blood, or honey, or red paint on the locks. That way, he said, they'd avoid doing serious property damage while making their symbolic point about the bloodshed occurring in Vietnam. In all likelihood, Hirschkop said, they'd be charged with simple trespassing. The meeting adjourned.

On the drive back home, Phil derided Hirschkop's idea as the tepid proposal of "just another bourgeois lawyer." But pouring blood in a draft office struck David Eberhardt as a prophetic stroke worthy of Amos and Hosea. After further discussion during a stop at a Howard Johnson's, Phil began to change his mind. A few days later he had worked out a whole theology for such a protest. The blood could be seen as a surrogate for the blood of Christ, he envisioned, and its pouring could be interpreted as a symbolic act of Christian purification—a kind of echo of the sacrifice of the Mass.[7]

Phil's friend Richard McSorley, an eloquent antiwar Jesuit based at Georgetown University, tried to talk him out the action when he heard the details. "I told Phil I was not sure to what degree he could be effective in jail," McSorley said later. "Phil, after all, is one of the four or five most valuable priests in the country. I pleaded with him for hours at a time to use a more Gandhian tactic, to pick out an action which a larger segment of society would appreciate. But then, I am less brave a man than he."[8]

The plan was set for late October. Four men would raid the Customs House, pouring human blood directly on 1–A draft files. The protest's goals were to stall a part of the Pentagon's induction machinery, possibly sparing a few young lives; stimulate debate about the morality of the draft; inspire others to assume greater personal risks in acting against the war; and use the courtroom as a public forum to denounce the war and the injustice of conscription. The four men pledged to the act were David Eberhardt, James Mengel, Thomas Lewis, and Phil Berrigan.

When Eberhardt had first met Phil in 1965, he, like many young people of that time, was idealistic, utopian, angry, and much taken with the biblical tradition of social justice, particularly as it related to racism and war. Born in Massachusetts, and raised on a blend of Episcopalianism and his parents' commitment to causes like civil rights, he often found himself wondering just what constituted legitimate authority, and in whom could one place one's trust? And that had led him to Phil.

James Mengel, age thirty-eight, was an air force veteran and a husband and father of two. He had served as a United Church of Christ missionary in Ghana (then the Gold Coast) and South Korea, and as a military chaplain during the Korean War. He and his ordained wife had worked many years with abandoned kids on the Korean streets and in orphanages. While working, he had found himself reflecting on the dead and wounded of the Korean War, and on the death of his uncle in the Second World War. These memories made him determined, he said, to "do something" for peace. Returned to the United States, the Mengels then settled in a religious commune in Baltimore. It was there, in churches and synagogues, he had heard Phil Berrigan speak about Vietnam.[9]

Thomas Lewis, age twenty-seven, was a military veteran, an artist and art teacher in the Baltimore area, a passionate Catholic whose work had been exhibited in the Baltimore Museum of Art and Washington's Corcoran Gallery. His younger brother was in the air force and, at the time, en route to Vietnam. Talking over beer and pretzels one day, Phil had urged Lewis to visit the Catholic Worker. Lewis did, and while serving in a soup kitchen there, underwent a kind of transformation, which had led him to help found the Baltimore Interfaith Peace Mission. It was then, as the Irish would say, that his troubles began. Listening and talking to Phil over several months, all the while loathing the war, Lewis reached the conclusion that he and the priest were the same kind of people.[10]

The day before the raid, Bill O'Connor brought in a nurse from Johns Hopkins University to draw blood from the four participants. But the syringe's thin tubing barely worked, causing Mengel to faint and Phil to stab his arm so many times in an attempt to improve the suction that the others begged him to stop. Someone finally ran out to buy duck blood at a poultry market, which was mixed in four empty Mr. Clean bottles with some calf's liver juices and the single pint of human blood they had been able to collect through a protracted and painful effort, mostly Phil's.[11] Then, having finished with their messy preparations, Phil cheered the group by marrying Eberhardt to his fiancée, Louise Yolton. It was a "dramatic thing to do," wrote Eberhardt in a memoir, "fitting that wonderful slogan of the time 'Make Love, Not War!' "

The four were ready. Their protest, they knew, would be shocking, and would probably bring down on them the full force of the law. As Mengel got to thinking about this, he confided to Phil his concern about being separated from his children during his no doubt lengthy prison term. "Jim," said Phil, smiling broadly, "Don't worry. You're about to enter the family of man."[12]

Early in the morning on October 27, 1967, Eberhardt, Lewis, and Mengel picked up Phil at the St. Peter Claver rectory and headed for the Customs House, accompanied by several reporters who'd been invited to witness "an unusual act of protest against the Vietnam War." The group repaired to Lewis's art studio across from the hulking Customs House, where they waited till ten past noon, when most of the building's employees would be at lunch. Lewis crossed the street to reconnoiter the scene. The plan was for Lewis to establish that the security guard was off-duty, then give the all-clear signal by waving a handkerchief. But as he came back out of the building, and before he was finished inspecting the site, a janitor appeared and began cleaning one of the Customs House's big windows with a rag. Watching from across the street, the others took this as the signal. False alarm! Lewis gestured frantically for everyone to retreat back to the studio, and after several confusing moments, the protesters and reporters turned around.

Several minutes later, when things seemed settled, Lewis waved the handkerchief. Eberhardt, Mengel, and Phil strolled leisurely across South Gay Street over to the Customs House and joined Lewis at the building's imposing front entrance. Mengel lingered at the door as a lookout—prepared to create a diversion by faking a heart attack should the guard appear—while the others entered the ground-floor office of the local Selective Service System, where the draft files were held. Phil, wearing his Roman collar and a wrinkled black raincoat, told a clerk he needed to consult the records of a congregant. Tom Lewis and David Eberhardt, dressed in suits and ties, both said they had problems with their draft cards. When the clerk moved away to investigate their requests, the three men hurried to the cabinets, pulled out some drawers, and rained down blood on the files. The clerks either screamed or stared horrified. Then the press burst in with cameras rolling as the head clerk rushed to slam shut the opened drawers, shouting, "Stop, get away from our files!" Another woman employee tried, with no chance of success, to restrain Phil as he "quite methodically, back and forth," according to later trial testimony, emptied the contents of his bottle on the files. Lewis began to read aloud from the Bible, while Reverend Mengel, who'd entered with the reporters, offered a paperback New Testament to a clerk. "He's one of those bastards!" she shrieked. The scene, though lasting all of thirty seconds, was so emotionally tumultuous that a photographer from the *Baltimore Sun* nearly fainted and had to be supported by O'Connor.

Their task accomplished, Eberhardt, Mengel, Lewis, and Phil—from then on known as the "Baltimore Four"—took seats on a wooden bench. The police arrived in minutes and stood a sullen watch over them, waiting for the FBI to show up and make the arrests. The first of the "stand around" draft board raids was complete. The actors had chosen to do their work in the open and then wait with Gandhian fortitude to suffer the consequences—the pattern Phil would follow in later protests. When the FBI showed up, they took some time to survey the evidence, allowing the four to offer leaflets or a Bible to the cops.

The reporters, realizing the event was done, tore open the sealed envelopes they'd been handed at St. Peter Claver's and took a few minutes to read the group's statement of purpose, written largely by Phil:

> **We shed our blood** willingly and gratefully in what we hope is a sacrificial and constructive act. We pour it upon these files to illustrate that with them and with these offices begins the pitiful waste of American and Vietnamese blood 10,000 miles away. That bloodshedding is never rational, seldom voluntary—in a word—non-constructive. It does not protect life . . .

> **We quarrel** with the idolatry of property and the war machine that makes property of men . . .

We charge that America would rather protect its empire of overseas profits than welcome its black people, rebuild its slums and cleanse its air and water. Thus we have singled out inner-city draft boards for our actions.

We invite friends in the peace and freedom movements to continue moving with us from dissent to resistance. We ask God to be merciful and patient with us and all men. We hope he will use our witness for his blessed designs.

A year and a half before, during one of the frantic Fort Myer raids, Mengel had remarked to an atheist member of the Baltimore Peace Mission, "I don't see how you can do this without religion." But then he had reconsidered, "Oh well, of course you can do it because of Phil . . . with all the faith I have I couldn't do any of these things without Phil Berrigan." The same held true for the Baltimore Four. A writer at the time described the magnetic force of Phil's leadership: "He exudes a terrifying energy, a terrifying impatience, and a maddening freedom. He is devoid of all the fears, the cautions, the proprieties that motivate normal men. His smile, like his brother's, is radiant and irresistible. The spell he casts over other humans is as great as Daniel's and more alarming. . . . His revolutionary zeal is like the cold blue center of a flame. . . . One recalls Camus' phrase: 'The revolutionary loves a man who does not yet exist.' "[13]

When the FBI had finished its preliminary work at the "crime scene," they handcuffed the four and moved them toward the door. A moment earlier, Mengel had offered a Bible to one of the clerks. The woman had accepted the gift and now used it to hit Eberhardt on the head. "Maybe," he said, "it gave her a Christian feeling."[14] The men were then carted to FBI headquarters a few blocks away, and were later arraigned on charges of mutilating government property and interfering with the working of the Selective Service System. Eberhardt and Mengel signed a promissory note to appear in court and were freed on their own recognizance. Phil and Lewis refused to sign. They were taken to the Baltimore City jail, where they started a fast that lasted until their hearing one week later.

The day of the action, Jerry Berrigan turned on the 4 o'clock news at home and learned of Phil's arrest. Though he shared his brother's hatred of the war, and much of his politics, he was unprepared to absorb the fact that Phil now faced a maximum eighteen-year penalty for attacking government property. So he sat down on his living room couch and wept.

Likewise, Dan knew nothing of the Baltimore raid beforehand. He heard about it while held in a Washington, D.C., jail, after his arrest with a group of Cornell students and chaplains at the massive October 22 Pentagon march. With his release five days later, he went to the Catholic Worker and phoned Freda in Syracuse with the latest news of her youngest sons. "My mother's calm touched me," he remembered. "This was by no means the first test of her equanimity, nor would it be the last. I explained things, as best I might. 'You mean,' she responded, 'that you are out of jail, and your brother is in?' "[15]

Not long after, one of Dan's friends in the Ithaca peace movement, "a modest man, not given to aphorism or prophecy," remarked to him about Phil, "You know, they'll have to kill your brother someday: he'll never change." The first part of the prediction was wrong, of course, but it captures the magnitude of the adversity Phil would seek out and face for the rest of his life, making the second part prescient. Perhaps sensing something of this, Dan had written in his journal on the day of the raid: "*Oremus pro fratribus in periculo*" (We pray for our brother in trouble); then added a quote from the Book of Isaiah, "Give honor to the Lord of Hosts, to Him only. Let Him be your only fear, let Him be your only dread."[16]

Looking about his jail cell, Tom Lewis saw a resemblance to a church. Even the FBI office seemed to him, in his ecstatic state, like a rectory waiting room, especially the green decor. Their interrogating agent addressed the pair as "Father Berrigan" and "Mr. Lewis." Like many of the marshals and prison guards they would meet in the coming months, he was a faithful churchgoer and a devout product of the Catholic parochial school system. He was also obedient and conventionally patriotic, and didn't think much of protest.[17]

In a letter, Phil explained his act to his Josephite superior, Father O'Dea. "It's perfectly natural that you would be confused and pained by what I have done with our other people, so I owe you a word of explanation," he began, then went on to speak of the war's impact and how most combat troops were from poor or lower-middle-class families, unlike the "rich" and powerful elites whose sons were "untouched by it to a shameful degree." Quoting Pope John XXIII's warning that, "in certain conditions, governments lose the right of jurisdiction," he also insisted that because the U.S. government was engaged in an illegitimate war, "I have a duty to withstand it as well as I can and then endure the consequences."[18]

Months later, with Phil and Lewis's release pending trial, the Baltimore Four got together with other Peace Mission members to discuss just what those consequences might be, and how they would deal with them. Phil brought a bottle of rye and some doughnuts to celebrate. But Mengel, who had shown up in bare feet (a gesture that struck Bill O'Connor as something of a penitential pose), objected to the liquor and the sweets. "Thinkest because thou art virtuous, there shall be no more cakes and ale?" recited O'Connor from Shakespeare's *Twelfth Night* in response to the dour Mengel—which broke the tension by getting everyone to laugh, including Mengel. The group's good humor, for the moment, would hold them together.

9

MORE VIETNAM

Each day it continues its grinding,
unrewarding way. For the Vietnamese,
it has been going on since World War
II . . . For the Americans recently
assigned here, it is all very new, and
from long years of ignorance about
Vietnam they have entered a world
where at times it seems that the only
thing that exists is this country, this
war, this enemy.

—*David Halberstam*
New York Times, *November 4, 1962*

HOWARD ZINN, A HISTORIAN AND ONETIME SECOND WORLD
War army air force bombardier, well-known for his progressive
views on civil rights and the war, remembered that while he was
teaching a political science class on January 30, 1968, at Boston
University, a department secretary knocked on the door, apologized for the interruption, and told him he had a pressing phone
call. "Can't it wait until I finish my class?" Zinn asked her. No, she
said, the call was urgent.[1]

David Dellinger, the veteran pacifist, was on the line. The North Vietnamese government had just wired him to say that as a good-will gesture in honor of the imminent Buddhist Tet holiday, three captured American fighter pilots would be freed. Would Dellinger and his antiwar people send "a responsible representative" to escort them home? Dellinger had immediately thought of Howard Zinn and Daniel Berrigan. So he called them up, explained the mission, and told them they'd have to drop everything and be on a plane to Southeast Asia within twenty-four hours. Both accepted, and the very next day found themselves with Dellinger and Tom Hayden of the Students for a Democratic Society in a Greenwich Village apartment.

That evening the professor and the priest boarded a flight at Kennedy Airport. It was an arduous trip. Dan had forgotten his Bible and was, as usual, plagued with back problems. They hopscotched from airport to airport for twenty-eight hours, landing and then taking off in Europe, the Middle East, and East Asia, until at last they reached Vientiane in ostensibly neutral Laos, where they hoped to catch one of the International Control Commission's aged four-engine Boeings which made the perilous Saigon-Phnom Penh-Vientiane-Hanoi run six times monthly.

But they arrived too late to catch the ICC plane and had to spend the week wandering around Vientiane, a dusty, backwater town on the Mekong River that belied the silent war under way between a motley horde of informants and spies of the various belligerents—the United States, the two Vietnams, the Pathet Lao, China, Taiwan, France, and the USSR. Outside the town, in the Plain of Jars and elsewhere, U.S. aerial bombing had begun attacking the Ho Chi Minh Trail, portions of which ran through Laos, in 1964; by 1973, several million tons of bombs, especially cluster bombs, had pounded Laos.[2]

Unaware of much of this when they landed, the men roamed the area, talking with journalists, Lao peasants, a Pathet Lao agent, and outspoken antiwar Americans living among Laotians and working for the International Volunteer Service. The distant fighting, the pervasive cynicism, the smell of corruption, and the prevalence of drugs and prostitution reminded Zinn of Bogart's wartime

Casablanca. At last, the ICC plane arrived and they flew on to Hanoi.

Left alone at first, the two wandered leisurely through the city. Dan, especially, was shocked at the immense damage done by American bombing raids: "the desolation and patience and cold," he recorded in *Night Flight to Hanoi,* his journal of prose and poetry, in which he also proclaimed, with poetic exaggeration, "I felt like a Nazi watching films of Dachau ... What will be the music I march to on my return?"[3]

The North Vietnamese finally showed up, putting them through dreary three-hour lectures, during which Dan insisted on criticizing them for their reliance on violence even as he sometimes tended to romanticize their cause. Finally, the playacting stopped and three American prisoners of war, all pilots, were brought to the rundown French-built hotel where he and Zinn were staying: Major Norris Overly, Captain John Black, and Lieutenant JG David Methany, all of whom had obviously been physically and psychologically battered by their captors. Though Dan says he was moved by their condition, he still thought they looked "better than us, better than the hundreds of thousands of people we have seen laboring and cycling through the streets."[4]

The bombing raids had stopped, but the day after their first meeting with the fliers, they resumed. As Dan huddled with ordinary Vietnamese in air raid shelters, his sympathies went out to the children hiding with them below the streets while the air raid alarms shrieked and bombs, napalm, and toxic chemicals detonated above, laying waste to hospitals, homes, and schools as well as to military installations. As in most of the twentieth century's wars, civilians were the main target. Dan's journal has him musing with empathy about the three fliers, two career men and the twenty-four-year-old Methany, still unsure of his future in the navy. But he also asked: Who will weep for the dead children of Vietnam? Seated in a shelter with three youngsters, he scribbled a touching poem in their honor, an illustration of how far he had traveled, how much the political poet he had become, so dissimilar was it from his infinitely more serene, *Time Without Number.*

Imagine; three of them.

As though survival
were a rat's word,
and a rat's death
waited there at the end

and I must have
in the century's boneyard
half of flesh and bone in my arms

I picked up the littlest
a boy, his face
breaded with rice (his sister calmly feeding him
as we climbed down)

In my arms fathered
In a moment's grace, the messiah
of all my fears. I bore, reborn

a Hiroshima child from hell.[5]

Living under bombs in a ravaged city, he was staggered by the degree of destruction and suffering he witnessed. For Dan, who had never before seen war's savagery firsthand, it was like being in a charnel house, the pain all the greater because he was living among people who had done him no harm. By the time he returned home he was a changed man, angrier, less forgiving.

He and Zinn flew back to Laos with the three ex-prisoners, and were met by U.S. Ambassador William Sullivan who insisted the pilots be flown home in a military aircraft. Sullivan was in his forties, a well-educated Ivy Leaguer and navy veteran. ("No single American had a greater effect on Laos than Sullivan, [who] was an ambassador with extraordinary powers—a virtual proconsul from 1964 to 1969," wrote Roger Warren.) According to Zinn, he laid it on the line to the pilots. "You men can choose whether you go home by commercial line or by military plane. However, you do understand that you are still members of the Armed Forces, and it is my duty to report to you that the Department of Defense has expressed the preference that you go home by military aircraft." The decision was "made in Washington. Indeed, it comes from the White House."[6]

That was all Dan had to hear. The affair had been designed to be a feather in the cap of antiwar forces, but the government had stolen their thunder, and their headlines. With no other choice, he and Zinn shook hands with the men they had liberated, though one of them mumbled out of earshot of the ambassador, "We're sorry." "Good luck," called back Zinn, the combat bombardier turned pacifist.

For Dan, the scene was the personification of a struggle between conscience and the military's ingrained obedience. For the pilots, compliance with military orders and loyalty to their country and still-imprisoned comrades came first. Nor were they comfortable cooperating with two celebrated antiwar leaders who had come to shepherd them home.

Years after, a questioner rose at a California college to ask Dan about his trip to Hanoi. "Perhaps intemperately in the heat of the narration," he admitted calling Ambassador Sullivan "Killer Sullivan." A young woman, Sullivan's daughter, came up to him after his lecture and said that when she was a child living in Laos, she had never before heard the story as Daniel had related it. "I could only advise her to repeat my version to her father, with my compliments," Dan told her, "and ask his reaction." And, years later, back at Cornell to speak, he was still rankled by Sullivan's action. This time he called him the man "who stole the freed POWs from us."[7]

In March, following their return home, events in and outside Washington, D.C. began to shake prowar opinion. Earlier that month, General William Westmoreland asked for 206,000 more troops, which, Hedrick Smith and Neil Sheehan of the *New York Times* reported, "touched off a divisive internal debate within high levels of the Johnson administration" and outraged Americans unwilling to accept the mounting numbers of dead and wounded. By then, a Gallup Poll revealed that almost half the population thought the intervention wrong. And, on March 13, Senator Eugene McCarthy won the New Hampshire Democratic presidential primary by 230 votes, "the loose thread," wrote historian Larry Berman, "which, when pulled, unraveled the Johnson presidency." Vermont's Senator George Aiken had been right all along: "Let's declare that we have achieved our objectives in Vietnam and go home." But if Johnson ultimately agreed, his successors and the prowar political forces at large did not—at least not yet. In any event, the pace was far too slow for the Berrigans and their impatient adherents.[8]

Back in Ithaca again, Dan received appalling news of another self-immolation, this time in Syracuse, and this time by a high school honors student. Straightaway, he drove to Syracuse to be with the dying boy, whom he had never met. "As far as I was able to piece things together his act was an act of hope; so he quietly and thoughtfully construed it . . . 'Just sensitive,' people said."

Visibly distressed, and overwhelmed by the calamities induced by the war at home and abroad, he sat down, prayed, and wrote a poem dedicated to the boy.

> He was living still a month later
> I was able to gain access to him
> I smelled the odor
> of burning flesh
> And I understood anew
> what I had seen in North Vietnam . . .
> I felt that my senses
> had been invaded in a new way
> I now understood
> the power of death in the modern world
> I knew I must speak and act
> against death

because this boy's death
was being multiplied
a thousandfold
In the Land of Burning Children.[9]

Jail time might well have been waived or reduced if the Baltimore Four, all first offenders, had agreed to a plea bargain accepting guilt and pledging never to violate the law again. But it was too late for that. There was a point to be made, and Phil, especially, was up to the challenge.

The trial of the four men was set for April 1968, a few months after the Tet offensive. Early that month, 24,500 reserves and National Guardsmen were ordered to report for active duty, about 45 percent of them assigned to Vietnam. This new draft was "after [Secretary of Defense Clark] Clifford had decided the war was unwinnable; after the *critical* White House meeting of the Wise Men on March 26 that finally convinced President Johnson that we had to get out of Vietnam," and after LBJ had decided not to seek reelection. The men called to war were "innocents," said an obviously angry writer in the *Washington Monthly*, "conscripted to die in a war their government, at the highest levels, had secretly decided was lost."[10]

The trial, nevertheless, proceeded on schedule. For four days the defendants tried unsuccessfully to explain and publicize their motives, but the judge ruled that the jury was not to draw any connections between the war and their break-in or involve itself in irrelevant issues of international law or references to any higher moral authority. The issue was simple: Did they or didn't they? Though not wholly persuaded that the raid was the right way to go, the veteran Catholic pacifist Gordon Zahn arrived to testify on their behalf, but was prevented by the judge's decision to limit testimony to the act itself, motivation be damned. Had he been permitted to testify, Zahn would have pointed out that had they been Germans living during the Nazi era who were fighting to save Jews slated for death, they would now be cheered.[11]

The courtroom was dominated by the stern Judge Edward S. Northrop, a former state senator. Stephen Sachs a well-regarded liberal, antiwar prosecutor, who was eager to uphold respect for the law in a democracy, argued that the country could not permit any belief, group, or person to decide for themselves what was and wasn't legal. As a defendant, Eberhardt, saw it differently, portraying the proceedings as conducted in "a leaden atmosphere of oppressive fear [since] we were only beginners [who] had put too much faith in the law." Faced with binding and uncomplicated instructions, the jury deliberated only ninety minutes before bringing in their inevitable guilty verdict, despite attorney Fred Weisgal's plea that the four men "had no evil motive, no criminal intent."[12]

With 150 supporters packing the courtroom, Judge Northrop sentenced Phil and Lewis to six years each and remanded them to jail. Eberhardt received three years but was released on $7,500 bail, and Mengel was handed eighteen years, a sentence the judge termed "technical" inasmuch as he was released on his own recognizance and ordered to undergo a psychiatric examination and return for resentencing. (He never served a day in prison). Two men in the courthouse hallway tried to distribute handbills backing the defendants and accused marshals of roughing them up. On the street, a single picket held up a sign, "Release Fr. Berrigan and Tom Lewis, Prisoners for Peace."

The trial was not only a measure of how much leeway the government would permit protesters while a war was on but an electrifying event for religious pacifists, especially dissenting Catholic clergy and religious. Father Joseph O'Rourke believed the raid "seemed *exactly* right at the time—to guys who had a history of militancy and were searching for ways to protest. You know: Why didn't I think of that!"[13]

But others were not as sure. The raid and the trial tended to set on edge some elements in the nonreligious peace movement. How to cope with so unprecedented a violation of the law? Did the raid (and subsequent ones as well) raise the ante so much that it could ignite far right crazies to turn violently against *them*? To what extent did it really influence the vital center? Or intimidate prowar political and military elites dead set on winning the war? And was the raid so extreme, so fraught with danger, that ordinary men and women could not expect to flout the law in this manner and endure the consequences?

"The important task is to create a new society and that means winning the people," wrote a Protestant pacifist. It is, he argued, "not one of seeking an outlet for one's rage; it is to build the widest possible support for new structures and for a new respect for persons."[14] Even more worrisome was whether a small portion of both the secular and Catholic Left was flirting with violence in the pursuit of "just" causes. Third World revolutionaries like Fanon, Debray, Che Guevara, and Ernesto Cardenal seemed more attractive than the nonviolent, religious Berrigans. It came down to this: How best to end the despised war? Standard pacifist gospel preached that not only was it essential to violate orders that breach the principles of conscience but it was just as important to accept the resulting punishment, since that put the government in the role of prosecutor. But what if the violated "law" is immoral? asked Howard Zinn. "When unjust decisions are accepted, injustice is sanctioned and perpetuated."

"It would be wrong," a legal scholar pointed out, "to say that there are no occasions, no circumstances under which the deliberate violation of law is justifiable, even in a decent society. There *are* times when one must say no to the state." Indeed, some laws were so diabolic—for example, Jim Crow legislation—and some property so heinous, such as Nazi concentration camps, that no respect was due them.[15]

Though he later rejoiced at news of the raid, Dan was at first taken aback, unaware it was to happen, and admitted he was at first "very far" from Phil's strategy. Anne Klejment, who has written extensively about the Berrigan brothers, noted that Dan brooded over whether the break-in was a violent act that might lead to real violence. Would he have to become involved? And what might it mean for his life as a Jesuit? Yet he detested the war, and all about him were draft-age Cornell students defying induction. He was, he said, slowly "drawn toward becoming involved in planning for acts of ultra-resistance." (Dan said later, not unkindly, to a lawyer friend, "If the government were coming for your TVs and cars, then you'd be upset. But, as it is, they're only coming for your sons."[16]) In the end, Anne Klejment believes, it came down to a moral judgment: "He could not claim religious leadership among students unless he began to take some actions against the war that entailed risks to himself."[17]

Despite his initial misgivings and lack of knowledge about what was to happen, Dan changed his mind in favor of personal involvement. "My brother Philip was working in the inner city of Baltimore; a community man, he drew the community around him like a magnet. The facts of life were his daily bread. He saw in his prophetic bones that our support of the student resisters was a game the government would tolerate indefinitely. So in [October] 1967 he and three friends decided to take their peaceable war into the enemy camp."[18]

Dan's explications were "pure Zen, but Zen for life in time of plague," thought Forest when he read these words. "The Zen spirit was needed, as events were rushing toward us at a pace we hadn't endured."[19]

Phil was censured by Lawrence Cardinal Shehan, the Archbishop of Baltimore. He was denied the right to say Mass publicly, preach, or hear confessions, though a church representative "explained that Father Berrigan may say Mass and give a brief homily in his prison cell where he is being held without bond."

Yes, declared the cardinal, freedom of expression is fine, "But I cannot condone and do not condone the damaging of property or the intimidation of government employees."[20] This was the same Cardinal Shehan who, on June 28, 1966, had issued a pastoral letter on the "patriotic duties of American Catholics," and praised the sacrifices of men and women in the military, who "should regard themselves as agents of security and freedom"; he had simultaneously defended the right of conscientious objection and insisted the war had to be waged in a "morally acceptable way." When they heard this, antiwar Catholics rejoiced, viewing the cardinal as a fellow traveler. Forest and Cornell reprinted copies of the cardinal's letter and distributed it widely to CPF members, while *Commonweal* interpreted his words to mean that in Shehan the peace forces had found an ally. Not so, declared the horrified cardinal to the extremely hawkish Catholic War Veterans. "Our presence in Vietnam and the reasons which have prompted us to involve ourselves there are honorable. I approved of them."[21]

The Josephites removed Phil from his duties at St. Peter Claver. The raid, meantime, led to an acceleration of FBI surveillance and harassment (The FBI, Bill O'Connor warned Phil, "is trying to drum up some sort of Communist conspiracy. They have been at my home as well as at the college where I teach.") Regardless, the Baltimore Interfaith Peace Mission was flooded with mail and phone calls from prominent people, publications, ordinary Americans, and GIs, offering their help and asking what they could do.

"Phil is in good health and his spirits are high," O'Connor wrote a mutual friend in Seattle, "a contradiction that breeds its own absurdities. Tom Lewis is his usual imperturbable self. The other two participants in the blood-pouring action vacillate between confusion, fear, and courage."[22]

The trial, however, didn't stir much interest outside Baltimore, even though it was the first of its kind, given that the national media was concentrating on the murder of Martin Luther King Jr., the ensuing ghetto and campus rebellions and riots, and the political challenges to President Johnson, as well as to the war itself.

More vexing for the Catholic resistance was what Dorothy Day and Thomas Merton thought about the Baltimore protest. Much like Merton, Day worried whether the destruction of property was truly nonviolent, and whether the Baltimore raid would lead to more destructive actions by less disciplined, more radical and violent nonpacifists.

"These actions are not ours," she would say over and again *after* Catonsville, which took place on May 17, 1968. She meant that the secrecy in which the protest was hatched vitiated traditionally non-violent Gandhian precepts of shunning what Tom Cornell, who was also seriously troubled by the raids, described as "conspiratorial, secretive activity" and "a violation of openness and truth." Day's injunction to "Do unto others as you would have others do unto you" underscored her fundamental belief that one's enemy should be persuaded peacefully and not turned away in anger.[23]

Her message, though, was mixed, supportive but troubled. Dan and other clergy of like mind, she once said, reflecting her social conservatism, were "underground" priests; she even compared Dan to St. Edmund Campion, a clandestine Jesuit priest in England executed when Catholicism was forbidden during the first Queen Elizabeth's reign. Still, Day, whose grandson Eric Hennessy was a combat Vietnam Ranger, continued to center the major thrust of her criticism on "the government itself, and all of us, of mass murders in Vietnam" as well as the American bishops for their acquiescence in the war and their timidity.[24]

Though hardly intimidated by the doyen of the anarcho-pacifist Christian movement, Dan felt unqualified respect for Day, and he always considered her one of his mentors. Yes, he confessed, he was "what you call an 'underground' priest" and it wasn't easy to oppose the church when he thought it was in error. "But stand I do. And I am strengthened by the reflection that you too have been, in the noblest sense, an 'underground' Catholic during most of your life." And now that she had "brought one revolution to pass," he asked, could she in good conscience "forbid others to carry forward the next wave?"[25]

Day did say, though, that in comparison with the vast bloodletting of the twentieth century, complaints about destroying property were "hair-splitting." Yet she herself would never join such an action. "But I have to admire all those who have been participating . . . they are laying down their lives and going to prison."[26] Dan returned the compliment, writing warmly about her and the impact she had on him in one of his most passionate and revealing books, *Portraits of Those I Love*.

It also took Merton a while to make sense of the break-in, but in the end, he lent his approval. He had planned to dedicate his forthcoming new book, *Faith and Violence*, to Dan and Phil, but because he had already dedicated an earlier work to Dan, he dedicated the new work to Phil and Jim Forest. He joked about Phil that, given the raid, he could very well have a "cloistered [prison] vocation" too. But "you have done what you could to draw attention to the mess, and for that I praise you and join you morally at least."[27]

After the subsequent and far more famous draft board raid at Catonsville, where files were actually burned, Merton wrote that Dan and Phil were his close friends, and while "I don't agree with their methods of action . . . I can understand the desperation which prompts them. They believe they have to witness *in jail* to the injustice of the war. That is their business. It is certainly not a necessary teaching of the Church." Still, he added, the war was an abomination, and neither Richard Nixon nor Hubert Humphrey, both running for the presidency then, was moving to end it.[28]

Whatever he thought about the break-ins, "there is no question but that Merton would have supported and honored those who took part in these raids in that they were following their consciences and had acted in a manner that avoided intentional physical violence to others or to themselves," commented Gordon Zahn, who himself had serious reservations.[29]

Back in Baltimore, some of the antiwar people were ecstatic, but few were prepared to take such risks and wind up in prison. The Baltimore Four raid had drastically ratcheted up the danger level; demonstrations and publications and baiting a university or church bureaucracy were one thing, but the FBI? The federal courts? Prison? Despite the outrage many felt and their sympathy for the defendants, they had quite understandable emotional responses, and felt growing consternation about what such actions would entail for themselves and their families.

Herman Heyn, for example, had written a letter to the *Sun* against the war as early as 1962, and was one of the founders of the Baltimore Peace Action Center. He was sympathetic, yes, but destroying government records was not something he could do. Other activists experienced what David Eberhardt later referred to as "psychological problems": fear of prosecution and prison life and menacing inmates. Still out on bail, Eberhardt turned down an invitation to join the Catonsville raiders in May 1968 because he was "scared" of prison, and afterward he was astonished to hear that Dan termed Catonsville "the happiest day of our lives." ("These are indeed parlous times," Dan said after the Baltimore raid, "but I would not want to live in any other. And for men who have some viable convictions about a human life, they are simply exhilarating and glorious."[30]) Nowhere, Eberhardt complained years after, did any of the many books on the sixties he had read refer to the pervasive dread of imprisonment he found among so many of the movement people he knew.

In 1991 he was asked by a psychologist, who sensed his animosity toward authority figures, if he hadn't harbored "anger toward the Berrigans." He later wrote: "I was angry at my father. I was angry at society. Phil Berrigan was a rebel, but at the same time he was an authority figure to me. But I wasn't angry at Phil. He had a right to be an authority; he was an authority who happened to be right!" Phil, he went on, "is the major historical figure, cast in the heroic mold [who] deserves the accolades. Phil's books don't dwell on self-analysis. It's just the way he is. Talk about courage. Talk about sacrifice."[31]

Once the trial was over in April 1968, the men were freed on bail pending their appeal. Phil contacted George Mische, an experienced organizer and antiwar activist who supported the raid and was looking for people willing to continue the onslaught. Before long they made contact with two ex-Maryknoll missionaries, Thomas and Marjorie Melville, who had worked in Guatemala with Mayan peasants. They all agreed to meet and do something "serious," as Phil presented it to them.

In late November Phil traveled to Cornell University, and there, joined by Dan, two other priests, a faculty member, and a student, helped inaugurate a ten-day Cornell resistance program. Citing the

Baltimore raid as an effective model of civil disobedience, Phil told his audience of 300 people: "You can make the draft quiver."[32]

Phil returned a few months later and spent the evening cloistered with Dan. The next morning, Dan mentioned to James Matlack that another action was coming soon. Did he want to join? Matlack, a married man with three children, including an infant daughter, and still battling the government ever since he had returned his draft card, politely refused.

On the morning of May 18, 1968, Matlack was startled to read that another draft board raid had occurred the day before in a place called Catonsville.

10

CATONSVILLE

The poet and the revolutionary are the
rampart of the people.
> —*Ho Chi Minh*

I think it is disgusting. [The Berrigans]
are on the lunatic fringe of the Church.
> —*Vice-commander of the Catholic War
> Veterans of Maryland*

"DAN'S IN," SHOUTED PHIL.

A few days earlier Phil and Tom Lewis had been in Ithaca trying
to get Dan to join in another raid, this time destroying and not
merely damaging files. Phil was consumed with anger. In Dan's play
about their subsequent trial, Phil defends himself: "We have been
accused of arrogance. But what of the fantastic arrogance of our
leaders? What of their crimes against the people, the poor and powerless? Still no court will try them, no jail will receive them. They
live in righteousness. They will die in honor."

Since the government relied on force; *they* would strike back in unexpected ways and confound the warmakers. At Cornell, in Dan's apartment, they drank and implored and argued well into the early hours of the morning to get Dan to commit himself. For Phil, the upcoming assault on the "Kingdom of the Blind" was a sacrament, a new rite of Baptism, a proclamation to believers that religious faith and their war against the war could not be separated. Did not Moses burn the wayward Israelites' pagan golden calf, and did not Martin Luther incinerate the papal bull of excommunication and the canon law?

In the end, "I couldn't not do it," said Dan. He put it this way: "I had seen myself in a different light before his [Phil's] visit—that we were out of the picture. Young men were faced with harsh choices." Could he do any less, given his role as "advisor and counselor" at Cornell? He faced the possibility "of losing everything, losing every way. Lose your good name, perhaps lose your place in the Order. At that time it was also quite possible that I would lose the exercise of priesthood." He explained his decision to Paul Mayer, a Benedictine monk, this way: "They slap me on the back and tell me how great I am—and nothing happens."[1]

Thirty minutes past noon on May 17, 1968, nine raiders—seven men and two women, all of them Roman Catholics—arrived at the nondescript Knights of Columbus Hall on 1010 Frederick Road in Catonsville, an untroubled Baltimore suburb, which housed Selective Service Board #33. They toted a ten-pound parcel filled with homemade napalm, concocted a few nights earlier by Dean Pappas, a local physics teacher, in Bill O'Connor's basement on St. Paul Street in Baltimore, from a formula printed in a United States Special Forces booklet and rumored to have been given them by a Green Beret sympathizer. Dan was there, too, the first time he met the entire raiding party. The napalm was made from two parts gasoline, which provided the flames, and one part Ivory Flakes, which provided the adhesive so the jellylike substance would stick to flesh. It was supposed to be cooked and allowed to harden, but since they wanted the stuff to pour easily out of gasoline cans, they bypassed the cooking.[2]

Posting a lookout, the raiders strode by two workingmen putting up an armed forces recruiting poster on the walk nearest the office. O'Connor was supposed to be stationed outside to circulate the group's statement, but he and a TV crew were stranded in a motel a few miles away because the driver who was supposed to pick them up had panicked and fled.

Lewis and the two women went first. Lewis knew where everything was since he had been there before, posing as someone wishing to rent the basement for a fictional upcoming wedding. Three women clerks were at their desks, one typing and the others leafing through papers. Lewis announced what was about to occur, but, caught up in their work, they seemed to pay no heed, until the other raiders burst in with wire trash baskets and went straight to the files. A clerk finally realized what was happening and screamed. Phil tried to calm her, saying no one would be harmed, while over the shouts someone yelled something about the war.

They began snatching up 1-A records and then moved on to 2-As and 1-Ys, stuffing them helter-skelter into a basket. Someone cautioned Dan about jamming them in too tightly because they might not burn as well. When one of the women clerks tried to phone the police, Mary Moylan put her finger on the receiver button and quietly advised her to wait until they were finished. Once they were done, she handed the woman the phone, saying, "Now you can call whoever you wish." Instead, the woman flung the phone out the window, hoping to draw help from the workmen outside. Another clerk thrust herself at Mische, grabbing for the basket and shrieking, "My files, my files, get away from my files," tearing the seam of his pants, but cutting her finger and suffering a small scratch on her leg and a torn stocking, though all the clerks were otherwise unharmed. Outside, the two workmen realized that something was up on the second floor, and they rushed toward the building.

In the parking lot, a small group of reporters and photographers and a TV crew were on hand, tipped off by Grenville Whitman, a former reporter working as an organizer for the Baltimore Interfaith Peace Mission.[3]

They gaped as the nine raiders walked slowly, serenely, out of the building with their package of napalm, and as John Hogan used his lit cigarette to set it ablaze. While Mische held on to his pants, Marjorie Melville frantically sewed up the torn seam. In ten minutes, they burned 378 files. Then, circling the pyre, they stood erect and intoned the Lord's Prayer and sang hymns while film and still cameras recorded the startling image. (When photos appeared the next day, only Dan and Phil were shown; the others had been cropped out, as if only the Berrigans mattered. To some of the raiders the Catonsville Nine had suddenly been transformed into the Catonsville Two).

"Who's responsible for this?" demanded a cop, pointing to the fire.

David Darst identified himself. "I wanted to make it more diffi-cult for men to kill each other," he told the bewildered officer.

Someone called out, "We speak out in the name of Catholicism and Christianity. We do this because everything else has failed."

Ignoring the speaker, the policeman turned to another raider and asked politely, "Your name, please?"

"Father Daniel Berrigan, S.J."

"Thank you, Father," he respectfully responded, as he carefully wrote the name in his pad.

Several cars pulled up and a jut-jawed, jowly FBI agent jumped out of the auto and stopped short. "Him again!" he cried out, glar-ing at Phil and recalling him from the earlier Baltimore Customs House raid. "Good God, I'm changing my religion."[4]

The plan may have sprung from George Mische as much as from Phil. Mische was an experienced and gifted organizer with a fertile imagination. By 1968 he and Phil believed that a more innovative approach was needed, possibly an act of civil disobedience that might involve as many as one hundred people, the harder for the law to prosecute them and the easier to make their case public. George Mische, age thirty, the son of a labor organizer, had worked to reeducate street gang members in Brooklyn and later joined the United States Agency for International Development in Central America and the Dominican Republic, organizing community development ventures, cooperatives, and housing projects, and working with Latin American unions taking part in the U.S.-run Alliance for Progress. He quit in 1964 to protest U.S. policies supporting undemocratic regimes. Back home, he tried unsuccessfully to persuade the Catholic bishops to help impoverished Americans. "George," said Phil, "is one of the few who has earned the label 'Christian revolutionary.' "

Mische approached several nuns, including Sister Elizabeth McAlister, a teacher of art history at Marymount College in Manhattan, and asked if they'd like to join, an invitation McAlister rejected because she didn't feel it was the "right time. At the time, I didn't have my own good reasons for doing it and I would not have been able to clearly articulate them."[5] She and Phil had been working together intensely against the war, and had by now begun to fall in love. Within a year, they would be "married by mutual consent" in a Bronx church office. (No one else would be present at their exchange of vows.) So Liz knew that the proposed raid at Catonsville, besides being risky, might mean years of separation for them both.

At some point, Mische handed over to Phil his list of possible raiders, among them John Hogan and Mary Moylan, both of whom later lived in Mische's rented house on S Street off Sixteenth Street in Washington.

Still awaiting sentence for the Baltimore raid, Phil was anxious to move again. The notion of clandestine operations directed at the soft belly of the warmakers continued to seize him. Doing something big and newsworthy had captured his imagination. What better way to clog up the system than by destroying the records of potential cannon fodder—many of whom were working-class and lower-middle-class kids, the very young men who were shipped out to Vietnam, while the children of the privileged were too often excused from the military.

David Darst, age twenty-six, volunteered after reading of the Baltimore raid. Born James McGinnis Darst and a summa cum laude graduate of St. Mary's College in Winona, Minnesota, he taught as a Christian Brother in various schools, most recently teaching religion in a black senior high school in Kansas City. Confused about the Vietnam War, he started reading extensively in the summer of 1967: "Senator Fulbright's book, some articles, some of the things by Bernard Fall [and] I remember going back to two articles by Michael Novak. . . . both of which appeared in *Commonweal*." By autumn, Darst was sure "that something was terribly wrong."

On December 4, 1967, Darst returned his draft card and as a result lost his clerical deferment and was drafted, only to refuse induction on April 4, 1968, shortly before Catonsville. He had corresponded with Jim Forest at the Catholic Peace Fellowship and sent a copy of his letter to Phil, whom he did not know personally.

Two weeks before the raid, Darst attended an all-day meeting and also received a message from Phil "asking me if I was interested in other things" besides draft refusal.[7]

John Hogan, age thirty-three, had been a Maryknoll Brother in Guatemala for seven years until recalled by his order for being too close to the Christian liberation movement. He resigned from Maryknoll the month before Catonsville. He hated the war, but more than all else, he wanted to publicize the savagery of the Guatemalan government and denounce "the marriage of U.S. economic imperialism to exploitative native oligarchies."

Marjorie Bradford Melville, age thirty-eight, was a former nun born in Mexico of American parents. As Maryknoll Sister Marian Peter, she had worked in Guatemala for fourteen years, teaching students from the elementary to the university level. After leaving Guatemala in December 1967, she married Thomas Melville, a Maryknoll priest.

Thomas Melville, age thirty-seven, had been ordained as a Maryknoll priest. Together with his brother Arthur, he and Marjorie had worked among the Indians of Guatemala, who comprised 56 percent of the Guatemalan population, as a parish priest and a pastor. They helped found credit cooperatives and organized the John the 23rd land-distribution project. They witnessed U.S. cooperation with the murderous Guatemalan government and its death squads. When Thomas returned to the United States in April 1968, he sought to publicize how U.S. policies were harming the poor by backing the military and political oligarchy, the prime reason they joined the others at Catonsville. "We intended to demonstrate," Thomas and Marjorie Melville wrote, "our belief that true loyalty to America as well as to Christ lies in active resistance to Nixon's continued propagation of it as well as to other expressions of American hate, destruction and inhumanity."

Mary Moylan, age thirty-two, was a registered nurse and midwife. The daughter of a Baltimore court reporter and a nurse-midwife, she had worked in Uganda with the White Sisters for three years under Catholic auspices. She later served as executive director of the Women Volunteers Association in Washington, preparing women to assist Third World countries. She also worked in Washington's depressed neighborhoods, saying it led her to understand that "law and order as a term is used, but in instances that I know of the law was broken by government agencies. Justice for a black person is just about impossible." Her interest in the antiwar movement had been motivated after she attended the trial of the Baltimore Four, though her connection with the Catholic ultra-resistance was only marginal. "I did just one action with them. It was the right thing to do at the time and I'm glad I did it."[8]

On May 24, one week after the Catonsville raid, Phil, Lewis, Eberhardt, and Mengel came before Judge Edward Northrop for sentencing for their earlier foray into the Baltimore Customs House draft board. Press accounts reported that almost 180 people jammed the courtroom, many of them nuns and priests. Fred Weisgal, their lead defense attorney, called several character witnesses, among them William Carter, the local black civil rights leader and head of Baltimore Model Cities, who called the four men "almost kingly" and likened them to Jesus. Others referred to the beliefs that had motivated them. Then U.S. Attorney Sachs rose and asked the judge to note that Berrigan and Lewis had committed a crime at Catonsville just seven days before.

Sentenced to prison, the felons were handcuffed and surrounded by court officers and marshals and moved toward the exit, when slowly a murmur began, mounting to a roar as spectators stood in respect for the four invaders. Afterward questions were raised. Was there no alternative to jail? No other way the government could reinforce its authority other than dispatching four otherwise peaceful souls into the misery of federal penitentiaries? But this was 1968, and someone had to pay for the collapse of "law and order"—be they draftees, college students, Dr. Spock, or the Baltimore Four.

On October 3, four days before the trial of the Catonsville raiders was to open, Selective Service announced that its December quota was 17,500 men, the highest number for the past four months. The very next day, George Wallace, running for the presidency on the American Independence Party ticket, announced that his running mate was retired general Curtis LeMay, former air force chief of staff. At the press conference declaring his candidacy, LeMay said that while he wouldn't use nuclear bombs "unless we have to," he didn't think "the world will end if we explode a nuclear weapon." And by now, another significant element was added to the mix: The Catholic Left and the secular antiwar movement had more or less converged, each with its own agenda but both with the identical aim of crippling the war effort.

On October 7, 1968, it was the turn of the Catonsville offenders. The trial in U.S. District Court was presided over by Judge Roszel Thomsen in the Federal Court House and Post Office Building on Calvert Street in Baltimore. In the short span of four days it became one of the more bizarre trials in American political history. In a country crackling with furious protests and counterprotests, the trial was remarkably thoughtful and orderly.

Outside the courtroom, 200 helmeted police armed with riot-prevention equipment surveilled 1,500 people (or 5,000, depending on who was estimating) who linked arms and paraded down Baltimore's streets, chanting "Free the Nine." Federal marshals patrolled the courthouse, and local police in black jackets held the leashes of their German shepherd dogs as they guarded a war memorial. A small army of American and foreign journalists and television reporters and cameras jammed Calvert Street. Some 600 students had come down from Cornell in support of Dan, many sporting "Free the 9" and "End the War" buttons. Everywhere there were placards and pins for every cause: farm workers, Guatemala, feminism, homosexuals, civil rights. Confronting them behind police barricades were a handful of counterdemonstrators who carried their own signs: "We Want Dead Reds," "Kill the Vietcong"; one placard was adorned with a communist hammer and sickle and a man wearing a Jewish Star of David and bearing the phrase "Peace Creeps Go Home." A local member of the extremist National States Rights Party showed up and wrestled a red flag from a peacenik.

Mayer, O'Connor, and local journalist Grenville Whitman persuaded the sympathetic Father J. William Michelman, a dedicated antiwar Jesuit and pastor of St. Ignatius Roman Catholic Church on North Calvert Street, to set aside its cavernous hall (out of "Christian charity and hospitality," said Father Michelman) for the hundreds of religious and secular leftists gathered there each day to listen to rousing speeches from the stars of the movement: Dorothy Day, Noam Chomsky, I.F. Stone, Robert Bly, Abraham Joshua Heschel, Harvey Cox, and a host of others. Dorothy Day announced her support but also cautioned the crowd against abetting violence of any sort, including violence against property. Others compared the break-in to liberation movements elsewhere and to the past, often calling on biblical themes and American history for substantiation. Jim Douglass, studying for his doctorate at the prestigious Catholic Gregorian Pontifical University in Rome and teaching religion at the University of Hawaii, was there, too, having flown in from Honolulu. "How to believe in the good news of men and women burning paper rather than children?" he asked. "What does one do with the Gospel when it comes to the front door? Have a chair, Phil. Sit down, Dan. Sorry, we've just been to Catonsville, on our way to jail now. See you there?" Though he originally had "real reservations about draft-card burning," Catonsville, he decided, could only be compared favorably to Jesus in the Temple and Gandhi's march to the sea, "a symbolic communion with . . . burning people, a homeless people, a crater-pocked land with napalmed children."[9]

Lutheran minister Richard John Neuhaus of CALCAV (years later he became a Roman Catholic priest) denounced the government and the Johnson Administration for "selling out the American dream of liberty for the mailed fist of repression." Dan's good friend William Stringfellow, the religious philosopher and attorney, was there, too, walking slowly with a cane, an "elegant skeleton." Slowly, in obvious pain, he mounted the rostrum and shouted, "Death shall have no dominion!" and then departed as inconspicuously as he had arrived.[10]

Suddenly, some men entered the basement shouting that peace people were being bitten by dogs and carried off to jail at a Wallace rally elsewhere in the city. Francine du Plessix Gray was there and recorded the dramatic scene as many made ready to leave and take on the cops and Wallaceites.

"George Mische grabbed the microphone and ordered the kids to cool it. 'We must abstain from violence at all times!' he shouted in a commanding voice. 'If you go out and call Wallace and the cops a bunch of pigs you're playing their game!' And then he added, threatening, magnificent, 'You'll go to that rally over the bodies of the Catonsville Nine.' "[11]

Later that week, in St. Ignatius Church Hall, Dean Pappas chaired a meeting (as an FBI informant reported) "until a fever pitch was reached. . . . At about 9:00 p.m. there was wild stamping of feet and shouting as numerous young men burned what were purported to be draft cards. As each card burned there was much spirited cheering . . . Some of the girls present appeared to be near hysteria."[12]

Draft cards were burned, twenty-seven on one night in St. Ignatius. Incredibly, two protesters were allowed to bring a cardboard coffin into the vestibule of the U.S. Customs House and to enter the very draft board office the Baltimore Four had attacked a year earlier and tell the Women's Army Corps officer present that the coffin depicted the dead of Vietnam and that all draft board employees were answerable for the deaths.

Inside the church and on the adjoining streets, there were both celebration and bedlam, an explosion of anger at the government and the war, and a very political, if inchoate, Woodstock. The reverberations of the Second Vatican Council and the civil rights and antiwar movements were all at the point of merging in their larger themes, and the trial was a watershed. To those men and women of religious faith, the raid and pending trial was a revelation and affirmation of their beliefs. For those who despised the war and warmakers, it was possible that never again would they experience the exhilaration, the sense of community, the solemnization and buoyancy of those few days.

"On the opening day of the trial," said Pappas (who, with forty others, had once picketed the home of the hawkish Walt Rostow and was under the FBI's constant surveillance) of the Baltimore Defense Committee, "I'll never forget it, we marched down Howard Street. There were 2,000 people—the biggest local march we'd had on the war."[13]

Judge Thomsen was no right-wing ideologue eager to mete out draconian punishment. A war veteran and a much-admired jurist in moderate liberal and conservative circles, as a Baltimore school board member he had helped end school segregation in 1952, before the Supreme Court's famous 1954 desegregation ruling. Afterward, as a judge, he declared that school segregation was illegal in Maryland. He also demanded reforms in Baltimore's police department and in the state prisons.

At the trial, he promptly ruled out the "justification" defense— which allowed defendants to speak to the court and jury about their motives; the charge, he repeated over and over, was that they had willfully destroyed government property and impeded Selective Service, charges the Nine gladly conceded—but he allowed them to speak out about their lives and rationale as an all-white jury listened. Stephen Sachs later said he thought that the judge was fascinated by the Nine, so different from the usual defendants in his court. "They were zealous, to be sure. . . . But Thomsen was intellectually engaged, more intellectually engaged than Northrop."[14]

Phil began, talking about his past life and military experiences in the Second World War. Catonsville, he said, was a way of anointing the draft files with Christian symbols of blood and fire. "As a Christian I must start from the basic assumption that the war is immoral." Thomas Melville said he wanted to "bring attention" to Guatemala *and* to Vietnam. Mary Moylan told the court, "We have to celebrate life. We have to learn not to engage in the dance of death that we are involved in." And the rights of property? "The only sacred thing is the life of people. Some property has no right to exist."

Dan took the stand, dressed in his priestly black suit and collar. Looking solemn, he proceeded to talk about his past, and how, after his return to Syracuse from exile in Latin America, he had learned to his horror that a teenage boy had entered a Catholic church, soaked his body with gasoline, and set fire to himself. When he visited the boy in the hospital, he "understood what I had seen in other ways in North Vietnam. The boy was lying in total torment upon his bed, and his body looked like a piece of meat that had been cast upon a grill. He died very shortly thereafter. . . . So I went to Catonsville. And I burned some paper because I was trying to say that the burning of children was inhuman and unbearable."

The prosecutor jumped to his feet. "Now Your Honor," but then stopped, sat down, and in an exasperated tone said, "Oh, go ahead," waving his hand.

Dan's lawyer asked about Catonsville.

" . . . I did not wish that any innocent people should be subject to death by fire, I did not wish that my flag be dishonored by my military and by my men of power and by my President." He said this slowly, in obvious fury, taut in the witness seat, his body stiff, pointing ahead, straining, "his gaunt face as grim and condemning as that of a medieval inquisitor," noted one observer.

"I did not wish that the American flag be steeped in the blood of the innocent across the world. . . . I was trying to be concrete about death, as I have tried to be concrete about the existence of God . . . and about Whom I read in my Testament."

When his Cornell colleague and lawyer Harrop Freeman asked him about the Jesuits, his manner lightened and he sat up straight. A group of them had only recently formed a support group because "Our Brother Is in Need."

"I ask you, Daniel Berrigan, was what you did on May 17,

1968, at Catonsville, carrying out that philosophy of the Jesuit order?"

Dan, the Catholic priest, and Harrop, the Quaker law professor, stared silently at each other.

"May I say that if that is not accepted as a substantial part of my action," replied Dan, "then the action is eviscerated of all meaning; and I should be committed for insanity."[15]

Then, incredibly, unexpectedly, with a great sense of melodrama, he asked Judge Thomsen if he would permit a recital of the Lord's Prayer. The judge was so startled that he turned to Sachs and asked if that would be acceptable. "To his eternal credit"—as defense lawyer William Kunstler put it—Sachs said he had no objection. Everyone rose, defendants, lawyers, judge, prosecutors, clerks, jury, and court officers and spectators, and recited the prayer. Had it ever happened before in a criminal case?[16]

For Harvey Cox, a Catonsville sympathizer and Harvard Divinity School professor, an amazing and wondrous scene was unfolding before his eyes—"a Pentecostal Moment." As the sacred words echoed through the austere room, "women sobbed, United States marshals bowed their heads and wiped their eyes, jurors and prosecuting attorneys mumbled ' . . . forgive us our trespasses as we forgive those' . . . City police, bearded peace workers, nuns, and court stenographers prayed together: 'For thine is the Kingdom and the Power and the Glory.'"[17]

"Suspend their sentences," pleaded Kunstler, after they were found guilty, "not because they are good and noble people . . . but solely because such an act on your part could affect the lives of your own grandsons as well as those of countless men, women and children in such separated places as Chicago, Guatemala City, Saigon and Hanoi."

"None of you has shown any remorse for your illegal act," Judge Thomsen told the Nine at sentencing. "Liberty cannot exist unless it is restrained and restricted," and he reminded them that change within the American political system is possible. "I can understand how you feel," he told the defendants. "I think the only difference between us is that I believe the institutions can do what you believe they cannot do."

Phil and Tom Lewis received three and a half years each to run concurrently with their six-year sentence for the Baltimore raid and were remanded to prison for another six weeks until Judge Thomsen granted them bail. The others were immediately freed on bail, pending their appeals. Dan, Thomas Melville, and Mische were given three years, and Darst, Hogan, Marjorie Melville, and Moylan, two years.

"I think we can agree," said Dan emerging from the courthouse to a group of applauding supporters, "that this was the greatest day of our lives."

After the jury's verdict, an FBI informant returned to St. Ignatius to observe 200 or so "sad, dirty-looking hippies" who had flocked to the Baltimore Defense Committee's final session. There were calls to "resist" but, reported the anonymous chronicler, "an air of depression hung over the hall."[18]

From his jail cell, Phil treated both the raids and trials and imprisonment as an act of Christian witness, a form of resistance and suffering of the prophets, Jesus, and the early Christians. "That's redemptive," he remarked, "and slowly, imperceptibly it turns people *if* they want it." Catonsville was rooted in "truth and love and justice. That is to say—about life."[19]

The Josephites quickly suspended his priestly functions at St. Peter Claver, yet an empathetic Father O'Dea handed him $1,000 toward his bail money and pledged another thousand, gifts from the Josephites. They also gave him the room on the top floor of their North Calvert Street house in Baltimore, so he might work on his federal appeal and prepare for a forthcoming state trial for the identical offense. He could, of course, come and go as he pleased, and they loaned him a Volkswagen, which he used for trips to gather more recruits for more raids.[20]

As always, Freda Berrigan backed her boys, as did Jerry. But not all her sons agreed.

Brother John was fifty-seven years old, unmarried, living a solitary life as a security guard in Minnesota, and also working during the summer on ore boats plying the Great Lakes. "I don't go along with all this destroying draft records and all the stuff that they've done. When they started out, they were conscientious priests. We were all proud of them. Now they're breaking the law by destroy-ing property. What they are doing is against the best interests of the United States." He even wrote a letter to the *Minneapolis Tribune:* "Who do they think they are to take the law into their own hands?"

Another Berrigan, Thomas, age fifty-nine, a combat veteran of World War II who earned a battlefield commission, pictured at the time as "a strong, wiry man with blue eyes, white hair and a bushy white mustache" labored in the identical Babbitt mine in Min-nesota where Dado, old Tom Berrigan, once worked. "There is a great block between us [Dan and Phil]. . . . With them, everything is so one-sided. They talk only of the terrible things they claim our government has done. There's never a word about the treachery and brutality of the Communists."[21]

Like Dorothy Day's army Ranger grandson in Vietnam, and Liz McAlister's career army officer brother-in-law, Tom Berrigan's son—Dan and Phil's nephew—had served two hitches in Vietnam as a marine. Yet another brother, James, was a civilian engineer in Vietnam, and his son was a helicopter pilot attached to NATO.

The irony was there for all to see: members of the Berrigan fam-ily in the military; prominent hawks' families safe at home.

In the end, however, nothing mattered more to Dan than Merton's opinion.[22]

For Merton, patience and compassion were the hallmarks of Christian nonviolence. "Without compassion," Jim Forest, one of his biographers, said, Merton believed "the protester tends to become more and more centered in anger and may easily become an obstacle to changing the attitudes of others," the identical point Day and Zahn were making.

In one of his final articles before his premature death, Merton laid out what could be interpreted as a personal testament of sorts. The Nine had accepted their inevitable punishment as a redemptive act "for the sin and injustice" they were protesting. The Berrigans might have a "jail mystique," but most Americans seemed to prefer "war and profits" to "peace and problems . . . And there is a certain indecency involved when Christians, even prelates, canonize this unpleasant fact by saying that the war in Vietnam is an act of Christian love." It is no surprise, then, that men and women of conscience and high moral principle are driven to extreme acts. Calling the raid a "prophetic nonviolent provocation," he nonetheless expressed concern that elements of the antiwar movement were moving too close to actual violence, though not—he took pains to emphasize explicitly—the Catonsville Nine. Even so, while he saw American foreign policy as morally tainted and driven, indeed, beholden to "big money," he still thought the raid "bordered on violence."

In fact, he went on, the Catonsville raid "frightened more than edified" since Americans were nervous, tense, utterly unsettled, even feeling imperiled, given the war, the demonstrations for and against the war, the swift and indigestible new styles of life, and the killing of Martin Luther King Jr. and Robert Kennedy. "There is then a real fear," he warned, "a deep ambivalence about our very existence" and thus the "use of nonviolence has to be extremely careful and clear," respecting just laws so as to stress the unjust. "But if nonviolence merely says in a very loud voice 'I don't like this damn law,' it does not do much to make the adversary confess that the law is wrong." Instead, opponents see such actions as revolutionary and zealotry, all very menacing to them. The unjustified draft, not the protesters' beliefs, was what counted. And as his ultimate bequest, Merton left these familiar phrases to his admirers and future generations: "What is truth?" "The truth shall make you free." "It seems to me that this is what really matters. If this is so, nonviolence is not a tactic you use one time and abandon the next. It is for keeps."[23]

On June 24, Merton wrote that, while "I don't agree with their methods of action . . . I can understand the desperation which prompts them. They believe they have to witness *in jail* to the injustice of the war. That is their business. It is certainly not a necessary teaching of the Church."[24]

Fluctuating between optimism and pessimism, and changing opinions at times, he was also quoted in an advertisement sponsored by the Catonsville Defense Committee, which claimed the raiders were "in essence, nonviolent." He compared his dismay expressed after the raid (the raiders were "in essence nonviolent") with the absence of "any shock at all when a Catholic bishop had the droll effrontery to speak of the Vietnam War as an act of Christian love."[25]

The truth is that Merton was critical *and* supportive, troubled yet pleased, and understandably ambiguous. Still, when he learned of the six-year prison sentences meted out, he turned despondent. "*Six years!* . . . how long will I myself be out of jail . . . I haven't deliberately broken any laws. But one of these days I may find myself in a position where I will have to."[26]

Perhaps no public disputation was more painful and revealing of the early signs of strain within the religious left than the theologian Rosemary Ruether's serious and disparaging comments. Had Dan asked her to join the Catonsville raiders, she would have declined, she wrote in an open letter to the *National Catholic Review*, because she detected an emerging us-against-the-world mood, "a kind of sectarian ethos" that rejects people who also hate the war and draft but have other responses. In the end, she concluded, perhaps "you don't believe change is possible either by revolution or by progressive change. The alternative then becomes apocalypse, the counsel of despair."[27]

Two weeks later Dan replied. Neither he nor Phil nor any of the others wanted to isolate themselves or excommunicate their antagonists. Catonsville, he argued, was "a substantial act of hope." And more: "As I conclude these notes . . . my brother, priest and convicted malefactor, awaits transfer to a federal prison. He is refused bail; the prosecutor has named him a public menace. . . . No one of us remember when he did harm to any man. But a war which seemed, so short a time ago, a cloud no bigger than a man's hand, has all but engulfed us."[28]

In December 1968, word arrived that Merton was accidentally electrocuted by a defective fan in Bangkok, Thailand. Dan was in Ithaca, and when he heard the news he went as quickly as he could to Linda and Dan Finlay's home and there wept inconsolably for his dear friend and teacher. "He really was in anguish," said Linda, recalling that day. "He felt like Merton was the other part of him, that they'd been through so much together, that they'd helped each other stay priests." That night he said Mass and then canceled all his appointments.[29]

Ten months later news of another loss reached him. David Darst was dead, killed in a car crash in October 1969 as he was driving to visit fellow draft resisters. The young idealist, who once told an interviewer he was certain "that the way of civil disobedience, the way of suffering love, the way of Gandhi and people like James Douglass, is the only hope left for peace among people," was gone. Dan and Phil were both deeply affected by his premature death.

"David Darst burned draft files," said a grieving Dan. "David Darst died by fire. Who let the symbol loose? Didn't they know that fire is a wild fire, a raving beast? Cold comfort. Burning the papers at Catonsville, burned to death on the road. On his way to visit prisoners of conscience in jail. Someone pushed his own words in his face, a burning brand. And he died of it. Listen: *It is better to burn papers than children; it is better to die by fire than to kill by fire.*"[30]

It is possible that the Catonsville raid and trial might have faded into obscurity had not Dan written his own impressive account of what transpired in that courtroom. He had returned to Cornell, weary of being a public figure, exhausted by the media and legal circus, and tried to "cool down" and write and pray.[31] It took him a while, but in the summer of 1969, he finished a play describing the trial and its implications. First produced in 1970, it may well become his best-remembered work, echoing in part the theme of Robert Bolt's play *A Man for All Seasons*, which centered on the fatal clash between Henry VIII and Sir Thomas More, his lord chancellor, over religious faith and politics and conscience. Dan's script exhibited all the tension that marks successful courtroom dramas and was stamped by Dan's remark to the court: "You cannot set up a court in the Kingdom of the Blind, to condemn those who see."[32]

Jim Finn, a onetime *Commonweal* and *Worldview* editor, who still admires Dan's "integrity and consistency," though not his politics, thought the play was proof of Dan's "moral arrogance, of self-righteousness that I have always liked in Berrigan. Here is no Uriah

Heep saying he did the best he could, pleading his sincerity and hoping for leniency. No. His is a voice which calls down thunder and lightning, his is the voice of judgment, and the judge is in the dock. And so too are those of us who stand with the judge."[33]

Dan's refuge was his poetry, but poetry that was becoming ever more political and angrier. And the more enraged he became, the more acrimonious his poetry. After Catonsville, he dedicated to Dorothy Day a poem about John Urey, a pseudonymous Catholic priest, possibly from Ireland (no one knows), who in the years before the American Revolution worked to rescue runaway slaves, and whose trial, execution, and final disposition was never recorded. Dan's poignant poem—tendentious to be sure ("I hoped to link our fate with his, even though we had not been tested as he was, or shown his degree of courage—and yes, willingness to defy the established 'law and order' and the 'traditions of his day,'" he told Robert Coles)—was so fervently personal that the pictures it paints calls out to the reader in describing how, "in the Manhattan sty . . . [Urey] ministered to slaves by night."

> . . . I think of John Urey . . .
> Wherefore, John Urey, make common cause with us
> indicted felons, for pouring blood and fire
> on murderous licenses;
> lead into court by hand the Great Society's dawn catch; the
>   dying
> children; burned, blinded
> in Washington rose gardens;
> give evidence upon that power
> wasted like seed or life blood
> on whoring and butchery. . . .[34]

And more outrage in "The Verdict":

> . . . *Everything else*
> *Is a great lie* Four walls, home, love, youth
> truth untried, all, all is a great lie.
> The truth

The judge shuts in his two eyes.
Come Jesuit, the university cannot
No nor the universe, nor murdered Jesus
Imagine. Imagine! Everything before
was a great lie.[35]

Give this much to Dan Berrigan. While he could admit, "I may not be without blame," obviously referring to himself and Phil, he could just as blithely add, "even though we may be wrong, where we are is right. I'm not interested in this or that issue being right. I'm interested in being in the right place when Christ returns." Pretentious and overbearing perhaps, and to some incensed critics a mark of an imperious nature, it was precisely the way he and Phil chose to live.

Free on bail, Dan traveled to Rochester to testify on behalf of Pat Farren, a former Peace Corps volunteer in the Ivory Coast, a life-long pacifist who was living and working at a Catholic Worker house his parents had helped establish. Farren had refused induction and been arrested. Trying to trap Dan, the prosecutor asked whether he had encouraged Farren to accept his legal responsibility of serving as a draftee.

DAN: "I would no more say that to a young man than tell him to go and burn draft files."
PROSECUTOR: "You told him not to serve?"
DAN: "I told him not to do anything—I told him nothing. I listened to him and read the gospel with him and encouraged him to be a Christian."[36]

Back at Cornell, Dan was unaware that Phil was disturbed by his return to bucolic Ithaca. Yet there Dan, not Phil, was the hero. His friends and colleagues had drawn up a petition with 1,400 signatures, urging the university to reinstate him despite his conviction. The university agreed, announcing that Catonsville was his personal affair "not involving" the school, and he could return to his job. "I feel relieved," said Dan on hearing the news, for "Catonsville was my way of striving to speak to the Cornell community. I wished, by placing my future in jeopardy, to raise questions connected with the very existence of the university."[37]

On April 9, 1970, their appeals denied, Hogan and Lewis surrendered to begin their prison sentences. Mische wanted to go on resisting but was picked up by Chicago police on May 16, almost two years after Catonsville.

The Melvilles were granted ten extra days to complete exams for their master's degrees at American University in Washington before turning themselves in. When they did, Marjorie's sentence was reduced to one year. "We took our final exam and went to prison," she said. "Civil disobedience is civil disobedience," she explained later. "You take what the law says. That's a major principle."[38]

Phil, joined by David Eberhardt, disappeared for ten days, as did Dan, who led government agents on a wild chase for four months before his capture in August 1970. And Mary Moylan, dying her red hair black, evaded capture for a decade until she finally surrendered in 1978.

Twenty-five years after the bonfire in the Catonsville parking lot, in 1993, six of the Nine, now well into and past middle age, came together again for the first time at a reunion at Goucher College in Baltimore.

Phil was there, for once not in prison for one of his innumerable Plowshares actions against nuclear missile sites, saying, "I don't have any second thoughts. I can't think of a better way to spend my life. I am not a martyr; I just found this the best course to follow." And Dan: "Things are worse than ever. There is no letup in the military under President Clinton. There is nothing for the poor."

Thomas Melville, now a cultural anthropologist in California, is still engaged in protests but not civil disobedience. Marjorie Melville was working at a California university and could not attend. Lewis carries on his artistic career and works with the very poor in Worcester, Massachusetts. John Hogan is a carpenter working for the city of New Haven. George Mische came, too, though not Mary Moylan, now jobless and near-blind (she died soon after); the organizers (not the Nine) said they couldn't locate her, though she lived in Asbury Park, New Jersey. Mische was now a labor organizer. Between 1986 and 1990 he was elected to the city council of St. Cloud, Minnesota.

Looking back, was Catonsville worth prison? Lewis said that while it wasn't backed by the entire peace movement, it was, however, morally right. Mische agreed. "People in power [in the future] who send military excursions abroad will have to realize that it won't be easy." Tom Melville said that "there's no way of telling whether it was worth it or not [but] we could not do otherwise . . . We could not *not* go and live with ourselves." And, as always, Dan seemed to have the last word, since for him the issue was basically the church. The contemporary Catholic Church, he admitted, was vastly different from the one he and the others fought so bitterly, "much more thoughtful on the idea of war. The whole atmosphere of the Catholic Church has changed."[39]

David Eberhardt, poet and former Baltimore Four raider, also present, overheard complaints about the Berrigans and once again about how the Catonsville Nine had been transformed into the Catonsville Two. Critics also saw "Phil as stuck in a mode of [Plowshares] protest that was not drawing in new adherents or building a mass movement." Eberhardt once again came to his defense, uncomfortable with the criticism and insisting that Phil had kept a "poetic flame alive" and that organizing a large following was not his style.

Eberhardt, ever reflective and introspective, thought: "Wasn't there room enough for George's [Mische] labor organizing, Brendan's [Walsh] Catholic Worker soup kitchen work, my work with [prison] offenders, Tom Melville's teaching as well as Phil's Plowshares actions?"

Seven men and two women, all but forgotten by a new generation, had raised the ante and posed thorny questions that are far from resolved. When is military intervention, governmental deceit, a nuclear first strike, or the overwhelming power of the state over individual rights justified, if at all? To what extent can American citizens opposed to their country's wartime policies carry out political activities unhindered by state police agencies? Can ethical and religious concerns play a role in shaping foreign policy? Can the Nuremberg laws ever be applied to American military and political leaders who may be implicated in war crimes? To the extent that some of these are reasonable questions, then the Nine could rightly see themselves as absolved from blame. They had, after all, broken the law, and served their time. Those who had dreamed up the war and filled the earth with the dead, had not.

After the final panel discussion, several celebrants drove to the corporate headquarters of the huge defense contractor Martin Marietta and poured blood on the doors.

David Eberhardt was near Dan, then seventy-two, on that day looking frail and sick. "I stood alongside Dan behind a banner held up at the main entrance to the Marietta plant on Sunday and listened to a discussion he was having with a young demonstrator. The youngster asked after the Buddhist monk Thich Nhat Hanh, whose sweet voice, gentle manner and inner peace was deeply admired by many pacifists. 'What is he doing now?' Dan had been with him recently, and he described Thich's serene approach to peace, sitting in meditation and saying to a nearby tree which he was observing, 'That tree has just won the Nobel prize for peace. As a matter of fact,' Thich said, 'I've conferred the prize on the tree.'"

"That sounds like Zen," Eberhardt broke in.

"Well," Dan replied, an elfin smile crossing his face, "Thich is a Zen master."[40]

Soon after the raid, when Dan was in Syracuse for one of his ubiquitous speaking engagements, a woman in the audience rose and asked: "I'm from Catonsville, so I've been curious why you and the other eight chose Catonsville for your draft board raid."

Dan, ready as always with a quip, and simulating a Maryland drawl, answered, "Well, ma'am. It just seemed like such a purty li'l town."[41]

11

UNDERGROUND

America stop pushing I know what
    I'm doing.
America the plum blossoms are
    falling . . .
My mind is made up there's going to
    be trouble.

                  —*Allen Ginsberg*

AFTER CATONSVILLE, BESIDES HELPING ON HIS APPEAL, PHIL worked with Vincent McGee on *Prison Journals of a Priest Revolutionary*, and spent time at the Catholic Worker House in Baltimore and at the local seminaries, where he was less interested in recruiting new people than in trying to school them in the group's ideas. He also offered liturgies and sermons at local colleges and seminaries and visited every month with his mother, now old and weak, and a widow since the death of her husband in 1969, stopping at Ithaca to stay with Dan. Once he drove to Washington, D.C. to the Josephite seminary, where black seminarians were in a state of incipient revolt. "I had some talks with them about black identity, black rights, the role of black priests in a white church, and of course, peace." But at every stage of his travels, he would sit with "movement types passing through, some veterans of civil disobedience." Often he found them "embittered or confused or just broke." Defying the law had "cost them jobs, severe misunderstanding, alienation. Sometimes marriages were slipping because of the pressures [and] often too, faith had suffered, or politics had gone violent."[1]

Just before David Eberhardt fled to delay serving his sentence, he published a lengthy letter in the Baltimore weekly *Harry*. "I agree with Phil Berrigan who feels men and women of vision have a duty to risk jail." But, he asked, "Will the actions of the Baltimore 4, Catonsville 9, etc., a) feed the future? b) feed the future of world socialism? c) feed the hungry of the world?"

George Mische also fled, refusing to surrender while the war was still on, determined to go on organizing against the endless war. He was caught by heavily armed FBI agents almost a year later when they broke down his door and streamed in, weapons drawn, scaring his fellow diners. "I'm the one you want," he quietly told the invaders.

Mary Moylan, by now a convinced feminist, also vanished, not resurfacing until she surrendered in 1978, when there was "no point in being underground anymore."

Phil made one last trip to Syracuse to see Freda and Jerry and Carol, and then, on April 8, 1970, he and Eberhardt accepted an invitation to stay at a Catholic sisters retreat house in Sea Girt, New Jersey, where they were joined by John Peter Grady and Paul Mayer, and where they worked on their statement, explaining their position which would be distributed to the media, and contacted reporters at *Newsweek* and *Time* about an upcoming rally in a Manhattan church, after which they planned to surrender. Then he and Eberhardt drove to a suburban residence in northwest New Jersey, where they met briefly with Dan and Liz.[2]

Their fallback scheme centered on a preposterous escape plan that they could carry out *if* anything went wrong (otherwise they would surrender) at the rally scheduled for St. Gregory's Church on Manhattan's Upper West Side. The idea was to exit by a rear door while two pretenders served as decoys to draw off their pursuers. While the pretenders were nabbed, Phil and Eberhardt were supposed to jump a barbed-wire fence and a ten-foot cyclone fence (which would be cut by a Jesuit armed with a wire cutter), race across an uninhabited lot, then leap down into an adjoining alley-way where a getaway car would be standing by. The "Young Lords," a radical group of Puerto Rican New Yorkers, were also supposed to start a diversionary street fight while one Young Lord would stand watch from a second-floor fire escape. "Lollypop revolutionaries," sneered a radical who learned of the plan, laughing aloud.

The St. Gregory rally, "Up From Under," was widely publicized and was to be yet another show of resistance, a way of snubbing their noses at the feds. The church's pastor, Father Harry Browne, a historian of the church and labor history, had, said one clerical admirer, a logical and absorbing mind, in addition to being funny, flamboyant, and deeply involved in neighborhood issues. His congregation was split between older, conservative people, who marched before the church the day of the rally with signs reading "Give Us Back Our Church," side by side with Berrigan backers. Browne was impatient with the church's traditionalists. "Some of them think Christianity is a Rotary Club," he shot back. Still and all, Phil and Eberhardt's pending arrival was causing problems, and the church's parish council was called into emergency session. What to do with men running from the law? And one of them a priest? Pat Burke, a lawyer in his eighties, as uncomfortable with the religious left as he was with the innovations introduced since Vatican II, rose and declared, "Phil Berrigan is one of our own and he has a right to be here," stoutly holding on to tradition and helping turn the tide, even if he personally couldn't abide Phil's politics or presumed flight from justice.[3]

Phil and Eberhardt told Father Browne that they planned to give up, and Browne, with their knowledge and approval, arranged with one of his parishioners, an FBI agent, to have them picked up as they emerged from the church after the rally. But Dan had started making asses of scores of FBI agents at Cornell a few days earlier, escaping from a huge demonstration at Cornell inside a puppet figure. The night before, FBI agents broke into Liz's quarters looking for Dan, but she had spirited him away thirty minutes earlier and sent him to Upper Montclair, New Jersey, her hometown. That was too much, too humiliating, and orders arrived from Washington to grab the two men immediately and forget about waiting till the end of the rally. What was to prevent them from escaping?[4]

At 4 P.M. FBI agents entered the church and started searching while awaiting their New York supervisor. Father Browne and several priests stood helplessly as an unsuspecting Jesuit walked up with a wire cutter. "I'd like you to meet J. Edgar Hoover," said Father Tom Farrelly jokingly, silently trying to warn the bewildered Jesuit, unaware he was surrounded by federal agents.

The agents turned to rooms near Father Browne's suite while the priests sat, holding their collective breaths. As the agents burst into one room, Father Browne shouted at them, "Stop, I'm the pastor here."

It made no difference. The agents were under orders to capture the fugitives. They turned to a large closet that held clothing on one side and a partition on the other. They started calling out softly, "Father Dan, Father Phil, are you there?" Father Philip Murnion, a diocesan priest who worked at St. Gregory's, knew Phil and Eberhardt were hiding behind the partition and was relieved when the agents found nothing and started to leave. Suddenly, one agent, still suspicious, spun around and opened the partition. "Here they are!" he yelled, shoving both men against a wall, frisking them for guns, and handcuffing them. As Father Browne burst into tears, Eberhardt, ever the gentle poet, turned to his captors and quietly asked, "Now what do you think about the Vietnam War?"[5]

The FBI's wrath then turned on St. Gregory's nonclerical administrator who was summoned to testify before a grand jury but pleaded the First Amendment and the Fifth Amendment to queries about whether he had given sanctuary to criminals. Federal prosecutors were just fishing in their high-priority hunt for Dan, their primary target. Father Browne was also summoned, but he declined to testify and instead wrote about the escapade in an open letter to Attorney General John Mitchell in his church bulletin:

"Please believe me, no one here at St. Gregory's knows the where-abouts of our beloved brother, Father Daniel Berrigan, and we are not impressed or overly frightened by the harassment from your trench-coated junior accountants." Denouncing his "ego-injured 'conspiracy' case," Browne taunted Mitchell, and by inference Hoover, who had ignored organized crime for decades, saying their time would be better spent "on Swiss Bank account cases, on the thieving of big business, and the really destructive conspiracy which allows heroin to flood our city."[6]

Just before he was to report to prison in April 1970, a few of Dan's friends threw Dan a farewell party in his $25 a month studio apart-ment. The FBI had been all over the campus questioning Dan's friends at Cornell "trying to get something sexual on me. It was," Dan said with annoyance, "so malodorous."[7] Toward the end of the evening, Jim Matlack was asked to pick up Dan and drive him to a parking lot opposite the gorge, though he had no idea Dan was going underground. When they pulled up, another car was waiting, and Dan, whether by plan or impulse (probably a bit of both), entered the second auto and vanished. He spent the first night in a rented Ithaca apartment and thereafter, for four months, from April 9 to August 10, moving from place to place, appearing and reap-pearing in publications, on television, and in person, further inflam-ing Hoover and frustrating his agents. "I wasn't avoiding punish-ment," Dan later explained, "just delaying it and protesting the war." He had with him a copy of Eberhard Bethge's *Dietrich Bon-hoeffer*, a hefty 867-page volume.[8]

On April 17 a massive crowd, variously estimated at 10,000 to 15,000 by the university's security police and local newspaper, gathered in Cornell's cavernous Barton Hall to celebrate Dan and "the spirit of militant nonviolence" at an "America Is Hard to Find" interfaith festival, the title taken from Dan's poem of the same name. Howard Zinn and Paul Goodman were there, along with Harvey Cox, Arthur Waskow, Leslie Fiedler, David Dellinger, John Cage, and Dr. Howard Levy. (Levy was the army physician who would not teach Green Berets heading for Vietnam, for which he received a three-year sentence in June 1967. At his court-martial Levy declared, very much in the spirit of the times, "It was just a prostitution of medicine. The medical art of healing was becoming the handmaiden of political objectives.") Also present were entertainers Country Joe and the Fish, Jerry Jeff Walker, Phil Ochs, Barbara Dane, and the Bread and Puppet Theater.

Matlack emceed most of the event while dozens of FBI agents swarmed through the arena, since it was widely rumored that Dan would make an appearance. Arthur Waskow, an advocate of Jewish religious renewal, flew in to help conduct his "Freedom Seder," an untraditional rendering of the Passover Haggadah.[9] Waskow was asked to drive to Lake Cayuga, away from FBI "bugs," where he was asked—hypothetically, they insisted—what if one of the Berrigan brothers came to the seder after Waskow recited, "Let all who are in need, let all who are hungry enter." Waskow backed away, uncomfortable with associating the Berrigans or any one else with Elijah the Prophet. Still, the show was also publicized as an interfaith happening, and unknown to Waskow, the Bread and Puppet Theater performers were to do a mime of Jesus and the Twelve Disciples at the Last Supper, suggesting—to an increasingly discomfited Waskow—that the Last Supper was merely a culmination of the seder. "Not in our tradition," replied the astonished Waskow.[10]

The seder proceeded. Someone read the portion about Elijah, the lights dimmed, the Bread and Puppet performers came on stage, and Mackendrie Spring, a rock band, began playing. By arrangement, Dan appeared on stage wearing a seven-foot costume, enveloped in a large burlap bag topped off with a papier-mâché head depicting one of the Twelve Disciples. He then left the stage, saying, "I have to go to the toilet." An FBI agent, recognizing the disguise, ran up to a faculty member standing nearby and demanded, "Where is he? Where is he? You know where he is!"

After Dan left, a student spontaneously raised his draft card and set it afire, and others followed suit. In the darkened arena, where Cornell's "Big Red" basketball teams played and ROTC units drilled, Matlack looked about the auditorium lit by candles held aloft by sympathizers. "It was an enormous, powerful, deeply inspiring event for what was going to be a long struggle."[11]

Accompanied by two allies, Dan walked quickly if awkwardly out the rear door and into a panel truck. Bob Fitch, a writer-photographer, tagged along, barely managing to reach the truck when someone inside yelled, "Hit it!" They drove for thirty minutes to an empty cabin. The next morning they moved on to a farmhouse. Another time he returned to Ithaca, where he stayed overnight in the attic of sympathizers. They then drove to their next hideout. "Dan, in his frumpy jacket, with a knit sailor cap flapping on top of his head, was the most suspicious-looking fugitive in disguise, particularly when he wore his bug-eye wire-rimmed sunglasses in dark roadside cafes," said Fitch.

They took a long, roundabout route to New Jersey. Fitch, who recorded the escapade with his camera, decided to leave, but not before he noticed Dan's shoes, so well-worn around the toes that he traded his good pair with the fugitive priest. When he returned home to Oakland, California, his wife put the damaged shoes on the mantel. "In one shoe there's a candle," wrote Fitch, "in the other a potted plant. Above them is a poster which reads: 'Thou Shalt Not Kill.'"[12]

"There is a mythology abroad in our country," wrote Dan early in his underground days, about "the moral necessity" of breaking unjust laws but then assuming the consequences; "otherwise, [the] act is necessarily tainted in the eyes of good men." This, he insisted, was simply another way of absolving the status quo and a "presumably beneficent public authority . . . If good men, acting in bad times on behalf of serious change," follow this line of reasoning, then "ethical men may, in such a way, even become a powerful support to an evil regime."[13]

Back in Ithaca, the FBI was more livid than ever, pressed hard by Hoover in Washington. Phones were indiscriminately and illegally tapped. People were followed, questioned, even threatened. Freda had broken her hip, and Dan bristled, remembering that agents had stood watch outside the operating room in the event her renegade son might decide to visit her. Dan and Linda Finlay, Dan's friends, were under constant surveillance, their phone conversations overheard. Finlay's mother was followed and his parents' bank assets were frozen for three days, because the FBI thought they might be funneling money to Dan. A onetime politician tried to befriend the

Finlays, visiting them, asking questions, and seemingly having all the time in the world. "That," says Dan Finlay, "was a sobering lesson in the importance of keeping your mouth shut." When they retrieved their FBI file under the Freedom of Information Act years after, it noted this about the experience: "Nothing of real interest learned from the Finlays." And when the Matlacks and another family sympathetic to Dan went coincidentally on separate vacations the same day, the local FBI wired Washington: "All six suspects left town on the same day and there's not enough manpower to follow them, but we're working on it."[14]

The hunt continued. *Commonweal* received a visit from the FBI, asking for its subscription lists. James O'Gara, the editor, turned them down. The agents then tried to intimidate him by threatening to return with a subpoena, but O'Gara stood his ground, telling them he'd never honor it. "Well, snapped one agent, "we'll see you in court." O'Gara shot back, "Then we'll get a lawyer and see you in court." He never heard from the FBI again.[15]

Dan popped up here and there. A friend saw him at a Holy Cross College alumni meeting.[16] In late July he met with Robert Coles, the psychiatrist and writer, and told him ("as he had on other occasions," noted Coles), "We are groping . . . We shouldn't be sure of ourselves, because we can't be, not now—not ever."[17]

He wrote a prose poem based on Dietrich Bonhoeffer's life for *Saturday Review*, and published his fourteenth volume, *Dark Night of Resistance*, a radical interpretation of "Dark Night of the Soul," by the sixteenth-century mystic St. John of the Cross. He delivered a sermon from hiding, describing his flight as a "metaphor for death itself," like prison, destitution, racism, severe infirmity, and sickness, "a kind of life outside the law, like 'Our Savior.' Death had no more dominion" over Jesus, who had chosen "to say no [and] put his life where his life should be," adding that, but for the war, he and Phil and the others would never have gone to Catonsville. And just as his pursuers had their reasons, so did they. "Their claim is declared null and void by Christ himself [and] we shall never obey them."[18] Paul Mayer says he even engineered an appearance on NBC-TV News for an interview with Edwin Newman in a Stamford, Connecticut, motel room.

Mayer, the former Benedictine monk and gifted organizer, had served as coordinator of the Catonsville defense committee, and was one of several people who helped find sympathetic yet unlikely people to harbor him: new people, not the usual movement ones, many of them Jewish, fearful but impelled by their consciences. From New England to the nation's capital, several hundred helped Dan elude the FBI. Called ahead on public phones, men and women—many of whom had no actual contact with the resistance or the Berrigans—were asked by activists if they would take a risk for peace and provide temporary sanctuary for the fugitive priest.

Mayer probably knew at times where Dan was hiding; most likely, so did Howard Zinn and a few others, though the FBI kept extremely close watch on them and tapped their phones.

Mayer arranged for safe houses, at times driving Dan around. On Philadelphia's mainline, William Davidon, a professor of physics at Haverford College, found havens for Dan in the homes of friends and arranged for a church in Germantown to have him deliver a sermon, the scene recorded by cameras. Accompanied by Mayer, Dan gave his sermon on August 2 at the First United Methodist Church (no Catholic church approached would let him speak) and asked the congregation: "Dear Friends, how do we translate in our lives the bombing of helpless cities? How do we translate in our lives the millions of Vietnamese peasants perishing . . . How do we translate to the truth of this morning's text the 50,000 children napalmed? How do we translate on this summer morning the 50,000 Americans dead? . . . There are a hundred ways of nonviolent resistance up to now untried or half-tried, or badly tried, but peace will not be won without . . . the moral equivalent of the loss and suffering and separation that the war itself is exacting."[19]

In Wilmington, Delaware, on August 7, his recorded remarks were delivered on Friday afternoon to hundreds gathered to celebrate raids on local draft boards two months earlier—tracked by the FBI, police in mufti, and photographers. "This is Father Daniel Berrigan speaking from the underground," he opened, and urged people who had taken personal and moral responsibility for the raids to remain "a community of resistance" since their fight to end the war brought on by "this misbegotten, war-ridden giant, America" shakes up the "chambers of American power . . . reflected, if only for a moment, in the ruthless faces of those men who sit in the cockpit of world power, who stamp upon others the stigma of criminality, whose exercise of power lies under no legal scrutiny, who hunt down good men, who police the wrong men, who are a law unto themselves, who decree—with an authority beyond question—who shall live and who shall die."[20]

Howard Zinn also helped hide Dan. After the St. Gregory Church rally he rented a car and drove to Dan's safe house in New Jersey (an FBI agent lived across the street) and found someone to take him to the Boston area, where he was sheltered by three Jewish families, all "very committed antiwar people," said Zinn. Never relying on his home phone, he and his wife Roslyn and "six or eight others" planned where Dan would stay the next night, when to move, when to stay, when to depart. His protectors were far more cautious than Dan. "We had to restrain him from taking walks along the Charles River, and going to films. Someone once suggested he wear a wig but when he tried it on he looked absurd. He didn't act like a hunted man. He certainly wasn't desperate."[21]

Mayer drove Dan to Point Judith, Rhode Island, to catch the ferry to Block Island, where Dan would stay, in disregard of the counsel of friends who thought it was a poor place to hide, with William Stringfellow, a lawyer and Episcopalian theologian, and the poet Anthony Towne, who had written a widely praised satire on the "death of God" craze. On the ferry, Mayer had Dan mask his identity by standing him alongside Naomi, Mayer's wife, and their infant son, Peter.

The house in which he would hide was owned by Stringfellow. He and Dan had been friendly for a few years, after Dan read his book, *My People Is the Enemy*, a moving interpretation of the seven years Stringfellow spent working as a lawyer on behalf of blacks and Hispanics in desperately poor East Harlem. They began to correspond, and later Dan visited the penthouse apartment Stringfellow and Towne rented in a neglected Upper West Side Manhattan apartment house. Their friendship blossomed, rooted in religious faith and their mutual adherence to the moral authority of nonviolence. At one point, the two men had talked about establishing an "underground seminary" or alternative community for the study of the Bible. Dan described their friendship this way: Stringfellow was a "staunch and taciturn friend, lawyer (though not in the pharisaic tradition), theologian (in the here and now tradition), harborer of criminals" and Towne as "Anthony, great bearded bear of man./At some point/he laid aside use, misuse, urban frenzies. follies, pride of place. Resolved like a Stonehenge circle, simply to be."[22]

The island was a joy to Dan, a place of rest and resurrection. There, on fourteen acres "sloping gently down and down like the domain of a land god, to the magnificent beatling cliffs," stood the odd-looking (to Dan, at least) main house—"maybe second-rate California cottage-cum-pretension."

Dan lived in a onetime one-horse stable, refurbished with bookcases and a large window that looked out on the fields and ocean beyond. Nights, the men engaged in leisurely conversations, while Fred, their Siamese cat, lay on Towne's lap. When they retired for the evening, the nocturnal Dan would go to work, writing, reading (including mysteries and Plato's account of the trial and execution of Socrates), or just watching old movies on television. So infatuated was he with films that, unrecognized, he visited the local movie house to see *Catch-22*, which he loved, and then *Patton*, Nixon's beloved film, trying to better understand that man in the White House. Days, he strode the bluffs and beaches in his bright yellow rain jacket, with Marmaduke, the pet Knickerbocker terrier, at his heels.

Until August 11. It was cloudy with the smell of a looming storm. Towne suddenly spotted someone wearing orange in the bushes. Dan was already up and about, out at the swimming pool in his shorts, shirt and a towel hanging from his neck. His suspicious hosts called him in. Towne's hands began shaking, and he poured himself a brandy. Dan refused a drink and went into the living room and sat down, waiting. It began raining hard and two cars roared into their driveway, while men came out of the bushes. Towne looked out and poured himself a second shot of brandy.

Dan rose, by now certain who the men were, and walked outside to be with Stringfellow, who had also spied a man in fluorescent orange, field glasses hanging from his neck, as if he were engaged in bird-watching.

The place was bustling with FBI agents. They were on and off-shore and closing in quickly.

"Who are you?" Stringfellow asked the man in the orange slicker.

"FBI," he answered. "Bird-watching."

"In a gale?"

"We're looking for Berrigan," he confessed, reaching for his identification.

The house was immediately surrounded. Dan's journey was over. "I suppose you're wondering who I am," he spoke up. "I am Daniel Berrigan." One of the capturing G-men mumbled aloud to himself, *"Ad majorem Dei gloriam"* ("For the greater glory of God"), the motto of the Society of Jesus. Ironically, the FBI had been inadvertently tipped off by one of Liz McAlister's intercepted letters to Phil in prison.

As Dan was manacled, Marmaduke, ignored by all, wandered about, carefully scrutinizing the tires of an FBI car, too distracted to bother with the inconsequential events around him. Satisfied, he dutifully lifted his leg. Towne, meanwhile, grabbed some of Dan's clothing, his watch, and his glasses, and handed them to him before he was shoved into a car. After the posse left, he also discovered a note Dan had left behind in the event of capture: "Call Jerry," his equally devoted brother who held both his and Phil's power of attorney. The next day, a photo flashed around the world depicting Dan in his yellow windbreaker, surrounded by agents, flashing his ironic, so Jesuitical, smile. One newspaper ran a headline: HE HID IN THE MANGER.

Stringfellow and Towne (though not Marmaduke) were soon indicted, charged with harboring Dan and accused of conspiring with the Catonsville Nine, allegations that were eventually dismissed. Calling their actions "Christian charity," the Right Reverend John Seville Higgins, Episcopal bishop of Rhode Island, defended the two. "Stringfellow and Towne," he declared, "were being hauled up for exercising Christian hospitality. I would have done the same thing if Berrigan came to me, even though I'm not necessarily one hundred percent behind the actions of the Fathers Berrigan, burning draft cards, all that sort of stuff."[23]

By 1980 Towne was dead, and Stringfellow decided to build an addition to his rambler house, overlooking the harbor near a cliff above the Atlantic, where Dan was welcome for the rest of his life. Dan, though, preferred a far smaller hermitage, and they were still discussing the project when Stringfellow died, five years later. At the funeral, Dan celebrated his life and death. "Well done good and faithful servant because you have been faithful over small matters. I shall place you over great ones."[24]

Stringfellow's will gave Dan lifetime use of somewhat more than an acre near the cliff, his for the remainder of his days. A small cottage was built, perched "at land's end, like an angelic sentinel. What was the cry of the landlocked and lost, as an epiphany opened before them? The sea, the sea!" There he lived and still lives whenever he withdraws to solitude, prayer, and reflection, lost in the changing face of the earth, sea, and sky.

Before dying, Stringfellow did one more favor for the man he so deeply respected, even loved, hiring a local gardener and carpenter, Jim Reale, to care for the cottage. Soon Dan and Jim became friends. Days, Dan often climbs down the cliff, spends the day walking and thinking, and then climbs back up and has dinner with the Reale family. In the 1980s Jim Reale linked up with Phil Berrigan's Plowshares movement and joined its Thames River Plowshares action.

The entire underground escapade was not without its bizarre moments. During the summer, Dan's onetime Cornell colleague and antiwar faculty member, Douglas Dowd, was invited to lecture in Sweden. Just before he and his wife departed for Stockholm, he met with a pair of nuns, one of whom was Sister Elizabeth McAlister, in Manhattan for a previously scheduled meeting to talk about

Dan's underground flight. Dowd said he asked "if they wouldn't like to have a couple of weeks respite at our nice place on Lake Cayuga, where they could also take care of Bianchino (our cat), the garbage, etc." Satisfied, the Dowds flew off to Sweden. On his return to Ithaca, Dowd was invited to deliver a lecture on economics at Bucknell University. The school was close by Lewisburg penitentiary, where Phil was incarcerated. Just before leaving Ithaca, he received a phone call from someone named Boyd Douglas, who asked to meet with him. Douglas said he was a fellow prisoner and friend of Phil's with special permission to study at Bucknell. He had seen an announcement of Dowd's coming lecture and had something crucial to tell him. When they met at an off-campus fraternity house, Dowd said Douglas told him, "Phil had convinced him that violent revolution was necessary." When Dowd objected that it didn't much sound like the Phil Berrigan he knew, Douglas ignored him and suggested "a series of violent actions."

Dowd dismissed him as a kook and forgot about it until early 1971. He was a visiting professor at the University of California at Berkeley, when two FBI men, carrying guns, suddenly leaped from an automobile and thrust a subpoena at him, ordering him to appear as a witness for the prosecution at the Harrisburg conspiracy trial, an indictment having been handed down a few days earlier by Attorney General John Mitchell, accusing Phil, Liz, and others of plotting to kidnap Henry Kissinger, among other allegations. That very evening, at an antiwar meeting at the University of San Francisco, Liz was present and her lawyer handed Dowd a copy of the *Saturday Evening Post*, which had printed one of her letters to Phil, composed after their meeting in Manhattan. "Evidently trying to perk up Phil's spirits," she had told him that Dowd was going to Sweden to raise $8 million for the movement and that she and another sister were driving to Kennedy Airport to see him "for instructions." "She didn't specify that the instructions were about a cat and garbage," noted Dowd.

And still another weird twist: "The man who arranged the Swedish trip told me that his brother had informed him that I had been trailed through Italy and Sweden, and when my friend asked his brother how *he* would know that, the latter was forced to tell my friend that he was secretly in the CIA," working in a publishing house.[25]

The war at home and abroad raged on. In February and March a wave of bombings occurred throughout the country, coupled with massive antidraft demonstrations on college and even some high school campuses. In late April 1970, President Nixon announced that American forces had bombed and invaded Cambodia, thereby enlarging the war. On May 4, 1970, Ohio National Guardsmen killed four Kent State University students, setting off huge protests across the United States. Ten days later, two Jackson State students were also killed and thirty were wounded, leading to even greater mass demonstrations throughout the country. Meanwhile, the Nixon White House made plans to win backing for the war by organizing "Americans for Winning the Peace." And that month, the Religious Heritage of America, a group "dedicated to preserving America's Judeo-Christian heritage," responded by honoring Richard M. Nixon as "Churchman of the Year."[26]

12

———

DRAFT BOARD RAIDS

> History cannot record that there was
> no resistance.
> *—Antiwar activist John Bach*

THE SUMMER AFTER THE CATONSVILLE BREAK-IN WAS SPENT planning new raids. "I remember driving . . . with Jim [Douglass]," said Jim Forest, "and just *reeling* from the impact of that sudden realization that this [Catonsville] was something which—at least in Dan's mind—deserved to be multiplied."[1]

That July, Forest and his wife, Linda, had visited Dan in Ithaca, where they found him very much at ease. He cooked dinner for the couple, after which they spent the evening drinking and sharing laughs and stories in a setting of warmth and conviviality. His ulcer, which had plagued him for months before Catonsville, had mysteriously vanished. "I am going to send the doctor bills to the White House," he said, chuckling. Forest, though, thought he sensed the subtle toll a life of rebellion had taken when Dan told them, in humor but probably half-seriously, "It's not the end, it's the beginning and the middle I find difficult." Some Jesuits still wanted to remove him from the order. And he fretted that, while many antiwar people were largely sympathetic to the raids, few were willing to assume the same risks he and a few others had taken.[2]

The next month, sixty ultra-resisters, still overwhelmingly Catholic and to a large extent nuns and priests, gathered on the grounds of the Benedictine Monastery in Newton, New Jersey, for a retreat to plan their next move. Dan and Phil and Liz were there, of course, along with George Mische; David Eberhardt; Dr. George McVey, the movement's dentist and the Berrigans' good friend; and Bill O'Connor, plus a host of friendly faces.

Paul Mayer ran the retreat, but it was Dan who set the tone. After hours of endless speeches, readings from the Scriptures and Revelations, and talk about the end of time, the theme that finally emerged was the "seriousness of the times, the destructiveness, the need for a community" of people willing to put themselves in jeopardy. "The upshot was that [we became] a more serious group about a particular action," said one participant, Father Bernard Meyer.[3] Before they departed, Michael Cullen, a twenty-six-year-old Irish-born noncitizen who arrived as a seminarian in the United States in 1961, spoke up. He had quit the seminary, founded the Casa Maria House of Hospitality in Milwaukee (a replica of the Catholic Worker houses of hospitality), and recruited people for another draft board bonfire, specifically a reprise of Catonsville in Milwaukee.

"The retreat was an incredible experience," said Cullen, "just beautiful. There was a great sense of joy and community, of working together." Dan Berrigan talked about the prophet Jeremiah and the need to be truthful and challenge evil. And then Mische offered an evaluation of political events.[4]

Father Jim Harney, age twenty-eight, who joined the group, was curate of St. Jerome Church in North Weymouth, Massachusetts (and a co-founder of the Baltimore Interfaith Peace Mission), serving the city's poor as part of Warwick House, a religious center run by priests in Roxbury, Massachusetts. Harney reached out to two brother priests, Fathers Robert Cunnane, age thirty-six, and

Antony Mullaney, age thirty-nine. A former parish priest, Cunnane was director of the Ecumenical Center in Stoughton and Roxbury, Massachusetts. Earlier, he had testified for the defense at the conspiracy trial of Michael Ferber, Mitchell Goodman, William Sloane Coffin, Marcus Raskin, and Benjamin Spock, and had collected discarded draft cards at the Arlington Street Church. Father Mullaney was a scholarly and soft-spoken Benedictine monk at St. Anselm's in Manchester, New Hampshire, who held a Ph.D. in psychology and been assigned to a church in the black ghetto of Roxbury.

If Cullen was the "heart" of the plot, then Forest was its "head." He was emboldened by his mentor, Dorothy Day, who praised Catonsville as "an act of liturgy . . . an act of prayer," saying her words left him "refreshed" and "challenged." And when he ran into Mische in Washington, the veteran of Catonsville had confronted him: "Well, Jim, are you going to be part of the next action?" To which Forest—twenty-six years old, a navy veteran who had been discharged as a conscientious objector, a Catholic Worker and co-chair of the Catholic Peace Fellowship—answered, "much to my astonishment," that he was ready.[5]

He and Dan drove to Milwaukee to meet with a few Franciscan nuns and afterward sat around discussing what might come next. "Out of that conversation," said Forest, "came the group that would become the Milwaukee 14."[6]

Others joined: Jerry Gardner, age twenty-four, Marquette University graduate and schoolteacher; Bob Graf, age twenty-four, a onetime Jesuit who worked at Casa Maria; Fred Ojile, age twenty-three, a graduate of Catholic University and a draft counselor; Brother Basil O'Leary, age forty-eight, a Notre Dame Ph.D., chair of the economics department and associate professor of theology at St. Mary's College; Father Larry Rosebaugh, age thirty-three, a member of the Religious Community of Oblates of Mary Immaculate, a group committed to helping the poor; Father Alfred Janicke, age thirty-three, a priest of the Archdiocese of St. Paul-Minneapolis; Don Cotton, age twenty-four, a graduate of St. Louis University, a Jesuit school, and former co-chair of its SDS chapter; and two non-Catholics, Reverend Jon Higginbotham, age twenty-seven, a

Scientologist; and Doug Marvy, age twenty-seven, a navy veteran, graduate student of mathematics and economics, and the sole Jewish member of the raiding party.

On a cool Tuesday evening on September 24, 1968, in downtown Milwaukee, while Phil was in prison and Dan in Ithaca, the Milwaukee Fourteen, as they came to be known, walked into an office building housing draft boards. A sixty-six-year-old cleaning woman tried to get them to leave. "You call yourself priests. You are a disgrace to the Catholic religion," she angrily shouted.

Another elderly woman spied the raiders and began shouting for help, at which point a few of the men tried to hold her, a clear violation of the principle of nonviolence. Shocked and ashamed, they fled earlier than planned, taking with them thousands of files, while leaving others. Outside, linking arms and singing "We Shall Overcome," they stood transfixed, staring at thousands of burning 1-A draft files. Like their predecessors in Baltimore and Catonsville, they relied on the identical rationalization, as they publicly explained their "crime."

"We use napalm and strike at the draft as a point of continuity in the nonviolent struggle recently carried forward in Maryland . . . last May, a community of nine burned the 1-A files in Catonsville. At that time they declared, as we declare today, 'Some property has no right to exist.' "

Now the Midwest had been hit and the conflagration was on the threshold of going national. The Fourteen's supporters handed statements to reporters from the Milwaukee *Journal* and *Sentinel* and weekly *Kaleidoscope* and briefed WTMJ-TV correspondents and cameramen, even telling them where the protesters could be found—a block away at the Brumder Building, waiting for the police to arrive.[7]

When Phil heard the news, he was ecstatic. To him, the two-party system was more than ever vacuous and impotent, torn between unbending hawks and fainthearted doves. Corporate liberalism, he believed, was comatose, unable to cope with its wars at home and abroad. The raid, he believed, now carried the fight to a higher plane.

The main event was the trial in May 1969 in Milwaukee's County Courthouse, an immense structure that reminded Mayer of the "bombastic, neo-Teutonic architecture" of Hitler's Reich, designed to reflect the new regime's authority. The prosecuting attorneys included a dovish Jew whose brother was a campus SDS leader; and a black civil rights advocate who also was opposed to the war. More than likely, they were deliberately selected because of their political beliefs, the better to persuade a jury and salve consciences. Both men were apparently personally appalled at their assigned roles, both were probably sympathetic to the defendants, and both resigned soon after the trial. At one point, the black prosecutor, after asking that the jury leave the room, told the judge, "It is impossible for the state represented by human beings to sit here any longer having it said that they believe in and of themselves that poverty and war are irrelevant. I just can't take it."

The central question (and the point the Fourteen's defense tried to make in every subsequent trial) came from a City University of New York scholar, John H.E. Fried. Citing the Nuremberg judgment that individuals' moral responsibilities surpass the duty of absolute allegiance to the state, Fried said, "Obedience to the higher, the world order, is more important." If, however, "such moral choice is in fact not possible for him, he will not be personally punishable for violating the international rule. But if he feels that he must make the choice even at personal risk, then he has to make the moral choice and do the things he considers morally proper. That is the great ethical and moral message of Nuremberg."[8]

A little more than an hour after they retired, the jurors returned with their verdict: All the defendants were guilty of burglary, arson, and theft. Then as the judge summarized the jury's findings and praised the jurors for a job well-done, the spectators exploded. "We thank you, men and women of the jury," roared a nun who herself would soon participate in an attack on the Washington offices of Dow Chemical, "for finding Jesus Christ guilty again!" A livid Paul Mayer, born Jewish in Germany, strode toward the Jewish prosecutor. Members of his own family had been killed by Hitler, he declared, and, looking straight at the shaken man, he told him that "this is how it began in Germany." Said Mayer afterward: "The district attorney turned visibly pale and his jaw dropped." As bailiffs dragged sympathizers gone limp out of the courtroom, the judge shrieked over the bedlam, "Good God," and called for more police. He then found three of the defendants guilty of contempt. "Judge, you just lost your authority, ," Father Harney cried out.[9]

Twenty-five years later, in 1993, much like the Catonsville raiders they imitated, the Milwaukee Fourteen came together again.

"I doubt if any of us had an ounce of sense as to what it would cost us—in energy, pain to family, pain of separation from spouses and loved ones," said Rosebaugh. Linda Henry, Forest's wife, had written movingly about her husband's incarceration, saying she detected personality changes in his correspondence: He "emerged not so much as politico as monk-poet, solitary, reflecting on life," writing during "bleak times . . . [of] famines of head and heart, whole hurricanes of void." He had, she thought, arrived at Merton's counsel of "balance" as opposed to an addiction to endless, mindless activism.[10]

"I'm not sorry we did it," said Forest, who has never abandoned his pacifist or religious principles. "We had wanted it to be a basically religious, liturgical act. It was. We had wanted it to reach a wide public. It did. We had wanted it to do something a little less symbolic than Catonsville; we wanted to take a whole city out of the draft. We did." And the lessons he learned? "Don't be bullied or manipulated or guilt tripped into obedience or disobedience. You have a conscience; learn to hear it; no one can hear it for you."[11]

Doug Marvy served fourteen months in prison. When he was released in late August 1970, he found the antiwar movement was radically different from the one he had known. He detected more factional infighting, shattered unity, and the powerful influence of feminism, which had driven many women away. Still and all, years later, Marvy ran into an old friend he hadn't seen since the fifties. After he told her what he had done in his life, she said, "God, you did all the right things."[12]

Though it was clearly inspired by Catonsville and the Berrigans, that impact of the Milwaukee action was felt in different ways throughout the movement. The "ultra-resistance"—a term coined by Francine du Plessix Gray—was about to dramatically step up its activities and draw in more people than simply estranged Catholics. Both secular and religious rebels were learning how to organize and agitate effectively and make publicity work for them; each was a corollary of the other even if the two segments of the resistance—and especially the Berrigans—had little contact with each other since the "revolutions" they were fighting for confronted an unbridgeable cultural and generational divide: one too often equating emancipation and peace with sexual and personal freedom, and the other (the Berrigans et al.) socially conservative, concentrating on a faith-based crusade.

"I believe in revolution," Phil wrote Forest at the time of the Baltimore raid in 1967, "and I hope to continue making a nonviolent contribution to it." Yet he also wrote Dan expressing a slightly different rationale: "The question is whether we are helping people get radical, whether we are content to stay small and do things . . . [or try to be] 'presentable' to large numbers of Catholics, and therefore morally neutral—or liberal—but not radical, not at the roots." The price to be paid was high, even for him: "jailings and the threat of jail to those we love [yet] the *equivalent risk* is going to be the only source of community worth talking about. And 'expressive' acts [like the Baltimore raid], once they are thoughtful and proceed from a sacrificing heart, must be multiplied. And that the masses may catch up as they wish, or not. But many will."[13]

Over the next three years, similar raids increasingly paralyzed Selective Service. In July 1969, five women broke into a draft board in Rockefeller Center, where they ripped up draft files. Calling themselves "Women Against Daddy Warbucks," they mailed pieces of the files to the head of Dow Chemical and to General Lewis Hershey, the Selective Service director, telling them they were holding in their hands a piece of someone's life. The fact that the raiders were female was deliberate. It was the first shot of the modern feminist antiwar movement. The women were never punished since investigators spent their time hunting for the men they believed had directed the women.[14]

People drawn to the movement were ready to undergo sacrifices. Certainly a prominent figure in the movement was John Peter Grady. Close to the Berrigans and a key player in the ultra-resistance and its draft board raids, Grady was a product of Catholic schools and Manhattan College. He was the recipient of a Fulbright Award, and subsequently taught sociology at Ithaca College. Phil described him as "quicksilver" because of his acumen, organizing skills, and fertile imagination. Grady met Phil after the publication of Phil's book *No More Strangers*. They became close, implicitly trusting each other. When Phil received a $1,000 advance against royalties for the book, he handed it to Grady, which helped pay for ten children's tuition in the Montessori school Grady and his wife had established. Grady found much to admire in the two priests. He liked their Irish working-class heritage, and their beliefs were similar to his. When his fifth child was born, she was baptized Teresa Berrigan Grady by Dan while Phil celebrated the liturgy after the Mass. When the Josephites shipped Phil north from New Orleans to their residence in the Bronx, he regularly visited the Gradys. Once Grady served as Phil's altar boy at a Mass in Fordham University. Occasionally Dan, too, would drop in at the Gradys. A family man and navy veteran, by the mid-sixties Grady was working as an urban planner when a Protestant pastor offered him an office in the shuttered "Iron Mountain" Episcopal Church on 219th Street in the Bronx, an offer he quickly accepted. Iron Mountain then became a central organizing center for draft board raiders.

It was there that he, Dan, and Phil, sitting on the stage in the abandoned Iron Mountain church auditorium, began hatching the notion of hit-and-run raids, improved media coverage, and attacks on FBI offices. A raid on a Bronx board was planned at Iron Mountain, as was the New York Eight attack. Grady saw the raids as an educational process. "As citizens," he explained, "we had a right to protest a war and the military-industrial complex—even if we destroyed property."[15]

Barbara Shapiro (later) Dougherty was one of the convinced. She was nineteen when she first encountered the ultra-resistance,

Phil and Grady. "Phil had the overall perspective on politics and Grady was the brains of the movement," she ultimately concluded. Born in California of Jewish parents, she was a student at the University of California at Davis but, bored and restless, she drove across the continent in her Volkswagen with her beloved golden retriever Kip, and ended up in Baltimore, teaching eighth grade in a Catholic elementary school. Soon she volunteered to teach in a school populated by black children, and drifted slowly into antiwar activities.

Young, sensitive, artistic, and idealistic, a self-described "naive, headstrong, California hippy" eager to do something to end the war, she eagerly sought out role models. Father Michael Dougherty, a Jesuit, was one hero (they later married), as was John Grady, the architect of hitting several draft boards simultaneously. "Grady made the movement," she wrote in her informative, unpublished memoir of those stormy times, "because he was creative and he could move the question along and change a group of dreamers into a group of actors ready to play their part." Strategy was vital, insisted Grady, "so that the dream did not get lost." Grady, she wrote, "was my midwife . . . I was his infant."

And then Barbara heard Phil speak. He invited her to one of his ubiquitous retreats in the Iron Mountain church in the Bronx. He also asked Michael Dougherty, a priest, to "check me out, to see if I had my guts together and my mind clear," she says. She discovered they were dead serious, demanding dedication, faithfulness, and possible sacrifice from people willing to break the law in the name of a higher law. She was fast becoming a trusted and valued member of the "resistance community," and later served as a "caser"—observing a building or draft board and reporting back so raids could be carried out efficiently and safely.

It was 1969. That summer she drove back to California to tell her parents she was going to take part in nonviolent draft actions, the principle of which her parents could accept, though hardly the possible consequences. While there, she found herself contrasting the idyllic, easy life of the West Coast with what she had experienced back East: the antiwar men and women prepared to defy the government and the impoverished black people she had worked among, contrasted with California's endemic drug culture and hedonistic boy-girl relationships on the campus at Davis. Then Phil called. He was at the Woodstock Seminary, with Michael Dougherty. "Be in Boston in twenty-four hours," he told her. Within hours she and Kip were aboard a plane headed for Boston. On arrival, a priest—"paranoid," she described him—approached her in the airport, and surreptitiously slipped a note to her. "If you're Barbara Shapiro," it read, "follow me out the door."

They drove to Cape Cod for a retreat, after which she took part in a raid on a draft board and discovered from chronological ledgers, alphabetical cross systems, and minutes of local board meetings that Puerto Ricans and blacks were being illegally conscripted out of the legal order of induction simply to fill quotas. Because the federal authorities feared the public airing of this fact, especially in a region with so many minorities and working-class people whose sons were bearing the brunt of the war, and with so many protesting college students, they did not prosecute. "Only nonviolent civil disobedience can effectively halt injustice," the raiding party's press release proudly proclaimed.[16]

Joe O'Rourke was yet another of the smart, tough, intellectual, activist Jesuit rebels drawn to the Catholic Left.

Born in Hudson, New York, he had taught philosophy at Canisius College and then Greek and English at McQuaid High School in Rochester, New York. Raised by a politically conservative, ardently Catholic mother, he slowly, *very* slowly, began to awaken during his long, thirteen-year Jesuit education. In the seminary, he heard and read about how many in the church had opposed the reforms of Vatican II. As he listened to Pope John XXIII on the radio, read Camus and Sartre and contemporary works like Charles Silberman's *Crisis in Black and White*, the travails of the impoverished Third World became real to him, and his life changed forever. He became convinced that the church and the Jesuits were isolated from the world of the poor and that the Kingdom of God only began with relieving the suffering of the poor. For two years, in 1962–63, he fought his superiors for permission to visit ghetto churches in New York City.

At Canisius in 1964, he sought to encourage students to tutor the less fortunate. He invited the intrepid organizer Saul Alinsky to visit the school, whose leaders were anti-union and opposed to community organizing. In Rochester, he met and worked with antiwar activists Allard Lowenstein and Paul O'Dwyer and joined the Eugene McCarthy-for-president campaign. Catonsville was electrifying to him, and soon he met and grew very close to Phil. Transferred to Woodstock Seminary, he started visiting Baltimore, becoming fast friends with Phil.

Ordained in 1971, he promptly joined in a protest against the church's silence on the war. Late in the 1970s, he was dismissed from the Jesuits for rejecting an order by his superiors and chose, instead, to baptize a three-month-old boy on the steps of a church in Marlboro, Massachusetts, after the infant had been refused Baptism because of his mother's views on abortion. O'Rourke disobeyed the Jesuit directive, insisting that canon law stipulated that Baptism could not be denied to anyone.

"You have your lawyers, your higher-ups, but, my friends, your church (*our* church) will not last without the common people," an anonymous priest wrote in anger to Jesuit superiors at Fordham University, protesting O'Rourke's suspension. Dan chimed in, too, declaring the dismissal from the Jesuits "intolerable from every point of view—ethical, human, Christian. It has once again underscored the reign of the 'armored men' against those who stand for life."[17]

It all came together in Washington, D.C., on March 22, 1969. Seven men (including O'Rourke and Michael Dougherty) and two women broadened the attack by targeting Dow Chemical offices, implicitly threatening other corporations that manufactured war material with exposure of their documents. Dow sought to defend itself against antiwar critics by arguing that it was only backing American fighting men in wartime. As early as late 1966, Dow recruiters were being harassed on several campuses—Illinois, Indiana, and Minnesota, for example—while at stockholders' annual meetings, antiwar Dow shareholders tried unsuccessfully to press the company to drop its napalm contract.

The invasion of Dow's Washington headquarters was an idea that emerged from retreats and conversations during which Phil and Grady were present. Some of the Milwaukee Fourteen defendants also started showing up at clandestine meetings in Washington and Baltimore, wondering what was next. O'Rourke told Phil he wanted to do something "serious." ("Serious," said O'Rourke—for a while, one of Phil's closest allies—was Phil's euphemism for "felonious action.") O'Rourke convinced Father Michael Dougherty, a Jesuit in his third year at Woodstock College and a onetime army paratrooper, to join.

Several days before the raid, they held their final retreat at Georgetown University, where the actual plan was laid out. It was, said Michael Dougherty, "kind of scary," and people asked worriedly, "Are we really going to do this?"[18]

At the close of the work day on March 22, they walked to Dow's offices at Fifteenth and L streets. Leaving Father Bob Begin, a member of Cleveland's Thomas Merton Community, downstairs as a lookout, they walked up the back way to the fourth floor, broke a window, and entered the suite of offices. They grabbed files, shattered typewriters and office equipment, and put antiwar posters on the walls along with streaks of blood, the religious movement's symbol of resistance. After making sure no one was on the street below, they smashed windows, destroyed some files, and dumped others out the window, the contents flying over several blocks of downtown Washington. Then they waited for the police to arrive while they sang peace songs and circulated their statements to newspaper and TV reporters, who had been advised to meet in the offices of the *DC Gazette*, from which they would be led to the action. When the call came from Father Bernard Meyer, also part of the Thomas Merton Community, reporters and cameramen raced to Dow.

Like earlier raiders, they wanted desperately to plead their case in open trial, but once again, this was denied. Eventually, only Katherine Melville and Father Meyer served time; the others were ultimately freed on appeal.

Once again, many wondered where the ultra-resistance was heading. After Milwaukee, the pacifist writer Barbara Deming—who had blessed Catonsville even when secular antiwar critics, unmoved by the religious left's metaphorical symbolism, often dismissed them as clerical cowboys—attended a secret weekend meeting with Dan and Phil present in Yonkers, New York, but she quickly departed, troubled by the intrigue and quixotic romanticism she detected, and by what she feared was a growing allure for violence among some of the people there. Then, too, over and over, one could hear the same questions: What had all these raids to do with *changing* America? How best to influence moderate and centrist Americans against the war? The organizers of the massive November 1969 Moratorium in Washington even refused to allow destroyed draft files to be exhibited on their platform. And everyone knew that for every trashed draft file, another young man was thrown into the "available for induction" category.[19]

Nothing, though, could persuade Phil that the Dow raid had not been worthwhile, especially because it increased public pressure on firms benefiting financially from war orders. "In its corporate conscience," he explained in 1970 about the Washington raid, "Dow felt no guilt—it merely served the government. In their turn, the defendants felt no guilt—they merely attempted to serve people. An impasse, one might say—and in whose favor would the court decide?" And always, in the background, serving as a rallying cry, was Dan's clarion call at Catonsville that "some property had no right to exist."[20]

The raids continued to mushroom. Draft offices were hit in Los Angeles; Silver Springs, Maryland; Chicago; New York City on four occasions; Akron, Ohio; Indianapolis (the Beaver Fifty-five, actually only eight people); Boston; Rochester, New York (the Flower City Conspiracy, the first raid on FBI offices by religious pacifists); Auburn, New York; Philadelphia; Midland, Michigan (where Dow's data center was raided and its magnetic tapes containing biological and chemical information were erased in November 1969); Providence, Rhode Island; Evanston, Indiana; and elsewhere. The East Coast Conspiracy to Save Lives (eleven people, among them four priests and two nuns, eager to "revive the spirit of Christ") destroyed draft files in Philadelphia and the General Electric files in Washington, D.C. A nineteen-year-old professor's daughter told police that she and a friend (dubbed the "Boston Two") had poured black paint over draft files. On Christmas Eve, December 24, 1970, in San Jose, California, a twenty-one-year-old

Episcopalian, John Williams, acted alone and burned draft files, for which he served two and a half years in prison. He was, he said, motivated "absolutely" by the Berrigans after he read Dan's *No Bars to Manhood*.[21]

Still, there were frequent dropouts. After Michael Dougherty helped organize the Boston Eight raid, he and Barbara married and stopped traveling and organizing, "exhausted," he said, by the constant wandering and tension. Some people also spoke of their discomfort with the pressures Phil applied. Time and again Phil put it this way: "If you're not doing this, you're not doing anything." Dan would occasionally apply the same sort of pressure. At the Catonsville trial, he met four "worshipful" priests who had organized the St. Ignatius Church rally. "Do something!" Dan told them. But what? Go to jail? Two priests broke into tears, unable to do what the Berrigans had done and would continue to do.

Edward Gargan, an eighteen-year-old who had invaded a Chicago draft board and had gone to prison, felt there was too much intimidation of potential raiders. He was, he said, irritated by Phil's trying to make reluctant, often frightened and unprepared people join him. "If someone didn't participate, they were frozen out of his circle. All of us were flawed and Phil Berrigan was no saint."[22]

Phil agreed, sort of.

In the late seventies he told the former priest Charles Meconis that many movement people were "traumatized. Many people were hurt by their friends. Only the hardiest survived. As for myself, I'm kind of a hard-nosed type and I could take the shit. But I dished it out too—much more than I should have."

And again, many years later: "I'd lay a heavy rap on them about the war, their Christian duty and then ask what they're doing about their lives. I'd tell them to stop underestimating yourself. I never tried to ask anyone to do whatever I wasn't prepared to do myself. And I don't want to let others off the hook any more than I am."[23]

The strains and ideological divides began, slowly at first, to erupt. The pressures to join the raids, the guilt of those who refused, and the anguish of those who went and were subjected to trials, punishment, ostracism, in addition to the distress it caused their families, were very evident. Many didn't think they could last years in jail, or withstand the movement's elitism, sexism, and, for some, reliance on a Gospel rather than "objective" economic analysis. Barbara Dougherty, whose admiration and respect for the Berrigans remains unshaken, nonetheless described many of the people who had enlisted in the ultra-resistance and then fled as "damaged people," never the same again after their harrowing, unforgettable experiences.

Phil's longtime Baltimore collaborator, Bill O'Connor, broke with him. Exhausted, jobless for two years because of his political work, O'Connor called a meeting at which he and Phil had it out. "Phil was like an icy wall," he recalled, adamant that he had chosen the right path. Months later, O'Connor visited Phil at the Josephite motherhouse on Calvert Street in Baltimore, again trying, he says, to mend fences, and finally saying, "We've done some good work but I can't work with you anymore." The break was final. Later, O'Connor mailed postcards to some movement people with whom he had worked. "Refuse to wage a joyless [fight] against injustice," he wrote, identifying with Rabbi Abraham Joshua Heschel's dictum: "Just to be is a blessing, just to live is holy." The more successful the draft board raids seemed to be, he concluded, the more the Catholic Left had become "a victim of its own mystique that these indeed were revolutionary times."[24]

All the same, many of those who gathered about Phil needed neither coaxing nor coercion. For Barbara Dougherty and for so many others, the era "was an incredibly emotional, tense, exciting time, with emotional ups and downs, a sense of being in the center of significant things." She will always treasure the retreats and the people as "the time of the best education of my life . . . a precious time" in spite of the fact that so many withdrew, never again to associate with Dan or Phil. But what she remembers above all is that they were part of a community in which one said, in essence, "I trust you with my life and you trust me with yours."

"I had an opportunity to find out what truth was about, to get radicalized, have courage to fight for a world that makes sense," and to uphold nonviolence and express concern for human life. "That's what we held in high esteem. Phil was always asking,

'What's the next step' while Dan was trying to explain what and why they were doing it. They were all gifts, all miracles."[25]

The last raid occurred in the early morning of Sunday, August 22, 1971, in Camden, New Jersey, when twenty-eight men and women broke into three local draft boards. (By then, Phil and Liz McAlister and others were awaiting a far more serious trial in Harrisburg, Pennsylvania.)

The Camden defendants appeared in court wearing "Camden 28" or "Resist, Now More Than Ever" buttons, fortified by parents and families in attendance, with ample funds raised by their "defense committee" and Dan's public backing. The trial was a disaster for the government. The jury quickly learned—and wisely believed—that the operation was an FBI setup, aimed at entrapping the defendants. The training and tools for the raid were supplied by an FBI informer, Robert Hardy, a member of defendant Father Michael Doyle's Camden Catholic congregation.

Doyle was Irish-born, reared with a healthy skepticism for authority (namely the British). In 1968, while teaching at Holy Spirit High School in Atlantic City, he was dismissed for objecting to a church-sponsored "victory rally" and sent into exile to the rotting south New Jersey city of Camden, where he worked for impoverished blacks and Latinos. He met Phil in 1964 at a Catholic Worker House in Philadelphia and attended a Mass conducted by Phil, who told him that when you see injustice, shout from the rooftops. Doyle honored the Berrigans and what he considered their Christ-like lives. So when the *Camden Courier-Post* reported that 300 men from the diocese had been killed in the war, he publicly urged that each man's name be attached to a brick and thrown at every military installation in the state.

"This city [Camden], sick and smelling of death, is the best visible and tangible [way] in America to demonstrate the tragic consequences of insane war abroad and 'benign neglect' at home. . . . The waste of the war has fallen heavily on this city, and buried it almost as [much] as the villages of Vietnam while its hundred thousand people—black, white and Puerto Rican—claw at each other in a trap of despair. The only two noteworthy buildings in this city of broken glass and boarded windows are City Hall and the Federal building—which houses Selective Service to draft local youth into the war machine."[26]

On March 15, 1972, the well-meaning ex-Marine Robert Hardy confessed to his role as an FBI informer and agent provocateur in an affidavit signed on a south Philadelphia street in the presence of Father Doyle and a notary public (after Hardy met with Doyle and Doyle's lawyer, David Kairys, in Woodbury, New Jersey), naively explaining that he had only wished to protect from imprisonment some raiders who were his friends. Hardy swore the FBI had pledged it would stop the raiders before anything actually happened. Hardy told the court the FBI not only had known of the plot to destroy draft records but had helped carry it out, enlisting him as an agent provocateur and then, rather than preventing the crime, gave him money to buy burglary devices and allowed the raiders two hours to destroy the files, only then moving in for the arrest.[27] All the defendants were subsequently acquitted.

Sometime after the trial, Hardy's nine-year-old son, Billy, died in a tragic accident and the Hardys asked Father Doyle, their priest, to conduct the child's funeral.[28]

Dan visited Sacred Heart years after the trial to honor Father Doyle and his desperately poor congregants. There, he offered a homily on "healing and the expulsion of demons" in a society where "evil is deliberate and institutionalized." Drawing on the Gospel of Mark, he preached:

I think he [Mark] means every claim upon human life by the powers of death. Every way in which a given culture, a given economy, a given social arrangement, lays a heavy claim upon people as its own, welcomes or enlarges the scope of death, hucksters it, sells it, as a good way of disposing of human beings. I speak also . . . of the spirit of control that governments exercise over citizens including Christians, urging them to silence and cowardice, inducting them into values that are death-ridden. I think of all the hidden persuasions and double dealing of consumerism that would make of us eternal children . . . that fosters racism, sets people in

competition. . . . One thinks of our professions, of professional-
ism, over service of human beings. The idea that one can pursue a
career irrespective of the poor or those in need of us, this of course
reaching its dead end in the degradation of the law, the degradation of medicine and teaching, and even the priesthood and the
ministry . . . [as] discussing with German doctors who had served
Hitler at Auschwitz what it meant to be a doctor in such circumstances, and 35 years after that still saying, "We came to believe
that killing was healing." . . . I submit to you that . . . where
Christians are, demons are put to flight.

Phil came, too. Citing the Scriptures' injunctions to "Love your
enemies, pray for those who persecute you so that you will become
children of your Father in heaven" and "do not take revenge on
someone who does you wrong," he wrestled with the delicate task
of not responding to violence with violence. "But—and this is a
very large BUT—we are commanded to resist evil. To submit to
evil with no resistance can be cowardly and slavish. . . . Christ commands us to resist—resist evil and injustice in ourselves and in our
government. Without that, good becomes impossible—evil and
injustice are too easy, too profitable, too highly rewarded by the
world."[29]

13

PRISON

Lay then the axe to the root, and
teach governments humanity. It is
their sanguinary punishments which
corrupt mankind. My country is the
world and my religion is to do good.
                              —*Thomas Paine*

THE BALTIMORE AND CATONSVILLE BREAK-INS HAD FINALLY
caught up with the Berrigans. Phil, in and out of various jails since
November 1967, was initially sent to the federal penitentiary at
Lewisburg, Pennsylvania, then to Allenwood in Pennsylvania, the
"country club" prison for white-collar felons, and eventually to
Danbury, Connecticut, on August 26, 1970, where he was assigned
to medium custody and put to work in the business office.

Lewisburg was hardest of all. A maximum-security prison, it was
hard time. He and Catonsville co-defendant Tom Lewis, escorted
by two federal marshals, were driven there in a Chevrolet sedan,
shackled by chains around their waists and legs. As they approached

the prison, they noticed clean and orderly small houses, with well-tended lawns, where many prison employees lived, and a prison farm outside the walls. Lewisburg prison, built by the WPA during the New Deal days of the thirties, had a macabre look—part Gothic, with icons and carved figures, it seemed like a medieval monastery, its stone floors and walls dominated by a tall Islamic-style structure overlooking the confluence of the Susquehanna and Buffalo rivers and nearby Bucknell University.

It was an extremely hot day when they arrived, still in chains until he and Lewis were removed from the stifling automobile and taken to processing, where they underwent a strip search and were allowed to shower. Later, they were examined by doctors and psychiatrists, generally young men who had volunteered to escape the military draft, most of whom, said Phil with a touch of irony, "didn't seem especially sympathetic to us."[1]

David Eberhardt arrived afterward, already uneasy at the horror stories he had heard in the West Street jail in Manhattan. "If one of those faggots comes at you, you have a nice razor ready," he was warned. Scary stuff, given the prison's well-deserved reputation for violence. "Fear ate at my brain," confessed Eberhardt. "My nervousness was going to be too obvious, I worried. I'm going to have to be cool, or I'll be marked for exploitation. They say Lewisburg is full of racists, hillbillies and right wingers, I worried. Thank God they cut my hair." Luckily, he had Phil as confidant, friend, supporter, and cellmate in a six-by-twelve-foot lockup.[2]

From May 1970 until August 1970, when Dan was finally captured, the U.S. Bureau of Prisons turned up the heat on Phil, feverishly trying to discover the whereabouts of his fugitive brother. Phil was initially assigned to the prison's maximum-security section and was from time to time shipped to the segregated punishment "hole" for a series of trivial offenses, which the prison officials denied were insignificant.[3]

Wherever he went, however, he was carefully watched, his mail censored, his cell and the chapel where he said Mass and vested for Mass inspected for weapons, though his keepers denied he was singled out for any special punishment. Clearly, Phil believed that other prisoners were encouraged to "rat" on him, and his tilt with his keepers went on day after day. To Phil, his guards were ultra-conservative, embittered, frustrated men venting their "petty persecution, and at worst, brutality" toward inmates, especially those jailed for antiwar acts. Phil fought back and was punished.[4] "Taken singly," observed Dr. Robert Coles, a visiting Harvard psychiatrist, "some of Phil's complaints may seem commonplace (his niece was not allowed to visit; he was searched in the yard; he was considered a 'dangerous organizer,' etc.)—together, they form a climate of oppression under which no one can humanly live."[5]

On July 6, Phil and Eberhardt protested the treatment and were sent to the "hole."[6] After several days, they refused release and started fasting. Coles, who had acceded to pleas by younger pro-Berrigan doctors in the Boston area to visit both men and examine their states of mind, was reluctantly allowed to interview them during their fast, though only in the presence of a warden. When Coles arrived on July 20, 1970, the irritated warden passed him one of Phil's love letters to Liz.

"Calls himself a priest! A priest! Read that, Doctor Coles. See what kind of stuff that 'priest' is writing! And to a nun! Read that!"[7]

Coles determined that continued confinement in Lewisburg might lead Eberhardt to a nervous breakdown; he was "agitated, frightened." And Coles thought that Phil, despite his external veneer of strength, was depressed. The Bureau of Prisons was skeptical, though, and sent its own psychiatrist to talk with Phil and Eberhardt. "You people are like salmon," he told Eberhardt, "trying to jump Niagara Falls. You can't take on the whole prison system. It's like lying down on the railroad tracks; the train is going to crush you!"[8]

Had Phil known of the diagnosis, he most likely would have waved it away as meaningless. "Things couldn't be better here, so no worries," he confidently wrote his brother Jerry and sister-in-law Carol Berrigan, hiding the fact that confinement and official pettiness were taking their toll. "Am coming out of segregation today to assume normality of life, whatever that means."[9]

It was all bravado. Masquerading as his cousin, Liz visited him and left filled with anxiety, disturbed by his appearance. She told Forest that Phil "was out of touch," and knew next to nothing about what was happening to the movement outside. In spite of his rugged and forceful disposition, he desperately needed Liz and Dan. To Forest, there was a flip side of Phil that few knew existed, "fragile and dependent"—one that needed desperately the loving relationship he had with his brothers and Liz. Nowhere was the tie between Dan and Phil more clearly expressed than in his inscription to Dan following the publication of his book *No More Strangers:* "To Dan, the first copy, with gratitude that defies my expression since I do not yet know what I owe you, with hope that Christ's Will come more to fruit in both of us. And with a brother's love."

Eberhardt was paroled on January 24, 1972, soon to begin his life's work of assisting former prisoners and composing poetry. He had, indeed, mastered a vital lesson in prison: "What's more psychically healthy than fighting for your rights?" He says he asked his parole officer which side he would have supported had he been present at the trial of Jesus. "I'd probably be doing the same thing I'm doing now," the official answered, "advising Pilate what would be a suitable penalty. After all," concluded the officer, "Christ got what he was looking for, didn't he?" The conversation reminded David Eberhardt of the Third Reich, with its multitude of willing bureaucrats and in particular, Adolf Eichmann, who told an Israeli court he was, after all, only doing his job and obeying his superiors.

The medium-security Federal Correctional Institute in Danbury, Connecticut, where Dan was serving time, was originally designed as a model prison in the late thirties by its reforming first warden, Sanford Bates. But his dream of reformation and humane treatment was soon discarded, especially as Danbury's population mushroomed, its cells filled with the Second World War's conscientious objectors and a growing number of white-collar criminals. By 1970, when the Berrigans arrived, it was just another bleak and cheerless federal penitentiary.

John Bach, the son of a United Church of Christ minister, and a fellow inmate, closely observed the brothers as prisoners. He himself was a draft violator who ultimately served thirty-five months in prison—the second longest term of any Vietnam draft resister.

Despising the war, yet never part of SDS, at eighteen Bach had no idea what being a Conscientious Objector even meant, but he dropped his 2-S deferment when he quit Wesleyan University and chose to stand alone and endure the consequences as a matter of conscience, so different from prominent contemporary "chicken hawks" who maintained their student and family deferments and then, when chronologically beyond the draft's grasp, turned hawkish.

"It was an honor to be in jail with Phil after he arrived from Lewisburg. He's a great man. He never told lies to the other cons, never bull-shitted anyone, always maintaining his self-respect. He was a born organizer and lots of inmates flocked to him." Not that Phil didn't have his own peculiarities. A real competitor in athletics, he picked Bach as his paddle ball partner for post-brunch Sunday games, and Bach says he and the other inmates never resented Phil's making calls favoring himself, since everyone saw him as a priest and a man, and they let him get away with it.[10]

Another inmate, in for armed bank robbery, felt the same way: "Phil wasn't involved in jailhouse politics. And he wasn't out to right the fuckin' system. He did what he had to do to get along. Everyone liked him. He didn't have any enemies. He did pretty good for a first-timer. He didn't get involved with gambling or homosexuals or drugs. *He was a man.* All the big shots liked him. They gravitated toward him. He wasn't a sycophant and he wasn't weak. He wasn't a whiner and complainer. He was an independent guy."[11]

Nor was Phil forgotten by the Josephites. Father Matthew O'Rourke, the order's vicar general, came to see him and wrote of his respect for Phil's "convictions and fidelity to conscience." While the order had its differences with him, wrote Father O'Rourke, "What you might not be aware of is the high esteem with which you are held by the men, and the concern they continually express for your welfare."[12]

Even so, prison time dragged on interminably, the days and months tedious, maddeningly boring, unstimulating. The brothers had to reestablish their relationship, too. Phil (it was believed by some) bore some resentment of his celebrity older brother, fantasizing that Dan could thrive just as well mixing with liberal intellectuals while he, Phil, suffered in prison. Prison life could easily set friend against friend and brother against brother.

Before long, however, these feelings, born during his isolation in Lewisburg, dissipated, and their remarkable brotherly love returned in force. After Phil's transfer to Danbury in late August, they found each other again and they heard each other's confessions and said private Eucharists. For both men, the central rock remained their faith; Jim Forest recalled that perhaps Dan's "most prized possession . . . [was] the frayed copy of that book [the Bible] he has that was used by Phil in several prisons. Page upon page is filled with notations in Phil's hand, lines and paragraphs underlined, exclamation marks in the margins." Dan interpreted it this way: "Philip reads from the New Testament and they [prison warders] couldn't stand it. That was his crime!"[13]

The two talked whenever they could, and some minor tactical differences arose on how best the movement should proceed once they were released. "Our approaches to the movement are quite different," Phil wrote Liz. "Dan is a superior propagandist and does it incomparably well. But I have different views about priorities."[14]

Jim Matlack, Dan's former Cornell colleague, visited monthly with a few Quakers and (particularly after the first Harrisburg indictment in January 1971) detected a change in their personalities. "The Berrigans are disappointed by the virtual collapse of the anti-war movement." They didn't want to be perceived "as saints or martyrs" but were eager to see more emphasis and work on "peace, poverty, racism, militarism, repression."[15]

Dan continued writing prose, poetry, and unconventional liturgies while prison authorities tried to watch the Berrigans' every move, every visitor, every correspondent. The Bureau of Prisons asked the FBI to investigate people "interested in [Phil] Berrigan" because "some could be couriers and/or religious people." Among those listed for background checks were Fathers George O'Dea and Matthew O'Rourke of the Josephites; Phil's erstwhile Baltimore colleague Bill O'Connor; book editors Jeremy Cott of Beacon Press and Elizabeth Bartelme of Macmillan; Dan's former companion on the trip to Hanoi, Howard Zinn; Robert Hoyt of the

National Catholic Reporter; and John Deedy of *Commonweal*. Dan's visitors and correspondents underwent the same scrutiny and surveillance.[16]

Prison routine rarely varied: wake up at 7:30; drink cocoa or coffee (Dan skipped breakfast); say a fast prayer, possibly a Psalm; make beds; wash and dress; and arrive at work stations by 8 A.M. (dental office for Dan; business office for Phil).

Then came lunch. ("[T]he food is like the religion is like the discipline is like the tenor and atmosphere of time—everything tastes alike . . . [no] odor, gusto, moral, sharp outline . . . nothing tastes like nothing. We are in prison," wrote Dan.)

Back to the dental and business offices where they worked until 1 P.M., break at 4, inmate count at 5:30 ("the hour when the zoo keepers render account of the bodies whose lockup is the rationale for the employment of some hundreds of key-bearing, goose-stepping custodians of private and public weal, the retention behind bars of menaces like himself").[17]

He and Phil were the Bureau of Prisons' star convicts, inmates-in-residence, as it were. The close watch over them never relaxed. They were both suspected of trying to figure out the prison's design, some officials probably fearful that they might try to escape. Four letters were discovered in Dan's shoes during the usual strip search after visitors' day, and he lost seven days' "good time" for the infraction. Actually, their defiance was subtle. In November, they composed a sermon, which the warden kept from the inmates but which they managed to smuggle out so it could be included in a First Amendment suit their supporters had instituted. Yet they also received privileges granted very few inmates. They were permitted to teach a Great Books course that met twice weekly for ninety minutes a session. The first assignment was to read the Gospel of Matthew, filled with enough insurrectionary and inflammatory themes with which to assail the status quo inside and outside the walls.

They were celebrities at the peak of their fame, and the Bureau of Prisons and Danbury's warden knew full well that when people joined together in a common cause, their power was a threat to their keepers. The bureau sought, generally unsuccessfully, through its minions and informers, to keep other prisoners, especially draft resisters, away from the Berrigans' subversive clutches. They weren't very successful. On visiting days, prisoners regularly brought their families over to meet "Father Dan" and "Father Phil." Once, when Phil was called out in the prison yard for a minor infraction, his fellow inmates rose spontaneously and cheered him.

Mitch Snyder, half-Jewish, half-Catholic, was in for auto theft. Slowly he gravitated toward the brothers, and they encouraged him to read seriously for the first time in his life, books like James Douglass's *Resistance and Contemplation* and Gandhi's autobiography. "He was both smart and very lost," Dan said, recalling their first meeting in 1969. "His background in no way helped him to find a way out. So with Phil and I, we tried to supply some new beginning to get away from what was a life of, well, thievery and stupidity. Mitch took hold of that and ran with it."[18]

Snyder was hardly unique. Inmates in their circle received birthday cakes, baked secretly or smuggled inside in guitar cases. They wrote and acted in musical skits, all designed to get inmates to share and not remain alone," as John Bach put it in his journal of prison life. Theirs was an informal ministry to forgotten men. Dan and Phil often made concoctions for evening discussions, instant coffee, nuts, hot chocolate with melted Snickers. "When they get your balls," Dan told Bach during a strip search, "and get your smile, they've gotten too much."[19]

"Don't let the bastards grind you down" was their slogan, their light at the end of the tunnel, "Stay strong" was their customary mantra at parting. It was this sense of invulnerability, of unyielding faith, that impressed inmates who had never known such men.

They also cooperated with an underground jailhouse newspaper, the *Shit House Press*. In one issue, Dan wrote: "Hardly 1 (one) Federal Employee Has His Own Life Together, Yet these 'correctional' officers are hired to help us put our lives together. They do this by working off their spleen eight hours a day. Like monkeys on ladders, the higher they climb, the more their asses show.

"Yet the fault is not entirely with them. Practically no inmates have their lives together. Count 'em: Whites, Blacks, Spanish . . . Not many love their brothers. Not many are outside the money game. Not many have thought through their lives and come up with anything new. Not many. Not in Attica, not in San Quentin.

"Moral: monkeys change when men change first; OR where were you Grievance Committee when we needed you? Answer: in the broom closet with old Mac."[20]

"Dan became a kind of resident chaplain at Danbury, warm, friendly, outgoing," said Rabbi Jerome Malino, the prison's part-time Jewish chaplain (he barely knew Phil), who shared many of the Berrigans' views on the war. During the Second World War, he had served as de facto chaplain for Danbury's imprisoned draft resisters, Jewish and non-Jewish.

Dan was much closer to David Saperstein, Malino's rabbinical intern, whom he had first befriended at Cornell, when Saperstein was a student. In Danbury, they talked for hours, and the young rabbinical student came away convinced by Dan that God had a simple test: What were we doing for the least among us? Who else, David asked himself, had "put themselves on the line" as Dan and Phil had? One time Saperstein showed a note from Joan Baez to Dan, urging him to "keep the faith." Someone saw Saperstein, and he was summoned to the warden's office, where the Roman Catholic chaplain ("God's snitch" inmates dubbed him; Dan and Phil's comments were not as kind) searched him for twenty minutes, missing the letter Saperstein had hidden in a magazine.

"I marvel at how sweetly Philip resists all this," Dan wrote admiringly in his journal, *Lights On in the House of the Dead*. Yet he continued to brood about how the Jesuits would view his conviction and confinement, a fear somewhat allayed by the visit of his sympathetic superior general, Father Pedro Arrupe, who believed the Jesuits' mission on earth was "to accompany Jesus as he carries his Cross in the world today."

If Dan's poetry is any barometer of his emotions, his most memorable poetic volume, *Prison Poems*, offers a forceful defense of nonviolent defiance. Taken as a whole, the collection is as striking a poetic depiction of prison life as has been published in the United States. Despite its occasional sweeping rhetoric and Dan's habit of resorting to superfluous, and at times puzzling, diction, the entire work, especially "Skunk," could very well be "one of the best resistance poems in American literature," rightly commented Michael True. It opens with the skunk entering jail. "He crept in under the full moon/like a moon thing, eyes dazed, moonstruck . . . foot-sore" and ends with a call to enlist in the resistance: "O skunk/raise against lawnorder, your grandiose/geysering stinking NO!" With enormous sympathy for his fellow "jailbirds," Dan writes in "Tulips in the Prison Yard": "I see prisoners pass/in the dead spur of spring, before you show face./Are you their glancing tears/the faces of wives and children, the yin-yang of hearts/to-fro liked hanged necks . . . Against the whips/of ignorant furies, the slavish pieties of judas priests/you stand, a first flicker in the brain's soil . . . . God is fire, is love."

Almost as revealing was Phil's introduction to *Prison Poems*, ask-ing the question that had become the basis of their stormy lives: "How does one maintain fidelity to God and to sisters and broth-ers when the overwhelming weight of culture, institutional reli-gion, and official Statecraft locks one into unbelief and alienation?" And he answers (for both of them), "what he [Dan] believed was obviously more important to him than his own life," concluding almost in reverence, "like thousands in prison and out, I remain profoundly in his debt. I cannot explain this debt, but merely acknowledge it—and wonder at it."[21]

There was occasional good news, too, as when Dan was given the Melcher Award (and $1,000) for his books promoting religious liberalism. The award cited *The Trial of the Catonsville Nine*, *No Bars to Manhood*, and *Trial Poems*, his three works most likely to be remembered by future generations. But always there was the fact that every day there were bars and guards. Phil grew uncomfortable at times, depressed and exasperated at his confinement. For Dan, the loss of freedom was more devastating. He became seriously ill, and almost died in a dental chair after he experienced a massive allergic reaction brought on by Novocain. Thinking he was dying, he told a visiting friend that while he no longer feared death, "It's not fair. To die now in this place." As he was rushed to a civilian hospital, the warden and Bureau of Prisons administrators in Wash-ington must have panicked. How could they allow Dan to die on their watch? What would this mean for their careers, and what would Dan's supporters in Congress, in the media, and on the streets do?

In the summer of 1971, ill and feeble because of his nearly fatal allergic attack, his endemic back problems, a herniated esophagus that required bland food not easily obtainable from the prison kitchen, arthritis, and a newly diagnosed kidney ailment, Dan became eligible for parole. Letters of support arrived from the Baltimore Roman Catholic Diocese's attorney, and from countless others, including several ex-prosecutors who had once tried to send him to prison. When the U.S. Parole Board in Washington turned him down, it triggered a dramatic hunger and work strike in August.

Led by Bach and Snyder, and joined (though not organized) by Phil—Dan was too weak and unwell to participate—several draft resisters and twenty other inmates participated in a thirty-three-day strike. They demanded parole for Dan and a shorter sentence for Phil Berrigan. After a perfunctory reference to South Vietnam's "tiger cages," they called on prison officials to allow prisoners the right to see their files at a parole hearing and learn why they were denied release.

The work stoppage was centered in the prison's electronics factory, which manufactured cables for missiles. The strikers were quickly sent to solitary, where they refused all food except liquids, until Phil, Bach, Snyder, and five others were shipped in chains to the dreaded Bureau of Prisons' Medical Center in Springfield, Missouri, and denied early parole.[22]

After Springfield, Phil was moved to Allenwood prison camp in Pennsylvania, where probably one-third of the prisoners were antiwar people, and where he was permitted to say daily Mass privately. There his lifelong love of physical labor gave him enormous pleasure as he happily, even joyously, worked on the prison farm six hours every day, "shoveling manure or splitting fence posts." He was, he said, in fine spirits and health. Energized, knowing that the woman he loved awaited his release, he felt that it was nothing less than "a new phase of resistance."

Dan's parole finally came through on February 24, 1972. The parole board explained that it was granted because of his poor health; Dan disagreed: It was granted because keeping him behind bars was "politically embarrassing" for the parole board. On the day he walked out the front gate to a bevvy of friends, he had with him the $50 given to all released inmates. At his first Mass he handed the money to Dorothy Day, who, while unhappy with the Berrigans' "prison mystique," nonetheless had it doused with holy water. Then, turning to Dan, she told him, smiling, "Now we can use this."

He arrived late that night at his apartment at Fordham University, only to find that all his possessions had been removed and dumped in the hall and his door had been locked. On his first night of freedom, he left the campus, deeply hurt, to look for somewhere else to stay.

John Bach, meanwhile, remained incarcerated, unbowed, proud of what he and others had done to oppose the killing. "History cannot record," he said more than two decades later with enormous and justifiable pride, "that there was no resistance."[23]

Out of prison, Dan was still a lionized celebrity. "In spite of everything," a friend wrote him, "the vibrations I get from people and from the atmosphere (not to mention some of your lovely writings) are good."[24]

Book editors were receptive to virtually everything he wrote, and magazine editors in the Catholic and secular press clamored for manuscripts. *The Trial of the Catonsville Nine* was being performed and hailed in regional and college theaters. Hard times in prison were past. The war was slowly grinding down, leaving in its wake tens of thousands of young Americans dead, wounded, exiled, or underground, and a million or more Asians killed, their lands devastated by incredibly destructive weapons. "America is hard to find." He had penned those words in 1970, and while there would surely be new battles ahead, it is hard to imagine they would be fought with the same intensity, passion, and enmity that had torn this country apart. Many antiwar people had wandered away, their singular sense of purpose, their high fervor diminished forever, exhausted; and like most Americans, they wanted a return to normality, real or imagined, wishing to return to an untroubled society, an end to mass demonstrations, street battles, police riots, political surveillance, and show trials. Congress was at last beginning to stir, hinting at investigations of the FBI, the CIA, indeed, the conduct of the war itself.

Years after, Dan remembered the war's end. "I was teaching in Detroit and I'm sitting alone watching images of the war on TV, which included Catonsville, and I'm weeping inconsolably for all those years of that harm in Vietnam, tears of relief that it's over. I didn't think of my contribution. I just thanked God that it was over, just, my God—at last, at last."[25]

Restless, peripatetic, he roamed the land as if in a biblical wilderness, lecturing and teaching in Catholic colleges and seminaries, accepting too many invitations to appear before too many audiences, but doing what he always did best—preaching, writing, and carrying on an extensive correspondence with family and friends despite the nearly constant discomfort and pain from his arthritic spine.

A self-described "token felon," he showed up in Worcester, Massachusetts, to deliver Holy Cross College's 127th commencement address in June 1973, "wearing an old turtleneck sweater, his long hair tousled, like an urchin's after a street fight," in Francine du Plessix Gray's graphic words. Surprise of surprise, especially to the school's old guard and prowar alumni, the graduating class chose him as its principal speaker, besting the political satirist Art Buchwald, while William Buckley came in a distant third.

"I'm with him on Vietnam, on the blacks, on poverty," Gray overheard one priest in the audience declaim, "but why can't he dress more properly?" And another groused, "Even when he taught me high school Latin back in Jersey [City] in the fifties, he had to be theatrical."[26]

On the road again, he headed for Winnipeg, Canada, hired to teach a course on the Book of Revelations in the University of Manitoba's religion department. Within days of his arrival, he joined a group of students picketing a Safeway store because he heard the store was buying non-union lettuce and grapes grown on farms struck by Cesar Chavez's United Farm Workers Union.

He also wrote faithfully to "Dearest" Freda, who was now living in the Loretto Rest Home for the Aged in Syracuse. On several occasions he explained why Phil and Liz had wed, and told her about the pending birth of their first child. Dan exulted in Liz's pregnancy: "The birth of a child is a blessing I look forward to with all my heart." After they were formally married in 1973, Dan wrote his mother: "Philip still considers himself a priest, as indeed do I. I hope and pray for the day when marriage will be no obstacle to full recognition of priesthood—as it was in our Lord's time!" In October he wrote her, "I keep trying to be faithful to all we were given in our family and church—especially by you. . . . I am sure Phil is trying in his way too—my recent visit to him and Liz made this clear once again. I hope you never worry about him—he is still an exemplary Christian and priest. He is meeting the ferocious realities of life in the way he has chosen—and I am sure he has God's blessing on this, with Elizabeth."[27]

There was trouble at the university. Soon after Dan appeared on the scene in 1973, he learned that the university's nontenured nonfaculty—clerks, maintenance people, office workers—were on strike. Though he told his mother he was "uneasy about living here"—he called it "my Canadian exile"—he threw himself into the fight, refusing to cross their picket line. "We have hundreds of underpaid workers on campus, and one simply has to stand with them." Other than students and the city's leftists, few Winnipegians of any influence or power sided with them publicly or dared defy the university's influential trustees. Dan, an outsider, did what he always did, resisting authority, boycotting school grounds, and teaching. Until the Franciscans invited him to stay with them downtown, he camped out in the apartment of Peter Jordan, his teaching assistant, where he conducted some classes and freely offered advice to visiting strikers on how to elude the Royal Canadian Mounted Police surveillance team parked outside Jordan's home. He was, he told Jordan, laughing, again at the "center of evil."[28]

Still, he was on familiar turf, even after the strike was settled. He wrote Ted Kennedy and his wife that he was praying for their son, who had lost his leg to cancer, and he corresponded prodigiously with many others about Canadian Indians and embattled local farmers struggling against far larger growers and distributors, defending as ever the powerless, and exercising, as he was prone to say, "the contrary virtues." In Peter's old Volkswagen, Jordan and Dan drove to several prisons, where Dan would chat with inmates. Once, on their way back to the city, Dan regaled Jordan with stories of Danbury, and how he nearly died there in its dental clinic. Jordan recalls him rolling his eyes, his voice dropping to a whisper, suggesting that maybe, just maybe, more than an accident was involved since he was treated with the wrong drug. And how, when he thought he was dying, he had thought of his friend Merton.

Winter was on the way in Winnipeg and it was already snowing and growing colder each day. One morning Dan arrived in his office to find that someone had anonymously left him a chrysanthemum plant. It bloomed the rest of that dreary season.[29]

14

THE TRIAL

If our system of jurisprudence is to survive, I deem it imperative that Americans reject this emotional self-serving claptrap.
—*Vice-President Spiro Agnew,*
January 25, 1971

"YOU PACIFISTS, WHADDYA YOU KNOW ABOUT ORGANIZING and picket lines? Goddamn, you're never gonna get anywhere. You need fists and guns!"

Jimmy Hoffa was talking to fellow prisoner David Eberhardt in Lewisburg penitentiary's exercise yard. And while the jailed resister could not agree with the former Teamster boss on methods, one thing Hoffa said was on target. Early on, Hoffa, convicted of tampering with a jury and wire fraud, concluded that Boyd Douglas, a fellow prisoner, was working for the government. Hoffa bragged about his prison communications network being far better than the warden's. Ironically, had Phil heeded Hoffa's warning, there would

266

have been no indictments for conspiracy, no show trial at Harrisburg, no calamitous impact on the religious, antiwar left.

Like most mob guys in prison, Hoffa backed the war, but he was generally respectful of Father Phil, as he occasionally addressed him. Jimmy was a traditional, if nominal, Catholic. Besides, anybody against the government was more or less OK with Jimmy. "I tried to help," said Hoffa, telling Phil "how to live in prison [and] who he should or should not talk to or be with. And last but not least, how to get along in prison." Hoffa seemed to know everything, even telling Phil that he'd be shipped to Allenwood and that once Phil was there, some of Hoffa's men inside could take care of his needs. Phil once asked him to protect Eberhardt, though he remained wary of Hoffa, disliking his Mafia connection. Once, said Phil, Mische, who could be outgoing and outspoken, asked Hoffa for a donation to the movement, and started to tell Hoffa why he was right and Hoffa wrong on the war. "Be careful," Phil warned Mische. "Hoffa can be dangerous." Mische backed off.[1]

Strolling around the cinder track one day, Hoffa asked draft resister Vincent McGee why Phil was hanging around with the wrong types. "Why are smart people like you and me and Father Phil in a place like this? Smart guys like us should be out on the streets picking the grapes."[2]

Phil claims he checked out Boyd Douglas with older, longtime cons, and when they said he was all right, Phil relied on Douglas to transmit letters to Liz and others, giving him a code name, "the local minister with portfolio," to try to confound the censors. He wrote Liz that Douglas was "the best thing hereabouts since polio vaccine."

Boyd Frederick Douglas Jr. was born in 1940 in Creston, Iowa, the son of an itinerant construction worker who separated from Douglas's mother when Boyd was a child. Boyd went to live with his father, while his mother took another son from an earlier marriage and a daughter. When Boyd was eight, his mother disappeared near Falls City, Nebraska, presumably drowned, her body never recovered.

Between ages nine and fourteen, his peripatetic life took him to sixteen different schools as his father moved from job to job. In 1952, possibly a troubled child, he was sent to Boys Town in Nebraska, and stayed four years, until June 1956, ending up at Indian Lake High School in Lewistown, Ohio, where he quit school after his third year because, as the principal informed reporters Jack Nelson and Ronald J. Ostrow, he allegedly stole $40 and was placed on probation. Two years later, he was found guilty of passing a bogus check, and the judge gave him a choice: the army or prison. At nineteen, he enlisted, serving for a time in Korea. But once back in the States, he deserted not once but twice, posed as an officer, renewed his fake-check scam, and received a six-year prison sentence and a less than honorable discharge.

By April 1963 he was in Lewisburg penitentiary. The next year he enlisted in a National Institutes of Health medical experiment that went badly, causing him much pain and scarring. As a result, he underwent a series of operations and sued the government (eventually receiving about $10,000). Paroled, he stayed on at the NIH a bit longer because his pain continued to plague him; he suffered abscesses from the experiments. Once he was out, though, his life of crime continued unabated. Back on the streets, he started forging checks again. When he tried to cash one at a Milwaukee bank, he pulled a Beretta on the customers and was finally cornered in a nearby parking lot. Rearrested and jailed again, he tried to kill himself at the U.S. Bureau of Prisons' Medical Center for Federal Prisoners in Springfield, Missouri. Later, resident doctors at the National Institutes of Health described him as "a sociopath and a pathological liar."[3]

Eventually, Douglas, alone among 1,400 Lewisburg inmates, was granted permission to study off-campus at Bucknell University, where he became a paid informer for the FBI.

It started on November 27, 1970, during the Thanksgiving holiday congressional recess. With most congressional representatives and the press away on holiday, J. Edgar Hoover appeared before the Senate Supplemental and Deficiencies Committee (an Appropriations Subcommittee) in support of his agency's $14 million supplemental budget request for the hiring of extra staff. Only two senators were present, but the testimony was promptly leaked to the press.

Without offering a shred of evidence, Hoover made the sensational announcement that a new and gigantic conspiracy was afoot in America: Dan and Phil, both imprisoned for months, were the leaders of "an anarchist group on the East Coast, the so-called East Coast Conspiracy to Save Lives," which was "concocting a scheme to kidnap a highly placed government official." The Berrigans, he charged, were also scheming to destroy underground electrical conduits and steampipes in Washington.

When he heard the news, the FBI's William Sullivan, rumored to be Hoover's successor and the third-ranking agent overseeing criminal activities, espionage, and intelligence, was flabbergasted, stunned that the case was publicized by Hoover, who for the first time in his long tenure had started coming under severe criticism. Sullivan, who had no sympathy for the antiwar movement, had nevertheless cautioned the director about moving too quickly on the Berrigans and the Catholic Left. "I don't think we'll even have a case against them, and they could have a case against us."

Sullivan and Hoover's long relationship had already begun to fray. Earlier that year, on October 12, at a United Press International editors meeting, Sullivan was asked, "Isn't it true that the American Communist Party is responsible for the racial riots and all the academic violence and upheaval?" and answered, "No, it's absolutely untrue."

"The Berrigans and their followers dreamed up and discussed hundreds of wild schemes to break into buildings and destroy federal property," declared an irritated Sullivan, in his break with Hoover, "ninety-nine percent of which never got beyond the discussion stage." In fact, Sullivan continued, "the Berrigans and their followers had no desire to hurt anyone, they just wanted to call attention to their cause."[4]

Hoover needed to personalize his indictment since that was the way he had always operated: Single out an enemy—Dillinger, the Rosenbergs, King, the Berrigans—and manipulate an uncritical or intimidated media to glorify the agency and make it easier for the public to grasp his and the FBI's role as the avenging and unrelenting enemy of their enemies, especially communists, real and imagined. As Lyndon Johnson's attorney general, Ramsey Clark lunched with Hoover once a month and never ceased to be amazed at the gossip about public figures the director delighted in amassing and how often he expressed his prejudice against "immoral" clergy like Martin Luther King Jr. and insurrectionary Catholic brothers, nuns, and priests.[5]

When they heard the charges, the Jesuit order was badly shaken. "To the Jesuits," went a Catholic weekly's report from Rome paraphrasing a Jesuit official, "destroying draft records is one thing, but conspiring to kidnap and bomb is another matter." Would all this tumult debase the Jesuits' good name?[6]

No one was more persuasive in denouncing Hoover's charges—before any indictments or trials—than an improbable Tennessee Democrat, Representative William R. Anderson. In fact, he was the only prominent personality with the courage to do so, since "no bishop, no cardinal, no senator, no governor" uttered a peep.[7] Anderson was a graduate of the U.S. Naval Academy, once the skipper of the *Nautilus*, the first nuclear American submarine, a recipient of the Legion of Merit, and a hawk turned dove.

Three days after Hoover's remarks, Anderson—who had actually read some of the Berrigans' books and visited them in Danbury—wrote Hoover. "Knowing the Berrigan brothers," said an angry Anderson, "and being reasonably well acquainted with their careers as priests, theologians, scholars and their dedication to Christian principles, and having read much of their writings, I [find] it impossible to believe that [your] allegations are true." In short, he became one of the first Washington politician to dare confront the still-powerful, always ominous director, telling him to put up or shut up.

Hoover reacted by doing what he loved doing—gathering all the unsubstantiated dirt he could on his critics and then spreading it around Washington. When an FBI field officer in Tennessee reported unverified gossip that the congressman had consorted with prostitutes, Hoover was ecstatic, urging the false story on his sycophants in the media. Like the equally vindictive Nixon, he firmly believed in the hoary adage about not getting sore, just getting even. "What a whore-monger this old reprobate [Anderson] is!" Hoover rejoiced, expressing his gratitude for the Memphis-based agent's "thoughtfulness." This bit of juicy rumor was promptly sent to President Nixon's Chief of Staff H. R. Haldeman, John Mitchell, and Spiro Agnew. Hoover's accompanying memo sanctimoniously noted that, while he did not view sex as a criminal act, he believed the report revealed "some insight into the character of the man."[8]

Anderson, though, was far more principled than most Washington politicians petrified of tangling with Hoover. He amazed sympathetic, silent House members by taking the floor and defending Dan and Phil in public. A fellow Tennessean, familiar with Anderson's district, expressed his sneaking, if anonymous, admiration. "It's not just the fact that he's taking on Hoover and defending radicals," he said. "Just speaking up for Catholic priests goes over like a pork chop in a synagogue down there."

Nor did the White House view the brothers with favor. Nixon's point man and attack dog, Vice-President Spiro Agnew, who had once called the Vietnam War a "moral war," lashed out at Anderson, advising the congressman to stop "popping off for political advantage prior to the trial."[9]

Hoover's reputation was on the line. He ordered his agents into action, and for the next fifteen months spent millions to get the Berrigans. Acting swiftly, on December 1 a grand jury was convened in the remote (from Washington, at least) small city of Harrisburg, Pennsylvania. Washington was too risky for a trial because too many potential jurors might very well sympathize with the defendants. Meanwhile, surveillance and wiretapping were accelerated and word spread through the ultra-resistance that its members were prime targets.

Going after the antiwar movement was nothing new in Washington. Lyndon Johnson started the ball rolling when, following the CIA's warning that communists might use the protests to harm the war effort, he ordered the FBI in 1965 to investigate the antiwar movement for subversive influences, a reprise of the infamous

McCarthy and House Un-American Activities Committee. Hoover was only too happy to oblige.

When the Organized Crime Control Act of 1970 was enacted, the government's power to call grand juries was greatly enhanced with severe restrictions on witnesses' right to invoke the Fifth Amendment. A willing presidential administration could prosecute those it wanted to see imprisoned and blur the distinction between criminal action and political dissent. In June 1971, for example, Attorney General John Mitchell told the Virginia Bar Association that he believed "domestic subversion ('in many instances directly connected with foreign interests') is as serious as any threat from abroad."[10] Indeed, from 1970 to 1973, the Justice Department worked overtime, convening some one hundred grand juries and winning a great many indictments. It went after the Black Panthers, the Vietnam Veterans Against the War, Daniel Ellsberg and Anthony Russo of Pentagon Papers fame, the American Indian Movement, Martin Luther King Jr., Students for a Democratic Society, SANE, Clergy and Laymen Concerned, and the Berrigans and their circle. So active was the FBI in probing every war resister organization and leading personality that it eventually kept files on more than hundreds of thousands of Americans, transforming the agency into a kind of federal thought police, and to all intents and purposes a political arm of the White House.[11]

Ten months after Hoover's outburst, after the indictments were secured and trial preparations under way, John Ehrlichman reported to Nixon, who was desperate to isolate and destroy dissent over the war, that the Ellsberg-Pentagon Papers case was "lagging" but the "Berrigan investigation is going very well. Mardian [Robert, assistant attorney general running the Justice Department's Internal Security Division, which had taken over the case from the Criminal Division] explains that Hoover's direct involvement in the Berrigan charges accounts for the difference."[12] Compliance with the law was not one of Richard Nixon's priorities. Nor Hoover's, for that matter. On the margins of reports submitted to him, Hoover scrawled: "expedite [the Berrigan case] . . . pull out all stops . . . push this hard." No wonder that Athan Theoharis, a scholar who has studied FBI documents for decades, could conclude that Hoover "created a culture of law-lessness within the ranks of the FBI."[13]

When news of Hoover's November 27 allegations reached him, Phil wrote Forest a rare confession, at least for him. "The evening was cold and snowy—like our hearts. For purposes of security, we walked in the handball courts to discuss Hoover's bombshell. The best reasons we could find for his statement were the FBI's incapac-ity to prosecute the recent draft board raids, Dan's impudent and effective underground, and Hoover's sagging reputation . . . I dared not conclude, at that point, that Douglas had betrayed us. A pon-derous gloom invaded us. I remember fighting to reconcile myself to the idea of life imprisonment . . . [I asked] what will God ask one to do? How many prison years will be required? . . . I remember thinking too—with astonishment—'Wow! they've finally got me!' . . . Finally, I thought of the others. Thanks to me, they were now in deep trouble. However I might excuse myself; however they might excuse me; however people might rally to our defense, the fact is, I had been guilty of imprudence and shallow judgment, asking for concern and services that few would have the arrogance to expect— information on the movement, requests for advice and speculation, etc., etc. I had no rational, or justifiable right to risk myself, let alone them."

He recognized the seriousness of the charges and realized that if found guilty, he could be imprisoned for life. Indeed, when Terry Lenzner (who became an investigator and lawyer at the trial) visited Phil and Dan at Danbury in early 1971, and attended a Mass with them, he found Phil and Dan "stoical but scared" about the forth-coming trial.[14]

On January 12, 1971, the U.S. government indicted Phil, Liz McAlister, Eqbal Ahmad, and three priests: Neil McLaughlin, Anthony Scoblick, and Joseph Wenderoth. The maximum penalty was indeed life imprisonment. Dan was inexplicably listed as an unindicted co-conspirator together with Sisters Beverly Bell, Jogues Egan, and Marjorie Shuman, plus William Davidon, Thomas Davidson, and Paul Mayer. They were alleged to have schemed to kidnap Henry Kissinger and destroy the heating pipes of government buildings in Washington, D.C. Six days later, on January 18, 1971, Attorney General John Mitchell sealed Douglas's prison files. When a few newspapers objected, Mitchell briefly relented before closing them again to public scrutiny. But not before reporters protested that some information was missing and other material remained sealed. The very next day, *Los Angeles Times* reporters Jack Nelson and Ronald Ostrow reported that the case "depended largely on a federal convict released last month," named Boyd Douglas.

Three months later, on April 30, the indictment was superseded by another far easier to prove. This time they were charged with conspiracy to destroy Selective Service records; the harshest penalty for this was five years' imprisonment. Mary Cain Scoblick, Anthony's new wife and an ex-nun, and John Theodore Glick, an antidraft activist, were added, while Dan and others—once again, inexplicably—were dropped. Though Hoover had named Dan and Phil as the masterminds, Dan was now out of the case.

Phil's response was to sneer, and he and his fellow defendants issued a statement rather than a plea, applicable to both indictments, old and new. The charge was a "potpourri of false charges, absurd allegations and acts labelled as crimes by the law . . . as sane or insane as our government's Indochinese war . . . one is a stepchild of the other, legal overkill following military overkill. Both are devious, ruthless and mad."

From his cell in Danbury, Dan wrote a mocking and scornful letter to Hoover, the original manuscript consuming eleven pages. He was, he told the director, "rehabilitated. This year I have counseled and befriended young prisoners, helped conduct classes in such books as 'St. Matthew's Gospel,' Gandhi's 'Autobiography,' 'Gulliver's Travels,' Erikson's 'Young Luther.' I have worked in the prison dental clinic, meditated on my crime and punishment, celebrated mass . . . I have not, after all, murdered children under military orders, nor tortured prisoners nor napalmed women, nor laid waste a foreign culture . . . I have burned papers instead of children. Let us rejoice that justice can distinguish criminal priests from military heroes."

Referring to Hoover's initial allegations, he asked the FBI director whether "American justice [applies] in his case," and offered,
"Justice does not apply." Finally, he reached his point: "How shall
we become men? How shall we live with other men? How shall we
so live that no man need die—whether of hunger, violence, of
despair, of the accumulated burdens of life, its injustice and poverty
pressing him into the earth before his time? . . . I have only the
most tentative answers to these questions," he concluded. "But I
have never heard, that in almost 50 years of voluminous public
utterance, you have framed such a single such question . . . have
you ever given thought to the victims, to the poor, to those who
seek a life worthy of human beings?"[15]

The government's case rested on Boyd Douglas and incriminating
correspondence, meetings, and Phil and Wenderoth's visit to
underground Washington, D.C., tunnels pretending to be General
Services Administration inspectors. There were no receipts for
explosives, no harassment or surveillance of Kissinger's office or
residence. In addition to Douglas, the case relied on a few hostile
witnesses who all refused to testify. "I talked about tunnels as an
incentive for people to get into actions and not just sit around,"
explained Phil.[16]

The revised indictment had to prove the existence of a conspiracy.
Conspiracy is ordinarily defined as a commitment between two or
more people to commit a crime or illegal overt act. It is, perhaps, the
vaguest, most elusive crime in the federal penal code and opens the
door to potential abuse of the law. "Conspirators" need not have ever
met or even known one another if their public behavior has been alike
enough to imply an agreement. For "conspiracy" to be proven, the
prosecution must show that there was a "conspiratorial agreement"
between the defendants and "overt" acts by one or more of them to
further the conspiracy. Yet the law of "conspiracy" allows prosecutors
to charge not the commission of a criminal act but merely to "con-
spire" to commit an illegal act.

The defendants were movement veterans, Catholics save Ted Glick
and Eqbal Ahmad. Ahmad was filled with scorn for his accusers. Born

in Pakistan, holding a doctorate from Princeton, New Jersey he specialized in Third World liberation movements and was a fellow of the Adlai Stevenson Institute of International Affairs at the University of Chicago.

Father Neil McLaughlin, age thirty, was active in West Baltimore's black neighborhoods and had been a participant in a draft board raid in New York City. Father Joseph Wenderoth, age thirty-five, was an assistant at St. Vincent de Paul parish in Baltimore in the black ghetto. Both priests worked together to establish a diocesan peace commission. When they were indicted they were released into Cardinal Shehan's custody. "It's almost like a father-son relationship," said the seventy-two-year-old prelate. "They are my priests and I am their bishop. I ordained them and I have a responsibility for their actions."

Father Anthony Scoblick, age thirty, was a Josephite, ordained in 1968, the son of a onetime Republican congressman from Pennsylvania. He, too, was also extremely active in Baltimore's black community. Jim Forest noted that Scoblick had petitioned Pope Paul— and been turned down—to allow him to marry. It was also said that he resented the constant reference to "the trial of Philip Berrigan and six others" and began sardonically referring to himself as Tony Other and to his wife as Mary Cain Other. She was a native of Baltimore, educated by the Sisters of Notre Dame de Namur. She had received a Fulbright Award to study French but refused, instead taking a job at a Kennedy family-supported school for retarded youngsters, before drifting into peace work.[17]

John Theodore (Ted) Glick, age twenty-two, a recipient of the God and Country Award as an Eagle Scout, a school wrestler and football player, and a faithful member of Lancaster Church of the Brethren, was added to the indictment though his case was soon severed because he insisted on the right to defend himself, and in the end he was never tried. Glick left Grinnell College in 1969, his sophomore year, turning in his draft card and refusing induction. "I met Phil in 1969 and later met Dan at Cornell. I liked what they and priests and nuns were doing. I liked their stronger actions against the war." In September 1970, as part of the Flower City Conspiracy in Rochester, New York, he and the others were arrested in the act of destroying draft files for which he served an eleven-month sentence.[18]

Maureen McAlister was born in Orange, New Jersey. Her Irish immigrant parents had arrived in the United States after the First World War and settled in the quiet suburban town of Montclair, New Jersey, not far from Manhattan. Her father was a general contractor and her mother helped out in the business as a bookkeeper and secretary. Maureen and her twin sister had four older siblings and one younger sibling. After graduating from Lacordaire, a Catholic secondary school for girls in Montclair, she went on to Marymount College, majoring in art.

"I became a nun because I had a call to that life. I wanted a life of prayer. I sensed I needed it. I had watched my brothers and sisters marry, have children and then lead ordinary lives. But I wanted to serve humanity though the distinction between charity and justice was then unknown to me, though I always instinctively had a sense of the importance of justice. There were no Peace Corps or Vista programs in 1959 when I decided to enter a convent and no other options were open. If there had been I might have chosen them."

By the close of her second year at Marymount she joined the Novitiate of the Religious of the Sacred Heart of Mary, where for the next two years she was permitted few family visits, since the order restricted such visits and the reading of newspapers and magazines. Nuns were allowed to gather in the common room to listen to a radio, but only to Bishop Fulton Sheen's homilies. She was an admirable sister, accepting the severe demands of her order, even the penance of genuflecting before breakfast and confessing her sins. Finally, in June 1961, she was renamed Sister Elizabeth and went on to earn her bachelor's degree, followed by a master's degree in art at Hunter College, a public college in Manhattan. Love of art consumed her; she even liked modernists such as Jackson Pollack, her favorite, much to the dismay of her more conventional superiors. She became an instructor of art history at Marymount, an exclusive college for young Catholic women.

In 1965 she was teaching Principles of Art Criticism, devoted to the philosopher Suzanne Langer's theory of symbolic forms. She was more or less still a political innocent, barely aware of the historic implications of the Vatican Council or of the fact that John Kennedy had previously dispatched American "advisers" to South Vietnam. A student suggested that David Miller's burning of his draft card illustrated symbolism in art. Liz nodded approval, saying, "I think you're right on target." Another student then piped up, "Well, if you think that way, you support David Miller," since presumably his act of burning his draft card was metaphorical. "I wasn't thinking in a political way, but simply as a concrete example of symbolism," explained Liz. Still, Marymount was a small school, and by the next day, "word had spread all over the campus that I was—suddenly—a pacifist!"

The war and the protective web cast around young, respectable Catholic women to shield them from external contamination was breaking down, and many students flocked to her, wanting to know more. She was also strengthened by Marymount's president Sister Brendan McQuillan, an Irish-born Ph.D. of French, and a pacifist to boot, and by Sister Jogues Egan, who also held a doctorate in French. It was Sister Brendan who gave Liz antiwar literature and took her to her first demonstrations and rallies. Sister Jogues had also turned ardently antiwar after the passage of the Tonkin Resolution in 1964, following a highly dubious American assertion that the North Vietnamese had twice attacked American warships, and she joined CALCAV and encouraged class and school discussions and debates. She knew Phil and helped recruit students to work with him at St. Peter Claver's Church in Baltimore as summer interns. She also knew Dan, who often dropped by to say Mass when he worked as an editor of *Jesuit Missions* close by on East 78th Street.

"Everyone talked about this Father [Dan] Berrigan," said Sister Jogues. "I was reluctant to become a Berrigan fan [until] I went to his Mass. He gave a homily which was unheard of at a weekday Mass. All of a sudden, despite myself, I was listening to him intently [and] the experience was a very profound one for me."

None of this was lost on Liz. She began to discover a community among the pious, antiwar Catholics she was now encountering. They would join rallies or vigils and then return to Marymount and celebrate the Eucharist together. Morally and spiritually, she said, "we came together and started exploring the phenomenon called community," often visiting the Catholic Worker downtown or going upstate to be with Maryknollers.

Toward 1968, as the war became more and more intense, and as the streets and campuses filled up with demonstrators, she was becoming convinced they were right. Her visits home were often punctuated with arguments with her patriotic family, who could not fathom the turn their daughter and sibling had taken. Nor could they overlook the fact that Liz's twin sister was married to a career army officer who would complete two tours in Vietnam. "Much anguish on the sisters' part," Phil wrote Dan, "not only because of hubby's dedication to Mars, but also because of Sister facing the music here with no twinly support. Both, however, will be able to hack it."[19]

William Davidon and his wife, Ann Morrissett Davidon, despised the war, too. He was a physicist who left the Argonne Laboratory at the University of Chicago, where he had opposed nuclear weapons and atom bomb tests. His wife was a writer well-known in peace and pacifist publications. In 1961 they arrived at Haverford College, a prestigious school near Philadelphia, where he taught physics and associated with the peace movement. When the first Harrisburg indictment was announced, he was with a group of Quakers on the tiny island of Culebra in Puerto Rico, protesting its use as a United States naval bombing practice site.

The Davidons and their daughters were on vacation in mid-August 1970, driving through the Connecticut countryside, when they phoned Julie Diamond, Eqbal Ahmad's wife, who invited them to drop in. The Ahmads were staying in Julie's parents' summer home in Weston while the parents were in Europe. Unbeknownst to the Davidons, Liz and Jogues were also there, Liz having just returned to her convent on East 81st Street after visiting her mother.

"Why don't the two of you drive out tomorrow?" asked Diamond. It was extremely hot, and she suggested they bring their bathing suits, adding, "I'll cook you a fabulous meal, we'll have a few drinks, and we can sit around and relax and talk things over with calmness."

After dinner, they gathered on the porch, drinking brandy and talking of Dan's four-month underground foray and how the FBI had discovered his Block Island hideaway only a few days earlier. (Liz's letter to Phil told the FBI all it needed to know: "Stringfellow . . . is part of Bruv's [the name she and Phil gave to Dan in their correspondence] next move.") On everyone's mind were the depressing and bloody events of the previous May when Kent State and Jackson State University students were killed and wounded and campuses had erupted as never before over the news of the bombing and invasion of Cambodia. It was as if a second civil war were possible. But, they must have wondered, why wasn't the war winding down?

Phil was becoming just as despondent, prison having taken its toll on him. He confessed his new pessimism to Francine du Plessix Gray just before the trial opened in January 1972: "I have absolutely no regrets about what I have done, and no regrets about doing it twice. But would I do it again? Probably not." Sadly, Gray observed his weariness and disillusionment. "He became silent, and I sensed some loss of that great hopefulness which had shaped the savage courage of his past five years."[20]

Frustrated, helpless, the men and women on that Connecticut porch began brainstorming an assortment of ideas, conjectures, and speculations, as they had always done. Such as: Could there be a "citizen's parole" of Phil when and if he was transferred to Danbury? How about pacifists conducting a nonviolent prison break? "Ridiculous," Ahmad shouted, but he soon advanced his own preposterous, even humorous, pipe dream. What about a "citizen's arrest" of a well-known hawk? And he mentioned Henry Kissinger. "He's a bachelor with girl friends and wouldn't want a lot of bodyguards around. And as a professor he wouldn't want police around his academic friends. We would invite him to a dinner with some anti-war intellectuals. Then, instead of serving him dessert, we would serve him with a notice of arrest."[21]

Gandhi, Merton, Martin Luther King Jr., even Jesus and the pacifist Gospels were thrown to the wind. Still, as stupid as it was, the idea was actually discussed, if only in a desultory fashion, as if they had momentarily taken leave of their senses, and values. Seated on that porch in Connecticut, hearing so bizarre an idea, Sister Jogues was appalled at the very notion of a "citizen's arrest" of anyone, let alone Kissinger. She would be ready to go to jail for refusing to testify before the grand jury in Harrisburg, but a "citizen's arrest" was for her unimaginable. Ann and William Davidon also spoke up in opposition, pointing out that it violated the theory and practice of nonviolence. Ahmad, too, quickly rejected the notion as worthless, laughing when he told Jim Forest, "And if he [Kissinger] doesn't talk, what the hell are you going to do with him?" They dropped the idea and forgot about it—only to be reminded of it soon after.

"Ours were freewheeling, speculative conversations," said Davidon, explaining what had happened that sweltering summer night in Connecticut, "just one of many ideas." "Liz's letters referred to our gathering as a 'planning group' and that gave what little basis Hoover had for the charges." Davidon, later named as an unindicted co-conspirator, wrote the *Philadelphia Inquirer* about the gathering and even called a news conference. It was "an abstract conversation," he maintained, since the people present—with the exception of Ahmad—were all thoroughgoing pacifists. Could such a grotesque act avoid violence? someone asked. "I expressed my reasons for believing it could not." Anyway, he repeated, they were just "casual conversations" and within their right "to explore ideas."[22]

Given the way the ultra-resistance operated, Davidon's version was true. It was just one more of their endemic wide-ranging, rambling, romantic, interminable mini-retreats. No one denied his or her part in clogging up draft boards or assailing corporations growing fat on war. But kidnapping Henry Kissinger was beyond them. They were impassioned, perhaps at times unreasonable in the absolute certainty of their views. But they were neither mad nor ready for martyrdom.

Liz, however, still a political innocent, proceeded to tell Phil about the idea in a letter transmitted by Douglas to the FBI and revealed publicly by the government in its second and superseding indictment. In it, she described in detail the suggestion that they detain "someone like Henry Kissinger" and then demand an end to B–52 raids and the freeing of political prisoners.

Kissinger would supposedly be held for a week or so while liberal VIPs would be allowed to speak to the captive—"also kidnapped if necessary"—and then Kissinger—and the liberal big shots—would be let go, unharmed. The letter, dated August 20, opened: " . . . this is in utter confidence & should not be committed to paper & I would want you not even to say a word of it to Dan until we have a fuller grasp of it." Her cover note to the intermediary and informer Boyd Douglas read, "The enclosed is dynamite & I mean it. The proposal (#3) is something no one and I mean no one should know about."[23]

When Ahmad learned of Liz's indiscretions in her letter to Phil, he exploded in fury, especially since he now knew about Douglas's role. Shouting at her for her witless letter even as she had noted "it should not be committed to paper!" he told her that Douglas was a government agent, though as late as December 1970, Liz says she found that hard to believe. Ahmad also asked Wenderoth about the tunnel idea just before the trial opened: "Why didn't you tell me about that idiotic tunnel idea?" The priest answered, "How could we, Eq, we were never serious about it."[24] Liz's letters were reckless but she defended herself by asserting that she was in fact trying to strengthen Phil's resolve, the man she loved and informally married in 1969 without telling anyone.

Sealed off in his cell and unable to join in the give-and-take, Phil actually, unbelievably, found some positive aspects in the Kissinger notion after reading Liz's letter. "About the plan," he wrote her on August 22, "the first time opens the door to murder. . . . When I refer to murder it is not to prohibit it absolutely . . . it is merely to observe that one has set the precedent, and that later on, when govm't resistance to this sort of thing stiffens, men will be killed . . . the project as you outlined it is brilliant, but grandiose . . . grabbing the gentleman will take a force of perhaps 10 of your best people—guarding him—getting communications out, perhaps moving him 2 or 3 times within a week. . . . Nonetheless, I like the plan and am just trying to weave elements of modesty into it. Why not coordinate it with one against capitol utilities? . . . This comes off the top of my head. Why not grab the Brain Child [Kissinger], treat him decently, but tell him nothing of his fate—or tell him his fate hinges on release of pol[itical] people or cessation of air strikes in Laos. . . . One thing should be implanted in that pea brain—that respectable murderers like himself are no longer inviolable."[25]

Even more damaging was the traumatic impact the letters had on the other defendants when they were disclosed in the superseding indictment. "Everyone in the movement was critical," said Joe O'Rourke, Phil's close friend and a former Dow Chemical raider.[26] McLaughlin and Wenderoth were stunned and felt they had been betrayed by the Kissinger idea, Liz and Phil's secret correspondence, and Liz and Phil's love relationship, particularly since Phil had been so strong a supporter of clerical celibacy.[27]

Not only did Hoover and people at the Internal Security Division read the letters, but so, of course, did Boyd Douglas, who was so excited at his find that he appended a note to Phil's August 22 letter to Liz, declaring his wholehearted support and offering to get a gun for her. Boyd's offer sickened and terrified her, and she ripped up his note.[28]

Douglas, meanwhile, continued writing and calling her. One day, he asked, "Where are things at with the Kissinger project? What can I do to help?" He asked her to arrange a meeting with Ahmad, but Liz, knowing Phil was by then in a Connecticut prison, closer to her, and still shaken by Douglas's gun offer, never passed on the message. In late November, Douglas was pressed by his FBI handler to get more out of her, and he wrote another letter about the tunnels and Kissinger. She never replied. Yet she acceded once more to Douglas's plea for a meeting, and the two talked briefly at the Sheraton Motor Inn in Manhattan on January 2, 1971, before Liz quickly departed, never again to set eyes on him until he appeared as a witness in Harrisburg.[29]

The case became "curiouser and curiouser." In January 1971, *after* the initial indictments were heralded to the country and world, William Davidon asked Kissinger for a meeting "so that we can

meet and think of each other as individual persons and not stereo-
types, and also so that we can discuss some foreign policy issues."

Actually, when Kissinger heard talk of the alleged plot to kidnap
him, he joked publicly that it was all the idea of "sex-starved nuns,"
which only set off howls from Catholics, and he apologized to Terence Cardinal Cooke, as well as unindicted co-conspirator Sister
Beverly Bell when he met her.

Early in March 1971, Davidon; Tom Davidson, an antiwar organizer; and Sister Beverly Bell of the Sisters of Notre Dame de
Namur, who had taught English for five years in impoverished East
Baltimore, entered the gates of the White House to meet the powerful Kissinger. The meeting was set up by Brian McDonnell, a
social worker Kissinger had encountered when McDonnell fasted in
Lafayette Park across from the White House to protest the 1970
U.S. invasion of Cambodia. Kissinger was impressed with his
"innocence," but perhaps, too, with his ethical stance, so different
from the amoral realpolitik of the Washington scene. In fact,
Kissinger seemed to have a passionate desire to be respected by his
erstwhile liberal and dovish colleagues, and had already met with
people like Senators George McGovern and Eugene McCarthy,
Rabbi Abraham Joshua Heschel, and the academicians Michael
Walzer, John Kenneth Galbraith, Ernest May, and Richard
Neustadt, among others, convincing none of the government's
position on the war.

Kissinger kept the meeting secret, neglecting to inform the
Secret Service or Department of Justice, let alone the vengeful
Nixon or H. R. Haldeman. The three Harrisburg defendants were
ushered into the White House basement; the only ground rule was
that discussion of their legal case was off-limits. Their talk was ami-
able, as Kissinger defended American strategy while he simultaneously sought to display his independence from the Washington
establishment and his irritation with Hoover. In the end, everyone
was satisfied. "We agreed to disagree," said Davidon, and they
handed him "Kidnap Kissinger" buttons the Harrisburg Defense
Committee had mockingly produced. "The scary thing is that he
really is a nice man," said another one of the trio, but he was "all
hung up over the communist threat."[30]

In December 1970, Douglas was released from prison and surfaced in Washington, D.C., where he suddenly appeared at a protest against J. Edgar Hoover. Bucknell University professor Gene Chenoweth saw Douglas on December 18, at a party for Boyd's university and movement friends. Douglas had begun planning it in October, and the invitation, and an accompanying slogan, "Persevere for Peace," went out to people he knew at Bucknell and to everyone soon to be cited as defendants and co-conspirators. But Hoover's charge intervened, and only a few Bucknell acquaintances showed up. And then Douglas vanished, not to emerge until he appeared on the witness stand.[31]

Most people who met Boyd Douglas were charmed with him. He spread tales about soldiering in Vietnam and how he had taken part in various antiwar actions in this country, then explaining that he was in prison because he had tried to attack a shipment of napalm in California. "Boyd," said David Eberhardt, "was not the sort of person we were used to; he was a clean cut, articulate confidence man. He was easy to get along with, had a sense of humor and suited Phil's purpose well acting as a courier for messages going out." Trusting letters were sent to him by members of the inner circle, one nun even signing off saying, "We need you badly." He fooled everybody—except, of course, Jimmy Hoffa.

To Christian pacifists especially, he was the epitome of someone whose life had been turned around. Now, at least to them, he was reborn as a man of peace. To the devout—and credulous—among them, Douglas was redemption personified. Besides, many of them had developed so much hostility to their government that they tended to view all prisoners as victims of a corrupt legal and political system.

Anyway, Douglas wasn't the kind of man the ultra-doves were accustomed to: young, athletic, good-looking, Middle-West wholesome, well-spoken though unread, a good listener, and even funny. In spite of a handful of skeptics, he was able to win people's confidence. He was, as Paul Cowan put it, an "intruder in a gentle community." He loved strutting about the untroubled campus, far removed from other turbulent colleges. At age thirty-four, much older than the students, he became a familiar and popular figure—an inmate gone good, smiling and handsome, calling out to the girls and flaunting the V-for-peace sign. He was in reality an "accomplished confidence man," said Delmar "Molly" Mayfield, his FBI contact, and an informer, but who outside the FBI knew? He delighted in reiterating to more ardent antiwar faculty members how much he respected Phil, and how badly he wanted to meet people fighting against the war. He wrote Professor Richard Drinnon that his "values have changed and I feel the system must be changed." In his sparsely furnished apartment on South Sixth Street, Douglas would bring together Liz, the newlyweds Mary and Tony Scoblick, Neil McLaughlin, and Joe Wenderoth, who was probably closest to him of all the defendants.[32]

Why Douglas turned against Phil is hard to fathom. Perhaps Boyd "loved" Phil. Phil was certainly different from anyone else Boyd had met. Who else had ever taken him into his confidence, trusted him, tried to be good to him? The supreme irony is that had he not turned on Phil and the others, his life might well have been transformed. During the trial, Phil told defense attorney Leonard Boudin, whose withering cross-examination left Douglas stripped of any credibility, "Don't be too hard on him." Others felt the same sort of empathy. "I remember him being terribly sad, neither lying on the stand nor telling the truth," said a member of the Harrisburg Defense Committee. Douglas, she thought, had been manipulated by his government, by his own character, and by Phil Berrigan. Zoia Horn, the Bucknell librarian who went to jail on contempt charges rather than testify before the grand jury said, "I suppose he victimized us, but he was misused, too. Sometimes I think of him as another victim."[33]

More dubious was his onetime teacher, the antiwar historian Richard Drinnon: "He would stand there with tears in his eyes, saying that he wanted to help the other prisoners. It was a consummate performance in 'conning' a faculty innocent." Drinnon suspected Douglas when he first met him, he says, but Douglas protested his innocence, and the professor and his wife reluctantly chose to believe him, as everyone else did, though not without misgivings. Even after Douglas sent a plaintive letter to him saying,

"My values have changed a great deal," something about him bothered Drinnon, and he cautioned Liz about using him as a courier, and even alerted Phil. But it was too late.[34]

Meanwhile, Douglas attended classes (he received a low grade in Drinnon's Recent U.S. History class) and settled into an off-campus apartment in a two-story white house at 204 South Sixth Street, which he shared with an unsuspecting antiwar student who had once set his draft card afire, whom he let live there rent-free. He had a ready supply of funds and attended rallies and bull sessions with students, subscribed to radical publications, and wrote pieces for the college paper denouncing the penal system. To the small antiwar community, he was initially an oddity and then a bit of a celebrity. On the top floor of the house lived two women students, Jane Hoover and Mary Elizabeth (Betsy) Sandel, and Douglas dated both of them, even proposing marriage to Jane Hoover, telling her he had cancer and only a few months to live. When she turned him down after conferring with Liz, who advised her to follow her best judgment, he turned to Betsy Sandel.

Inmates like "Buzzy" Mulligan saw a different Douglas, a man who misstated the amount of money he received in his lawsuit, the epitome of conspicuous consumption, "smoking boxes of large cigars, buying fifty-dollar pipes, attache cases, loafer shoes"—anything "to show other convicts he was a big man." And after he was allowed out to attend Bucknell, he would often brag to Mulligan about his apartment in town, "the booze he had stashed there, the women he romanced there, the car he was planning to buy"—"all the trappings of the 'big man' Boyd wished to be."[35]

Gene Chenoweth met him in early 1970. The school was interested in recruiting some prisoners for part-time study on campus, and when Douglas arrived on his bike that summer of 1970, he was hired to work on the buildings and grounds and allowed to take a few courses. Once he walked into Chenoweth's office and asked if he could leave his attaché case; with no reason to distrust him, Chenoweth handed him a key to an empty office. A few days later, Douglas arrived "all nervous." The FBI, he told Chenoweth, had entered the office and stolen his case. Chenoweth recalls that Douglas was extremely worried lest his upcoming December 1970 date of release from prison might be jeopardized. More than anything else, Douglas wanted out of prison, and he worked hard to impress outsiders, even local businessmen. Their Buffalo Valley Chamber of Commerce had a chapter inside Lewisburg, and during one of their sessions Boyd introduced Phil to Chenoweth. "Douglas was really impressed, even awed" with Phil.[36]

Despite his criminal record, any definitive judgment about why Douglas turned informer is as yet impossible. Still-classified FBI documents have never been released, and he has long since vanished from public view. Had he finally found a place for himself with the peace movement and then panicked when caught by the prison authorities? Or was he hired by the FBI months before to penetrate Bucknell's minuscule antiwar movement and then, later, assigned to get Berrigan and his allies? Or was he just another con man who saw them as a promising meal ticket, an opportunistic squealer, a false witness, a man irreparably damaged by his past? Or someone who so loathed authority—government, priests, all of them—that he was cynically ready to serve anyone prepared to inflict mayhem on them? Phil had high hopes that in Douglas—whose code names were "Pete" and "minister without portfolio"—he had found a way to communicate with Liz and to guide the movement. "He is more and more immersed with the idea of being of service," he wrote Liz, and shrugged off jailhouse talk "that Pete was a courier of contraband." Even so, Phil kept asking himself why Douglas had turned on him. "He had a compulsion to identify with so-called leaders, and especially with people of conscience," and then appealed to them on the grounds that he was a victim of government brutality and society in general. "Behind it, there were his true needs: the acceptance and love required of a profoundly insecure person; evidence of capability to dominate and master others, especially women; recognition of intelligence, charm, conviction, courage. . . . It was as though we were not responding fast enough, or in a manner he desired, to his cries for help."[37]

We do know that when a letter to Liz was found in Phil's cell during a shakedown in June 1970, Douglas confessed to the assistant warden that he was their intermediary. To a fellow prisoner,

Douglas described the scene: He had been called to the assistant warden's office and greeted sardonically, "Good morning, Peter." Then, presumably, he met with FBI agents Delmar Mayfield and Philip Morris and was told he faced a ten-year sentence for smuggling mail. He was squeezed: Cooperate and win his release or spend another decade behind bars.[38]

Father Neil McLaughlin was the first defendant to seriously conclude that Douglas was working for the government. When Douglas was paroled on December 17, 1970, he had invited Liz and others to a party celebrating his freedom. McLaughlin was on his way to a religious vigil in front of the Justice Department, scheduled for the next day, when the notion struck him. Boyd was an informer![39]

"Where are all these kids coming from?" asked a middle-aged man near the federal courthouse in Harrisburg. His companion stared at the lunchtime crowd. "They're probably in there watching that trial that's going on—some crazy nuns and priests or something."[40]

Greater Harrisburg, Pennsylvania, numbered some 250,000 people in 1972, so conservative that in the 1964 presidential race between Lyndon Johnson and Barry Goldwater, it contained a black electoral district that voted Republican. The city was ruled for decades by an entrenched political machine, and enrolled Republicans dominated Democrats by four to one, "very far to the right" as one of the natives described it in 1972. "If you wanted a conviction you couldn't pick a better town."[41]

Once more, sympathizers poured in, eager to defend the Harrisburg Eight but just as eager to lambaste what was to them an unresponsive, bellicose, repressive government, sentiments reinforced by the publication, on June 13, 1971, by the *New York Times*, of the Pentagon Papers, which documented the government's deceit in the conflict in Southeast Asia. For the moment at least, the delicate balance of trust between the governed and the governors had been upset. Once you bloody a trusting people, once you take a loyal and believing population into a baffling war, once you tear apart the membrane that holds things together, you set in motion ill-defined forces that threatened to sever the bond. It was no coincidence, then, that in August, for the first time, a Harris Poll reported that most Americans believed the war was wrong, and more than 60 percent told Gallup pollsters that they wanted all U.S. troops withdrawn.

Energized by the changing national mood, a defense committee was promptly organized in Harrisburg, New York City, and more than twenty states. In all, more than 125 local committees were operating when the trial opened in early 1972. Nuns, priests, seminarians, and antiwar amateurs flocked to Harrisburg, viewing the issues as clearly moral and spiritual. Along with them came hardened veterans of the secular antiwar movement, who saw the trial as a political sideshow, however necessary it was to humiliate the Nixon Administration.

Sister Evelyn Joseph Mattern arrived from St. Augustine's (Episcopal) College in Raleigh, North Carolina, where she was teaching literature and writing, to spend her spring vacation working for the committee in Harrisburg. Mary Daly, the Catholic daughter of an army colonel sympathetic to the antiwar movement, the civil rights movement, and Vatican II's reforms, arrived at Liz's invitation to organize a staff. Robert Hoyt, the *National Catholic Reporter's* founding editor, and his wife, Mig, took over press relations. Paul Mayer, the veteran coordinator of the Baltimore and Catonsville trials, was also on hand.

The Harrisburg Defense Committee (HDC) made prodigious efforts to raise money, not to strategize, for that was left to Phil's inner circle. Its rallies were closely monitored by federal agents and informants. Sister Jogues Egan was reported (falsely) to be planning a trip to Russia; Paul Mayer was reported (falsely) to be in Cuba "to obtain funds to finance antiwar activities." An FBI memo urged that Mayer's tax returns be scrutinized "for past three years, possibility exists that a good income tax evasion case can be made against him." An ominous warning was issued from the FBI's Buffalo office: "All individuals involved in New Left extremist activity should be considered dangerous because of their known advocacy and use of explosives, reported acquisition of firearms and incendiary devices and known propensity for violence." The HDC's office at 156 Fifth Avenue was mysteriously ransacked, and committee worker Sue Susman's notebook was stolen and then mysteriously returned. Was there an informer among them? No one knew, though all suspected it was so. Paranoid about infiltration, they had no alternative but to trust one another, possibly the most memorable recollection for many of the participants. "Each of us," said Stewart Schaar, "gave up our lives to this [cause]."[42]

HDC headquarters was set up near the courthouse in a shabby building that also housed CALCAV and the *Harrisburg Independent Press*, which was started with HDC seed money and was perpetually jammed with college journalists. HDC also helped start a breakfast program for poor black youngsters, did draft counseling, served communal meals, and offered talks by the defendants and sympathizers. Local Catholics and non-Catholics were not generally sympathetic, but the defendants were not alone. Thirty-four local priests (of the diocese's 180) came to their defense, publishing a letter of support that alluded to Pope Paul's denunciation of war. Another priest described the Eight as "family" in his Sunday sermon.[43]

As the months dragged on, there were signs of strain among the defenders. Staff women began to resent their exclusion from "important" meetings, attended only by males, adding evidence that a fissure between the sexes was about to erupt in the antiwar movement. Serious differences started cropping up between the religious and secular left, too. The talk was that the pros and amateurs, and the religious and secular on the defense committee, were at odds. Dedicated HDC staff people were often at a loss; one priest complained that he didn't know any of the movement pros who had descended on Harrisburg and who, he believed, wanted control. He had expected to be surrounded by clergy, nuns, and seminarians, by prayer and liturgies. The new scene hit Mayer hard and led him to think of leaving. "HDC," he explained, "felt more like employees after a while than part of an activist community. The defendants were in heavy jeopardy yet we seemed to have abandoned the sort of camaraderie and information-sharing as before and instead had a quasi-elitist scene." But he stayed on, and composed a little ditty: "Oh Harrisburg, oh Harrisburg, I'd rather be in Parisburg."[44]

Few outside the small coterie of defendants and lawyers were aware that serious differences had also arisen between them about how their defense should be conducted. Four defendants—the Scoblicks, McLaughlin, and Wenderoth—dreaded the idea of prison. They, and Ahmad, were furious at the use of Douglas as a middleman. Only Phil, Liz, and Ahmad wanted to make the trial a public statement (as did Glick, but his case was severed and he was never tried); the others wanted to mount a conventional legal defense that would give them a reasonable chance at acquittal. Dan advised Phil to fight back in open court, saying he owed it to the movement and the American people to answer the charges. "The politics of the case required a defense, and people generally expected one," wrote Phil. Dan's reasoning was that "painful and unanswered questions existed about the charges, about our relationship with Douglas, about the letters themselves. I agreed."[45]

It was an onerous decision. Do you go after the government, putting it on trial for Vietnam? Or do you try to use every legal tactic for an acquittal? Paul O'Dwyer warned that if they took the stand, "they must supply to the government evidence it could not otherwise present to the jury." But Phil fantasized that "our attack will shift from Douglas to the government." And some, like Ahmad, wanted to represent themselves, a suggestion O'Dwyer dismissed out of hand, even threatening to quit.

Their debate took on an ugly, harsh edge. "Pressures on people were mounting," Phil said, "and exacting a heavy toll." To his chagrin, "less and less did we talk together, pray together, plan together." Finally, a meeting was held at the Dauphin County Jail. All the defendants were present, together with Dan and Terry Lenzner. Everyone spoke in what can only be described (by Phil's account) as an agitated, embittered, scared, vituperative atmosphere. Accusations were flung at one another—and more often than not at Phil and Liz—and many would never again speak with the couple once the trial was over. "Apparently," Phil said, "the daily feeling of standing in that suffocating court like a clay image in a shooting gallery, had its price tag. Voices became emotive, strident, accusatory." In the end, they voted to heed their lawyers, who recommended a conventional legal defense. Harrisburg, one of the defense lawyers said, summing it all up, was "a real ordeal."[46]

On January 24, 1972, Judge R. Dixon Herman, a sixty-one-year-old alumnus of Bucknell and Cornell Law School, a Mason, and a Sunday school teacher who had served with the navy in the South Pacific during the Second World War, entered the starkly furnished courtroom. Balding, wearing glasses, he had been an assistant district attorney and county juvenile judge, and had been elevated to the federal district by President Nixon in 1969. His reputation was that of a strict constructionist, as conservative as his community.

The night before the trial opened, hundreds of people appeared before the Dauphin County Jail to celebrate Phil. On the morning of the trial, hundreds, including Vietnam veterans, collected outside the courthouse to carry a coffin to an adjoining federal building. When the coffin was thrown open, the demonstrators tossed in scraps of paper, symbolically representing shredded draft files. Judge Herman, meanwhile, had numerous guards stationed inside and out, and bullet-proof windows installed. Outside the austere courtroom, spectators queued up, hoping to be among the few allowed to enter the smallish room. The judge's daughter was a frequent spectator, and gossip had it—though it was *never* verified—that she opposed the war and was tormented by the trial over which her father presided.[47]

The prosecutor, William S. Lynch, was a formidable figure, a onetime subordinate of Ramsey Clark during the latter's tenure as U.S. attorney general, and each man held the other in high professional esteem. Clark called Lynch the "most highly-regarded prosecutor in Justice's Criminal Division."

As experienced as he was, Lynch faced an equally impressive battery of lawyers: Leonard Boudin; Ramsey Clark; Father William Cunningham, S.J.; Charles Glackin; Terry Lenzner; Tom Menaker; Paul O'Dwyer; and two younger members of the team, William Bender, who had worked with the Center for Constitutional

Rights, and Diane Schulder, who had worked on the Spock conspiracy case.

They promptly set out to find a jury willing to consider the case fairly, the first time "scientific" jury selection was used. Jay Schulman, a sociologist and antiwar scholar, was brought in to see—in his words—whether "a few favorable jurors could be found, in a fundamentally conservative area, to try unpopular antiwar activists."[48]

While the lawyers wrangled over procedural questions, Phil read books, looking cool and collected but anxious and self-pitying nonetheless, "the huge temptation of the political prisoner." Helpless to do otherwise throughout the three-month ordeal, he says he sought to strengthen himself by thinking of the South Vietnamese tiger cages at Con Son, or the Passion, or Liz, the love of his life, who sat next to him. "I watched your lips get red as we talked," he wrote to her in one of his intercepted letters, "knew once again the life surging in you, inviting my own and responding to it. . . . You enkindle me as no woman can. Fathom, if you can, how much I love you . . . that my pride in you is limitless." Even so, the public release of their romantic letters was "terribly mortifying" to both. It was, after all, a private exchange. Still, as Phil acknowledged, clerical critics were justified in being angry at their love affair. But, he insisted, "our views had changed." They had been separated for years by prison. They were normal human beings. How else could they express their love for each other?[49]

Dan arrived, recently released from Danbury, and was greeted with genuine exhilaration at HDC offices. The night he arrived, he was introduced at a rally as Father Daniel Ellsberg (Ellsberg was observing the trial, because his own trial was scheduled to begin in June). "No, no," shouted Dan over the crowd noise, grinning, "I'm Dan Berrigan and that bad Jesuit"—pointing at Ellsberg—"is sitting behind me."[50]

His appearance in the courtroom the next morning was met with an audible buzz. Wearing his conventional turtleneck shirt and a cross, his black beret in hand, he appeared thin and drawn after prison and his near-fatal reaction to a proscribed drug. His presence caused the judge to summon defense lawyers to the bench, telling them Dan could stay "as long as he is a normal spectator," but "if any demonstrations start in this courtroom or if any of this hilarity that begins every once in a while, then I will have a different thought on it."[51]

Boyd Douglas took the stand. Heavier by some twenty pounds since his Bucknell days, dressed fastidiously in a gray pin-striped suit, wide tie, and pink shirt, he left his seat (where he was surrounded by five U.S. marshals) and walked briskly to the witness chair. Lynch had him detail his relationship to Phil and Liz and Wenderoth. He answered softly and deliberately. At one point in his testimony, he sounded so convincing a witness for the prosecution that, at the close of the day's testimony, Boudin whispered to a colleague that he'd be a hard nut to crack.

He had worked for the FBI, he said, because he was afraid he would be charged for smuggling letters and because his deep feeling for America led him to choose sides. Lynch then read aloud the incriminating letters (but not the "love" letters, by agreement between O'Dwyer and Lynch). The letters' contents were extremely painful for the couple to hear in open court. "Mr. Lynch read our letters—with proper emphasis," Phil wrote Jerry. Liz and Phil "sat rooted [for five days] while our hopes and affections and lives were stripped layer by layer—sat there impassively helpless, lest the jury and press interpret reaction as guilt. Privacy was shattered, non-violence ridiculed—everything about us reduced to a caricature, a hideous, incompetent, frantic plot—worthy only of the irresponsible, or the mad."[52]

After fourteen days on the stand, including seven days of grueling, pounding, nonstop cross-examination by six defense lawyers, Douglas began to falter. He admitted that he had received FBI payoffs of $200 for helping them find and arrest Dan on Block Island, and that he had demanded $50,000 from the government for his testimony plus an honorable discharge from the army. It was the first time the fact that he was a paid agent was revealed. In fact, on October 3, 1970, Douglas wrote his FBI handler, "Molly" Mayfield, about "an incipient plot" to kidnap Kissinger and destroy the heating pipes, thereby severely hampering government work in Washington. He then thanked Mayfield "for the reward," adding,

"This will be used for a new car soon"—he bought a blue Javelin for $3,800—and then said, "I request a minimum reward of $50,000 (tax free)."

When it was O'Dwyer's turn to question the witness, he was merciless, tearing into Douglas, since he never saw the same Boyd Douglas that Phil and Wenderoth and Liz had. He repeatedly labeled him a paid informer, a "pathological liar," and cited over and over his past history of criminality and use of aliases. To O'Dwyer, his sharp Irish brogue pounding at the witness, the handsome young man on the stand "was an informer who had betrayed the confidence good people had placed in him. He had deliberately led them into a position that made an indictment and jail inevitable . . . I felt no scruple, as my clients and my colleagues did, in attacking his character."[53]

Lynch, on redirect, spent another hour with Douglas, trying to get the jury of nine women and three men to see Douglas in a sympathetic light. He had Douglas tell them that since his release, he had been living under an assumed name in Des Moines, Iowa, employed as a clothing salesman, and that his firm had sent him a letter of commendation. Now it was defense's turn.

The next day, Ramsey Clark—who was President Lyndon Johnson's attorney general when Phil was indicted for the Baltimore and Catonsville raids—rose. To the amazement of everyone, he proclaimed, "The defendants will always seek peace, the defendants continue to proclaim their innocence, and the defense rests."[54]

There was silence, then "What did he say?" in the press section, incredulous at the unexpected maneuver. The decision had been reached a few hours earlier. The defense wanted to underscore the absurdity of the government's case, but it wanted to keep Phil and Liz off the witness stand, since prosecutors would surely demand, among many other details, to know the identities of the people who had hidden Dan while he was underground. They also worried lest transforming the case into a political trial—as Phil, Liz, and Ahmad's testimonies surely would have—not only would fly in the face of what the other defendants wished but could possibly turn the jury against them.

The prosecution, shocked (though later Lynch said that he was "not very surprised" by the tactic), protested. Judge Herman, wrote a bemused Phil, at first snickered, then, "alternately fumbling papers, grinning inanely, uttering incoherences of bewilderment and surprise" turned visibly angry, but there was little he could do, other than send the case to the jury. After almost sixty hours, the jurors returned, expressionless, staring straight ahead at the judge. They could not reach a verdict, they announced, forcing the judge to declare a mistrial. Ten of twelve of Nixon's "silent majority" had voted against the charges of conspiracy. Originally convinced they could not get a fair trial, Phil was jubilant. "It was a tribute to people, that cautious group of mid-Pennsylvanians who wouldn't be finessed out by outrageous bullshit."[55]

Phil and Liz received a relatively modest though unprecedented sentence for smuggling letters in and out of a federal prison, though no one present could recall anyone ever being sentenced to jail for this "crime." To Phil, it was just another travesty of justice, "manufactured reality," he called it. "Money, drugs, pornography, weapons" were smuggled into prisons, but he and Liz were singled out for punishment.[56] (The sentence was later voided by an appellate court.) In the end, Phil proudly confessed to Carol and Jerry Berrigan: "I did not communicate my fear to others; and secondly, . . . I did not begin to hate."[57]

It was a mortifying setback for Hoover and the Nixon White House. Boyd Douglas then disappeared into an early version of the government witness protection program, name and identity changed forever. Still, he continued to press the FBI for money. He called the FBI's attorney Paul Killion and told him that he "was somewhat agitated," because he had supposedly been promised additional moneys by the Philadelphia FBI office. "In view of his propensity to institute unjustified claims against the Government for money he does not deserve," the acting FBI director instructed the Philadelphia office on October 20, 1972, "you should be most circumspect in any future contacts with him, none of which should be initiated by your office." And anyway, noted an FBI memo sent on September 22, Douglas will probably "write a book or otherwise record his experiences, including his relationship with the Bureau."[58]

The ultra-resistance disintegrated at trial's end, exhausted and dis-illusioned by the ordeal. Phil admitted to making "several mistakes in dabbling in violence, such as with the D.C. tunnels" and vowed never to commit himself to any action that might hurt someone. To his brother and sister-in-law he tried to delineate the ultra-resis-tance's weaknesses: too defensive, an "elitist . . . male . . . leader-ship," a movement that "cannot sustain itself [or] sustain continu-ity." Later, he added, "our movement wasn't religious in the deep sense of having deep roots and a sense of identity to sustain us," and as time passed, it became more secular. "[W]e used nonviolence only as a strategy, as something to be used against our enemies. We didn't work the evil and hatred out of ourselves."[59]

The movement's women were among the first to drift away. Nuns were outraged at privileges accorded male priests in Harrisburg and in movement retreats and caucuses. The "priest as hero" and the "priest as stud" disgusted numerous movement women, lay as well as religious.[60]

As John Deedy, an early biographer of Dan, pointed out, "the drainage to Catholicism in the communities of resistance was espe-cially pronounced among women," a significant number of them feeling the church was unsympathetic to their needs, and that many of the Catholic Left's men, Phil more than Dan, were blind to their complaints and aspirations. Long before Harrisburg, the draft board raids had been interpreted as male attacks on the war while mothers and wives of the card burners and draft board raiders had to wait, caring for their families or participating in the resistance's more servile tasks. Before the trial opened, an HDC woman member, in an open letter to her "dear sisters," made the point that women, too, were suffering from police surveillance and harassment by grand juries, and that women lawyers and a raising of the issues of sexism and discrimination were badly needed.[61]

"So we're being called sexist, huh?" wrote Phil from Lewisburg during the trial. "That's a gas! While admitting possibilities in that regard, esp. in myself I still question the myopic, shrill one-issue shit these termagants cling to. Some of them would ignore mass murder to get resolved the issue of the clitoral area [and] the vaginal orgasm."[62]

Dan, far more moderate on the subject, however, thought feminism could wait while the exigencies of war and peace were being resolved, but he "approved of women as priests." Still, he remained a target of radical feminists for years after, especially by those furious at his opposition to abortion, even as he expressed no sympathy for violent, latter-day anti-abortionists.[63]

Others wandered away as well. Jim Forest, now quite estranged, accused Phil and Liz of deceiving the HDC and their fellow defendants about the letters rather than confiding in them, for Forest a blatant disregard of the Gandhian notion of the need for truthfulness. Forest abandoned the book he was writing about the trial, for which he had a book publisher's contract. "We deserved better," he wrote, his close relationship with Dan and Phil ruptured for the moment, and perhaps forever. Joe O'Rourke, Phil's lieutenant and close friend, was also disappointed, but for different reasons. "The real failure of Harrisburg was that out of every single trial came action, but nothing came from Harrisburg." The movement was in shambles but for an isolated raid on Hickam Air Force Base near Honolulu, which attracted little or no media attention or new recruits. Like it or not, everything was built around Phil's energy and leadership and Dan's moral standing. After the trial, little was left on which to build their new world.[64]

As if in response, Phil wrote his mother, "I know why I'm here and would not have it otherwise." And to Dan he added: "To my mind, our greatest achievement in jail was learning our meaning to one another, and trusting it implicitly. We are not done yet—just beginning. I love you, and wish only that I could love you more." As if in response, Dan wrote a loving "prison poem to philip"

> with us it was never
> winner and loser
> but you, a big AND
> and i and our two hands,
> who cared if overhead

napkined and beaked
in the air a buzzard stank
in the air the wrong gods;
heel to heel, we ran.
both
made it, death to life
so no hindmost and no
devil to take either.[65]

Liz decided that what they now needed was "a deeper form of community as a witness to the presence of the 'kin-dom,' as a magnetism for good, as an antidote to the culture. That is where Jonah House was born." Rather than concentrate on building a large, political movement, they would shrink dramatically in size, dedicating the remainder of their lives to living among the poor, bearing witness, and suffering imprisonment in their contempt for the consumerist, excessively materialist, and nuclear Mammon. They would continue confronting the state nonviolently, even if they were abandoned and ignored. "I only have my life in this permissive culture," Phil explained, obviously speaking for both of them. "I can only give up my freedom. We speak of jail as a witness, an extension of action and resistance in a courtroom. Jail is a form of resistance, the kind of resistance practiced by Prophets, Jesus and early Christians. That's redemptive and slowly, imperceptibly, turns people *if* they want it."[66]

Yet above all else, conscience and protest did count, and millions of others opposed to the pointless and bloody war were right. Had there been no demonstrations, no draft board raids, no campus upheavals, no alternative weeklies, no centrist opposition, and, yes, no Dan or Phil Berrigan and the Catholic Left, there is no telling when it might have ended, how many more Asians and Americans would have died, and even whether nuclear weapons might have been used. "More than any other war in history, it is a foul carrion bird coming home to roost [and] physical death for the Indochinese brings about moral death in us," a caustic and unchastened Phil said when he was finally released from prison in 1972.[67]

Phil was welcomed back into the Josephites. Two of their priests greeted him at the Danbury prison gates when he was freed. "What appeared to be 'arrogance,' was rather his [Phil's] conviction based on Christian principles that our nation could better serve mankind through a more positive policy," his superior general explained, oblivious to the fact that Phil and Liz had exchanged marital vows in the sacristy, next to John Peter Grady's office, in 1969, in the unoccupied Iron Mountain Episcopal Church in the Bronx.

"Dear Mary and Dick," Phil wrote friends in Seattle in 1973. "It's our 4th anniversary (Liz and myself) and we're going public." They had renewed their marital vows at Danbury in January 1972—witnessed by Dan and Sister Jogues—and legalized the marriage on May 28, 1973, with a gala party in June in Upper Montclair. Later, nine guests gathered with the couple in Dan's eleventh-floor Manhattan apartment to celebrate the union. Someone asked Phil when he had changed his mind about celibacy; he had, after all, urged it on others as the cornerstone for a complete commitment to the "revolutionary lifestyle." But now he said he had changed, a rationalization that failed to persuade the church's religious who had placed great trust in his words. "Celibacy was instituted in the fifth century," he explained at the party, "for the sake of bureaucracy," an explanation he repeated over the next few months. "I am resisting the attempt to make this the central thing in Christian life."

Within the movement, or what was left of it, there was dismay and disenchantment. Others, outside, gloated about priestly hypocrisy and made abundant sexual jokes. Even Dan was suspect: Was he any different? detractors asked. At the celebration in his apartment, Dan said he was overjoyed, though he was silent about it in his writings. The Josephites, though, were not silent. Phil was promptly ousted from their order. "We are sorry to lose a brother who in the past had given years of service as a parish priest, as a teacher, and as a man of great energy and dedication," they declared, though not every Josephite priest agreed with the sentiment. Still, he had his supporters, like an eighty-five-year-old woman, a parishioner at a Josephite Baltimore church, who decided the marriage was fine with her. She said that Liz "got a good man. Let me tell you—if I were younger . . . "[68]

J. Edgar Hoover died on May 2, 1972. Asked by a reporter for a comment, Dan said he hoped Hoover had gained the mercy he had for so long denied others.

15

THE SPEECH

The tragedy of the Jewish-Arab encounter is not, as Berrigan would have it, that the Arabs were right and the Jews were wrong, but that both were right. The reality is in ambiguity, in proximate justice.

—*Rabbi Arthur Hertzberg*

IT WAS 1973 AND THE YOM KIPPUR WAR (TO JEWS) AND THE October War (to Arabs and Palestinians) had drawn to its unsatisfactory conclusion, with all sides more unreconciled and resentful than ever.

Israel was torn internally with harsh recriminations directed at its old-line leaders. America's Jews were especially concerned, their nerves on edge, alarmed that Israel had come within a hair's breadth of being overwhelmed by invading armies. The bulk of American Jewry had awakened during the 1967 Six-Day War with visions of David slaying the powerful Goliath, and a sense of triumphalism spread everywhere, as America's Jews basked in tales of

Israeli daring and military prowess. One best-selling poster had portrayed General Moshe Dayan in a Superman suit. Israelis as Supermen. Unbeatable in war. Tough as cactus plants in peacetime. Noble idealists. It was no wonder that so many Vietnam hawks, bogged down in a civil war that could not be won, so admired Israel's military prowess.

Less than three decades from the stench of Auschwitz, America's Jews believed that Israel's position was precarious—friendless, dependent on its own grit and fortitude, save for fellow Jews in the Diaspora who provided badly needed money and political support in Washington, though few immigrants, and, generally, American government blessings.

To American Jewish organizations, then, any public criticism of Israel, especially after the Holocaust, was troublesome, and to the more passionate, it was biased, indefensible, anti-Zionist, and anti-Semitic. Consequently, Israel's friends and allies in this country—from left to right—did all they could to form a solid phalanx against any and all reproaches, both from within and from without. Any suggestions by dovish Jews, however modest or timid, that Palestinians, too, had rights, were stigmatized and their proponents condemned as anti-Israel and pro-PLO (Palestine Liberation Organization). American Jews, as the saying went, were often "more Israelis than the Israelis." And if dovish Jews could be driven to cover, how could critical outsiders expect anything else?[1]

The antiwar movement in general, and Dan and his community of friends in particular, rarely mentioned the Middle East, since Southeast Asia held the greatest priority. There was another factor: So many Jews had opposed the war in Asia, and their backing—financial, literary, moral, political, and, in Dan's case, often personal—was essential.

There is yet another clue to his thinking about this issue. In his syllabus at Cornell for one of his noncredit discussion courses, Gandhi: This Man Is Disarmed and Dangerous, Dan wrote: "Gandhi's life and death are an example of a constant law; most human beings (but not all) fall far short of humanity. The Bible has said the same thing for a long time. The Jews, probably because they have always had a classic minority stance before the onslaught of the goyim, have placed their act of trust in what the prophets call a 'saving remnant.' Which is to say, their hope is simply in their own historic situation, as God has cast some measure of light upon it. It is better, the times inevitably being what they are, to be the victim rather than the predator. Even from the point of view of survival, it seems to be better. The incapacity of the victim for survival is unproven, simply because he has been chewed up in this or that instance. Indeed, this or that instance may show him how to escape next time. But the predator who becomes a congenital predator, that is to say, who needs seriously to disturb the natural balance in order to survive, becomes too big to survive."[2]

While teaching at the University of Manitoba in Winnipeg, Canada, Dan received an invitation to speak in Washington, D.C., on October 19, 1973. It was yet another speech among dozens he delivered each year, and he would challenge the shibboleths of everyone concerned, writing the speech without help, deleting and editing until he had a final draft. The invitation was from the Association of Arab-American University Graduates, a group he had never heard of. When he finally mounted the rostrum, he faced a pro-Palestinian, clearly anti-Israeli audience.

"When he left Winnipeg to deliver the speech," said Peter Jordan, his teaching assistant in the religion department, "Dan knew he was going to stir things up," though clearly he had no idea of the thunderstorm his speech would arouse and how it would alter his life. Living in Winnipeg, a city of 600,000 far removed from major cosmopolitan centers—"the center of nowhere" says native Winnepegian Jordan—Dan had, it seemed, momentarily lost touch with the harsh and unforgiving world outside.

When Dan arrived in Washington for the specch, Arthur Waskow says he visited with Eqbal Ahmad at the Institute of Policy Studies but failed to drop into Waskow's adjoining office, where "Dan could have gotten a serious radical Jewish view of Israel." Waskow later explained: "The socialist and Christian lefts have never quite learned to live with the anomaly of a religiously covenanted but not universally religious Jewish people and its stubborn fusion of particularism with universalism and of commitment to the world with commitment to a single land," he wrote in a pacifist magazine after the speech.[3]

Years later Dan insisted that his decision to speak on so contentious, so impassioned an issue, was a "calculated choice," though whether he had ever really seriously examined the Mideast's complex and hoary issues or even had written much of anything on the subject is problematical.[4] Certainly he had no real grasp of the trouble that lay ahead. "It was a considerable mercy that I knew nothing of the outcome," he wrote in *To Dwell in Peace*, his autobiography.[5] Perhaps he experienced an epiphany and, as always, honed in automatically on the side of people he believed to be impotent victims. Of Jewish memories and Israeli fears he knew little; Palestinians, after all, were opposed to their Israeli conquerors and masters. Their homes and property were expropriated, their young men were killed and imprisoned. Tens of thousands still languished in dismal refugee camps. It was all he had to know.

He opened his talk, typically presenting himself as a "nonexpert" and pacifist. "Shit," muttered a young man in the audience, "another damn pacifist," and marched out.

What, actually, did he say?[6]

Dan began by damning Arab and Israeli policies. The equivalence was deliberate, though few in the legions of the outraged cared one whit about what he had to say about Arab governments; Arabs, after all, had no influential lobby or sophisticated public relations apparatus in this country, other than their sycophants in the oil business and here and there among State Department Arabists. Israel, home to hundreds of thousands of Holocaust survivors, and the source of much Christian guilt about historical Christian anti-Semitism and its widespread reluctance to condemn publicly the Nazis' mass murders during the Second World War, was all that mattered.

He opened with a statement of his absolute pacifism, saying he didn't wish to align himself with one side or the other. "I am sick of 'sides'; which is to say, I am sick of war; of wars hot and cold . . . sick of foreign ministers and all their works and pomps . . . sick of torture and secret police and the apparition of fascists and the rhetoric of the leftists."

Then on to a succinct, though no less biting, critique of the Arab states and "their capacity for deception . . . their contempt for their own poor . . . their willingness to oil the war machinery of the superpowers making them accomplices of the American war criminals. . . . No, I offer no apologia for the Arab states any more than I do for Israel." The character of Jews had been transformed. "The wandering Jew became the settler Jew, the settler ethos became the imperial adventure." He argued that "the coinage of Israel is stamped with the imperialist faces whose favor she has courted, the creation of millionaires, generals and entrepreneurs. And the price is being paid by Israel's Oriental Jews, the poor. . . . Zionist violence and repression joins the violence and repression of the great (and little) powers; a common method, a common dead end."

And much more. Israel "has not passed from a dispossessed people to a democratic state, as she would claim, she has passed from a dispossessed people to an imperial entity. . . . And this (I say with a sinking heart) is to the loss of all the world." The world had always witnessed "criminal Christian communities"; it "had never known a criminal Jewish community. We had known Jewish communities that were a light to the gentiles, that were persecuted, all but erased, that remained merciful, eloquent, prophetic. But something new was occurring before our eyes. . . . The Jews arose from the holocaust, a cause of universal joy; but the Jews arose like warriors, armed to the teeth, They took possession of a land, they exiled and destroyed old Arab communities."

Turning to American Jewish leaders, he insisted—somewhat inaccurately—that they offered support for the war in Vietnam in return for American weaponry to Israel. "Mrs. Meir [Golda, then Israel's prime minister] wanted Phantom jets and Nixon wanted re-election. . . . To put the matter brutally, many American Jewish leaders were capable of ignoring the Asian holocaust in favor of economic and military aid to Israel. . . . The fate of the Vietnamese was as unimportant to the Zionists in our midst as was the state of the Palestinians," though he clearly and properly exempted "the great majority of the Jewish community which refused the bait offered by Nixon, and peddled by their own leaders . . . and for that we must honor them."

How, Dan asked, does a Jesuit priest bring himself to utter these forbidden words? Because, he explained, his is a "debt of love, more properly, a debt of outraged love" by a Christian battling his church and country. "I am a Catholic priest, in resistance against Rome. I am an American, in resistance against Nixon. And I am a Jew, in resistance against Israel"—a phrase that infuriated many Jews. "In America, in my church, I am a Jew. I am scarcely granted a place to teach, a place to worship, a place to announce the truths I live by. I stand in front of St. Patrick's Cathedral to pray for the victims of our ceaseless rage. I stand in front of the White House. And a question arises from both powers; how shall we deal with this troublesome Jew?"

He continued, "How does a Jesuit, a member of the church elite, come to such trouble? How does the son of the oppressor come to be oppressed even while the oppressed, the Zionist, the state of Israel, becomes the oppressor?"

Concluding, he maintained, "Israel has betrayed her exodus by turning it into military conquests. And the Arabs have often betrayed their resistance to rhetorical violence and blind terrorism. The question . . . is: What else can we do?"[7]

"This was potent criticism" to the Arab audience and worse than outrageous to American Jewish pro-Israelis, wrote John Deedy.[8]

The speech delivered, he flew back to Winnipeg, utterly oblivious to the explosion he had unwittingly fashioned. Ironically, the speech would have gone largely unnoticed had it not been reprinted in the antiwar newspaper *American Report* on October 29. Not many people read that paper, but when the *New York Times* and the wire services picked up the story, all hell broke loose.

A friend working in the campus ministry at Boston University tried to warn him: The school's Jewish chaplain was sending around a memo to all the campus ministers, expressing grief that someone (Dan) he had admired for so long could express such "calumnies."[9]

Establishment apparatchiks and political right-wingers began damning him, as was inevitable, but that they were joined by his erstwhile sympathizers and advocates, many themselves longtime critics of some Israeli policies, transformed the parameters of the argument. Dan Berrigan, a Jesuit priest and valued iconoclast of the antiwar movement, had crossed a line, alienating them with what they maintained were bizarre hyperbole and misstatements.

Not only had he delivered his words to an assembly of Israel's enemies, but Dan's description of Israel was offered in the same uncharitable way that he and Phil had had to endure during the height of the war. Who, his dovish critics demanded, were the real victims of the Israeli-Palestinian eternal conflict? Only the Palestinians? Or were both victims of a mutual calamity only partly of their own making?

Dan's text was one of many similar ones he had delivered on a variety of topics. You merely had to substitute aggressors and victims. It certainly wasn't dissimilar from the sorts of things he had spoken and written about his church, as when he assailed "the pervasive cultural witness of the American Church, its illusions about moral superiority, its massive spiritual victimization by racism, cold and hot war fervor, anti-Communism."[10] Even so, he had never even been to Israel or visited Palestinians inside Israel or in the West Bank or Gaza.

An early biographer, John Deedy, formerly an editor of *Commonweal*, noted that Dan "still insists that there is a critical distinction … between the whole prophetic and historic content of the Old Testament on the one hand, and the state of Israel on the other," a distinction unacceptable to Jewish theologians, let alone to American Jewish supporters. This attempt at so subtle a distinction seemed to them mere sophistry.[11]

From the Jewish iconoclast Arthur Hertzberg, the highly regarded rabbi, historian, and Zionist, who had been an early and forceful opponent of the Vietnam War, came the most crushing critique. Despite his lack of any organized constituency, Hertzberg had considerable intellectual influence, and he opened and defined the attack by categorizing Dan's speech as "old-fashioned theological anti-Semitism," a shattering accusation and one that simply was *not* the experience of every Jew who had ever known Dan Berrigan.

To his early critics, Dan snapped back: "I'm as anti-Semitic as I am anti-Catholic."

Hertzberg, who was frequently critical of American Jewish and Israeli policies and was hardly a shrinking violet himself, angrily declared that Dan had allowed for "no decency, no honor, no compassion, no social justice—only unrelieved wickedness . . . against a neighbor whom he has never seen in the flesh." Dan had overlooked a crucial element in his concern for the refugees as victims: Neither side was totally right or wrong but—and this was constant and a central element in the refutations offered by his dovish critics—"both were right. The reality," said the rabbi rightly to the priest, "is in ambiguity, in proximate justice," a nuance that Dan had missed, despite his commendable attempt to bring the issue of the Palestinians' plight to the fore. It was a struggle not between absolute right and wrong, as Dan saw it, but rather between two peoples who saw themselves on the side of God and justice.[12]

Paul Jacobs, who had also been branded a pariah by some American Jewish true-believers because of *his* disapproval of Israel and its policies toward Palestinians, and who had written an aptly named book about the Mideastern imbroglio, *Between the Rock and the Hard Place*, also found Dan's speech troublesome. As critical as he was of conservatives who unjustly compared Dan to discredited Jew-hating Catholic priests like Father Charles Coughlin, and of those Jews who insisted Zionism and Judaism were "virtually identical," Jacobs nevertheless argued that Dan simply didn't understand Israeli life and politics, neither its "ambiguities" nor the stresses and tensions resulting from its past or present. Rather, Dan offered his friendly audience a "good guy, bad guy scenario" without citing the deep divisions among Israelis, their peace movement, and the difficulty in finding enough influential, peace-minded Palestinians and Arabs with whom to do business.[13]

Dan didn't help matters by proclaiming, "I am a Jew, in resistance against Israel," as if trying, some interpreted, to equate his own suffering with the history of millions of Jewish victims. The model of Israeli Jews as subjugators and Palestinians as Jews (symbolically at least) was hardly novel, given that a few pacifists and leftists had already begun writing in this vein. But American and

Israeli Jews, already sensitive to Christian anti-Semitism, and acutely aware of Israel's encirclement by unremittingly hostile Arab states and threatened by internal terrorism, were not too inclined to allow a Roman Catholic priest to preach to them. Similarly, philosopher Martin Buber and Judah Magnes, the first president of the Hebrew University, both advocates of a pre–State-of-Israel binational entity with Jews and Palestinians sharing power, had once rejected the Hindu Gandhi's suggestion that Jews confront the Nazis with nonviolence—as if it were a viable option, and as if Nazi brutality could in any way be equated with the actions of imperial Britain. Once Dan's words were aired in public, and despite his best intentions, they precipitated anger among Jews because of the church's historic anti-Semitism.

Arthur Waskow said that he was "angry as hell" after he learned of the speech, and that for Dan to have the temerity to state "I am a Jew" was to use that definition to buttress an attack on Jews and Israel that could delegitimatize Israel. He added, as others had, that Dan had no sense of the complexity of the issue and the profound emotional responses it was sure to arouse. "By claiming Jewishness and asserting that the Jews have betrayed the Covenant, he triggers in Jews the oldest image of the dangerous Christian: the Christian who claims the Church is the New Israel; the Christian who honors the suffering Jew, but cannot hear that the Jewish hero is not Jesus crucified or even Akiba tortured, but the Moses who won his peoples' liberation; the Christian who leaps toward sainthood, and is baffled by the plodding Jews. Dan Berrigan is no anti-Semite, but what Jews remember was that from roots like these in the past have flowered the most serious, the least brutal, the loftiest anti-Semitism—and the deepest."[14]

It was a far more enigmatic and perplexing Middle East than Dan had ever imagined.

But he had a few defenders, such as his friend, the writer and Jew James Munves. "My own point of view is that Dan hasn't an anti-Semitic bone in his body," said Munves. "I believe it was because of his awareness of this that he felt safe in saying what he did. I also believe in a way that he [still] thinks of himself as more Jewish than many Jews. His Jesuit training included study of biblical Hebrew

312 DISARMED AND DANGEROUS

(although, really, he has retained little) and his theology, which is very much liberation theology, derives from the prophets of the Tanach. (He is always talking about the Shekinah.) His criticism of Israel thus came out of the knowledge of what Jews could and should be, as inheritors of the prophetic tradition."[15]

The ensuing uproar divided the pacifist and largely leftist antiwar movements and grew so savage in its unrestrained animosity that Dan, his sense of humor strained, yet still intact, said he had somehow replaced God "in prime pulpit time." But the fact remains that even his most ardent admirers were appalled by portions of the speech, by its sweeping, unsupported generalizations, its flawed use of certain phrases that led many to think he had actually or implicitly compared Israeli Jewish behavior toward Palestinians to the Nazis, which he hadn't. "The word 'Nazi' was never used" an irritated, upset Dan told Hans Morgenthau, his discussion partner in a televised interview. He had only accused Israeli of using "racist language." It was hard to appreciate the nuance. "Settler Jew, imperial entity, repression, cruelty, militarism" were all that could be heard above the shouting and denunciations. Dreadful words invited enraged retorts.

Morgenthau, a very early and effective antiwar critic, asked Dan if he had learned anything from the affair.

Dan answered that the indictment of him as anti-Semitic was not only inaccurate but "has to do with an effort to warn me and others to keep quiet." Still, the counterattack had been so *unexpected* and so harrowing, agonizing, and painful. "I stepped in where it was forbidden to step in. I took a chance. On the other hand, I don't want to say that I think it's a rational response for people to say this man is suddenly functioning out of hatred or irrationality, or anti-Semitism or insanity. I think the supposition of someone about someone like myself ought to be, 'Well, he certainly irritated us, and he probably was wrong on a lot of points, but maybe he's worth listening to.' "

Morgenthau responded: "I would fully agree with the last sentence. My personal respect for Father Berrigan has not been diminished at all. Perhaps, my evaluation of his political wisdom has been somewhat impaired."[16]

"That was a speech he should have shown me," said Paul Mayer, coordinator of the Catonsville, Milwaukee, and Harrisburg defense committees, a major strategist of the movement, and an unindicted co-conspirator at the Harrisburg trial, someone Dan once described as a "peacemaker, Jewish Catholic, priest, monk, friend."[17]

Mayer believed that had he seen the speech beforehand, he would have used different language and different "formulations," though he agreed with the sentiments and opinions expressed. Writing to Dan, Mayer elaborated, saying that although a portion here and there might have been changed, "it was a statement that badly needed to be made but it is a hard word and 'who will hear it'? The Jewish community is so closed on this issue. I try to avoid it when I can with my father," a committed Zionist.[18]

Paul Mayer was born in Frankfurt, Germany, into a Jewish Zionist family. Fleeing the Nazis, he arrived in the United States with his parents in 1938, much like Henry Kissinger and his family. Paul and Henry never met, but as young immigrants they lived in the same Washington Heights neighborhood of upper Manhattan (dubbed the "Fourth Reich" because of the many German Jewish refugees there), and graduated from George Washington High School. Kissinger's family joined an Orthodox synagogue founded by Mayer's grandfather in Germany. It was a marvelous paradox that the Nixon Administration charged Mayer in 1971 for conspiring to kidnap Kissinger.

When he was sixteen, Mayer converted to Catholicism and entered St. Paul's Abbey in Newton, New Jersey, where he served as a Benedictine monk until 1966, when he married a former nun. He was, he joked, "an all-around apostate (church, synagogue, state)."[19]

Several months after the speech, his father, Ernest, visited Sylvia Heschel, Rabbi Abraham Joshua Heschel's widow. "My father told me last night," he wrote Dan on December 25, 1973, "that during a conversation with Mrs. Heschel your infamous piece in *American Report* came up. She spoke very warmly of you [and] also wants very much to have you visit her when you are next in New York—perhaps together with the Mayer clan."[20]

Dan was heartened and extremely delighted to hear this. The attacks were showing no signs of abating and he had been close to Heschel. Before Heschel's death in December 1972, they had planned to collaborate on a book in response to the anti-Catholic tone Heschel said he thought he detected in some book. "You and I have to write a rejoinder to this awful book," he told Dan, who had himself been moved and inspired by Heschel's seminal book, *The Prophets*.[21]

Both men shared a common view of politics, the war in Vietnam, the prevailing domestic racism. They also felt a common brotherhood in their fervor for their religious faiths.[22] After Catonsville, Heschel was one of six clergy who signed a full-page ad praising the nine men and women who "did confront the evil of our times."[23] Dan, in fact, had recently composed an admiring essay about Heschel: "Simply put, he was my friend." In his autobiography, he also portrayed Heschel as "a father to me, in more sense than one . . ." a "saint, before the judgment." Both of them were "more and more isolated in America" because of their stand on the war. While neither was friendless, if Dan was an outcast in the eyes of his church's bureaucracy, Heschel was occasionally criticized by some of his colleagues and co-religionists for the ardor of his antiwar views and his association with Martin Luther King Jr.

When a bishop he respected and honored died, Dan wrote his mother that the late cleric had the very qualities of "dear goodness and love and genius," which reminded him "(I do not hesitate to say it) of Dr. Heschel."

In December 1972, when Phil was released from Danbury prison, Heschel and his daughter, Suzanne, were there to greet him. Ten days later, Heschel was dead of a heart attack.

"Dearest Momma," Dan wrote his mother, "I do not know if I got to tell you; Phil and I had an invitation to take tea with himself and Mrs. Heschel and their daughter. Phil was resting; I picked up the phone, an hour before we were to go down to the street to their apartment. It was their daughter Suzanne, in tears; Dr. Heschel was dead. He was truly a light to the people. We will not see his like again."[24]

Dan had found and lost a soul mate, who, he firmly believed for years after the speech, would have raced to his defense, even though Heschel clearly loved Israel and the Jewish people. But would he have? In 1967, in the midst of the Six-Day War, Dan sensed that "a shadow fell across our friendship." He asked himself if his friend would oppose the war as he had opposed America's war in Vietnam. "Heartsick," Dan wrote Heschel a letter asking where he stood on the question. Then Dan had second thoughts. Heschel was not well, and "I had no heart to raise an issue bound to be painful beyond measure." He destroyed the letter and never again posed the question.[25]

"My life goes like this," went Dan's poem about the speech and its aftermath.

"The Christians decided to make a Jew of me/I ended up around someone's neck, an albatross or crucifix—anyway, a 'saving metaphor.' . . . And the Jews?/When I came round, they laid it down hard; 'Love us, love yeretz Israel!'/When I stammered out distinctions, distinctions . . . they would have none of it, fists came down/ So my destiny (big deal) is marginal as a cockroach or a crucifix . . . "[26]

It was all bravado. Many of his friends say he was devastated, and still suffers from the wounds. Anonymous hate mail poured in, overwhelmingly from scandalized Jews, a people he had always felt were his special allies, people he often felt closer to than many of his fellow Catholics in their opposition to the war and their votes against Nixon. And nowhere in all his writings and speeches, even in his ad lib remarks, was there even the slightest hint of anti-Jewish sentiments.

The repercussions and retribution continued. The pacifist Rabbi Everett Gendler, a longtime member of the Jewish Peace Fellowship, said, "I could have wept," because the substance and tone of the speech were too damning, too absolute. "Are human tangles so simple as to warrant such an approach? Whatever may have been the case with Vietnam, the Middle East today defies such oversimplification."[27] And David Saperstein, who so admired Dan at Cornell and spent much time with him at Danbury while he was a student rabbi, was shocked. While he didn't talk with Dan about it, he sent him a copy of the veteran Israeli peacenik Amos Kenan's letter to Fidel Castro, which said that being pro-Israel was consonant with freedom. By now Saperstein had been ordained as a rabbi, and while officiating at the Bar Mitzvah of the son of the actress Phyllis Newman and playwright/lyricist Adolph Green, he encountered composer Leonard Bernstein, who had once hosted Black Panthers in his posh East Side apartment and been friendly with Dan. Bernstein, says Saperstein, expressed a sense of betrayal.[28]

And Dan had so few defenders. Phil was one, of course. Speaking at St. Joseph's College in Philadelphia in late November, he struck out against his familiar foes—Nixon; Kissinger; Alexander P. Haig, Nixon's chief of staff after H.R. Haldeman departed; "war mongers who fight one war and prepare for the next with the people's money," before assailing Israel for having deserted the prophetic tradition and establishing a "minor superstate in imitation of our major superstate."[29]

Dan's paramount shield, however, was Jim Forest, editor of *Fellowship* magazine and a principled veteran of the war against the war. Forest played the major role (with Allan Solomonow) in the editing and publication of a pamphlet, *The Great Berrigan Debate*, arranging for financing and advertising.

He maintained a steady stream of correspondence exonerating Dan. Courteous to a fault, he typed long letters to seething correspondents threatening to withhold donations from the Fellowship of Reconciliation (FOR), the magazine's sponsor, or to abandon peace activities. He did not hesitate to admit the speech had flaws, such as the biased audience and the preponderance of criticism directed largely at Israel. But when someone complained that Dan had no right to call himself a Jew, Forest explained in *Fellowship* that while it properly angered critics, "it was revelatory of his own vocation within the Christian tradition, but hardly established a foothold for communication with Jews." He also time and again directed aggrieved readers of *Fellowship* to Abraham Joshua Heschel's book *The Prophets*. The book opens with a portrayal that to Forest was "astonishing," given the battle over the speech and the true character of Berrigan: "To us, a single set of injustices—cheating in business, exploitation of the poor—is slight; to the prophets a disaster. To us injustice is injurious to the welfare of the people; to the prophets it is a deathblow to existence; to us, an episode; to them a catastrophe, a threat to the world." Quoting Heschel's portrait of the Hebrew prophets, Forest could only think of Dan Berrigan.[30]

Two months after the speech, on December 16, 1973, Dan was turned down for the Gandhi Peace Award, originally offered him by Promoting Enduring Peace, located in Woodmont, Connecticut, a group whose officers included the religious scholar Roland Bainton, Yale law professor Thomas Emerson, and many liberals and doves. Once the *Times* account of the speech was out, the group had to swallow hard; it decided to poll its board, putting its previous selection of Dan into question. The Reverend Donald Harrington, a Protestant liberal minister of the Community Church in New York City and a board member of Promoting Enduring Peace, castigated Berrigan for having "trailed off into anti-Semitism." CALCAV, the organization Dan had helped form in 1965, backed away from co-sponsorship of the award ceremony. Only 103 people were left with tickets, many others having canceled or demanded refunds.

With characteristic bravado in the face of condemnation and antagonism, Dan was really beside himself, filled with contempt at the very idea of a popularity poll. Clearly bruised but certainly proud and very angry and very hurt, he wrote Roy Pfaff, PEP's executive director, that his "conscience is not subject to your constituency" and that PEP had collapsed before outside pressures. Dan recalled his earlier experience with the church when he was driven into exile because he objected to Cardinal Spellman's prowar views and asked Pfaff who he thought "was at that time speaking for the honor of the church." Some things that cannot be debated and discussed publicly become a form of idolatry. "[H]as Israel itself become your idol? And in service to the idol are you urging, as a solution to violence, ever more violence—including psychological violence against those who seek another way. . . . Thus my offense. I had pursued a critique and urged in consequence, a search for alternatives. Of this I am beyond doubt guilty."[31]

Dan flew off to Paris, to his Buddhist friends, where he often went in search of solace. But it was impossible to forget the debacle. To his closest friends and allies, the shrinking community of people he trusted most, he wrote, "I am grateful for the sympathy and debate and heat and ice and anger; for everything but the hatred (which one confronts in fear and trembling)," ending up with his deepest belief, of his vision of witness and Jesus on the Cross, and enclosed this:

> We want to bury your dead.
> We want to stand with your resisters.
> We want to bind the wounds of your victims.
> We want to weep with your widows.
> We want to suffer with your displaced persons.

And then, finally, a practical restatement of his and Phil's moral imperative: "I had seen nothing in our scripture which allowed us to take sides, to approve of war."[32]

Seven years earlier, he had written "Dachau Is Now Open for Visitors" about the horrors of the concentration camps.

> The arabesque scrawled by the dead
> in their laborious passage,
> leaf and flower mould of their spent bodies, faces frost touch
>   gently and coldly
> to time's geometric—
>
> a multitude of skeletal men
> presses forward; such cries
> the patient poor speak, whose despair
> leaves no man's peace intact, no coin
> for death's foreclosing fist.[33]

To his legion of critics, it made no difference then and now. Dan Berrigan was a marked man, less for what he had done than for what he had said.

In April 1974 he was home in New York City, mornings striding the streets of upper Broadway, fraternizing with his fellow Jesuits in the mammoth apartment house on West 98th Street where they lived. How the small-town boy from rural Minnesota and upstate New York loved the city! "I miss it every time I'm away," he said lovingly.

Had he missed anything while he was gone? Was there anything to learn from the experience? Determined to see for himself, he abruptly decided to travel to Israel, Lebanon, and Egypt. He and Paul Mayer would make the trip, and they would tape extensive interviews for a book they hoped to publish. Their notion was to spend two weeks in Israel, the West Bank, Lebanon, and Egypt, and, if possible, to visit Syria and other Arab states.[34]

Berrigan was the eternal expatriate and exile, and for the moment at least an outcast, and Mayer was the former Jew and Catholic monk, whose father, a passionate Zionist, had once worked with Martin Buber in Germany. Mayer had many Israeli family members, among them his uncle, once the dean of the Hebrew University's medical faculty, and his mother's sister.

They also wanted to go beyond contemporary events, to search out their religious roots, or so Dan said toward the end of their journey. Both wanted to see the places where Jesus was born and died, and where "the prophets and kings and sinners . . . who have shaped and misshaped us actually lived."[35]

Arriving at Tel Aviv's Ben-Gurion Airport while throngs of Christian pilgrims were departing following Holy Week in 1974, they were driven to Jerusalem to meet Paul's cousins and their children and Paul's aunt. In Israel, they were constantly on the go, talking day and night about the war with Palestinians and Jews of all political views. They met scores of people eager to share their many opinions—academics, rabbis, writers, Knesset members, Israeli Palestinians. They visited two refugee camps on the West Bank. They were invited for lunch at a kibbutz and given a tour of the grounds. "Fine, intelligent people," Dan described the Israelis he met in letters home to "Maywood" (Jerry and Carol), "the Baltimores" (Phil and Liz and the gang at Jonah House), and "Momma."

Many they met tried to get them to understand the imbroglio and how the situation often defied simple solutions, how hard it was to differentiate between absolute right and wrong, and how much more of a convoluted tangle it was than Vietnam, given the region's history, its religious passions, and the variegated interests involved.

It was quite an education.

Dan watched in horror as a poor Palestinian tried to offer an Israeli bus driver an orange as a peace offering to atone for a murder of Jews the week before. The driver recoiled in fear, alarmed that it might contain a bomb, and refused the gift. "War madness," Dan called it. But who could blame the driver? Or the Palestinian? "Apart from the burnoose, etc., one can hardly tell Jew from Arab, especially as Sephardic, Asian, African Jews are so dark and Semitic-looking," lending reinforcement, if that was even needed, of his previsit conclusion that there was "never a more absurd, useless war. In the last phase, 2600–3000 dead Israelis, which in our country would be equivalent to 2–300 thousand. Everyone has lost someone, almost a new whiff of holocaust."[36]

Talking, taping, trying to take in everything, Mayer thought the journey was moving and informative, given the "enormity and complexity of the problem."[37]

One day they wandered around the Old City and were, as Dan wrote, deeply affected by "the golden light, the pilgrim places worn by centuries of pilgrims, the three faiths holding tight on three beginnings, nurtured and bled for. And then the complete absence of *anyone* from any faith, Moslem, Jewish, Christian, who might shed some light on present bloodletting. Sad indeed."

Another day, they spent time with a friend of Martin Buber, a Bergen-Belsen concentration camp survivor, and then with a Quaker couple and their Palestinian friend. These long, relaxed conversations pleased Dan, his mind open to new revelations and experiences, "a week of rebirth, frustration, great highs and lows, pounding the pavements talking to all sorts from moderates to at least one great old radical save one." Yet if nonviolence as a way out of the darkness was for both men a natural corrective, no one in the Middle East dared risk it, would ever dream of disarming, or would accept it as a possible means of coping with the impasse. Except for Haifa's bishop, they couldn't find one religious figure of any denomination whom people might "want to turn to and see some reconciliation through—part of the tragedy indeed."

Soon to depart, more sensitive to Israeli fears, sensing the deep reservoir of mutual hostility and dread, an enigma apparently without resolution, Dan still grieved for the stateless Palestinians he had visited in the West Bank. But—and this was the difference between the pre- and post-speech Berrigan—he could see the Jews of Israel more sympathetically, a people and country still in "shock" and "still mourning the dead, still furious over recent Palestinian terrorism on a village apartment house."

He had, indeed, learned much. The Israelis, he wrote home, were exhausted by repeated wars and the threat of wars, "death-ridden," understandably unable to exorcise the pain of the Holocaust and the woes inflicted on them by earthly and ecclesiastical despots. Yet many, he found, were willing to explore possible solutions, whatever they were and whenever they might arise.[38]

In Beirut the two men were guests at the Jesuit University, and they pursued the same course they had in Israel. Meetings, late-night conversations, wandering. They met Yasser Arafat of the Palestine Liberation Organization and George Habash of the Popular Front for the Liberation of Palestine, one of the most irreconcilable of Palestinian extremist groups. Yet Arafat and Habash denounced terrorism and said they now eschewed violent acts against civilians except in unavoidable instances.

Dan was hardly encouraged when one young Palestinian pointed to his automatic weapon, proclaiming that the gun, not the Lebanese card he carried, was his identity, and that one day it would help him return to a Palestine he had never set eyes on.

One evening, close to 6 P.M., Dan and Mayer were guided to a safe house where they spent more than two hours with Nayif Hawatmeh of the ultra-extremist Popular Democratic Front for the Liberation of Palestine, while Mayer taped the conversation. Hawatmeh insisted that "his branch" had since 1969 ruled out hijacking airplanes, attacks on civilians, and other violence. As he spoke, Dan glanced at a poster on the wall glorifying the killing of Jews several weeks earlier.

When they flew to Cyprus on May 11, they had in their possession taped interviews; Dan variously thought they had twenty-five, thirty, thirty-five, or forty tapes, "spectacular tapes, conversations, with all kinds of people on all kinds of sides." The idea of doing a book on what they had seen and heard excited them, and they packed the tapes carefully and mailed them home. It was the last time they would ever see them. Sent from Nicosia, the parcel never arrived at its destination. Dan suspected foul play. Mayer thought, and still does, though naturally can never prove, that they were "stolen by some combination of Israeli intelligence and CIA." Or, perhaps, by an Arab intelligence group. No one will ever know, or tell.[39]

The trip nearly over, Dan said it made him "feel inadequate enough—a midge in a whirlwind of anguish, displacement, fury and redemption. The place seems like a vortex into which the God of Arab, Jew and Christian has poured the juices and distempers of history . . . . My first love, of course, is the Arabs. I only wish they had better leaders." And while Israel was still a "settler state perhaps" he thought there was time to set things right with Palestinians because he was impressed by the way Israelis lived under fire. They then flew to Israel to tell Israeli peacemakers that there was, in fact, a sense of humanity and integrity among Palestinians, qualities that should be explored and encouraged as a way out of their never-ending war. They made no mention of the possibility of nonviolence.[40]

Returning to Tel Aviv, Dan rejoiced at the pile of letters awaiting him. After dinner at the Mayer family's home, both men heard the latest news: Palestinian terrorists had struck again, killing twenty-one Jewish grade-school children and wounding sixty other youngsters in Ma'alot, a town in the west Galilee in northern Israel. Hawatmeh's group claimed responsibility.

Too trusting of the Palestinian leaders he met, Dan felt

"betrayed"—a sure expression of his naiveté in such a volatile, hate-filled war; how, he wondered, could one have faith in peaceful reconciliation when children on all sides were routinely dispatched without remorse? Hawatmeh and the other Palestinian leaders had brazenly lied to him, and he knew it. They told him, he said, that "crimes as today's [were to be] unacceptable and publicly abominated." In Tel Aviv, an outraged and scandalized Dan held a well-attended press conference to castigate the murders and murderers.

He described his reaction in an article addressed to "Dear revolutionary leaders—Hawatmeh and Arafat—" blaming them for their act of terror in Ma'alot.

"Then you, Arafat, you violated your word . . . you made a pact with us." And after the inevitable retaliatory bombing raids, "by what authority do you decide who in Israel . . . (as Rabin [then prime minister] must be asked . . . who in the camps) shall live and who shall die? . . . who will consent to die, by napalm or anti-personnel weaponry or shelling? Do you leaders, together with your families, consent to be the first victims . . . to push your own children into the furnace. . . . You chose to meet us, and to lie to us."[41]

It was Dan at his most furious, his anger harsher, more caustic than his censure of judges, prison officials, and the detested Spellman, Hoover, and Nixon. It was, he now knew, far more daunting and complicated and possibly unresolvable than Vietnam.

He was exhausted, sleeping "like a defeated animal," wanting badly to keep on struggling for decency and a disarmed region and world, but "unconvinced that any words will make a hair's difference."

On his last day in Israel, Israeli planes bombed a refugee camp in Lebanon in retaliation for Ma'alot, the same camp he and Mayer had visited ten days before. "God help us all!" he said before flying home.

Would Dan have made the same speech after such a trip? Surely yes, though the tone and the phraseology would probably have been different and the polemical tone avoided. But especially after his mission to the Mideast, Arab states were still "fat oil cats" utterly indifferent to their poor; Palestinians were repressed exiles, and he continued to trust that nonviolence could be a sturdier, more effective weapon against the Israeli rulers of the occupied territories.

"I am no longer angry at Israel," he wrote two years after his trip. "I reserve my anger for the mythmakers and kingmakers, Israelis and Americans, who shuttle like voracious locusts between Washington and Tel Aviv, bargaining away the lives of people, upping the military ante, fanning the fires of mythology and fear."[42]

Two decades later, he believed people still held the speech against him, and his memory of it remained "very sharp, bitter, extant."[43] What hurt him most of all was the false allegation that he was anti-Semitic, a condemnation that belied his entire life's experience, then and now.

16

THE REST OF THEIR LIVES

> The drop of rain maketh a hole in the
> stone, not by violence, but by oft
> falling.
>
> —*Bishop Hugh Latimer*
> *Seventh sermon preached before*
> *Edward VI, 1549*

PHIL WAS NOW A MARRIED EX-JOSEPHITE PRIEST. BUT HE STILL occasionally corresponded with his old Josephite friend Matthew O'Rourke, keeping him apprised of what he was up to. After prison, he began traveling again to various and sundry points, trying to drum up support for renewed campaigns against arms makers and the Pentagon. "Generally I try to get people to reflect on what this war has done to us spiritually (good Americans after good Germans); on mustering pressure to keep us from reinvolvement; on doing something to free the 2 hundred thousand political prisoners in S. Vietnam; on getting people to say something rational and humane about amnesty" for American exiles and deserters who refused military service during the Vietnam War.[1]

In 1973, their first child, Frida, was born, followed by Jerome (Jerry) in 1975, and, six years later, Katy. By every measure and by all testimony, family life was and is sweet despite the comings and goings of friends and strangers, and despite Phil and Liz's continual protests and jailings. Jonah House, an Edward Hopper lookalike brick-face building, on Baltimore's Park Avenue, was set in a black neighborhood not far from a renovated upscale area and a park where few dared venture after dark. It was typically old Baltimorean, with its facade of white marble steps and weather-softened window frames; it was christened Jonah House in 1973, marking the birth of their new community. So began a new phase of their biblically based nonviolent resistance. They and the tiny band of loyalists supported themselves by house painting and lectures. Well into the nineties Phil was climbing high ladders in all weather; past seventy, he fell on a picket fence and broke a rib, while Liz worried about him: "My husband is seventy-one and I don't want him perched on ladders anymore," she said.[2] Dan sent them checks and came as often as he could. They lived in voluntary poverty, simply, denying themselves the benefits of manic consumerism, managing on the food supermarkets could no longer sell, sharing with their black neighbors when they could, donating whatever extra funds they had to various war victims and groups.

"We embraced a Judeo-Christian ethic," explained one member. Sunday morning there would be a liturgy with Phil or Liz, and then a reflection on how the Gospel reinforced their active opposition to warmakers, then on to Phil's breakfast specialty, pancakes filled with all sorts of fruit. "Life in Jonah House," said Esther Cassidy, who gave birth in the house, was "monastic, with lots of prayer. We were all up by 7:30 and four nights a week we would have meetings, reading Scripture, praying, planning actions." When Dan visited, the whole house would relax and Phil seemed transformed, elated that Dan was present. Dan, in turn, would kid his younger brother, calling him "Philly" and telling him not to be so serious. Esther's husband, Barry, had known Phil since he was thirteen, when he was Phil's student in Newburgh. To him, life at Jonah House was "stark

and risky," and the actions they undertook left him "very frightened." Even so, he and Esther came away deeply respectful of the
powerful commitment to political activism and religious faith, especially in the post-Vietnam decades of hedonism, passivism, and self-
absorption. "It was," said Barry Cassidy, now a nurse at St. Rose's
Home for terminally ill impoverished cancer patients, in Manhattan,
a "remarkable experience, very stimulating, very difficult."[3]

Liz and Phil's kids tried to understand their unusual lives and the
periodic disappearance of their parents.

"I longed for a normal time . . . I longed for a normal household
. . . I wore second hand clothes. I cared so little about my appearance that my classmates were convinced that I was rich, and
strange," Frida wrote in a poignant recollection of her growing-up
years. When she was nine and Jerry seven, Liz received a three-year
sentence for walking into Griffiss Air Force Base in Rome, New
York, with a small group to symbolically disassemble a B–52
bomber that carried cruise missiles. After her mother's sentencing, "I wiped the tears away as they fell, [but] I couldn't find my
father, or hug my Mom goodbye." A frightened child, she ran to
the women's room, where a family friend, a Buddhist nun, comforted her as she cried in her arms.

When Liz was finally released, Frida remembered, they all hugged
and kissed. "Connected, reunited, moving as one person we went to
a greasy spoon diner and ate the most delicious hamburgers and fries
I've ever tasted. I never longed for normal parents."[4]

It wasn't any easier for Liz and Phil. They missed their children
terribly. Once Liz and Jerry returned from visiting Phil in prison
and Jerry became ill and exhausted. Another time, upon hearing a
judge sentence her to six months' imprisonment, Liz grabbed
Frida, hugged her, and wept. Phil, a doting and loving father, was
no less worried about the kids. "The children bloom," he wrote a
friend, "despite the shuffling around. Of course, Joan C. [a former
nun] and Ladon [a military veteran and onetime businessman] and
others give them careful and loving care. Were it not for a community such as ours, Liz and I could not both join these rhubarbs with
the warmakers. Not at once."[5] And this: "Liz and I have pain,
inconvenience. But what is it next to the pain of those in the

Ukraine or Armenia or Indonesia or El Salvador, or wherever superpowers grind their iron heels? Perhaps, however, the Lord will show us what we must yet suffer."[6]

In July 1974 Dan was hired to teach in Ithaca College and then abruptly dropped because the school's "mandarins" ruled (or so friends told him), "he does not respect property and will transmit that disrespect to the students." Of course he would. "May the fires of Catonsville be fed and fed by the lovers of life!" It would happen time and again. In 1990, Professor Earl Crow, a theologian and dean of High Point University in North Carolina, hired him to teach an eight-week course, but after the Persian Gulf War erupted the next year, the school turned him down. Shortly after, he was rejected as a speaker for being too controversial. "I'm frequently disinvited that way," he told the *Los Angeles Times*. "Gandhi's grandson invited me to speak at the Gandhi Institute, but then I was disinvited by his trustees. I think I'm the only one too peaceful for even Gandhi." In the following years he was twice turned down for an honorary degree by Colorado College, the second time in 1995. In the past he had taught there, preached in the college chapel, and delivered the 1990 baccalaureate speech, but the school's board of trustees chose to reject him; he could teach there, but honoring him was out of the question.[7]

Back home again on Manhattan's Upper West Side, he returned to his apartment on West 98th Street near his Jesuit friends. In his long poem "Fidelity," he graphically portrays his New York life:

"Coming up Broadway, a fruitless evening/reception at UN . . . It rains on Broadway, tears of knowledge. I look for a store to buy a pen . . . where my old friend the picture framer/propped a photo of his dead wife in the window."

    Rain worsens
    knowledge goes under

"He was inefficient and faithful/she slumped in a wheel chair, a cauliflower/in a stall, months and months. Every hour or so"

he lit a cigarette
put it to her lips.
One day
a crazy old black woman
came by
leaned convivially over
the speechless, mindless creature, yelled
"how are you dearie?" and kissed her like a luv. . . .
She died that night in his arms. On this foul foot path mule
    track, death mile, oblivion alley, bloody pass Broadway,
    pith and paradigm of the world, splicing the 50 States of
    Amnesia, swollen Styx and Augean drain ditch
a lotus blooms . . . .[8]

On the move again, he taught briefly in Michigan and then returned home to Syracuse to be with his aging and frail mother. "It was the longest time I have spent with her in the 35 years since I entered the Jesuits. I took away with me the image of the soul as sphere; the perfect form of spirit; both gift and achievement . . . I think she will not die; because I believe that our God is He 'of the living, not of the dead.' And because she has chosen to live, all the years (88) among 'things unseen.' . . . I wish every prisoner could know her, all the tortured and abandoned, the victims and the outcast. She understands, she stands there." He also smarted because his parents too had been ostracized. "A lot of those [parish] priests and the Irish blackballed them because of our being in jail and being against the war."[9]

He and Phil had been one of the central symbols of the turbulent sixties and seventies, in open rebellion against their country and church bureaucracy. Once they had been endowed with the mantle of heroism by their impassioned supporters, but the curtain was now down, their "fifteen minutes of fame" supposedly past, according to a culture that had a difficult time focusing on long-range implications. For more than two decades after Harrisburg, Dan and Phil were either cherished, excoriated, or, as is more likely, simply ignored. "Whatever became of Phil Berrigan?" asked Dan sardonically, and answered that while the "uglifiers, yuppies, developers, corporate pirates, are positively celebrated," Phil and the Plowshares people are still "unrepentantly opposed to nuclear violence and its lethal spinoffs; domestic violence on a spiraling scale, sexism, and the vile social triage being worked against the poor."[10]

Having argued and acted on the basis of their understanding of the Gospel, Dan and Phil offered no solace to those seeking either practical answers or instant spiritual gratification. "We can't save the world," Dan said in 1994 at a talk he gave recalling his life. "We can't do the big things . . . we can't do what we thought we could do in better times. Most of us in my generation will not live to see serious changes in a pro-human direction in our country. But that is not the point. The point is the integrity and the consistency of our actions, the ability to concentrate and be refreshed by the quality of things to be done," such as rearing children in a lasting marriage, and leading work lives and everyday lives morally, without avarice and violence toward others.[10] (Michael Novak, who became one of their sharpest critics, thought, however, that the brothers had ignored the very people from whom they had sprung. "*Which* public" he asked, were they trying to reach? And "what was it [they were] trying to say? . . . [writing] of ordinary Americans with contempt."[11])

Undaunted, they were condemned and revered by the "elite" as well as by "ordinary" people even as their names vanished from the national press and television. When Dan was still "underground" in the mid-1970s, he reminded one admirer of the character Dr. Rieux, in *The Plague* by Albert Camus, battling against despair and failure in the afflicted city of Oran. In London, a young couple, Sue and Tom Wesselkamper, named their newborn son after Dan. They had never met the Jesuit but were deeply moved by his life's work. When, ten years later, young Daniel was tragically killed in a bicycle accident, Dan wrote the grieving parents, "I wept when I received your letter," and dedicated "Zen Poem" "in loving memory of Daniel." He wrote, "Listen; blessed is the one/who walks the earth/5 years, 50 years, 80 years/and deceives no one/and curses no one/and kills no one/Of such a one/the angels whisper in wonder; behold the irresistible power/of natural powers—of height, of joy, of soul, of non belittling!"[12]

The conservative-inspired "culture wars" of the late twentieth century had their own meaning for Dan. It was "a culture that teaches in many tongues and tones and nuances; by consuming, by segregating and ignoring the poor, by investing, by hiding in churches, by voting clowns and cretins into the shambles of public office—teaches us quite simply that human life (including our own) is valueless, expendable, absurd. And by implication it teaches us that property, ownership, bank accounts, corporate arrangements, the voracious deep-throat and breakaway arms race, the nukes, the junk standard of living and dying—that these are the absolutes, the land marks, the true measure of worth, the macho-macha ideal; finally, the gods."[13]

Above all, their protests, including the melodramatic and metaphorical trashing of draft files at Baltimore and Catonsville, were a logical corollary of how they saw their roles as priests, to show by deeds as well as by words the power and authenticity of an earlier Christianity. Catonsville, the highlight of their public lives, was born of their religious dimension—a theological clue to their fiery admonitions and relentless, uncompromising, often too-bitter judgments of those with whom they disagreed. Early on, Dan concluded that the new technological age, which can bring good and bad, was a major watershed: The new age, and its idolatry of technology, is marred by a fundamental flaw, for it has no spiritual base and is severed from its Judeo-Christian heritage, bringing in its wake a potential "death agony of the spirit." The alternative, Dan argued, was not dehumanization and a mechanized, computer-driven society that disregards human beings, but the life of Jesus and his message of love, amity with all men and women, peace and justice—a Catholic tradition of witness that cannot deny, however, as Novak argued, yet another American Catholic legacy of "pragmatic accommodation, skillful brokerage, and *winning*."[14]

Yet Catonsville was a liturgy directed at Catholics—and at the raiders' respective orders—Jesuit, Josephite, Maryknoll, Christian Brothers—and at the bishops, Cardinal Spellman, and, indeed, the Roman Catholic Church. It was as well an effort to establish a connection between preparing for and making war and delegitimizing nuclear weapons, war, and public worship of property, the very things the brothers believe buttress an inequitable system and are intimately associated with abuse and manipulation of ordinary people and the continued plague of racial discrimination and violence.[15]

That doesn't mean that every day was filled with dark, moody depression. There was fun, too. For Dan, there were precious visits by dear friends. Jaunts to Baltimore where they were a family again. Becoming an uncle again and again as Liz gave birth to her children. Dan's devotion to Liz and Phil and Jerry and Carol. His fellow Jesuits at Ninety-eighth Street. Gordon Zahn presented Dan and Phil with "the (fictional) Shaft of Loyola," a long-standing gag among people he respected and loved. Dan also received the "justly prestigious PASS-THE-PLATE AWARD (formerly the Gold Crown Award)" as "the Jesuit qua Jesuit who has been the best dental technician qua technician in the Society." Phil got his, too: the "GREAT ESCAPE AWARD" for "having matriculated at Holy Cross College and done graduate work at Danberrigan Tech and wound up a Josephite."

At the Jesuit School of Theology at Berkeley, where Dan was teaching, when he was forced to give his students a final exam for his course, which he dubbed "Unsystematics 24387," he devised questions (students were told to reply to "all or some, or none") such as these: "Reflect on the Seven Deadly Sins. Describe how you have integrated these into your life. Be specific." "Make an ethical critique of a hypothetical proposal to establish a papal sperm bank." "In light of the protestant theology of the 60s, discuss the congruence of the neo-gothic towers of NY's Riverside Church." "If God is indeed dead, has the church buried him standing?"[16]

In 1985 he produced another volume of poetry, *Block Island*, about fellowship, reputation, loss, qualms about religion, and the island itself. He also went off to Colombia and Argentina to act as a consultant and extra (with one spoken line) in Ronald Jaffee's film *The Mission*, which starred Jeremy Irons, Robert De Niro, and Liam Neeson in a drama about a Jesuit mission among the Guarani tribe and their eighteenth-century clash with and defeat at the hands of secular state power and an acquiescent Rome.[17]

His closest friends among the Jesuits seemed to know him in ways that few ever did.

"He's suffered with the Jesuits," says a priest who knows both brothers well. "By and large he's ignored by the Jesuits. People don't talk about him. He means nothing to the Jesuits. Yet, to my mind, he's the greatest Jesuit since Ignatius."[18] By now, the Jesuits pretty well left him to his own rights and he had become a freelance apostolate to the peace movement and other assorted causes. He remained as always a traditional Catholic priest, but was driven—as are Phil and Liz—by his reading of the Gospel.

Another Jesuit, who once served as Dan's superior, noted that so many people, including his Jesuit brothers, misunderstood him. For one thing, he did not love all the publicity. "He is a terribly sensitive and prickly person. He is also incredibly vulnerable. The first thing he needs after he goes out and pulls one of these actions is for you to go up to him and give him a hug and tell him you love him. He has this permanent feeling of being an outsider, of not belonging, in exile. He needs to be constantly welcomed back into the fold; told 'you're forgiven, come.' What I notice about him in public situations is generally how ill at ease he is. The celebrity business he finds very taxing."[19]

Both Dan and Phil continued to serve as lightning rods. As early as the spring of 1973, they wrote to North Vietnam's prime minister "in grief and distress of spirit" because of news that American prisoners of war had been tortured. "Please believe that we are brothers who rejoice to name you our brother," they went on, asking for an answer to the allegations. Their letter brought dismay to many antiwar activists, persuaded that it lent credibility to the American rationale for intervention. In any event, Hanoi's answer came several months later, calling the charges an absolute lie. But the Berrigans remained dissatisfied and insisted the peace camp in this country needed to avoid seeing Hanoi as blameless. What was required instead was to avoid romanticizing everyone, including the United States and the two Vietnams, and instead to draw up a credo that violence against humans for whatever reason cannot be condoned or committed.[20]

Jim Forest and Richard John Neuhaus (representing CALCAV) drew up an "Appeal to the Democratic Republic of Vietnam to Observe Human Rights." In their draft copy, they described a variety of outrages against South Vietnamese and Buddhist opponents (as well as urging amnesty for draft-age Americans who refused to serve, and assistance to Vietnam veterans), thereby opening up a huge rift in the antiwar movement. A savage, intense public and private war erupted. Was criticizing the North Vietnamese the right course to follow? Forest doggedly pursued the issue, writing an editorial in the October 1976 *Fellowship*: "Vietnam: Unification Without Reconciliation." An open letter was distributed, championing the cause of human rights rather than refighting the Vietnam War. Among antiwar people and pacifists—and supporters of the war, too, who sought justification for their stand—it caused yet another firestorm.

The Berrigans and three bishops, Carroll Dozier of Memphis, Thomas Gumbleton of Detroit, and John Dougherty of Newark, signed, as did Dorothy Day, Paul O'Dwyer, Tom Cornell, and Jim Finn. When the document was leaked to the media, the American Friends Service Committee and some in the War Resisters League, and some of FOR's staff, parted company, believing, among other objections, that it would only encourage American retribution against Hanoi. Forest, explained one historian, "was accused [by some antiwar activists] of being too pure in his quest for human rights and in turn was hurting the broader aims of the movement." He was also victimized by bitter attacks and fabrications, including, he says, a charge that he was a CIA agent. In December 1976, though he enjoyed the work, he was disgusted by his reception, and the FOR reluctantly agreed to let him leave the magazine and move to the Netherlands to direct its International FOR group.[21]

When the statement was published, Dan and Phil suddenly withdrew their sponsorship, Dan explaining rather weakly that he would never have signed originally had he known it would be made public, though he pledged "to question our friends in Vietnam" about the criticisms Forest and Neuhaus had raised. Neither Dan nor Phil had ever taken the nonpacifist, antiwar hard-left line lionizing Hanoi or wishing for a Vietcong-National Liberation Front victory. Then, too, for Dan as well as the FOR, the gentle Buddhist monk

Thich Nhat Hanh's influence in urging a third, nonviolent response to the bloodletting was significant, so much so that Dan wrote an apologetic note to Forest and then, learning that Nhat Hanh was furious at the withdrawal of Dan's name, apologized again. "It was not his finest moment," said Forest. "I never saw Dan so ashamed of himself."[22]

Still, the issue would not die. On May 30, 1979, Joan Baez and other antiwar veterans, such as Allen Ginsberg, Ed Asner, I.F. Stone, and Staughton Lynd, paid $52,000 to place a similar ad in various newspapers, rebuking the new Vietnam and condemning it for the ruthless treatment it was meting out to 150,000 to 200,000 political prisoners. This time, Dan and Phil signed, though Phil again changed his mind and withdrew his name.[23]

Bad news arrived. On December 22, 1977, their mother Freda died at age ninety. As she approached death, with family members gathered about her bedside, she sounded out, "I love you."

At the funeral, Phil said that he, Dan, and Jerry would honor their mother's life by standing in protest before the Pentagon on December 28. Twenty-nine people were arrested for spilling their blood on the columns and chaining themselves to the doors.[24]

Years later, they both publicly supported Soviet political dissenters, both of them signing a *New York Times* ad, "American dissenters demand amnesty for dissenters in Communist countries. . . . [T]o protest U.S. policies in Indochina but to acquiesce in the Soviet occupation of Czechoslovakia would not only be immoral but would quite properly call into question the sincerity of our commitments at home."[25]

Dan, more pensive than Phil, kept going back in his mind to the decades that marked his life. In the summer before Freda died, he marked the twenty-fifth anniversary of his life as a priest. Asking himself, "[A]re your symbols thriving? Are you still able to imagine the real world? Are your eyes seeing, your ears hearing, your heart beating—and this in a world that is largely dysfunctional, in a culture that lies there, terminally ill but still kicking?" To which he responded, happily, that he was still surviving and thriving, middle-aged now, still writing his beloved poems, "happy, cross-grained, angry, loving," working among the desperately ill, occasionally sticking his tongue out at the Pentagon and its think tanks, nagging a country (not nearly as much as Phil and Liz) that no longer cared to listen that nuclear annihilation was still possible, observing his "beloved order," so many of them seduced by assimilating in the consumer, materialistic, hip culture, "talking psychobabble and corporate management and liberal politics." Yet he, too, was very much a part of this climate, trying, in his words, however, to be "less guilty" than the clerical brothers he satirized, trying—paraphrasing Paul's counsel—"to be as marginal as possible to madness."[26]

Meanwhile, Phil and Liz and the Jonah House community had begun a series of actions that would eventually number a hundred or more, here and abroad, and would last well into the nineties, though they were rarely reported in the broadcast or print media. In the summer of 1973 they began "White House Pray-ins" calling for an end to the bombing of Cambodia. They held a vigil in front of Henry Kissinger's home; dug a grave on Secretary of Defense Donald Rumsfeld's front lawn; planted trees as a life symbol at the naval base housing Trident nuclear submarines; tried to visit the newly elected president Jimmy Carter in Plains, Georgia, in 1976 and, denied the opportunity, proceeded to raise banners protesting nuclear weapons; and repeatedly disrupted lavish arms bazaars in Washington, which Phil acidly painted as "the obscenity to eclipse all obscenities—big hoopla, blacks and Hispanics offering cocktails, scantily-clad hostesses beckoning on the military jocks and dignitaries to buy the wares." As always, he lambasted liberals. "You know what they say about liberals," he told a priest, " 'scratch 'em and you'll find a fascist. Or at the least, a weathervane.' "[27] Repeatedly arrested, often jailed, he, Liz, and their loyalists would not, could not desist.

There were other deeds, far from public mention. Perhaps moved by Mother Teresa and the Catholic Worker, Dan learned of St. Rose's interracial, interfaith hospice for destitute cancer patients from a friend serving there as a volunteer orderly. His writing, his protests at the Pentagon, and his teaching must have left a hole within his soul: Something was missing; "whether true icons, physical work, or self-testing." He called the hospital, founded by Rose Hawthorne Lathrop, daughter of Nathaniel Hawthorne, who in 1896 had come to live in the slum tenements of New York's Lower East Side to tend those dying of cancer. A true commune developed from her dedication, and St. Rose's Home is now operated by the Hawthorne Dominican Sisters, one of seven such homes they operate throughout the country.

"Could I hire out as a part-time volunteer?" he asked.

For five years he labored unobtrusively, without fanfare, without accolades, doing what virtually all our public personalities, politicians, corporate and media giants, and celebrities (with the exception of Jimmy Carter) would not do, engaged as they are in amassing power, influence, wealth, applause. Emptying bedpans of the dying, feeding them, being there. "I appear at bedside . . . hold their hands . . . ready for whatever service seems required or helpful. They can take me or leave me, as can the nuns, orderlies, families. I do not bring the holy oils, or pray the sacrament of the sick, or give communion, except on special occasions. . . . I come and go, a kind of marginal figure in that shell-shocked lunar, no-person land which is laid claim to by both life and death." In a poignant book he never allows the reader to forget there is death all about him, and he asks again if he will be "in the right place when the Lord comes." To a reporter he later described the environment: "I don't know whether you have ever smelled cancer. Cancer of the nose, cancer of the face, which is the most terrible to look upon and to smell; cancer of the brain; cancer of the lungs. We see it all, smell it all, hold it all in our arms."[28]

Then one day on the New York City subway, a young Jesuit in mufti eyed Dan wearing his elf cap, clad in old clothing, "looking like a ragman, like a leprechaun, his hair sticking out of his cap" and approached him with trepidation, introducing himself. Dan sat and stared serenely "like a Buddha" at the young priest, who suddenly asked: "How have you made it as a Jesuit all this time?" to which Dan answered, "how have *you* made it?"

Their conversation deepened and extended into dinner, and continued afterward, on many walks and ferry rides to Staten Island. The young Jesuit, Father William Hart McNichols, had read Dan's books, especially *No Bars to Manhood*, and thought of him as the "perfect gift of what God was calling him to do." Later, McNichols described his work with AIDS patients. It was spring 1984 and the disease was still largely unknown, and if Dan joined McNichols's ministry, that would surely give rise to rumors about Dan being gay. Even so, again doing what few other famous people ever do on a year by year basis, helping the dismal and hopeless, Dan chose to join McNichols in his ministry to the afflicted. He learned very quickly that AIDS patients produce buckets of diarrhea, bleed, vomit. The sick—Buddhists, Jews, Moslems, Orthodox—were all estranged from their faiths. Dan came to St. Vincent's Hospital in Greenwich Village in July 1984 and has remained there. For two years he walked the wards with a list of AIDS patients, trying to get to know them, until he was asked if he would consider taking under his personal care two or three people who had no family, no friends. One of them lived six years, and just before dying asked Dan to give him Communion. Dan conducted their funerals and dealt with alienated Catholics, some so depressed that nothing but suicide could relieve their agony. Young people. Betrayed, but by what and by whom? By an indifferent and inured society that despises and fears their ailment? By a church that failed to reach them? By themselves? "The brutal question insinuates itself like a demon at the door: Can this terror strike me also?"[29]

Controversy followed on controversy. Opposing abortion and the death penalty and war and racism were part of Dan and Phil's "consistent ethic of life," their version of the "seamless web." Dan especially—but Phil and Liz as well—were assailed by Catholic and non-Catholic pro-choicers outraged over Dan's unwavering opposition to abortion.[30] In the spring of 1980 Dan taught at the Jesuit School of Theology in Berkeley, where he and others were soon arrested for a sit-in on Ash Wednesday during a "liturgy for peace" at the University of California, trying to draw attention to the "notorious" . . . "death trap" of Livermore and Los Alamos nuclear laboratories, "where every nuclear weapon in these United States is concocted."[31]

Dan and Phil were now in the eighth decade of their lives. Phil's Masada complex, undaunted, bull-headed, courageous, no doubt believing that suffering was a crucial part of Catholicism, more religious but still too intolerant with those who no longer believed in his form of witness, led him to repeated clashes with the law. Quite different from Dan, he remained an earthy, streetwise organizer, rough and tough if need be. "Phil reminds me of revolutionaries I met in Central America," says John Dear, a young Jesuit who was his cellmate for a while after they were both arrested for trespassing at Seymour Johnson Air Force Base in North Carolina in 1994, "FMLN commandantes, Sandinistas, except that Phil's committed to nonviolence. There's a tough 'we've got to organize, give our lives if we have to'" attitude about the country's willingness to fight wars. By late 1995 Phil had spent seven and a half years in some of the worst prisons in the eastern United States, yet Dear believes that, instead of becoming dehumanized and bitter, "Phil's like Jeremiah, like Ezekiel, like an Old Testament personality. And when he's house painting, he'll spend hours reciting the Jesus prayer. One day I found a writing pad and on the back of it was written, 'Prince of Peace; Son of God; Root of Jesse; Suffering Servant; Wonder Counselor; Peacemaker; Christ; Anointed One; Messiah; Good Shepherd; The Way; The Truth; The Life; and I asked him 'What is this?' And he told me, 'I read these names and reflect on them when I lie in bed at night.'"

Imprisoned for his North Carolina action, he rose early, cleaned his cell, exercised, and as soon as he had time, sat down to read his Bible and the Lectio Divina, a compendium of the current year's readings and prayers for daily Mass. Evenings, he read murder mysteries for escape (Liz and Dan are also addicted to them).[32]

Dan, too, stood with protesters every month before a military research laboratory in New York City, content now with trespassing and vigils. One had a sense that he and Phil had accomplished what they set out to do decades earlier. "Dan's ready to die at any time now," said a fellow Jesuit, David Toolan. "He's finished his life's project."

"I had a conversation with Dan about a friend of his who's been involved in many Plowshares actions, about this guy's annoying habit of giving the message that you're not good enough. Dan was appalled. 'That's dreadful,' he said. But then you have the chapter in his book about Israel—the in-your-face, tough attitude. The mood of being an outsider, of being in exile, the ambivalence. As if he were saying, this is where God or my genes have placed me, this is where I have chosen to take my stand."[33]

It was a stand directed essentially at their church when they thundered over and over and over, to the irritation and thorough exasperation of so many: What did it mean to be a Catholic? To be a Christian? To be a human being? Pope John XXIII had blazed an alternative way with his *Mater et Magistra* in 1961 and *Pacem in Terris* two years later, stimulating Latin America's bishops, gathered in Medellin in 1968, to takes sides with the continent's impoverished and repressed millions and helping give rise to liberation theology, which then started defying the traditional bonds among the Catholic Church, the armed forces, and the privileged governing aristocracy.

By the 1980s and well into the following decade, the American bishops' policies on economics and foreign policy reflected many of these events as well as the Berrigans' witness, expressing a profound concern for the poor and most vulnerable. And if not yet pacifists, they were being transformed into peacemakers. Like Dorothy Day and Thomas Merton, they and the Berrigans were neither liberals nor Marxists; many bishops were Gospel radicals, as were the Berrigans. And all these American Catholic peacemakers were "a peace movement and not [just] an antiwar movement," noted the historian Patricia McNeal, though the Catholic Left accelerated the process of moving the church away from uncritical cold war policies and turning its attention toward the arms race and United States backing of repressive oligarchies in Latin America. As early as 1968, the bishops, collectively and individually, were condemning the bloodshed in Southeast Asia. In 1971, for example, Bishop Carroll

Dozier of Memphis issued a pastoral letter at Christmas denouncing the war and insisting that a Christian could not countenance war. In 1983, thanks to various papal declarations and encyclicals over the years, to other bishops, and especially to Dan and Phil, the National Conference of Catholic Bishops' pastoral letter, *The Challenge of Peace: God's Promise and Our Response*, proclaimed that selective and conscientious objection, nuclear pacifism, resistance to war, even pacifism are integral parts of church tradition, just as much as its contemporary opponents.[34] Detroit Auxiliary Bishop Thomas Gumbleton played a major role in various bishops' resolutions aimed at the war and the arms race. Gumbleton believes the Berrigans' witness "had a strong influence on my thinking," and especially on the Catholic peace movement within the church. Indeed, Bishop Walter F. Sullivan sees them as "modern-day prophets. Their witness is prophetic, like the prophets of the Old Testament . . . [they] will always be remembered in history as taking the Catholic Church in the United States away from a militaristic war-like stance to a much stronger commitment to peacemaking. They were the first to bring peacemaking to the agenda of the bishops." Bishop Charles Buswell is a believer, too. "Both Dan and Phil appear to many to be on the fringe; as a matter of fact, they are true prophets for our time . . . to be put in prison is not unusual for a prophet."

And though the Berrigans' and the bishops' counsels on war and peace continue to be disregarded by their government and many Americans, a good many ordinary Catholics and clergy have undergone a sea change in their thinking. In June 1995 the bishops continued to press their religiously grounded case, as the Vatican and African bishops had in 1994, this time turning their criticism against "excessive" American sales of weapons abroad. *Sowing Weapons of War* declared, "Jobs at home cannot justify exporting the means of war abroad," and concluded, "the United States needs to put its energies into building peace, not supplying arms"—words that also clearly reflected the Berrigans' lives and works.[35]

Try as he might, though, Dan couldn't forget the reception to his Israeli-Arab speech. Speaking at Willamette University in Oregon, after debating a prison warden on the treatment of prisoners, he confided to a Jewish law professor his continuing personal grief at alienating some of his Jewish friends.[36]

In 1987, Dan's autobiography was published. In one passage, he advises anyone wondering about the speech, "My reaction to all this . . . is simply gratitude. I am grateful for having spoken the truth, as I saw it, as it was given to me to understand. And this from three vantage points. From my religious belief . . . from my tendency to speak up and let the chips fly. And closest of all, from the Vietnam decade, its chills and fevers and nightmares and bloodletting and courts and jails. Having endured a few of these makeshift delights, one is apt to pay small tribute to shibboleths."[37]

To Dwell in Peace was greeted with critical reviews in the *Boston Globe* and the *Washington Post* and two *New York Times* reviews in the daily and Sunday editions. The *Wall Street Journal* coupled its review with a review of a new book by the Christian fundamentalist Jerry Falwell, "two wackos for the price of one," said Dan, laughing, with no little sarcasm. *Commonweal* couldn't get anyone to jointly review Dan's and Andrew Greeley's new books, because prospective reviewers told editor Peter Steinfels (who had reviewed Dan's book for the *Globe*), "Who needs a twenty-year fight with them?"[38] Even so, Steinfels's review was far more incisive than most, by reverent admirers and unforgiving critics alike. "Like many others, I conduct my own life on the carefully examined conclusion that he [Dan] is seriously wrong," he concluded. "But not a day goes by that I do not think he may be right."[39]

Why, then, the generally unappreciative reviews, especially in the major mainstream media? Dan thought he knew. To his friend Patrick Henry, he explained: "The invisible writing and unmentionable rub is the chapter on Israel," a remark he has made repeatedly. (Henry, a professor of French literature at Whitman College, took great umbrage at the Sunday *Times* review and wrote an objecting letter that was never published.) "I believe the reason that book was pilloried," Dan concluded, "was because of that [Israel] chapter. The book was judged on that one chapter."[40]

Actually, the autobiography was an impressive, rich, and stimulating, if sometimes rambling, life story, decidedly unsympathetic to
opponents, as are many memoir writers who have led controversial
lives, and here and there prone to ambiguous metaphors that
obscured more than clarified. In retrospect, the chapter on Israel
was relatively tame, given the blunt, often cruel and vulgar criticism
of Israel that arose among hard-line conservative American Jews
after the start of the peace process in 1993 between Israel and the
PLO. Even so, it was a book that could surely have used some judi-
cious editing and excisions despite Dan's propensity to reject copy-
editing by others. Harper & Row, the publisher, suggested some
revisions, some reorganizing and deletions, but according to a close
friend, Dan resisted. To Dan, it was not merely a book but a work
of art. As it turned out, it was a substantial, significant, if imperfect,
book, a highly personal memoir by a man and priest whose life had
been richer, more worthwhile, and more ethical than most.[41]

Yet it was hard to take seriously his belief that some reviewers still
considered his 1973 censure of Israel so important that they would
allow it to color their reviews and deliberately call it into question.
The war and the draft were long past, and a whole new set of foreign and domestic challenges and issues had appeared. Yes, old
scores were being repaid in kind, but where was the conspiracy?
However he rationalized it, though, the negative reviews hurt him
badly, as they would any writer, and still do.[42]

At a party celebrating the book's publication, he candidly spoke
to his friends, as if offering his final testament.

"I wake up in the world each day, and don't know what to do. I
don't know what to do about what I see. Since I see, I can't rightly
deny what I see. But what to do? I feel like a blind man ordered to
paint a sunset or a quadriplegic in a marathon. The best thing one
can do in such a fix (the best I can do) is—not to do nothing. . . .
Thus my fix. Burdened with fevers and chills, incapacity and outrage at the goings on of fools and rogues in church and state, laying their heavy hand on shoulder, heart and mind—and worse, a
very septenary of demons whispering in my ear a befouled gospel;
words like 'Why not adjust, why not calm down, why not die before
you die?'—in such a fix what can one do? Not do nothing."

Well, hardly nothing. Through the turbulent decades of their secular and theological revolt, neither Dan nor Phil veered from his absolute refusal to sanction murder, by individuals, by the state, by abortion (which they condemned; Dan was sentenced with four others to forty hours of community service in 1990 in Rochester, New York—they were promptly dubbed the "Fervent Five"—for blocking the front door of Planned Parenthood), or by war, braced, as one who knew the brothers aptly put it, "not by ideology but by a core of religious beliefs and a Zen-like conviction that patience is the only revolutionary virtue."[43]

Dan's Jesuit friend, Dan Toolan, joked, "Dan, when you get into the promised land and get through that St. Peter's Gate, you're not going to be happy. Eternal paradise will not be enough."

Dan put on a face of mock amazement, looked at Toolan, and came back, "Who me?" And they both roared with laughter.

Soon after the book's appearance and the reviews in the major papers and magazines, Dan's brother John was hit by a car, and another brother, Tom, suffered a stroke. Phil was back in prison in Norfolk, Virginia. Jerry was awaiting a sentence in Syracuse for trespassing on a military reservation, while Dan and Phil and the other Plowshares activists were still waiting for their appeal to be heard for marching into a General Electric plant in King of Prussia, Pennsylvania, to protest the manufacture of the nuclear bomb's delivery system.

Otherwise, things were normal.

Especially for Phil.

Bob Smith's Brandywine Peace Community had been conducting peace vigils and acts of civil disobedience since 1977 at the front gates of General Electric's nuclear Re-entry Division assembly facility in King of Prussia, not far from Philadelphia, the Delaware Valley's main weapons industry at the time and a major employer. Born into a working-class Philadelphia family, Smith had founded the community some years earlier. John Schuchardt, a former marine officer, an attorney and public defender in Vermont for five years, and a member of Jonah House, was so appalled at the development of first-strike weaponry that he joined with Brandywine to demonstrate peacefully before GE's front gates.

As the two men talked, they kept asking themselves what they could do to publicize what GE was producing. Schuchardt came up with the idea of using a hammer to disarm a partially assembled warhead—the Mark 12A reentry vehicle, a first-strike weapon that prevents the H-bomb from melting as it came back into the atmosphere. The Mark 12A rests on a missile, which enters space and then drops off, speeding toward its target. Only the vehicles were made by GE, after which they were put into canisters and shipped to Pantax in Amarillo, Texas, for assembly. Schuchardt mused, "We could just walk in here and get one of those things."

Intrigued, the two men took counsel at Jonah House with ten others, including Phil and Liz. If they entered the plant, how would people react? Would it make a contribution to the cause? They checked the law and learned that "sabotage" carried a very stiff penalty. "I had the feeling," said Schuchardt, "I'd spend the rest of my life in prison." Still, he asked whether they had a moral responsibility to risk their lives to challenge nuclear first-strike weapons.

He spent months trying to recruit people to join, since no one but a handful of specialists really understood much about reentry vehicles. Phil then contacted a onetime nuclear engineer turned nonviolent advocate who educated him and the others about the mechanism's intricacies. By late August 1980, as he had before Catonsville, Phil persuaded Dan to join them. Finally, on a weekend retreat on September 9, the would-be raiders came together for the first time at the Concord Friends House in Concordville, Pennsylvania: Father Carl Kabat, an Oblate priest; Sister Anne Montgomery, daughter of a Second World War admiral and sister of an air force pilot who had died in an air crash; Dean Hammer, a Yale Divinity School graduate; Molly Rush, a wife and mother of six from Pittsburgh; Elmer Maas, a former college teacher; and Schuchardt. They decided that Smith would not join them, inasmuch as he was on parole for past "actions," and, besides, after they were jailed, he would be able to organize a support group. Dan arrived by train, his back pain plaguing him so much that during the retreat, Schuchardt kept massaging his back.

The morning before the raid, Phil called Charles Glackin, a lawyer. "Charlie, I may need you tomorrow. Will you be where I can reach you at 7:30 in the morning?" Glackin had no idea what Phil was up to until he received a call that the eight were being held in the local jail.

Using a GE phone directory and floor plan, and information given to them by a disaffected GE employee, the invaders carried clawless hammers (Dan, not feeling well, was unarmed and never reached the site of the hammering) and moved quickly and unimpeded into the building, and diverted two guards. Six of them entered a building—Father Kabat and Sister Anne were told to distract the guards—and proceeded to shatter part of two Mark 12A casings (the damage was estimated at $28,000) and then dumped blood—a reprise of draft board raids—onto blueprints, work orders, and assorted equipment. Then they knelt in a circle, held hands, and sang hymns. Three-quarters of an hour later police arrived to arrest them. When he learned of the raid, Glackin phoned the Jesuit provincial in New York, who agreed to post a bond for $75,000, telling Glackin the Jesuits were very concerned about Dan's health and wanted him home. Ailing, in pain from a herniated esophagus, Dan was the first to be bailed out.[44]

Meanwhile, the judge called Glackin and Michael Shields, a local attorney, into his chambers, telling them that he didn't want another Harrisburg and that the district attorney was ready to make a deal: He'd drop all charges and give them one hour to make their speeches. "They came here to make a statement, your Honor," Glackin explained, adding that in all likelihood they would want a trial. Take the deal, the judge urged. The sentence, if they were found guilty, could run as long as ten years. But Schuchardt and Phil were adamant. They wanted everyone to know what GE had been manufacturing, and, above all, that they were defending international law established at the Nuremberg trials, which they insisted allowed people to interfere with those preparing to wage war.

Outside, on the streets, though it certainly wasn't Catonsville or

Harrisburg II, pro- and anti-Plowshares demonstrators arrived, and verbal battles were fought between the defenders and the opponents. Meanwhile, a new and far more uncompromising judge was assigned, and all were eventually found guilty; Dan, Phil, Father Kabat, and Schuchardt received three to ten years, and the others one and a half to five. Ramsey Clark appealed, and their appeal stretched across the decade of the eighties, a small but stubborn challenge to ascendant Reaganism. Eventually, the case was brought before a new judge, who then sentenced all to time served, with twenty-three months' probation tacked on. Judge James E Buckingham, while not supporting this action, also added a personal note: "The defendants were attempting to make a statement of their deep-felt convictions. I agree with many of those convictions. We are all concerned about nuclear war." When he walked out of the courtroom, Dan, grinning, pulled out a toothbrush from his shirt pocket, telling reporters he had come ready for "anything, including jail." Phil had "mixed feelings. We got a warm, decent judge who was lenient and then slapped probation on us," reminding his listeners that he was "ready to go to jail"—again and again.[45]

It was the opening shot of Phil's new brainchild—the Plowshares movement, the name drawn from the call to "beat swords into plowshares" in Isaiah (2:4) and Micah (4:3). They would attempt this quixotic effort with a little more than one hundred committed men and women, hammering and pouring blood on MX missiles, Trident submarines, B–52 bombers, and components of the strategic nuclear triad. To drastically shrinking media attention, they tenaciously insisted that the government's nuclear weapons' first-strike strategy was a crime, that indiscriminate sales of extraordinarily devastating weapons abroad was obscene, and that politicians and generals alike are bound by precepts of international law.

Throughout the eighties and well into the nineties, Phil and his miniscule, fearless, loyal band walked into military camps, onto naval and air force bases, into the mouths of war industries with astonishing ease, prepared to accept occasional draconian punishments far greater than that meted out to many violent criminals or to the Iran-Contra defendants who escaped imprisonment. Plow-shares people were routinely convicted, barred from arguing in court about who the "real" criminals were. Who really had violated international law and abetted in the killing of others—the Plow-shares people or the realpolitikers in Washington, D.C., and other world capitals? Once, when he appeared in court in support of Liz and seven other Plowshares defendants and was denied the oppor-tunity to speak against a laboratory engaged in weapons research, Phil called the trial a "disgrace," refused to apologize, and was given *five years* for contempt of court, though he served very little time. "Arrogant terrorists," one federal prosecutor called them. "Fanatics," said another, and yet another told the court that Plow-shares defendants were "misguided anarchists who have failed to respect the law."[46]

In their cell in Robison County in North Carolina in 1994, Phil paraphrased Pascal to his cellmate, the young Jesuit John Dear, obviously describing his life's journey: If you speak peace and jus-tice, 50 percent are for you. After a few years, 30–40 percent are and you have lost some friends. Twenty years later, 10 percent are with you. But at the end of your life, if you're still saying the same thing, there'll be no more friends. "That's my life story," Dear remembers Phil telling him. "And that's what happened to Jesus."[47]

Some of their most loyal followers and erstwhile friends charged Plowshares and Phil—they were synonymous—with the same accu-sations leveled at Phil during the draft board raids. He was, they said, still coercive. Moreover, they had found alternative ways of resistance. Besides, many of them were married with children, and some were exhausted. Others saw little or no results for their efforts, and still others thought that working with the poor or oth-ers in need of assistance was more enriching and empowering than "actions," and that constant struggle with the courts and jailers was personally destructive.

Then, too, critics repeatedly asked if their illegal assaults were not a rejection of the democratic process. Did it not exalt a secret and militant resistance to the detriment of nonviolent means—like voting, lobbying, and legal mass protests? Was not conventional war, and the propensity for violence here at home—not simply nuclear war—equally a problem? And, among veteran pacifists, one heard the complaint that their tactics would never bring about the true goal of nonviolence: the reconciliation of opposing groups, the need to be open and honest to all, including one's antagonists. Or was Plowshares merely pointless personal martyr-dom that only enhanced mutual animosities and phobias, however unwittingly?[48]

Some of their old Catholic Peace Fellowship allies wanted no part of it. One decried it as "too much romanticism, too many retreats, too much indoctrination." Plowshares' obsession was the threat of nuclear warfare. But, suggested other former sympathiz-ers, many other problems had emerged and demanded serious attention, too, especially the mushrooming number of unemployed and how the working poor were forced to endure and suffer in a pitiless economic and political environment. "Can John Dear," asked the well-known Jesuit pacifist Richard McSorley, "do more for peace in jail than being outside?" For that matter, could Phil and Liz do far more through teaching, writing, lecturing, picketing the IRS against war taxes (which might not be dramatic enough, said McSorley, but would be far more effective than Plowshares raids), and organizing on a larger scale, than they could do simply by becoming professional prisoners? But in prison, Phil told Dear that Plowshares had done more than Gandhi ever had. Others might respond by saying that to Gandhi, civil disobedience was a last resort, to be attempted after all else had failed, and that rather than resort to clandestine plotting, Gandhi had sent advance warn-ing to his adversaries. Besides, while Plowshares' nearly fifty actions have given the Lilliputian movement honorable and decent mar-tyrs, it still has no way of seriously changing an armed society in a violent world, or expanding its influence, and thus no impact on the media, on public policy, or on public opinion.

This time, Phil's movement contained very few priests and nuns. Many in the peace movement came to believe that going to prison was Phil and Liz's way of life, a ritualized, frozen-in-time tactic that sought to legitimize themselves as the only ones doing effective work today, but it was irrelevant. Nearly three decades after their initial defiance of the law, what had they accomplished with Plowshares? There were infinitely more nuclear weapons throughout the world, and the United States, their nation, was a major exporter of weapons to the Third World. Then, too, Plowshares ran the serious risk of confusing ends and means and possibly setting a precedent for extremists of all political shades and causes.

And Dan?

John Dear tells this story: "I was sent to Georgetown University to do the Long Experiment [a step in Jesuit training]. I talked to the Georgetown rector about doing civil disobedience and he said, 'I know that Dan Berrigan will be the only Jesuit remembered in U.S. history in the twentieth century. He is the epitome of the American Jesuit. But the last thing I need is another Dan Berrigan at Georgetown. Don't do it.' "[49]

By the nineties, Dan rarely involved himself in any more Plowshares actions, though he continued his monthly vigils before the Riverside Research Institute in Manhattan. The Plowshares movement, he said with pride in 1994 at Cornell University, is composed of "spiritually disciplined and well-prepared people who can do these things and who can take the heat." Prison was out of the question for him, and the less of a celebrity he became, the more he had become a holy man, perhaps even a prophet, arriving at some sort of peace, to be admired, read, and reread fifty and one hundred years from now. Sustained by the Catholic Church's tradition and his Jesuit training, his devotion to past Jesuit poets and Jesuit writers and martyrs, he continued to wage his battle in his own way. "You keep on keeping on, praying," he said. "The nub: faithlessness on our part is no response to dereliction on theirs."[50]

Phil, past seventy now, still climbs forty-foot ladders painting houses in Baltimore, is still political, and is more fascinated than ever by biblical studies and the Scriptures, buoyed by Liz and their kids, still enthusiastic and joyful.

Father McSorley recalls inviting Phil to address a class he was teaching at Georgetown University. A student asked Phil, "If the Catholic Church is so bad, why are you still a Catholic?" Phil thought for a moment, then quietly answered, "Where else can I go? My roots are in the Church, in Thomas à Becket, the Christian martyrs of Rome, Thomas More, the Apostles."[51]

In April 1994, a retired managing editor of a small-town Ohio newspaper, Joe Lersky, and his wife, "for no particular reason," drove into Elizabeth City, North Carolina, soon after four Plowshares raiders were condemned for damaging an air force jet at a nearby base. Unaware even that such raids were still occurring, he read in the local newspaper that "longtime peace activist Philip Berrigan, 70" was one of the convicted. The following day, Richard Nixon died, an event followed by accolades and tributes from America's mighty and powerful. Lersky pondered the curious juxtaposition of one man's death and another's prison time, of the unrepentant former president and the incorrigible dissenter.

"So, on the one hand," Lersky wrote in an essay for *Commonweal*, "beneath the sod of Yorba Linda, there is the dead Richard Nixon, his primary legacy the sanguine knowledge that James Madison was an ass and the Constitution exists mainly to be subverted when the moon is right or the need arises; and on the other, jailed in North Carolina, the live Philip Berrigan, paying one more time the price of an unswerving devotion to the message of Jesus Christ."[52]

It had been Dan and Phil Berrigan's hope to inspire a spiritual metamorphosis and help heal the "moral rot" at the heart of the modern state by finding a way attuned to Judaic-Buddhist-Christian ideals: patience, justice, mercy, tolerance, worship, peacemaking, trust, community, and love of family, friend, neighbor—and enemy. Nothing of the sort had happened, and the movement and their flaws were evident for all to see. The years had taken their toll. In 1994, invited once again to speak at Cornell in Merton's honor, Dan told students and faculty: "We can't save the world. There are too many calloused hearts in people of power." Fatigued from a tiring and interrupted flight, he sounded momentarily dispirited. "We do what we can, salvage a few lives, including our own . . . we can't do what we thought we could do in better times." What conclusions, then, had he reached? Drawing on the "modesty of human endeavor" of Albert Camus, he counseled marriage, family, faith, and trust—and upon the strands of Buddhism and Christianity he had himself embraced, of doing good for its own sake "because it is good and true not because it goes somewhere."

Whatever their successes or the lack of them, despite their imperfections, their failure to delineate how to get from here to there, politically and economically, the Berrigans honored the country and the world in this, the bloodiest century in human history, by their moral balance, in public and private. Their disturbing questions about nurturing spiritual and ethical values remain essentially untested and unexamined, scorned by a new generation of avaricious cynics and demagogues. Dan and Phil were gifts, transient perhaps, possibly myopic in what they thought might be accomplished, but gifts nonetheless.

When they finally pass from this life, we will need a new generation of Berrigan brothers to remind us once more, if we need any reminder at all, that they tried to do as beckoned by the prophet Amos (5:14): "Seek good, and not evil, that ye may live; And so the LORD, the God of hosts, will be with you, as ye say, Hate the evil and love the good, And establish justice in the gate."

NOTES

Prologue: "How Do They Keep Going?"

1. From a July 28, 1995, interview with an employee, who refused to be identified, in the financial department of the Riverside Research Institute (RRI) at 330 West 42nd Street in New York City. Citing the institute's biomedical and electromechanical projects, the employee complained that the Berrigans and the Catholic peace group, Pax Christi, "picket us all the time, but they have no idea what we're really involved in." However, RRI's president, Marvin King, made no effort to shed light on his company's work, refusing comment. Nor did the chief of security, William Jackson, who would only say, "We don't comment one way or the other about the demonstrators or any project having to do with the Berrigans." Interviews with King and Jackson, August 8, 1995.

2. Thomas Merton, *Thomas Merton: The Nonviolent Alternative,* rev. ed. of *Thomas Merton on Peace,* ed. Gordon Zahn (New York: Farrar, Straus & Giroux, 1980), 160–61.

3. Philip Berrigan, "On Blindness and Healing," in *Swords Into Plowshares: Nonviolent Direct Action for Disarmament,* eds. Arthur J. Laffin and Anne Montgomery (San Francisco: Harper & Row, 1987), 49.

4. Daniel Berrigan, *America Is Hard to Find* (New York: Doubleday, 1972), 95.

5. Daniel Berrigan, "Letter to Ernesto Cardenal," *National Catholic Reporter,* May 5, 1978, 12.

6. Interview with Joe Cosgrove, July 31, 1995.

7. Daniel Berrigan, *The Mission: A Film Journal* (New York: Harper & Row, 1986), 73.

8. John Dear, ed., *Apostle of Peace: Essays in Honor of Daniel Berrigan* (Maryknoll, N.Y.: Orbis, 1996), 1.

9. Daniel Berrigan, *The Dark Night of Resistance* (New York: Doubleday, 1971), xviii–xix.

10. Interview with Michael Chinsolo, chief jailer, Chowan County Jail, September 19, 1995.

11. Interview with Tom Cornell, March 24, 1994.

12. Longtime Catholic pacifist Gordon Zahn, quoted in Michael Gallagher's *Laws of Heaven: Catholic Activists Today* (New York: Ticknor & Fields, 1992), 259. Zahn also says that in the Plowshares movement, "getting arrested has been romanticized."

13. Philip Berrigan, "Imprisonment Could Hardly Be More to the Point," *National Catholic Reporter,* February 11, 1994, 1.

14. John Dear, *Peace Behind Bars: A Peacemaking Priest's Journal from Jail* (Kansas City: Sheed & Ward, 1995), 79, quoting from Daniel Berrigan, "The Peacemaker," in *Thomas Merton/Monk,* ed. Patrick Hart (Kalamazoo, Mich.: Cistercian Publications, 1983), 226.

15. Daniel Berrigan, *Dark Night of Resistance*, PAGE.

16. Philip Berrigan, *Prison Journals of a Priest Revolutionary,* ed. Vincent McGee (New York: Holt, Rinehart & Winston, 1970), 18–19.

17. Ibid., 23.

18. Daniel Berrigan, *To Dwell in Peace: An Autobiography* (San Francisco: Harper & Row, 1987), 3.

19. Interview with "Spike," outside the Pentagon, August 7, 1995.

20. Interview with Philip Berrigan, January 21, 1995.

21. Michael Novak, "The Oranging of the Berrigans: Neither in Their Political nor in Their Moral Judgment Are the Berrigans Suitable Models for Thought and Action," *Christian Century,* April 17, 1974, 420–21. See also, Dale Vree, "'Stripped Clean': The Berrigans and the Politics of Guilt and Martyrdom," *Ethics,* July 4, 1975.

22. Philip Berrigan, *Prison Journals,* 17.

Chapter 1: Pater Unfamilias

1. Daniel Berrigan, *To Dwell in Peace: An Autobiography* (San Francisco: Harper & Row, 1987), 8.

2. Interview with Jim and Rosalie Berrigan, January 18–19, 1995.

3. "Berrigan–Fromhertz Roots," a family tree with commentary by James W. Berrigan, 1988, 4.

4. Thomas Berrigan, "Daily Encounters," 1904, from his unpublished poems in the Rare and Manuscript Collections, #4602, Carl A. Kroch

Library, Cornell University, Ithaca, New York (hereafter cited as Cornell), Box 68.

5. Thomas Berrigan, "To My Sister Agnes," 1915, Cornell, Box 68.
6. Daniel Berrigan, *To Dwell in Peace*, 11.

Chapter 2: Bloodline

1. Daniel Berrigan, *To Dwell in Peace: An Autobiography* (San Francisco: Harper & Row, 1987), 17.
2. Francine du Plessix Gray, *Divine Disobedience: Profiles in Catholic Radicalism* (New York: Knopf, 1970), 61.
3. Sister Bernard Coleman, O.S.B., and Sister Verona LaBud, O.S.B., *Masinaigans: The Little Book*, a biography of Monsignor Joseph F. Buh (St. Paul, Minn.: North Central, 1972), 160.
4. Ely's local newspaper reported that the 1901 dedication of St. Anthony's Church attracted "a concourse of such people as have never graced a public occasion in this city," at which the presiding bishop delivered an extended oral history of the Roman Empire, "showing the advancement of the Catholic church from the time of St. Peter" to its modern recrudescence in Minnesota. Ibid., 180.
5. Daniel Berrigan letter, included in "Berrigan–Fromhertz Roots," a family tree with commentary by James W. Berrigan, 1988.
6. "Berrigan–Fromhertz Roots."
7. Ibid.
8. Interview with Jim and Rosalie Berrigan, January 18–19, 1995.
9. Interview with Jerry Berrigan, March 12, 1995.
10. Interview with Daniel Berrigan, March 17, 1995.
11. Interview with Philip Berrigan, January 21, 1995.
12. The Great Potato Famine was Malthusian in the way that war, an avoidable human event, causes death on the scale of natural disaster (in this case, some 1 million people in Ireland between 1845 and 1849). Queen Victoria's culpability is complicated, but indisputable. Throughout 1845, she supported the Tory prime minister, Robert Peel, and his assistant secretary to the treasury, Charles Edward Trevelyan, who argued in *The Irish Crisis* that the famine was God's prudent corrective to overpopulation. Trevelyan was in charge of famine relief, which he undermined by maintaining Ireland's traditional level of food exports, lest the entrepreneurial initiative of the starving masses be blunted, and, more importantly, European markets suffer upset. Viscount Palmerston's prime ministership, beginning in 1846, was little better at stemming the crisis.

And the English-dominated landlord-tenant farming system, in many cases, thwarted organized relief. See R. F. Foster, *Modern Ireland: 1600–1972* (New York: Viking Penguin, 1988), 318–44; Laim de Paor, *The Peoples of Ireland from Prehistory to Modern Times* (Notre Dame, Ind.: University of Notre Dame Press, 1986), 243–47; and T. W. Moody and F. X. Martin, eds., *The Course of Irish History* (Dublin, Ireland: Mercier, 1929), 263–74.

13. "He Who Plants a Tree Plants Hope," a narrative of the Dohertys in America, 5, Cornell, Box 68.

14. Many have remarked on the modern Irish character's paradoxical combination of radicalism and passivity. Francine du Plessix Gray provides a useful synopsis of its impact on American grassroots politics during the 1960s in "The Ultra-Resistance," from her collection, *Adam and Eve in the City* (New York: Simon & Schuster, 1987), 16.

15. "Berrigan–Fromhertz Roots."

16. "He Who Plants," 5.

17. Ibid, 2.

18. Foster, *Modern Ireland*, 345–72.

19. "Berrigan-Fromherz Roots."

20. Foster, *Modern Ireland*, 279.

21. Interview with Daniel Berrigan, March 17, 1995.

22. David M. Ellis, James A. Frost, Harold C. Syrett, Harry J. Carman, *A History of New York State* (New York: Cornell University Press, 1957), 188, 245.

23. Daniel Berrigan, *Prison Poems* (Greensboro, N.C.: Unicorn, 1973), 58.

24. Thomas Berrigan, "Sleet Storm," Cornell, Box 68.

25. Thomas Berrigan, "Winter Song," unpublished poem from Jerry Berrigan's private collection.

26. Thomas Berrigan, "Written in Memory of One I Deem It a Privilege to Mourn," Cornell, Box 68.

27. Thomas Berrigan, "To My Sister (To Winnie)," Cornell, Box 68.

28. Interview with Jim and Rosalie Berrigan, January 18–19, 1995.

29. Interview with Jerry Berrigan, March 12, 1995.

30. Thomas Berrigan, "To My Sister (To Winnie)," Cornell, Box 68.

31. Thomas Berrigan, "To My Mother," Cornell, Box 68.

32. Interview with Daniel Berrigan, March 17, 1995.

33. Thomas Berrigan, "Au Revoir," from Jerry Berrigan's private collection.

34. From *The Iron Range: A People's History,* a video documentary produced by Twin Cities Public Television, 1994.

35. "My Brother Fire . . . "

36. Jim Berrigan; see also Gray, *Divine Disobedience*, 66.

37. "My Brother Fire . . . "

38. Ibid.

39. Daniel Berrigan, "My Father," in *Daniel Berrigan: Poetry, Drama, Prose,* ed. Michael True (Maryknoll, N.Y.: Orbis, 1988), 18–28.

40. Daniel Berrigan, *Prison Poems,* 59; Daniel Berrigan, *Portraits of Those I Love* (New York: Crossroad, 1982), 119; also, interview with Daniel Berrigan, September 9, 1994.

41. Anne Klejment, "The Berrigans: Revolutionary Christian Nonviolence," in *Peace Heroes in Twentieth-Century America,* ed. Charles DeBenedetti (Bloomington: Indiana University Press, 1986), 230.

42. Thomas Berrigan, "Spring and Summer," Cornell, Box 68.

43. Interview with Jim and Rosalie Berrigan, January 18–19, 1995.

44. Interview with Daniel Berrigan, March 17, 1995.

45. Daniel Berrigan, *Portraits,* 115.

46. Interview with Daniel Berrigan, March 17, 1995.

47. Daniel Berrigan, *To Dwell in Peace,* 6.

48. James Berrigan, "Family History II," an unpublished collection of anecdotes about the Berrigans' early years in Minnesota and Syracuse, New York, from his private collection.

49. Daniel Berrigan, *To Dwell in Peace,* 12, 13, 20.

50. "Berrigan–Fromhertz Roots."

51. James Berrigan, "Family History II."

Chapter 3: Fighting Irish

1. Daniel Berrigan, *To Dwell in Peace: An Autobiography* (San Francisco: Harper & Row, 1987), 22.

2. Ibid., 23.

3. Ibid., 19, 22.

4. Interview with Philip Berrigan, January 21, 1995; Daniel Berrigan, *To Dwell in Peace,* 57.

5. Interviews with Philip and Daniel Berrigan.

6. Interview with Jim and Rosalie Berrigan, January 18–19, 1995.

7. Interview with Daniel Berrigan, September 9, 1994.

8. Thomas Merton to Daniel Berrigan, August 4, 1964, Cornell, Box 68.

9. Daniel Berrigan, *To Dwell in Peace,* 38; interviews with Jerry Berrigan and Jim Berrigan.

10. Daniel Berrigan, *To Dwell in Peace*, 28.
11. Interviews with Jerry Berrigan, Jim Berrigan, Philip Berrigan, and Daniel Berrigan.
12. Michael True, ed., *Daniel Berrigan: Poetry, Drama, Prose* (Maryknoll, N.Y.: Orbis, 1988), 19.
13. Interview with Jerry Berrigan, July 23, 1994.
14. Interview with Daniel Berrigan, March 17, 1995.
15. Interview with Jim and Rosalie Berrigan, January 18–19, 1995.
16. Philip Berrigan with Fred A. Wilcox, *Fighting the Lamb's War: Skirmishes with the American Empire* (Monroe, ME: Common Courage Press, 1996), 2, 3.
17. Interview with Jim and Rosalie Berrigan, January 18–19, 1995.
18. Interview with Daniel Berrigan, March 17, 1995
19. *Fighting the Lamb's War*, 5, 6.
20. True, *Daniel Berrigan*, 32.
21. Interview with Philip Berrigan, January 21, 1995.
22. Daniel Berrigan, *Lights On in the House of the Dead: A Prison Diary* (New York: Doubleday, 1974), 14.
23. Daniel Berrigan, *To Dwell in Peace*, 43.
24. Interview with Daniel Berrigan, February 19, 1994.
25. Interview with Philip Berrigan, January 21, 1995.
26. Ibid.
27. Interview with Daniel Berrigan, March 17, 1995.
28. Interview with Jerry Berrigan, March 12, 1995.
29. Interview with Jerry Berrigan, July 23, 1994.
30. *Fighting the Lamb's War*, 8.
31. Daniel Berrigan, *To Dwell in Peace*, 54.
32. Interview with Philip Berrigan, January 21, 1995.
33. Interview with Jerry Berrigan, March 12, 1995.

Chapter 4: Formations

1. Daniel Berrigan, letter to family, August 14, 1939, Cornell, Box 68.
2. Interview with Vinnie Quayle, May 12, 1995.
3. Interview with Jim and Rosalie Berrigan, January 18–19, 1995.
4. Loye Miller Jr., *Philadelphia Inquirer*, September 12, 1971, 14.
5. Peter McDonough, *Men Astutely Trained: A History of the Jesuits in the American Century* (New York: Free Press, 1992), 4–5.
6. Interview with Jim Kelly, May 20, 1995. The choices Kelly and others faced in 1959, when he decided to enter the priesthood, were even starker twenty years earlier when Daniel Berrigan faced them.

7. McDonough, *Men Astutely Trained*, 6.

8. Daniel Berrigan, *Portraits of Those I Love* (New York: Crossroad, 1982), 92. The quote applies to Berrigan and another Jesuit, John McNeil, whose paths first crossed as young priests in Paris, but it describes the mindset of most Jesuit novices in an era of church stability.

9. John W. O'Malley, *The First Jesuits* (Cambridge, Mass.: Harvard University Press, 1933), p. 37.

10. John L'Heureux, "The New American Jesuits," *Atlantic,* November 1963, 63.

11. Ibid., 61.

12. Daniel Berrigan, *To Dwell in Peace: An Autobiography* (San Francisco: Harper & Row, 1987), 96–97.

13. Daniel Berrigan, "Open Sesame: My Life and Good Times," in *Daniel Berrigan: Poetry, Drama, Prose*, ed. by Michael True (Maryknoll, N.Y.: Orbis, 1988), 6. First published in *Katallagete* (Winter 1968–69).

14. Daniel to Freda Berrigan, July 30 c.1940's (exact year unknown), Cornell, Box 68.

15. Daniel Berrigan, *To Dwell in Peace,* 117.

16. George Reimer, *The New Jesuits* (Boston: Little, Brown, 1971), xvi–xvii.

17. Interview with Daniel Berrigan, September 9, 1994.

18. Daniel Berrigan, *To Dwell in Peace,* 90.

19. Daniel Berrigan, *The Mission: A Film Journal* (New York: Harper & Row, 1986), 79.

20. Daniel Berrigan, *To Dwell in Peace,* 94.

21. Ibid., 94–95.

22. Ibid., 92.

23. Ibid., 125.

24. Interview with Vinnie Quayle, May 12, 1995.

25. Daniel Berrigan to family, August 15, 1939, Cornell, Box 68.

26. Interview with Jim and Rosalie Berrigan, January 18–19, 1995.

27. Philip Berrigan with Fred Wilcox, *Fighting the Lamb's War: Skirmishes with the American Empire* (Monroe, Maine: Common Courage Press, 1996), 9.

28. Michael True, ed., *Daniel Berrigan: Poetry, Drama, Prose* (Maryknoll, N.Y.: Orbis, 1988), xiii.

29. *Fighting the Lamb's War,* 13, 14.

30. Ibid., 16, 17.

31. Interview with Philip Berrigan, January 21, 1995.

32. Ibid.

33. Philip Berrigan, *A Punishment for Peace* (New York: Macmillan, 1969), 113–16.
34. Loye Miller Jr., "Why Did Mild Phil Berrigan Turn Firebrand?" *Philadelphia Inquirer,* September 13, 1971.
35. *Fighting the Lamb's War,* 15, 16.
36. Richard Curtis, *The Berrigan Brothers: The Story of Daniel and Philip Berrigan* (New York: Hawthorn, 1974), 21.
37. Interviews with Philip Berrigan, August 9, 1994, and January 21, 1995.
38. Interestingly, this is the opposite of the spiritual journey taken by Dorothy Day, whose activism and friendship would later shape the thinking of both Berrigan brothers. Day was an accomplished radical with celebrated jail time and hunger strikes under her belt when she embraced Catholicism in her late twenties, much to the dismay of her communist friends. In contrast, Catholicism seems to have been bred in the bones of Daniel and Philip. Interview with Philip Berrigan, January 21, 1995.
39. *Fighting the Lamb's War,* 29.
40. Interview with Jim and Rosalie Berrigan, January 18–19, 1995.
41. Interview with Philip Berrigan, January 21, 1995.
42. Interview with Daniel Berrigan, March 17, 1995.
43. Interview with Richard Cusack, July 7, 1995.
44. Interview with Phil Berrigan, January 21, 1995.
45. Loye Miller, Jr., *Philadelphia Inquirer,* September 13, 1971.
46. Interview with Philip Berrigan, January 21, 1995.
47. Ibid.
48. Interview with Jim and Rosalie Berrigan, January 18–19, 1995.
49. Interview with Philip Berrigan, January 21, 1995.
50. Interview with Jerry Berrigan, July 23, 1995.
51. Francine du Plessix Gray, *Divine Disobedience: Profiles in Catholic Radicalism* (New York: Knopf, 1970), 67.
52. True, *Daniel Berrigan,* 4.
53. Gray, *Divine Disobedience,* 66.
54. Interview with Daniel Berrigan, March 17, 1995.

Chapter 5: Awakenings

1. In late 1944, Camus wrote, "For years now we've been waiting for the greatest spiritual authority of our times to condemn in clear terms the ventures of dictatorships. For this condemnation may be found in certain encyclical letters if they are read and correctly

interpreted. But these letters and the language in which they are written have never been very accessible to the vast majority of men. . . . This great majority have waited all these years for a voice to raise itself and clearly state . . . where evil lies." See Albert Camus, *Between Hell and Reason: Essays from the Resistance Newspaper, "Combat," 1944–1947* (Middleton, Conn.: Wesleyan University Press, 1991), 97, 98.

2. Stanley Windass, trans. and ed., *Chronicle of the Worker-Priests* (New York: Humanities Press, 1966), 18.

3. Daniel Berrigan, *To Dwell in Peace: An Autobiography* (San Francisco: Harper & Row, 1987), 129.

4. Windass, *Chronicle of the Worker-Priests,* 81.

5. Adam Gopnik, "The Virtual Bishop," *The New Yorker,* March 18, 1996, 60.

6. Windass, *Chronicle of the Worker-Priests,* 57–58.

7. F. Gray, *Divine Disobedience,* 67.

8. Daniel Berrigan, *No Bars to Manhood* (New York: Doubleday, 1970), 14.

9. Daniel Berrigan, *To Dwell in Peace,* 137.

10. Interview with James Loughran, S.J., February 17, 1995.

11. Interview with Larry Holfelder, May 12, 1995.

12. Interview with Bill Carrington, June 12, 1995.

13. Interview with James Loughran, S.J., February 17, 1995.

14. Interview with Vinnie Quayle, May 12, 1995.

15. Interview with James Loughran, S.J., February 17, 1995.

16. Interview with Peter McDonough, June 13, 1995.

17. Interview with Father Joseph Roccosalvo, S.J., April 4, 1994.

18. Philip Berrigan with Fred A. Wilcox, *Fighting the Lamb's War* (Monroe, ME.: Common Courage Press, 1966), 48, 49,

19. Philip Berrigan, *No More Strangers* (New York: Macmillan, 1966), chapters 4 and 5, and 135. See also Daniel Berrigan, "Notes for Sermons, Lent, 3rd Sunday," Cornell, March 21, 1954, Box 35. Also, Anne Klejment, "In the Lion's Den: The Social Catholicism of Daniel and Philip Berrigan, 1955–65" (Ph.D. dissertation, State University of New York at Binghamton, 1980), especially chapters 6 and 7. See, too, Daniel Berrigan, *The Dark Night of Resistance* (New York: Doubleday, 1971), 15.

20. *Fighting the Lamb's War,* 49.

21. Daniel Berrigan, *Lights On in the House of the Dead: A Prison Diary* (New York: Doubleday, 1974), 68.

22. Interview with Peter McDonough, June 13, 1995.

23. Daniel Berrigan, *To Dwell in Peace*, 143.

24. Daniel Berrigan, *The Bride: Essays in the Church* (New York: Macmillan, 1959), 142.

25. Interview with Father John Dear, S.J., January 20, 1995.

26. Much of the information about New Orleans is gleaned from the Josephite Archive in Baltimore, and the *Philadelphia Inquirer* interviews with Philip Berrigan and others.

27. Thomas Merton to Daniel Berrigan, 1963, Cornell, Box 135.

28. Philip Berrigan, "Lay Leaders in Action," *Josephite Harvest* 75 (Sept.–Oct. 1963): 18–21. As late as mid–1966, Phil was praised by the Josephites. See *Josephite Harvest* 78, no. 2 (May–June 1966): 18–21, which notes, "People who are suffering every type of social neglect cannot take Christ seriously if those who profess to believe in the Gospel are not concerned about social injustice. It was with this spirit that Fr. Philip Berrigan, SSJ, initiated efforts at community action in [West Baltimore]."

29. Loye Miller Jr., "Why Did Mild Phil Berrigan Turn Firebrand?" *Philadelphia Inquirer*, September 13, 1971, 1, 8, for Coffey, Welch, and Willard quotes.

30. Philip Berrigan, *The Catholic Church and the Negro* (St. Louis: Queen's Work, 1962), and Philip Berrigan, *No More Strangers*, 133–34.

31. "NAACP Leader Pleads for End of Violence," NCWC News (Domestic), August 18, 1964.

32. Richard Gilman, *Faith, Sex, Mystery* (New York: Penguin, 1988), 141.

33. Interview with Philip Berrigan, September 25, 1990.

34. Philip Berrigan, *Prison Journals of a Priest Revolutionary*, ed. Vincent McGee (New York: Holt, Rinehart & Winston, 1970), 182–83.

35. "Priests, Nuns in Viet War Protest," *Baltimore Catholic Review*, March 12, 1965.

36. Interview with Barry Cassidy, June 28, 1994.

37. Thomas Merton to Daniel Berrigan, November 10, 1961, Cornell, Box 90; *The Hidden Ground of Love: The Letters of Thomas Merton on Religious Experience and Social Concerns*, ed. William H. Shannon (New York: Farrar, Strauss & Girous, 1985), 71.

38. Thomas Merton, *The Road to Joy: Letters to New and Old Friends*, ed. Robert E. Daggy (San Diego: Harcourt Brace Jovanovich, 1989), 241–42.

39. Michael Mott, *The Seven Mountains of Thomas Merton* (Boston: Houghton Mifflin, 1984), 383–84, quoting from Merton's *Restricted Journals*, August 21, 1962. Philip Berrigan claimed Merton did not have the same impact on him as he obviously did on Daniel. See Patricia F. McNeal, *The American Catholic Movement, 1928–1972* (New

York: Arno, 1978), 161–62. McNeal's interview with Philip was conducted February 4, 1970, and Daniel's comments on Merton were contained in a letter to her dated June 12, 1969. See, too, interview with Philip Berrigan, January 21, 1995, and Daniel Berrigan, "Recollections of a Friend: Berrigan on Merton," speech, Westbury, N.Y., St. Brigid's Church, December 2, 1993.

40. Elena Malits, *The Solitary Explorer: Thomas Merton's Transforming Journey* (San Francisco: Harper & Row, 1980), 76–78, 95. See, too, Thomas Merton, *Faith and Violence: Christian Teaching and Christian Practice* (Notre Dame, Ind.: University of Notre Dame Press, 1968), 6–7; Thomas Merton, "Nuclear War and Christian Responsibility," *Commonweal*, February 9, 1962; and Daniel Berrigan and Thich Nhat Hanh, *The Raft Is Not the Shore: Conversations Towards a Buddhist/Christian Awareness* (Boston: Beacon, 1975), 44. On nuclear weaponry, see Thomas Merton, "Peace, a Religious Responsibility," in *Breakthrough to Peace: Twelve Views on the Threat of Nuclear Extermination* (New York: New Directions, 1962), 90.

41. On the retreat at Gethsemani, see Mott, *Seven Mountains,* 406–7; *Thomas Merton: A Vow of Conversation, Journals 1964–1965,* ed. Naomi Burton Stone (New York: Farrar, Straus & Giroux, 1988), 100–101; Michael True, "Nonviolence and Contemplation: The Legacy of Thomas Merton," *Fellowship* (Nov.–Dec. 1994): 10; Jim Forest, "A Great Lake of Beer," in *Apostle of Peace: Essays in Honor of Daniel Berrigan,* ed. John Dear (Maryknoll, N.Y.: Orbis, 1995), 120-21; and Jo Ann Ooiman, *Abraham Went Out: A Biography of A. J. Muste* (Philadelphia: Temple University Press, 1981), 188.

42. Forest's essay, "No Longer Alone: The Catholic Peace Movement," was published in *American Catholics and the Vietnam War,* ed. Thomas E. Quigley (Grand Rapids, Mich.: Eerdmans, 1968), 139–50.

43. James Finn, "Pacifism and Justifiable War," in *War or Peace? The Search for New Answers,* ed. Thomas A. Shannon (Maryknoll, N.Y.: Orbis, 1980), 12–13. See also John Courtney Murray, S.J., "Morality and Modern War," in *The Moral Dilemma of Nuclear Weapons: Essays from Worldview,* ed. William Clancy (New York: Church Peace Union, 1961), 7–16; James Finn's *Protest: Pacifism and Politics. Some Passionate Views on War and Nonviolence* (New York: Random House, 1967), a valuable guide to pacifist thought, including conversations with A.J. Muste and many others.

44. David J. O'Brien, "American Catholic Opposition to the Vietnam War: A Preliminary Assessment," in Shannon, 119–50, esp. 121;

Constance Rosenblum, "A History of the Vietnam Protest Movement," *Ave Maria*, December 23–30, 1967, 10–14.

Chapter 6: Exile and Shunning

1. Jonathan Roberts, "Voices of an Antiwar Movement: Baltimore During the Vietnam War," 38 pp., unpublished, Johns Hopkins University, Department of History, 1991, 23.
2. Daniel Berrigan, *To Dwell in Peace: An Autobiography* (San Francisco: Harper & Row, 1987), 176.
3. Daniel Berrigan, *They Call Us Dead Men: Reflections on Life and Conscience* (New York: Macmillan, 1966), 186, 188.
4. Xavier Rynne, *Letters from Vatican City* (New York: Doubleday, 1963), 15–42.
5. Philip Berrigan, *No More Strangers* (New York: Macmillan, 1966), 31, 159.
6. Daniel Berrigan, *To Dwell in Peace*, 170.
7. Pierre Teilhard de Chardin, "The Meaning and Constructive Value of Suffering," in *Jubilee*, June 1962, quoted in Philip Berrigan, *No More Strangers*.
8. Interview with Father Henry Offer, November 1, 1994.
9. Ibid.
10. Stephen J. Ochs, *Desegregating the Altar: The Josephites and the Struggle for Black Priests, 1871–1960* (Baton Rouge: Louisiana State University Press, 1990).
11. Jim Forest, "Fall of '64, Spring of '65," unpublished manuscript, Cornell, Box 74; and Jim Forest, "Philip Berrigan: Disturber of the Sleep," in *The Berrigans*, eds. William Van Etten Casey, S.J., and Philip Nobile (New York: Praeger, 1971), 166–79.
12. Philip Berrigan, *No More Strangers*, 95.
13. Francine du Plessix Gray, *Divine Disobedience: Profiles in Catholic Radicalism* (New York: Knopf, 1970), 81.
14. Philip Berrigan, *No More Strangers*, 110, 111, 115, 117–19.
15. Gray, *Divine Disobedience*, 110, 111.
16. Ibid., 83, 87.
17. Interview with Rev. Peter Hogan, S.S.J., September 25, 1994.
18. Stanley Karnow, *Vietnam: A History* (New York: Viking, 1983), 214.
19. Interview with James O'Gara, February 2, 1994. See also Rodger Van Allen's, *The Commonweal and American Catholicism: The Magazine, the Movement, the Meaning* (Philadelphia: Fortress, 1974), 92–93, which details the evolution in opinion of this important mag-

azine toward the war, from early backing to outspoken opposition.

20. Interview with Bill O'Connor, January 21, 1995.

21. Karnow, *Vietnam*, 366–76.

22. Philip Berrigan to Martin Corbin, ca. 1965, Dorothy Day–Catholic Worker Collection, Marquette University, Series W–3, Box 5.

23. Daniel Berrigan, introduction in Philip Berrigan, *Prison Journals of a Priest Revolutionary,* ed. Vincent McGee (New York: Holt, Rhinehart & Winston, 1970), xvii.

24. Philip Berrigan, *Prison Journals,* 74.

25. Robert Weisbrot, *Freedom Bound: A History of America's Civil Rights Movement* (New York: Norton, 1990), 196–206.

26. Philip Berrigan interview in *From Camelot to Kent State: The Sixties in the Words of Those Who Lived It,* eds. Joan Morrison and Robert K. Morrison (New York: Times Books, 1987), 146.

27. Robert S. McNamara with Brian VanDeMark, *In Retrospect: The Tragedy and Lessons of Vietnam* (New York: Times Books, 1995), 216. See also Nancy Zaroulis and Gerald Sullivan, *Who Spoke Up? American Protest Against the War in Vietnam, 1963–1975* (New York: Doubleday, 1984), 1–3.

28. Interview with Philip Berrigan, January 21, 1995.

29. Karnow, *Vietnam,* 281.

30. Interviews with David Eberhardt, March 10, March 18, and April 4, 1994; and from his insightful, though unpublished, autobiography (hereafter cited as Eberhardt Memoir).

31. James H. Forest, "Reflections on the Self-Burning of Roger LaPorte," *Ave Maria,* December 18, 1965, 20, 22; interview with Jim Forest, November 6, 1994.

32. James Terence Fisher, *The Catholic Counterculture in America* (Chapel Hill: University of North Carolina Press, 1989), 253.

33. Jim Forest, *Love Is the Measure: A Biography of Dorothy Day* (Maryknoll, N.Y.: Orbis, 1994), 114–15.

34. Thomas Merton, quoted in Gordon Zahn, "Original Child Monk: An Appreciation," introduction to *Thomas Merton: The Nonviolent Alternative,* rev. ed., ed. Gordon Zahn (New York: Farrar, Straus & Giroux, 1980), xxxiv.

35. Ibid. See also Thomas Merton to Jim Forest correspondence, March 21, 1967, Cornell, Box 90; Michael Mott, *The Seven Mountains of Thomas Merton* (Boston: Houghton Mifflin, 1984), 427–49; and *The Hidden Ground of Love: The Letters of Thomas Merton on Religious Experience and Social Concerns,* ed. William H. Shannon (New York: Farrar, Straus & Giroux, 1985), 88–89.

36. Forest, *Love Is the Measure*, 114, 115.

37. David Miller interview in Morrison and Morrison, eds., *From Camelot to Kent State*, 107–10.

38. John Cooney, *The American Pope: The Life and Times of Francis Cardinal Spellman* (New York: Times Books, 1984), 287.

39. Gray, *Divine Disobedience*, 99, 100.

40. Daniel Berrigan, *To Dwell in Peace*, 179–80; Daniel Berrigan and Thich Nhat Hanh, *The Raft Is Not the Shore: Conversations Towards a Buddhist/Christian Awareness* (Boston: Beacon, 1975), 59–60.

41. Ross Labrie, *The Writings of Daniel Berrigan* (Lanham, Md.: University Press of America, 1989), 75.

42. *New Catholic Encyclopedia* (New York: McGraw-Hill, 1967), 315, citing Thomas Aquinas's *Summa Theologica*, which is predicated on Augustine's *City of God*.

43. Gray, *Divine Disobedience*, 102; and "The Politics of Salvation," Parts 1 and 2, June 1, 1972, 34–40 and June 15, 1972, 14–21, *New York Review of Books*.

44. Jim Forest, "Daniel Berrigan: The Poet and Prophet as Priest," Cornell, Box 74, and published in *The Witness of the Berrigans*, eds. Stephen Halpert and Tom Murray (New York: Doubleday, 1972).

45. Daniel Berrigan to John Deedy, January 4, 1994, Deedy Collection; interview with John Leo, April 25, 1994; interview with Rev. James Patrick Cotter, S.J., February 1, 1995.

46. Gray, *Divine Disobedience*, 104.

47. Father James Patrick Cotter, S.J., untitled and unpublished memorandum, May 1966.

48. James H. Forest, "Thomas Merton's Struggle with Peacemaking," in *Thomas Merton: Prophet in the Belly of a Paradox*, ed. Gerald Twomey (New York: Paulist, 1978), 40–46.

49. Daniel Berrigan, letter to Jim Forest and Tom Cornell, February 17, 1966, Cornell, Box 90.

50. Daniel Berrigan, letter to Tom Cornell and Jim Forest, December 7, 1965, Cornell, Box 90.

51. Interview with Daniel Berrigan, July 7, 1995.

52. Daniel Berrigan, letter to Freda Berrigan, February 20, 1966, Cornell, Box 90.

53. Gray, *Divine Disobedience*, 105.

54. Daniel Berrigan, letter to Patrick Henry, November 1965, Cornell, Box 90.

55. Daniel Berrigan, *Consequences: Truth and . . .* (New York: Macmillan, 1967), 80.

56. Daniel Berrigan, *To Dwell in Peace*, 183.

57. Interview with Rev. Alden Stevenson, S.J., February 1, 1995; Daniel Berrigan, *Consequences*, 104, 113.

58. Richard Curtis, *The Berrigan Brothers: The Story of Daniel and Philip Berrigan* (New York: Hawthorn, 1974), 57.

59. Interviews with Joseph Mulholland, February 24–25 and June 29, 1995; *New York Times*, December 12, 1965, E4.

60. Daniel Berrigan, *Consequences*, 80, 104.

61. Shannon, *Hidden Ground of Love*, 89.

62. Thomas Merton to Daniel Berrigan, February 14, 1966, Cornell, Box 90; Shannon, *Hidden Ground of Love*, 89–90. See also Daniel Berrigan and Thich Nhat Hanh, *Raft Is Not the Shore*, 139.

63. Daniel Berrigan, *Consequences*, 104, 119, 123.

64. Ibid., 186.

65. Ibid., 109.

66. German Guzman, *Camilio Torres*, trans. by John D. Ring (New York: Sheed & Ward, 1969), 22 and passim. John M. Swomley Jr.'s *Liberation Ethics* (New York: Macmillan, 1972), 136–43, deals with Torres's romanticizing of Fidelista guerrillas.

67. "South America: The Church at the Edge," *Jesuit Missions*, September 1966, 13–19. On clergy and laity working in slums, 13; on violence and nonviolence, 16.

68. Ross Labrie, *The Writings of Daniel Berrigan* (Latham, Md.: University Press of America, 1989), 84.

69. "South America," *Jesuit Missions*, 13–19.

70. Interview with Rev. Alden Stevenson, S.J., February 1, 1995.

71. James Forest, *Prophet*, 18, 19.

72. Shannon, *Hidden Ground of Love*, 91.

73. Twenty-eight years later, Dan said he felt compassion for the late Cardinal Spellman, inasmuch as "he was totally forgotten and discredited." Interview with Daniel Berrigan, August 11, 1994.

74. Jim Forest, "Daniel Berrigan: The Poet and Prophet as Priest," in *The Witness of the Berrigans*, eds. Stephen Halpert and Tom Murray (New York: Doubleday, 1972), 98–99.

Chapter 7: Kennedy and Cornell

1. Daniel Berrigan, *They Call Us Dead Men: Reflections on Life and Conscience* (New York: Macmillan, 1966), 187, 188.

2. Daniel Berrigan, "The Sistine Chapel," in *Daniel Berrigan: Poetry,*

Drama, Prose, ed. Michael True (Maryknoll, N.Y.: Orbis, 1988), 54. Originally published in *Spirit*, May 1964.

3. Daniel Berrigan, *Consequences: Truth and . . .* (New York: Macmillan, 1967), 86, 103.

4. Interview with Daniel Berrigan, July 21, 1995; Daniel Berrigan, *They Call Us Dead Men*, 183; Francine du Plessix Gray, *Divine Disobedience: Profiles in Catholic Radicalism* (New York: Knopf, 1970), 96.

5. Daniel Berrigan letter to Father General Pedro Arrupe, S.J., June 4, 1966, Cornell, Box 90.

6. John Deedy, *Apologies, Good Friends: An Interim Biography of Daniel Berrigan, S.J.* (Chicago: Fides/Claretian, 1981), 73.

7. Richard Curtis, *The Berrigan Brothers: The Story of Daniel and Philip Berrigan* (New York: Hawthorn, 1974), 65.

8. Interview with DeAnne Mimms, August 12, 1994; interview with James Mengel, August 4, 1994; and interviews with David Eberhardt, March 10, 1994, and March 29, 1995. See also Gray, *Divine Disobedience*, 111–16; and Curtis, *Berrigan Brothers*, 71–75.

9. Interview with Philip Berrigan, August 9, 1995.

10. Jim Forest, "Daniel Berrigan: The Poet and Prophet as Priest," in *The Witness of the Berrigans*, eds. Stephen Halpert and Tom Murray (New York: Doubleday, 1972), 102–3; and interview with James Forest, November 6, 1994.

11. Ibid.

12. Daniel Berrigan, *America Is Hard to Find* (New York: Doubleday, 1972), 56; Daniel Berrigan, *No Bars to Manhood* (New York: Doubleday, 1970), 22.

13. Michael Useem, *Conscription, Protest, and Social Conflict: The Life and Death of a Draft Resistance Movement* (New York: Wiley, 1973), 62–63.

14. Walter Berns, "The 'Essential Soul' of Dan Berrigan," *National Review*, November 9, 1973, 1231–33.

15. David W. Connor interview with Anne Klejment, October 7, 1976, Cornell, 3.

16. Allan Bloom, *The Closing of the American Mind* (New York: Simon & Schuster, 1987), 313.

17. Daniel Berrigan to James A. Perkins, September 11, 1967, Cornell, Box 90.

18. Harry J. Cargas interview with Daniel Berrigan, unabridged and unpublished, 1969, 182. An edited version appeared in *U.S. Catholic*, January 1970, 6–11.

19. Interview with James Matlack, July 6, 1994; Daniel Berrigan, *The*

Dark Night of Resistance (New York: Doubleday, 1971), 153–54; Daniel Berrigan, *No Bars to Manhood*, 202–6.

20. Gray, *Divine Disobedience*, 139; interview with John Leo, April 15, 1994.

21. Interview with Daniel and Linda Finlay, July 26, 1994; and Daniel Finlay, "Personhood and Poetry," in *The Witness of the Berrigans*, eds. Stephen Halpert and Tom Murray (New York: Doubleday, 1972), 69.

22. David W. Connor interview with Anne Klejment, October 7, 1976, Cornell, 14.

23. Interview with David Saperstein and letter to authors, both June 30, 1994.

24. Douglas Dowd, untitled and unpublished memoir, 1994, 53 (hereafter cited as Dowd Memoir); interview with Bruce Dancis, August 21, 1994.

25. Interview with Dancis, August 21, 1994; and Tom Wells, *The War Within* (Berkeley: University of California Press, 1994), 284.

26. Thomas Merton to Daniel Berrigan, September 2, 1962, Cornell, Box 135.

27. Gray, *Divine Disobedience*, 140.

28. Daniel Berrigan, *To Dwell in Peace: An Autobiography* (San Francisco: Harper & Row, 1987), 225, 226.

29. Thomas Merton to Daniel Berrigan, October 10, 1967, Cornell, Box 90; and *The Hidden Ground of Love: The Letters of Thomas Merton on Religious Experience and Social Concerns*, ed. William H. Shannon (New York: Farrar, Straus & Giroux, 1985), 97-98.

30. Gray, *Divine Disobedience*, 136; Daniel Berrigan, *To Dwell in Peace*, 186.

31. Daniel Berrigan, *To Dwell in Peace*, 215–16; interview with Father Joseph Roccosalvo, S.J., April 4, 1994.

32. Anonymous, "Prophets of the Human Spirit: The Brothers Berrigan," Cornell, Box 157; interview with Fred Solway, July 14, 1995; interview with Rev. Jack Lewis, July 19, 1994.

33. Interview with Jerry Berrigan, July 23, 1994; interview with Daniel Berrigan, September 9, 1994.

34. Interview with Carol Berrigan, July 23, 1994.

35. Peter McDonough, *Men Astutely Trained: A History of the Jesuits in the American Century* (New York: Free Press, 1992), 467.

36. Daniel Berrigan, *To Dwell in Peace*, 226.

37. Daniel Berrigan, *The Discipline of the Mountain: Dante's Purgatorio in a Nuclear World* (New York: Seabury, 1979), 101, 102.

38. Gray, *Divine Disobedience*, 141.

39. Daniel Berrigan; interview with Carol Berrigan, July 23, 1944.

40. Daniel Berrigan, *Discipline of the Mountain*, 101, 102.

41. Interview with Father John Dear, S.J., December 14, 1994; interview with Father Joseph Roccosalvo, S.J., April 4, 1994.

42. Interview with Rev. Fred O'Connor, S.J., March 12, 1994.

43. Gray, *Divine Disobedience*, 96.

44. Interview with Mickey Myers, July 16, 1994.

45. Interview with Daniel Berrigan, September 9, 1994.

Chapter 8: Vietnam

1. Philip Berrigan to Father O'Dea, October 31, 1965, and May 8, 1967, Archives of the Society of St. Joseph.

2. Philip Berrigan, *A Punishment for Peace* (Toronto, Ontario: Macmillan, 1969), 87.

3. Philip Berrigan, "The Priest and Society," *Ave Maria*, January 8, 1966, 19.

4. David J. O'Brien, "American Catholic Opposition to the Vietnam War," in *War or Peace? The Search for New Answers*, ed. Thjomas A. Shannon, (Maryknoll, N.Y.: Orbis, 1980), 119–50; John J. Conley, "Catholic Pacifism in America," *America*, December 14, 1974, 381–83; letters to the editor from Richard McSorley, S.J.; Edwin G. Kaiser, C.P.P.S.; and Gordon Zahn, *America*, January 18, 1975, 22.

5. John Deedy, *Apologies, Good Friends: An Interim Biography of Daniel Berrigan, S.J.* (Chicago: Fides/Claretian, 1981), 87.

6. Robert S. McNamara to Philip Berrigan, January 14, 1967, Dr. George J. McVey Collection. See, especially, Robert McNamara with Brian VanDeMark, *In Retrospect: The Tragedy and Lessons of Vietnam* (New York: Times Books, 1995), 266.

7. Eberhardt Memoir, 11–12, quotes Bill O'Connor saying, "Hirschkop's face went white," upon hearing Phil's remark; Philip Berrigan interview in *From Camelot to Kent State: The Sixties in the Words of Those Who Lived It*, eds. Joan Morrison and Robert K. Morrison (New York: Times Books, 1987), 146; interview with Bill O'Connor, January 21, 1995; interviews with Philip Hirschkop, January 30, 1995, and July 22, 1996.

8. Francine du Plessix Gray, *Divine Disobedience: Profiles in Catholic Radicalism* (New York: Knopf, 1970), 117.

9. Interviews with James Mengel, August 4 and October 31, 1994.

10. Tom Lewis interview with Rosalie R. Troester, Dorothy Day–Catholic Worker Collection, Series W–9, unprocessed, Marquette University; "Tom Lewis, Catonsville 9 and Baltimore 4" interview with Charles Meconis, November 1975.

11. Richard Byrne Jr., "Revolution," (Baltimore) *City Paper*, January 29–February 4, 1993, 14.

12. Eberhardt Memoir, 12–13.

13. Gray, *Divine Disobedience*, 119–23, 78–79.

14. Eberhardt Memoir, 13–15; interviews with James Mengel, August 4 and October 31, 1994; interview with Bill O'Connor, January 21, 1995.

15. Daniel Berrigan, *To Dwell in Peace: An Autobiography* (San Francisco: Harper & Row, 1987), 210.

16. Ibid., 206, and Gray, *Divine Disobedience*, 203.

17. Thomas Lewis, "Some Reflections of a Catholic War-Protestor While in Jail with Fr. Philip Berrigan," October 28, 1967, Cornell, Box 76.

18. Philip Berrigan to Father O'Dea, October 28, 1967, Archives of the Society of St. Joseph.

Chapter 9: More Vietnam

1. Interviews with Howard Zinn, July 6 and 7, 1994; Howard Zinn, "The Prisoners: A Bit of Contemporary History," in *The Witness of the Berrigans*, eds. Stephen Halpert and Tom Murray (New York: Doubleday, 1972), 3–18, the latter a more thorough version than is found in Zinn's autobiography, *You Can't Be Neutral on a Moving Train* (Boston: Beacon, 1994), 126–34; Howard Zinn, "Peace Pilgrim to Vietnam," in *Apostle of Peace: Essays in Honor of Daniel Berrigan*, John Dear, ed., (Maryknoll, N.Y.: Orbis, 1996), 63–66; and Daniel Berrigan, "In Vietnam and Laos," in *Daniel Berrigan: Poetry, Drama, Prose*, ed. Michael True (Maryknoll, N.Y.: Orbis, 1988), 149–53.

2. Henry Kamm, "Decades-Old U.S. Bombs Still Killing Laotians," *New York Times*, August 10, 1995, A12.

3. For a highly critical account of the Berrigans in general and the Hanoi trip in particular, see Max Geltman, "The Berrigans vs. the United States," *National Review*, May 4, 1971, 470–74.

4. Daniel Berrigan, *Night Flight to Hanoi: War Diary with 11 Poems* (New York: Macmillan, 1968), 61, 85–92.

5. Michael True, ed., *Daniel Berrigan: Poetry, Drama, Prose* (Maryknoll, N.Y.: Orbis, 1988), 154.

6. Zinn, "The Prisoners," 12–15. David Corn's *Blond Ghost: Ted Shackley and the CIA's Crusades* (New York: Simon & Schuster, 1994), 120–70, portrays Ambassador Sullivan and the CIA in the "secret war" in Laos. See, too, "In Vietnam and Laos," in True, ed., *Daniel Berrigan*, 149–53; and Roger Warner, *Back Fire: The CIA's Secret*

Army in Laos and Its Link to the War in Vietnam (New York: Simon & Schuster, 1995), 276–78, 371.

7. Daniel Berrigan, *To Dwell in Peace: An Autobiography* (San Francisco: Harper & Row, 1987), 214, Dan described Sullivan as "overseer . . . of the extermination bombing of the Plain of Jars," and "amicable advisor to the unspeakable shah [of Iran]. After further denigrating Sullivan as "stony of face . . . devious . . . the perfect chattel, in sum, of imperial criminality," he noted that he was as well a "practicing Catholic. In the circles I move in, one seldom encounters so astonishing a figure." See Daniel Berrigan, "Nonviolent Citizen in the Warmaking State," unpublished speech, Cornell University, April 14, 1994. Ambassador Sullivan did not respond to an invitation sent to him care of the State Department to be interviewed for this book. See, too, William H. Sullivan, *Obbligato: Notes on a Foreign Service Career* (New York: Norton, 1984), 196–235, for his view of events in Southeast Asia. He does not mention the Berrigan-Zinn incident.

8. Larry Berman, *Lyndon Johnson's War: The Road to Stalemate in Vietnam* (New York: Norton, 1989), 184 and 202–3 for President Johnson's remark to Leonard Marks, director of the United States Information Agency, that Aiken was correct.

9. The Syracuse suicide and the poem are from Jack Lewis, "Prophets of the Human Spirit: The Brothers Berrigan," Cornell, Box 76, 2–3.

10. Bill Kovach, "How Vietnam Came to Main Street," *Washington Monthly*, June 1994, 52–53.

11. Interview with Gordon Zahn, September 27, 1994.

12. Roberts,"Voices of an Antiwar Movement: Baltimore During the Vietnam War," Johns Hopkins University, History Department, Unpublished, 1991, 17–18. Roberts describes the prosecuting U.S. Attorney Stephen Sachs as "a committed civil libertarian who was well-known in the Baltimore liberal community [who] decided to try the case personally, in order to vindicate due process and the rule of law." Roberts interviewed Sachs on February 5, 1991, and was told the raid "was a misnomer for civil disobedience. It was an aggressive affliction of views on others to make a political statement." Even so, Sachs felt it necessary to treat the case "sensitively" since the "process was fragile" and the case a "clash of moral passion and the rule of law." Interview with Stephen Sachs, February 14, 1996.

13. At his sentencing the following spring, Phil Berrigan tried to get in the last word. "[We] while under conviction and awaiting sentence,

have acted once more [at Catonsville in May 1968] against the apparatus of war. And for that, many people have judged us 'irresponsible,' or 'untrustworthy.' One prominent and respected friend called us 'a danger to the community.' A remark we accept with equanimity if not pain, since we feel our friend has the equipment to understand better." Philip Berrigan, "Statement at Sentencing," 2 pp., 1968, Richard Cusack Collection. As might be expected, Dan defended his brother at the time of the Baltimore Four trial by attacking the church once again for its silence during the Nazi era. Then, he added: "I think both of us were also cooled by our sense of the pervasive cultural illness of the American Church, its illusions about moral superiority, its massive spiritual victimization by racism, cold and hot war fervor, anti-Communism." He concluded, "Philip is not of that landscape, not of that war; indeed, not of that Church. Which is why he is in this courtroom, on this day." Daniel Berrigan, "My Brother, The Witness," *Commonweal*, April 20, 1968, 180–82.

14. John M. Swomley Jr., *Liberation Ethics* (New York: Macmillan, 1972), 162–82.

15. William R. Miller, "Nonviolence: A Christian Interpretation," in *War and Conscience in America*, ed. Edward LeRoy Long Jr. (Philadelphia: Westminster, 1964), 118–19. "The greatest danger of all is that an excessive focusing on the legality of situations tend to blind one to the obligation to make humane judgments," concludes Joseph L. Sax, "Civil Disobedience: The Law Is Never Blind," *Saturday Review*, September 28, 1968, 22–25, 56.

16. Barry Bearak, "Berrigan at 70: Still Protesting," *Los Angeles Times*, April 10, 1993, A–1.

17. "He could not claim religious leadership," from Anne Klejment, "The Berrigans: Revolutionary Christian Nonviolence," in *Peace Heroes in Twentieth-Century America*, ed. Charles DeBenedetti (Bloomington: Indiana University Press, 1986), 241–42.

18. True, ed., *Daniel Berrigan*, 14.

19. Jim Forest, "Daniel Berrigan: The Poet and Prophet as Priest," in *The Witness of the Berrigans*, eds. Stephen Halpert and Tom Murray (New York: Doubleday, 1972), 103–4.

20. *Catholic Review* (Baltimore), May 31, 1968.

21. David J. O'Brien, "American Catholic Opposition to the Vietnam War," in *War or Peace? The Search for New Answers*, ed. Thomas A. Shannon (Maryknoll, N.Y.: Orbis, 1980), 126–27; and *Commonweal*, July 22, 1966.

22. Interview with Bill O'Connor, January 21, 1995; Bill O'Connor to

Richard Carbray, November 21, 1967, Carbray Collection, University of Washington.

23. Interview with Tom Cornell, March 24, 1994. After the third raid on a draft board, in Milwaukee, very few Catholic Workers joined the many subsequent ones. By then, both Dorothy Day and Gordon Zahn had turned a cold eye on the burning of draft files.

24. Jim Forest, *Love Is the Measure: A Biography of Dorothy Day* (Maryknoll, N.Y.: Orbis, 1994), 117–18.

25. William D. Miller, *Dorothy Day: A Biography* (New York: Harper & Row, 1982), 489. This sentiment mirrored Dan's much earlier letter to Day in April 14, 1964, following his two-week stay in apartheid South Africa, which reminded him of Hitler's Germany. "Indeed, Gordon Zahn's book [*German Catholics and Hitler's Wars*] could be read there and the implications for the Catholic community could be played there without changing a major note." He added that Archbishop Patrick Hurley of Durban told him after a meeting with Daniel and the clergy "that what was needed in [Durban] was fewer Masses on Sunday and a few priests in jail." William D. Miller, *A Harsh and Dreadful Love: Dorothy Day and the Catholic Worker Movement* (New York: Liveright, 1973), 315.

26. Her sentiment was restated in October 1968 when she praised the clergy and laypeople, "amongst whom are so many of our friends," who "have offered themselves as a living sacrifice, as hostages" for destroying draft files of men classified as 1-A "in our criminal drafting and enslavement of young men for our immoral wars." Dorothy Day, *On Pilgrimage: The Sixties* (New York: Curtis, 1972), 344.

27. Thomas Merton to Philip Berrigan, December 31, 1967, Cornell, Box 90.

28. Thomas Merton to Mary Lanahan, June 24, 1968, in *Witness to Freedom: The Letters of Thomas Merton in Times of Crisis*, selected and edited by William H. Shannon (New York: Farrar, Straus & Giroux, 1994), 118–19.

29. Gordon Zahn, "Original Child Monk: An Appreciation," introduction to Thomas Merton, *The Nonviolent Alternative*, ed. Gordon Zahn (New York: Farrar, Straus & Giroux, 1980), xxxv. Zahn believed that had Merton lived, he would have disapproved of the many draft board raids that followed beyond "one or two reasonable" actions.

30. Daniel Berrigan to Willard Uphaus, December 14, 1967, Cornell, Box 56.

31. Interview with Herman Heyn, August 10, 1994 and September 16,

1996, Eberhardt interviews, March 10, 1994 and May 16, 1996 and Eberhardt Memoir, 17–24.

32. "Mass Meeting on the Draft" leaflet, November 28, 1967, Annabel Taylor Auditorium, Cornell University, and "Draft Protestor Says Violence Nothing New," *Ithaca Journal*, November 29, 1967.

Chapter 10: Catonsville

1. Daniel Berrigan to Harry J. Cargas, 202; Jim Forest, "Daniel Berrigan: The Poet and Prophet as Priest," in *The Witness of the Berrigans*, eds. Stephen Halpert and Tom Murray (New York: Doubleday, 1972), 106. "Advisor and counselor" and "couldn't not do it" are from Daniel Berrigan lecture, Cornell University, April 14, 1994.

2. Interview with Bill O'Connor, January 21, 1995; interview with Dean Pappas, February 22, 1995.

3. Interview with Grenville Whitman, February 23, 1995

4. Richard Byrne Jr., "Revolution 9," (Baltimore) *City Paper*, January 29–February 4, 1993, 12–21; and Francine du Plessix Gray, *Divine Disobedience: Profiles in Catholic Radicalism* (New York: Knopf, 1970). David Darst told the interviewer Harry James Cargas, "We were very sorry for this assault. We meant no harm to any persons whatsoever; we just wanted to destroy, as Dan Berrigan calls it, the technological garbage, these killing licenses, the draft files." See Cargas interview with David Darst, *Year One*, July–August 1993, 4–5.

5. Interviews with Philip Berrigan and Elizabeth McAlister, October 26, 1990, and January 21, 1995; and Hoag Levin, "Sister Elizabeth: A Quiet Nun Becomes a Peace Extremist," *Philadelphia Inquirer*, September 14, 1971, 1, 6–9.

6. Eberhardt Memoir, 66–67.

7. Cargas, *Year One*, 4–5.

8. Interview with John Hogan, May 19, 1994; Thomas and Marjorie Melville, "The Catholic Resistance: I," *New York Times*, April 26, 1971, 33–34; Philip Berrigan, *Prison Journals of a Priest Revolutionary*, ed. Vincent McGee (New York: Holt, Rinehart & Winston, 1970), 25; Charles Meconis interview with George Mische, November 1975, unpublished; portions of many of Meconis's interviews also appeared in his book, *With Clumsy Grace;* interview with Mary Moylan, May 17, 1994.

9. "Real reservations about draft-card burning" in James Douglass's interview with Charles Meconis, January 1976, unpublished, 3; and James W. Douglass, *Resistance and Contemplation: The Way of Liber-*

ation. The Yin and Yang of the Non-Violent Life (New York: Doubleday, 1972), 105.

10. "Selling Out the American dream," Gray, *Divine Disobedience*, 163–64. The description of William Stringfellow as an "elegant skeleton" from Daniel Berrigan, "My Friend," 6 pp., unpublished.

11. Byrne, the street scene from "Revolution 9," 17, and Gray, *Divine Disobedience*, 162–65.

12. FBI reports on Dean Pappas and the Baltimore Defense Committee, April 4, 1968, and thereafter, courtesy of Dean Pappas.

13. Elizabeth Fee, "Dean Pappas: Antiwar Activist," in *The Baltimore Book: New Views of Local History*, eds. Elizabeth Fee, Linda Shopes, and Linda Zeidman (Philadelphia: Temple University Press, 1991), 197–99.

14. Byrne, "Revolution 9," 17.

15. Dan Finlay, "Notes on the Catonsville Trial," n.d., Cornell, Box 67.

16. "To his eternal credit" from William Kunstler with Sheila Isenberg, *My Life as a Radical Lawyer* (New York: Birch Lane, 1994), 190.

17. Harvey Cox Jr., "Tongues of Flame: The Trial of the Catonsville Nine," in *The Witness of the Berrigans*, eds. Stephen Halpert and Tom Murray (New York: Doubleday, 1972), 22–23, Gray, *Divine Disobedience*, 165–225.

18. FBI reports on Dean Pappas and the Baltimore Defense Committee, April 4, 1968, and thereafter.

19. Philip Berrigan, "After the Trial, Hope," *National Catholic Reporter*, October 30, 1968, 3, and interview with Philip Berrigan, January 21, 1995.

20. Initially preoccupied with his upcoming state trial and his federal appeal, Phil had little or no hope that he would prevail in either. Philip Berrigan to Nancy and Richard Cusack, February 7, 1969, Richard Cusack Collection; interview with John Dear, January 20, 1995; Philip Berrigan's letter to "Sue and George," February 4, 1969, George McVey Collection, and *Josephite News & Views* 6, no. 6 (January 15, 1969), for reference to bail money, Josephite Archives. On Phil traveling to organize more resistance, interview with Monsignor Frank Scollen, October 5, 1994.

21. John and Thomas Berrigan in Loye Miller Jr., "Berrigans Controversial Even in Own Family," *Philadelphia Inquirer*, September 12, 1971, 15.

22. Two examples of the high esteem so many Catholic peacemakers felt toward Merton can be seen in Michael True, "Nonviolence and Contemplation: The Legacy of Thomas Merton," *Fellowship* (Nov.–Dec. 1994), 10–11 and Jim Forest, "Thomas Merton and the Catholic Worker: Waking from a Dream of Separateness," in *A Penny a Copy:*

Readings from the Catholic Worker, eds. Thomas C. Cornell, Robert Ellsberg, and Jim Forest (Maryknoll, N.Y.: Orbis, 1995), 319–24.

23. *The Hidden Ground of Love: The Letters of Thomas Merton on Religious Experience and Social Concerns*, ed. William H. Shannon (New York: Farrar, Straus & Giroux, 1985), 136, 262; "In one of his final articles," from *Ave Maria*, September 7, 1968, reprinted in *Soundings* (Washington, D.C.: Council of International Lay Associations, 1968) and *Fellowship* magazine, March 1969. See, too, Thomas Merton, *The Nonviolent Alternative*, ed. Gordon Zahn (New York: Farrar, Straus & Giroux, 1970), 231–33, and William H. Shannon, ed., *Witness to Freedom: The Letters of Thomas Merton in Times of Crisis* (New York: Farrar, Straus & Giroux, 1994), 82–83.

24. Shannon, *Witness to Freedom*, 118.

25. "A Call to Men of Conscience," advertisement placed by the Catonsville Nine Defense Committee in the *National Catholic Reporter*, September 18, 1968, 2; *The Road to Joy: The Letters of Thomas Merton to New and Old Friends*, ed. Robert E. Daggy (New York: Harcourt Brace Jovanovich, 1989), 116.

26. Daniel Berrigan believes that Merton, his mentor, ultimately approved of Catonsville, interview with Daniel Berrigan, August 11, 1994, though the authors could not locate a specific reference. "*Six years!*" from Merton's journal entry, May 28, 1968, and Mott, 524. See Jim Forest, *Living with Wisdom: A Life of Thomas Merton* (Maryknoll, N.Y.: Orbis, 1991), 195.

27. Rosemary Ruether, "Ruether's Open Letter to Daniel Berrigan," *National Catholic Reporter*, June 5, 1968, 4; Rosemary Ruether, "Tactics Fail the Vision," *National Catholic Reporter*, June 26, 1968, 4. See, too, defenses of Berrigan by David Darst, June 12; and Richard McSorley, July 10, *National Catholic Reporter*. David McReynolds, a socialist and pacifist, long associated with the War Resisters League, was also troubled by Catonsville, calling it "a very Catholic, Jesuit tactic," adding, "The burning of the files meant no willingness to built a mass system." Interview with David McReynolds, January 13, 1994.

28. Daniel Berrigan, "Dan Berrigan Answers Rosemary Ruether," *National Catholic Reporter*, June 19, 1968, 4.

29. Interview with Linda Finlay, July 26, 1994.

30. Daniel Berrigan, "David Darst," in *America Is Hard to Find* (New York: Doubleday, 1972), 179.

31. Interview with Daniel Berrigan, February 24, 1994.

32. Daniel Berrigan, *The Trial of the Catonsville Nine* (Boston: Beacon, 1970), xi. In his introduction (p. vii), Daniel Berrigan explains his use

of trial testimony dialogue as the technique of "factual theater," which necessitated "essential adherence to the letter of a text . . . I have been as faithful as possible to the original words, spoken in the heat or long haul of the trial, making only those minute changes required for clarity or good sense." The quotation attributed to Philip Berrigan ("We have been accused of arrogance") is from the play, 30.

33. James Finn, "The Trial of the Catonsville Nine," March 1971, Cornell, Box 74; and interview with James Finn, January 13, 1994. The play, produced by Leland Hayward, opened in Los Angeles at the Mark Taper Forum. In New York it was shown Off-Off Broadway at the Good Shepherd–Faith Church because the Phoenix Theater, the producer, had no theater of its own, and because "the spirit of the work, and of the brothers themselves, seemed to require an austere setting," said Daniel Freudenberger, the production stage manager. The play was turned into a film directed by Gordon Davidson and produced by Gregory Peck. See, too, Nora M. Alter, *Vietnam Protest Theatre* (Bloomington, IN.: Indiana University Press, 1996), 41–46.

34. "I hoped to link our fate," to Robert Coles, published originally in *New York Review of Books,* April 8, 1971, and reprinted in *Daniel Berrigan: Poetry, Drama, Prose,* ed. Michael True (Maryknoll, N.Y.: Orbis, 1988), 69; Daniel Berrigan's poem on John Urey, *National Catholic Reporter,* November 20, 1968, 3.

35. Harry James Cargas, *Daniel Berrigan and Contemporary Protest Poetry* (New Haven, Conn.: College and University Press, 1972), 104; Harry James Cargas, "A Protest Poet Becomes Angrier and Angrier, *National Catholic Reporter,* April 30, 1969, 9; and "The Verdict," in *Tulips in the Prison Yard,* ed. Father Patrick O'Brien (Dublin, Ireland, 1992; dist. Baltimore: Fortkamp, 1994), 38.

36. *United States of America v. Patrick George Farren,* transcript of testimony, October 28, 1969. The jury returned in twenty minutes with a guilty verdict. Farren received a suspended two-year sentence, with the stipulation he leave Rochester, New York and do alternate service. He worked for two years at a mental health center in Boston. Pat Farren letter to the authors, dated August 4, 1994.

37. Ellen Kirk, "Berrigan Given Option to Return," *Cornell Daily Sun,* May 12, 1969, 1.

38. Byrne, "Revolution 9," 18.

39. Ibid., 20.

40. Eberhardt Memoir, 65–69; Robert A. Erlandson, "Moral Passion Still Burns Among 'Catonsville Nine,'" *Baltimore Sun,* May 17, 1993, 5A–6A. For Daniel Berrigan on Thich Nhat Hanh, see "Their

Speech Is All of Forgiveness," and his foreword to Hanh's book, *Love in Action: Writings on Nonviolent Social Change* (Berkeley, Cal.: Parallax, 1993), 3–8.

41. Margaret Rusk letter to the authors, September 14, 1990.

Chapter 11: Underground

1. Philip Berrigan, "Cover Activities, December 12, 1968–April 21, 1970," unpublished, 2–3, Ramsey Clark Papers, Box 166, LBJ Library.
2. Ibid., 6.
3. Interview with Father Thomas Farrelly, February 24, 1994.
4. "The night before" from Philip Berrigan, "Cover Activities," 6.
5. Interview with Father Thomas Farrelly, February 24, 1994; interview with Father Philip Murnion, February 24, 1994; Margaret O'Brien Steinfels, "Philip Berrigan, Eberhardt Seized," *National Catholic Reporter*, May 1, 1970, 2 and Eberhardt Memoir, 35.
6. Father Harry Browne, Letter to Attorney General John Mitchell. Quoted in John Deedy, "St. Gregory's revisited," *Commonweal*, May 29, 1970, 258.
7. Interview with Daniel Berrigan, February 19, 1994.
8. "I wasn't avoiding punishment," ibid.; Bonhoeffer book from Larry Rasmussen with Ranate Bethge, *Dietrich Bonhoeffer: His Significance for North Americans* (Minneapolis: Fortress, 1990), 43.
9. The *haggadah* is the text established for home Passover Seder services when Jews recount the events associated with their flight from Egypt. Like Waskow's haggadah, many Jews have abandoned the Orthodox version, from committed Jews like socialist kibbutzniks in Palestine and Israel to Reform Jews, Reconstructionists, vegetarians, and feminists.
10. Interview with Arthur Waskow, September 26, 1994. Elijah the prophet lived during the ninth century B.C.E. and supposedly did not die, often returning to assist Jews in dire peril, according to religious tradition.
11. Interview with James Matlack, July 6, 1994.
12. For Daniel Berrigan's adventures underground, interview with Jack Lewis, July 20, 1994; interview with Daniel Berrigan, February 19, 1994; and Bob Fitch, "Berrigan Dons Burlap, Eludes FBI," *National Catholic Reporter*, May 1, 1970, 1.
13. Daniel Berrigan, "From the Underground #1," unpublished, 2.
14. "Freda broke her hip," from interview with Daniel Berrigan, February 19, 1994; interview with Daniel and Linda Finlay, July 26, 1994;

interview with James Matlack, July 6, 1994. Additional information from interview with Rev. Jack Lewis, July 20, 1994.

15. Interview with James O'Gara, February 2, 1994.
16. Interview with George McVey, July 18, 1994.
17. Robert Coles, "Thinking About Those Priests," in *The Berrigans*, eds. William Van Etten Casey, S.J., and Philip Nobile (New York: Praeger, 1971), 219.
18. Daniel Berrigan, "Berrigan Raps," Caedmon cassette, n.d.
19. Interviews with Paul Mayer, April 22 and August 25, 1994; interview with William Davidon, March 16, 1994.
20. The Germantown speech is in *Christianity and Crisis*, September 21, 1970. The Wilmington speech is in the John Schuchardt Papers, State Historical Society of Wisconsin. See, too, Daniel Berrigan, "Notes from The Underground; Or, I Was a Fugitive from the F.B.I.," *Commonweal*, May 29, 1970, 263–65; and Elizabeth McAlister to Phil Berrigan, August 13, 1970, FBI, EASTCOM, File No. 100–460495, Section 3.
21. Interviews with Howard Zinn, July 6–7, 1994 and July 19, 1996; and Howard Zinn, *You Can't Be Neutral on a Moving Train* (Boston: Beacon, 1994), 135–37; "Dan Berrigan With Families in the Underground: Four Sketches by People Who Sheltered Him," in *The Berrigans*, eds. William Van Etten Casey, S.J., and Philip Nobile (New York: Praeger, 1971), 191–202; and Philip Nobile, "The Priest Who Stayed Out in the Cold," *New York Times Magazine*, June 28, 1970, 9.
22. Daniel Berrigan, *Block Island* (Greensboro, N.C.: Unicorn, 1985), 7, 103. On the "alternative seminary" idea, Bill-Wylie-Kellerman, "The Seminary Underground," n.d., i–xi.
23. William Stringfellow and Anthony Towne, *Suspect Tenderness: The Ethics of the Berrigan Witness* (New York: Holt, Rinehart & Winston, 1971), 13–55; and Robert Wool, "The Harboring of Daniel Berrigan: An Exercise in Christian Charity," *Esquire*, November 1971, 156–206. After their indictment was dismissed, the two men wrote to Daniel in prison:

> Let Dr. Kissinger resign; let Mr. Hoover step aside; let General Westmoreland be discharged; let all spies, informers, wiretappers, undercover agents, secret policemen, as well as assorted bird-watchers, be fired; let the President quit—even as his predecessor did. . . . Those who warn us to 'play it safe' by practicing quietism are not alone in betraying fear of the authorities. Through-

out our ordeal we have been astonished to hear ourselves described as courageous.

William Stringfellow and Anthony Towne, Carbray Collection, 9 pp., unpublished.

24. Daniel Berrigan, "To Celebrate the Death and Life of William Stringfellow," March 5, 1985, 5 pp., unpublished.

25. Interview with Douglas Dowd, August 1, 1994; Dowd Memoir, 59–61.

26. John Deedy, "Onward, Christian," *Commonweal*, May 29, 1970, 258.

Chapter 12: Draft Board Raids

1. Jim Forest in Charles Meconis, *With Clumsy Grace: The American Catholic Left, 1961–1975* (New York: Seabury, 1979), 26.

2. Interview with Jim Forest, November 6, 1994.

3. Interview with Bernard Meyer, May 18, 1994.

4. Michael Cullen in Meconis, *With Clumsy Grace*, 27; interviews with Paul Mayer, April 15 and August 25, 1994; interview with George McVey, December 15, 1994; interview with Bernard Meyer, May 18, 1994; and interview with Bill O'Connor, January 21, 1995.

5. Meconis, *With Clumsy Grace*, 27; Meconis interviews with Harney and Mullaney, November 1975 and October 1975.

6. Interview with Jim Forest, November 6, 1994, and Meconis interview with Forest, November, 1975.

7. Meconis, *With Clumsy Grace*, 29–32; interview with Jim Forest, November 6, 1994; Pegi Taylor and Stanley Wallach, "The Impact of the Milwaukee 14," *Milwaukee Journal Wisconsin Magazine*, September 19, 1993, 4, 7–13; and "Six Draft Cards Blaze at Mass in Milwaukee," *National Catholic Reporter*, November 6, 1968, 9.

8. John H. E. Fried, letter, *New York Review of Books*, October 29, 1969, 60–61.

9. Francine du Plessix Gray, *The Ultra-Resistance* (New York: New York Review of Books, 1970), 125–61; Paul Mayer, "A Courtroom Outside the World: The Milwaukee Fourteen vs. The State of Wisconsin," in *The Witness of the Berrigans*, eds. Stephen Halpert and Tom Murray (New York: Doubleday, 1972), 24–44; and Stephen E. Barkan, *Protestors on Trial: Criminal Justice in the Southern Civil Rights and Vietnam Antiwar Movements* (New Brunswick, N.J.: Rutgers University Press, 1985), 127–28; and Meconis, *With Clumsy Grace*, 52.

10. "I doubt if any of us," Taylor and Wallach, "Impact of the Milwaukee 14," 13; Linda Henry, "The Incarcerated Heart: The Prison Experiences of Jim Forest as Revealed in Letters to His Wife," *The Critic*, July–August 1971, 70–78.

11. Interview with Jim Forest, November 6, 1994; Taylor and Wallach, "Impact of the Milwaukee 14."

12. Interview with Douglas Marvy, February 25, 1995.

13. Jim Forest, Cornell, Box 74, 8–9.

14. Terry Lenzner and Dolores Donovan, "Chronology," Ramsey Clark Papers, Box 192, LBJ Library, 17 pp., unpublished, contains the names of people, places, and dates of numerous raids; Molly Finnegan, Maggie Geddes, Jill Boskey, and Valentine Green, "Women's Day at the Draft Board," *WIN*, 7, August 1969, 1, 38–39; interview with Jill Boskey, August 13, 1994.

15. Interview with John Peter Grady, April 13, 1994.

16. Interviews with Barbara Dougherty, April 12 and August 26, 1994, and July 21, 1995; Barbara Dougherty Memoir, unpublished. See, too, "Boston 8," *Catholic Radical* 3 (December 1969): 9.

17. Daniel Berrigan, "An Open Letter to Joe O'Rourke," *Commonweal*, October 18, 1974, 61; interviews with Joseph O'Rourke, February 9 and 25, 1994, July 11 and 12, 1994, August 27, 1995, and September 11, 1996.

18. Interview with Michael Dougherty, April 11, 1994.

19. Interview with Bill O'Connor, January 21, 1995.

20. Philip Berrigan, "Resistance and the Warfare State," ASUH Symposia Committee, Honolulu, 1970.

21. Mark Arnold, "The Berrigan Affair," *National Observer*, April 5, 1971, 25, estimates that more than 300 draft boards were raided; Frank Femia, "Letter from the Boston Two," in *Trials of the Resistance* (New York: New York Review of Books, 1970), 163–67; Frank Femia, "Destroying Draft Files Was My Duty," *Peacemaker*, 6, October 24, 1970, 3; interview with John Williams, May 15, 1994, on the San Jose raid.

22. Interview with Edward Gargan, March 2, 1994; Joseph Gallagher, *The Pain and the Privilege* (New York: Image, 1983), 47; Meconis interview with James Gorman, October 1975, 9, 12; interview with Bill O'Connor, January 21, 1995. All speak of undue pressure.

23. "Traumatized," Philip Berrigan in Meconis interview, May 1976; "I'd lay a heavy rap," interview with Philip Berrigan, January 21, 1995.

24. Interview with Bill O'Connor, January 21, 1995.

25. Barbara Dougherty Memoir, 3, 8; interviews with Barbara Dougherty, April 12 and August 26, 1994.

26. Father Michael Doyle, "The Camden 28," unpublished, 1971, 2 pp.; interview with Father Michael Doyle, July 15, 1994; (Philadelphia) *Common Life*, April 1994, 1–7.

27. Paul Cowan, Nick Egleson, and Nat Hentoff, with Barbara Herbert and Robert Wall, *State Secrets: Police Surveillance in America* (New York: Holt, Rinehart & Winston, 1974), 222–27; Donald Janson, "F.B.I. Is Accused of Aiding a Crime," *New York Times*, March 16, 1972; and "Camden Jurors Cite Role of U.S.," *New York Times*, May 22, 1973; and the editorial "The Camden Acquittal," *New York Times*, May 23, 1973.

28. Interview with Father Michael Doyle, July 15, 1994

29. Daniel Berrigan, untitled sermon, ca. 1980; Philip Berrigan, "A Letter to Sacred Heart Parish," February 22, 1981.

Chapter 13: Prison

1. Philip Berrigan, *Prison Journals of a Priest Revolutionary,* ed. Vincent McGee (New York: Holt, Rinehart & Winston, 1970), 27–37.

2. Eberhardt Memoir, 39–50.

3. Liz, meanwhile, told the reporter that Philip was punished for two "minor" reasons: standing too long in the hallway after Sunday liturgy and inadvertently being with an unassigned lunch group. Betty Medsger, "FBI Searches N.Y. Convent," *Washington Post*, July 14, 1970, B1, B4.

4. On Lewisburg, Eberhardt Memoir, 40–53; Tom Lewis, "A Free Ride to Lewisburg Prison Complements [sic] of the U.S. Government," unpublished, Cornell, Box 76; Philip Berrigan, *Widen the Prison Gates: Writing from Jails, April 1970–December 1972* (New York: Touchstone, 1973), 23–58; and Philip Nobile, "Phil Berrigan in Prison," in *The Berrigans*, eds. William Van Etten Casey, S.J., and Philip Nobile (New York: Praeger, 1971), 121–48.

5. Robert Coles, *The Geography of Faith: Conversations Between Daniel Berrigan, When Underground, and Robert Coles* (Boston: Beacon, 1971), 2 , 16–18.

6. A warden insisted the two men were "in the hole" voluntarily. An associate warden told a reporter, "We just talked with Berrigan a few minutes ago and he says he won't come out. It's very unusual for a man to ask to go into segregation. Sure beats me why he wants to be up there." Medsger, "FBI Searches N.Y. Convent."

7. Jim Forest, Harrisburg Memoir manuscript, unpublished, Cornell, Box 74, 24. A slightly different version later appeared as "Harrisburg

Conspiracy: The Berrigans and the Catholic Left," *WIN*, March 15, 1973, 3–31.

8. Coles, *Geography of Faith*, 16–18; John Kifner, "The Berrigan Affair: How It Evolved," *New York Times*, February 21, 1971, 56–57 and Eberhardt Memoir, 51.

9. Philip Berrigan to "Dear Carol and Jerry," Cornell, Box 103, ca. 1971.

10. Interviews with John Bach, March 14 and July 25, 1994.

11. Interview with Robert Kristiansen, December 5, 1994.

12. Very Rev. Matthew J. O'Rourke to Philip Berrigan, October 8, 1970, quoted in *Holy Cross Quarterly* 4, no. 1 (January 1971): 36.

13. Fred A. Wilcox, *Uncommon Martyrs: The Plowshares Movement and the Catholic Left* (Reading, Mass.: Addison-Wesley, 1991), 40, and Forest, Harrisburg Memoir, 5–6.

14. Philip Berrigan to Elizabeth McAlister, August 24, 1970, FBI, EASTCOM, File No. 100–460495. The letter was one of many transmitted to Boyd Douglas, who, unknown to Berrigan or McAlister, sent a copy to the FBI, and then mailed the original letter to McAlister.

15. James Matlack, *Tiohero* (Ithaca, New York) 1, no. 4.

16. FBI, U.S. Bureau of Prisons File No. 70173–158; FBI, EASTCOM File No. 100–460495, 8–17; and FBI, EASTCOM FILE No. 100–20708.

17. Daniel Berrigan, *Lights On in the House of the Dead: A Prison Diary* (New York: Doubleday, 1974), 161–62.

18. Sarah Ferguson, "Walking a Tightrope: Mitch Snyder Hovered Between Hope and Despair," *Village Voice*, July 17, 1990, 17–18. After his release, he joined the Community for Creative Non-Violence in Washington, D.C., which soon became a center for homeless people. See Charles Meconis's interview with Snyder, August 1975, unpublished, Philip Berrigan on Snyder, July 29, 1990, Cornell, Box B21, and interview with Daniel Berrigan, August 11, 1994.

19. Interview with John Bach, July 25, 1994.

20. John Bach Collection.

21. Daniel Berrigan, *Prison Poems* (Greensboro, N.C.: Unicorn, 1973), 83; 23–24; Philip Berrigan, foreword, and Michael True, "Poetry and the Vietnam Vortex," *Cross Currents*, Summer 1976, 251–56. In "Poetry and the Vietnam Vortex," True adds that despite his high regard for *Prison Poems*, "Berrigan is not a careful writer. . . . He sometimes throws lines away, comically and unnecessarily. He pays too little attention to the integrity of an individual line or stanza and its relation-

ship to the whole poem," 252. Interview with Michael True, September 28, 1994; and letter from M.L. Rosenthal, June 17, 1994.

22. On the Danbury prison strike, interviews with John Bach, March 14 and July 25, 1994; John Bach and Mitchell Snyder, "Danbury: Anatomy of a Prison Strike," Cornell, Box 67; Bach, "Numbers: A Season's Prison Journal," unpublished; John Deedy, "From a Cellblock in Connecticut: Denial of Parole to the Berrigans Was an Act of Revenge," *New York Times*, August 13, 1971, 29; and John Deedy, "The Berrigans: From Behind Prison Walls, a Cry of Rage," *New York Times* (News of the Week in Review), August 15, 1971, 4.

23. Interview with John Bach, March 14, 1994. On September 14, 1988, Bach and sixteen religious peace activists arrived in Tegulcicapa, Honduras, to participate in nonviolent civil disobedience against U.S. policies in that country and in Guatemala. *Year One*, November 1988, 4–5.

24. Paul Mayer to Daniel Berrigan, May 1973, Cornell, Box 135.

25. Interview with Daniel Berrigan, September 9, 1994.

26. The Holy Cross quotes are from Francine du Plessix Gray, "Commencement 1973," *New Yorker*, June 23, 1973, 28–30.

27. "Philip still considers himself a priest" from Daniel Berrigan to Freda Berrigan, [no month or day] 1973, Cornell, Box 95; "I keep trying to be faithful," Daniel Berrigan to Freda Berrigan, October 2, 1973, Cornell, Box 95.

28. "Uneasy about living here" and "my Canadian exile" from Daniel Berrigan to Freda Berrigan, November 19, 1973; also, Daniel Berrigan, November 1973, Carbray Collection.

29. Interview with Peter Jordan, October 3, 1994. About Ted Kennedy, see Daniel Berrigan to Freda Berrigan, November 19, 1973, Cornell, Box 95.

Chapter 14: The Trial

1. Interview with Philip Berrigan, January 21, 1995, and Eberhardt memoir, 48.

2. Interview with Vincent McGee, March 21, 1994; Jack Nelson interview with Jimmy Hoffa, in "Father Philip Berrigan/Boyd Douglas," 3 pp., Cornell, Box 75; interview with Philip Berrigan, January 21, 1995.

3. Jack Nelson and Ronald J. Ostrow's *The FBI and the Berrigans: The Making of a Conspiracy* (New York: Coward, McCann & Geoghegan, 1972), 138–42, is the most thorough account of the Harrisburg trial

and events surrounding the case; "Special Progress Report," Ramsey Clark Papers, Box 192, January 27, 1964, LBJ Library; U.S. Bureau of Prisons, March 28, 1995, letter to authors; the "Boyd Douglas Chronology" and Memo, Francis X. Gallagher, "Life at Lewisburg," Ramsey Clark Papers, Box 167, March 29, 1971, LBJ Library. Our efforts to locate Boyd Douglas were fruitless.

4. William Sullivan on the American Communist Party in Curt Gentry, *J. Edgar Hoover: The Man and The Secrets* (New York: Norton, 1991), 659. Richard G. Kleindienst told Ovid Demaris that Hoover's November public allegation about the Berrigans was "an oversight." But Sullivan argued: "Of course he [Hoover] pushed on the Berrigan case. He pushed hard." Ovid Demaris, *J. Edgar Hoover as They Knew Him: An Oral Biography* (New York: Carroll & Graf/Richard Gallen, 1994), 236, 239, 241. On Sullivan and Hoover's testimony and the Berrigans, William Sullivan, with Bill Brown, *The Bureau: My Thirty Years in Hoover's FBI* (New York: Pinnacle, 1982), 153–55. Hoover forced Sullivan out on September 30, 1971. On November 9, 1977, Sullivan was killed while hunting in New Hampshire. Wild rumors flew that he was "murdered" by the FBI, but co-author Bill Brown said the Sullivan family and local police believed the death was accidental. *The Bureau*, 10.

5. Interview with Ramsey Clark, May 10, 1994.

6. "To the Jesuits" from "Fathers Daniel, Philip Berrigan giving superiors complex questions to answer," *Long Island Catholic*, January 21, 1971, 8; Douglas Robinson, "Catholics Are Shaken by the Berrigan Case," *New York Times*, February 6, 1971, 34.

7. William Van Etten Casey, S.J., *Holy Cross Quarterly*, January 1971, 3.

8. Athan Theoharis, *J. Edgar Hoover, Sex, and Crime* (Chicago: Dee, 1995), 75–76.

9. William R. Anderson letter to J. Edgar Hoover, November 30, 1970; address by William R. Anderson to the House of Representatives, December 9, 1970; Jack Nelson, "Court Nominee Powell Hit on Berrigan Story," *Los Angeles Times*, November 7, 1971, 5, Section B; and Norman C. Miller, "Congressman Anderson's Daring Deed," *Wall Street Journal*, December 18, 1970, 8. Anderson was defeated for reelection in 1972. Agnew's statement, January 25, 1971.

10. Ronald L. Goldfarb, "Politics at the Justice Department," in *Conspiracy: The Implications of the Harrisburg Trial for the Democratic Tradition*, ed. John C. Raines (New York: Harper & Row, 1974), 106.

11. Morton H. Halperin, Jerry J. Berman, Robert L. Borosage, and Christine M. Marwick, *The Lawless State: The Crimes of the U.S. Intel-*

ligence Agencies (New York: Penguin, 1976), 118–21, 212–13, 234–35; John Prados, *The Hidden History of the Vietnam War* (Chicago: Dee, 1995), 282–97; and Kathryn S. Olmstead, *Challenging the Secret Government: The Post-Watergate Investigations of the CIA and FBI* (Chapel Hill: University of North Carolina Press, 1996), passim.

12. Bruce Oudes, ed., *Richard Nixon's Secret Files* (New York: Harper & Row, 1989), 323; on Robert Mardian, David Wise, *The American Police State: The Government Against the People* (New York: Random House, 1976), 376.

13. "Expedite" from Forest, Harrisburg Memoir, 59; "created a culture of lawlessness" from Theoharis, *J. Edgar Hoover, Sex, and Crime*, 154, 158.

14. "The evening was cold and snowy," Philip Berrigan to Jim Forest, Harrisburg Memoir, 71; "stoical but scared," interview with Terry Lenzner, May 4, 1994.

15. Philip Berrigan, "Statement in Lieu of Plea," U.S. District Court for the Middle District of Pennsylvania, *United States of America v. Philip Berrigan*, Criminal No. 14950, May 25, 1971; Daniel Berrigan, *America Is Hard to Find* (New York: Doubleday, 1972), 120–27.

16. Mark Arnold, "The Berrigan Affair," *National Observer*, April 5, 1971, 24; "I talked about tunnels," Terry Lenzner interview with Philip Berrigan, June 18, 1971, Ramsey Clark Papers, Box 166, 6, LBJ Library; Dolores Donovan memorandum and information on Boyd Douglas, December 30, 1971, Ramsey Clark Papers, Box 192, LBJ Library; Philip Berrigan, "Cover Activities," Dec. 12, 1968-April 19, 1970," Ramsey Clark Papers, Box 166, LBJ Library, 4–5. In 1995, Philip Berrigan said that he truly regretted the tunnel escapade and denied ever considering using explosives. Interview with Philip Berrigan, January 21, 1995. See, too, Paul L. Ross, "'Conspiracy' Law," The Washington's *Birthday Defense Committee*, n.d., 3pp.

17. Scoblick's remark from William O'Rourke, *The Harrisburg 7 and the New Catholic Left* (New York: Crowell, 1972), 173.

18. Forest, Harrisburg Memoir, 61–63, 74–75; interview with Theodore Glick, June 7, 1994.

19. Interviews with Elizabeth McAlister, September 25, 1990, and January 21, 1995; Hoag Levin "Sister Elizabeth: A Quiet Nun Becomes a Peace Extremist," *Philadelphia Inquirer*, September 14, 1971, 1, 6–9; Francine du Plessix Gray, "The Politics of Salvation," *New York Review of Books,* June 1, 1972, 34. Philip on Liz's twin sister, Cornell, Box 104, February 4, 1972.

20. Gray, "The Politics of Salvation," 37.

21. On the invitations to Connecticut and the porch discussions, interview with William Davidon, March 16, 1994; interview with Ann Morrissett Davidon, March 17, 1994; interview with Julie Diamond Ahmad, July 21, 1994. William Davidon's "'Only Casual Conversations'" and a *Philadelphia Inquirer* editorial, January 25, 1971; William Davidon's letter to the newspaper, February 4, 1971. O'Rourke, *Harrisburg 7*, passim; Nelson and Ostrow, *FBI and the Berrigans*, 111–14; Max Geltman, "The Berrigans vs. the United States," *National Review*, May 4, 1971, 470–74; and Max Geltman, "How About It, Sister?" *National Review*, May 18, 1971, 516–17.

22. Interview with William Davidon, March 16, 1994.

23. Elizabeth McAlister to Philip Berrigan, and Elizabeth McAlister to Boyd Douglas cover note in FBI, EASTCOM, File No. 100–460496, Section 3; Nelson and Ostrow, *FBI and the Berrigans*, 116–17.

24. Eqbal Ahmad to Elizabeth McAlister in Elizabeth McAlister, "General Background," Ramsey Clark Papers, Box 166, n.d., LBJ Library, 16; Ahmad to Wenderoth, Gray, "The Politics of Salvation," 39.

25. United States Indictment No. 14950, April 30, 1971. Excerpts from the exchange of letters also appeared in Bill Kovach, "Berrigan Case Broadened; Letters on 'Plot' Released," *New York Times*, May 1, 1971, 1, 12. Nelson and Ostrow, *FBI and the Berrigans*, 120–24.

26. Interview with Joseph O'Rourke, August 1, 1994.

27. "Douglas Material: McLaughlin," Ramsey Clark Papers, Box 192, n.d., 8; Father Neil McLaughlin, July 1975, 6–7, and Father Joseph Wenderoth, July 1975, interviews with Charles Meconis, stating they had no idea of the secret love letters. John Theodore Glick, "Getting at the Truth," unpublished memoir, asserts that the attorneys and defendants were told of the marriage, and that Phil wanted to tell them even before the trial, "feeling that he had [a] responsibility to the movement," but backed away on the recommendation of lawyers, 432–35.

28. Forest, Harrrisburg Memoir, 53, and *WIN*, March 15, 1973, 21.

29. Forest, Harrisburg Memoir, 55; Elizabeth McAlister's letter to Boyd Douglas, Cornell, B-VII, G–43, Box 10. On the Sheraton Motor Inn meeting, Terry Lenzner and Dolores Donovan, "Chronology," Ramsey Clark Papers, Box 192, LBJ Library, 17 pp., unpublished, n.d.

30. William Davidon to Henry Kissinger, January 21, 1971, interview with William Davidon, March 16, 1994, Walter Isaacson, *Kissinger*

(New York: Simon & Schuster, 1992), 282–83, and Marvin Kalb and Bernard Kalb, *Kissinger* (Boston: Little, Brown, 1974), 178.

31. On the anti-Hoover demonstration, Bayard Brunt, "Douglas Attended Capitol Protest Against FBI Director," *Philadelphia Evening Bulletin*, March 25, 1971, F–13. On Hoover and the Berrigans, Frank J. Donner, *The Age of Surveillance: The Aims and Methods of America's Political Intelligence System* (New York: Knopf, 1980), 87–90; Richard Gid Powers, *Secrecy and Power: The Life of J. Edgar Hoover* (New York: Free Press, 1987), 468–69.

32. "Boyd was not the sort of person" from Eberhardt Memoir, 49; "Intruder in a gentle community," Paul Cowan in *Village Voice*, April 16–22, 1972, 1; "accomplished confidence man," in Rem Rieder, "FBI Agent Concedes He Called Douglas an 'Accomplished Confidence Man,'" *Philadelphia Evening Bulletin*, March 22, 1972; "He wanted to meet people . . . ," Ramsey Clark Papers; Box 192, February 1970, and "values have changed" from Ramsey Clark Papers, Boxes 167 and 192, August 19, 1970; Francine du Plessix Gray's, "The Politics of Salvation: II," *New York Review of Books,* June 15, 1972, 14–42, is replete with information and insights.

33. "Don't be too hard on him," interview with Terry Lenzner, May 4, 1994; "I remember him being terribly sad," interview with Mary Daly, January 24, 1994; "I suppose he victimized us," interview with Zoia Horn, May 19, 1994, and Zoia Horn, *Zoia! Memoirs of Zoia Horn, Battler for the People's Right to Know* (Jefferson, N.C.: McFarland, 1995), 130–32, 142, 146; Nelson and Ostrow, *FBI and the Berrigans,* 81–110; and Philip Berrigan, two decades later, while expressing no hate, stated, "Douglas had the instincts of a rat; he knew how to survive." Interview with Philip Berrigan, January 21, 1995.

34. "He would stand there," interview with Richard Drinnon, April 8, 1994; Boyd Douglas to Dick [Drinnon], August 19, 1970. Douglas's letter concluded: "the only way I can help is by nonviolent civil disobedience."

35. Statement, "Buzzy" Mulligan, n.d., Ramsey Clark Papers, Box 167, LBJ Library.

36. See Chenoweth letter to the *Washington Post* disputing a previous article, "Berrigan Witness Under Fire" (February 12, 1971), that suggested he may have known that Douglas was a courier. "I have no such knowledge," he wrote, that Douglas was carrying "contraband messages." "A Response to 'Berrigan Under Fire,'" March 5, 1971, A23; interviews with Gene Chenoweth, June 9, 1994, and September 5, 1995.

37. Philip Berrigan to Elizabeth McAlister, Cornell, Box 10, May 24, 1970, and on Boyd Douglas's possible motives, Cornell, Box 104, February 28, 1972.

38. John Kifner, "The Berrigan Affair: How It Evolved," *New York Times*, February 21, 1971, 1; Nelson and Ostrow, *FBI and the Berrigans*, 225–26, 242, 262; Philip Berrigan, *Widen the Prison Gates: Writing from Jails, April 1970–December 1972* (New York: Touchstone, 1973), 201; Statement, "Buzzy" Mulligan, n.d., Ramsey Clark Papers, Box 167, LBJ Library.

39. On McLaughlin's suspicions, see Forest Harrisburg Memoir, 59–60; Douglas's activities following his parole, Bayard Brunt, "Douglas Attended Capitol Protest Against FBI Director," *Philadelphia Evening Bulletin*, March 25, 1971, 13.

40. Evelyn J. Mattern, "Vacation in Harrisburg," *America*, April 22, 1972, 424–28.

41. "Very far to the right," interview with Charles Glackin, May 11, 1994. Glackin had been elected as tax director of the Auditor General of Pennsylvania and worked in Harrisburg.

42. On Sister Jogues Egan, FBI EASTCOM, File No. 100–46095, Section 19, January 22, 1971; on Paul Mayer FBI, EASTCOM, File No. 100–460495, Section 51, March 23, 1971; for the warning about the New Left, FBI, EASTCOM, File No. 100–460495, Section 51 April 2, 1971; on the HDC, interview with Mary Daly, January 24, 1994; interview with Sue Susman, July 16, 1974; interview with Stewart Schaar, August 24, 1994.

43. Jack Freed, "What Goes On in Harrisburg," *Nation*, April 12, 1971, 464–66. Freed was a reporter for the *Harrisburg Patriot-News*.

44. Interview with Paul Mayer, August 8, 1995.

45. Philip Berrigan, *Widen the Prison Gates*, 208.

46. Philip Berrigan to Carol and Jerry Berrigan, March 26, 1972, Cornell, Box 104; on the rift among defendants and lawyers, Philip Berrigan, *Widen the Prison Gates*, 206–09; on internal disagreements, Paul O'Dwyer, *Counsel for the Defense: The Autobiography of Paul O'Dwyer* (New York: Simon & Schuster, 1979), 252; also, interview with Arthur Waskow, September 26, 1994; interviews with Mary Daly, January 24 and February 2, 1994, and April 18, 1995; interview with Robert G. Hoyt, February 7, 1994; Philip Berrigan to Daniel Berrigan, March 6 and March 23, 1972, Cornell, Box 104; and interview with William Glackin, May 11, 1994.

47. Judge Herman died on April 9, 1990.

48. For "scientific" jury selection, Jay Schulman, Philip Shaver, Robert

Colman, Barbara Emrich, and Richard Christie, "Recipe for a Jury," in *In the Jury Box: Controversies in the Courtroom*, eds. Lawrence Wrightsman, Saul M. Kassin, and Cynthia E. Willis (Newbury Park, Cal.: Sage, 1987), 13–47. "A few favorable jurors" from Stephen J. Adler, *The Jury: Trial and Error in the American Courtroom* (New York: Times Books, 1994), 87.

49. Interview with Philip Berrigan, January 21, 1995; Philip Berrigan to Elizabeth McAlister, FBI, EASTCOM, File No. 100–460–495, May 26, 1970.

50. Interview with Daniel Ellsberg, April 1, 1994.

51. Nelson and Ostrow, *FBI and the Berrigans*, 269 and passim; and Gray, "Politics of Salvation," passim.

52. Philip Berrigan to Jerry Berrigan, March 5, 1972, Cornell, Box 104.

53. O'Dwyer, *Counsel for the Defense*, 253; Sharon Dickman, "Harrisburg Defense Asks If Informant Got $50,000," *Baltimore Evening Sun*, February 29, 1972, A2; Rem Rieder and H. James Laverty, "Douglas Admits Lying to Berrigan as 5th Lawyer Cross-Examines Him," *Philadelphia Evening Bulletin*, March 13, 1972; Rem Rieder and H. James Laverty, "Government Informer Leaves Stand; Testified 14 Days Against Berrigan," *Philadelphia Evening Bulletin*, March 16, 1972; Rem Rieder, "FBI Agent Concedes he called Douglas an 'Accomplished Confidence Man,'" *Philadelphia Evening Bulletin*, March 22, 1972; and Duncan Spencer, "Berrigan Informer Asked for $50,000," *Washington Star*, March 20, 1972. FBI, EASTCOM, File No. 100–460495, Section 6.

54. Phil Berrigan recalls Clark's statement slightly differently: "The defendants proclaim their innocence, and state that they will continue working for peace. The defense rests." Philip Berrigan to Daniel Berrigan, March 24, 1972, Cornell, Box 104.

55. "Not very surprised," interview with William Lynch, May 11, 1994; "alternately fumbling papers," Philip Berrigan to Carol and Jerry Berrigan, March 26, 1972, Cornell, Box 104; "it was a tribute to people," Philip Berrigan to Richard Cusack, April 10, 1972, Cusack Collection.

56. Philip Berrigan to Carol and Jerry Berrigan, April 2, 1972, Cornell, Box 104.

57. Philip Berrigan to Carol and Jerry Berrigan, April 7, 1972, Cornell, Box 104.

58. The FBI memos are from FBI, EASTCOM, File No. 100–460495, Section 111, October 13, 1972; memoranda to Mr. E.S. Miller, n.d., September 22, October 19, and October 20, 1972.

59. Made "several mistakes," interview with Philip Berrigan, January 21, 1995; "Elitist . . . male . . . leadership," Philip Berrigan to Jerry and Carol Berrigan, April 11, 1972, Cornell, Box 104; also, Philip Berrigan to Freda Berrigan, May 11, 1972, Cornell, Box 104. On related matters, see, too, Philip Berrigan interview with Charles Meconis, May, 1976, Philip Berrigan to Daniel Berrigan, April 7, 1972, Cornell, Box 104.

60. See, for example, Valerie Hendy interview with Charles Meconis, December 1975, and Sister Anne Walsh interview with Charles Meconis, November 1975. See, too, interview with Sue Susman, July 16, 1974.

61. "The drainage to Catholicism," John Deedy, *Apologies, Good Friends: An Interim Biography of Daniel Berrigan, S.J.* (Chicago: Fides/Claretian, 1981). 91; "dear sisters," Cookie Cirillo, Harrisburg Defense Committee, Swarthmore College Peace Collection, December 9, 1971.

62. "So we're being called sexists," from Philip to Daniel Berrigan, March 18, 1972, Cornell, Box 104.

63. "Approved of women as priests," Daniel Berrigan to Linda Finlay, October 13, 1971, Cornell, Box 93, expressing his growing understanding "of man's inhumanity to women: and most of all for us, how the same tactic infected the movement as well," and Deedy, *Apologies, Good Friends*, 117; Anne Klejment, "In the Lion's Den: The Social Catholicism of Daniel and Philip Berrigan, 1955–1965" (Ph.D. dissertation, State University of New York at Binghamton, 1980), 224–28, and Anne Klejment, "From Holy Homemaker to Madonna of the Movement: Daniel and Philip Berrigan's Ideology of Social Reform and Its Implication for Catholic Women," February 1979, Cornell, Box 75.

64. "We deserved better," Jim Forest, "Reflections After a Demonstration," *Fellowship*, March 1976, 17; interview with Jim Forest, November 6, 1994; "The real failure of Harrisburg," interview with Joe O'Rourke, July 12, 1994.

65. Philip Berrigan to Freda Berrigan, n.d., Cornell, Box 104; Daniel Berrigan's poem, Richard Carbray Collection, University of Washington Libraries, Manuscript Division, #3073, Box 9, Folder 20.

66. On Jonah House, Elizabeth McAlister, "William Stringfellow: Continuing Clarification of Ethic and Action," in *Radical Christian and Exemplary Lawyer*, ed. Andrew W. McThenia Jr. (Grand Rapids, Mich.: Eerdmans, 1995), 45. She defined "kin-dom of God" as avoiding "both the sexist and hierarchical implications of the term "kingdom of God," 43; "I only have my life," interview with Philip Berrigan, January 21, 1995.

67. "More than any other war," Philip Berrigan, "Statement of Fr. Phil Berrigan," December 20, 1972, 2 pp.

68. "It's our 4th anniversary," from Philip Berrigan, "Dear Dick and Mary [Carbray]," May 2, 1973, Carbray Collection; John Deedy, "Fr. and Mrs. Philip Berrigan," *Commonweal*, June 15, 1973, 325–26; Deedy, *Apologies, Good Friends*, 108–10; "Celibacy was instituted," Religious News Service, November 21, 1973; and on their marriage, see "Phil and Liz: Statement," 1973, 2 pp.; "Some Responses to Meconis' Thesis on the Catholic Left . . . Liz," Cornell, Box 112, 4 pp., n.d.; "She's got a good man," Josephite News Views, 11, no. 1 (January–February 1973) *Josephite News Views* 11, no. 3 (May–June 1973).

Chapter 15: The Speech

1. One such group was Breira ("Alternatives"), which emerged in the mid-seventies, and its statement, "Our Anxieties Should Not Bind Us," which urged that while "the Israeli Government's unwillingness to talk with the PLO terrorists is understandable . . . as long as Palestinian self-determination remains unresolved and unfulfilled, there can be no hope for peace for Israel." See David Friedman, "B'nai B'rith to Study Involvement of Hillel Directors in Breira," *Jewish Telegraphic Agency Daily News Bulletin*, March 4, 1977; "ADL for B'nai B'rith Probe," *Jewish Week* (New York), February 27, 1977; William Novak, "The Breira Story," *Genesis 2* (Boston), March–April 1977, 1; Paul Foer, "The War Against Breira," *Jewish Spectator*, Summer 1983; Marjorie Hyer, "Jews Ask Boycott of Meetings Here on Middle East," *Washington Post*, February 13, 1977; also, "Breira" papers, American Jewish Committee Proskauer Library for a collection of miscellaneous articles, clippings, and memoranda; Rael Jean Isaac, "Breira Counsel for Judaism," Americans for a Safe Israel, 1977, Carolyn Toll Oppenheim, "American Jews and the Middle East Dilemma," *Progressive*, August 1979, 28–35; and Edward Tivnan, *The Lobby: Jewish Political Power and American Foreign Policy* (New York: Simon & Schuster, 1987), 90–97. The campaign of vilification against American Jewish dissenters continued until the historic "handshake" on the White House lawn in September 1993 between Yitzhak Rabin and Yasser Arafat, and subsequently the Oslo Accords. After that, secular conservatives and many Orthodox rabbis and lay leaders regularly and publicly assailed the peace agreement and Israeli government leaders in terms far harsher than Breira, the New Jewish Agenda (a later peace group that confronted

similar opposition), and Daniel Berrigan ever used. For the New Jewish Agenda, see Ezra Goldstein, "What's Left?" *PS*, no. 25, August 31, 1994, 1.

2. Daniel Berrigan, *No Bars to Manhood* (New York: Doubleday, 1970); Spring Seminar Syllabus, March 5, 1969, James Matlack Collection.

3. Interview with Arthur Waskow, September 26, 1994; and "The Middle East: Two Justices Crossing Each Other, Colliding," *WIN*, September 12, 1974, 4–6.

4. Interview with Daniel Berrigan, January 13, 1994.

5. Daniel Berrigan, *To Dwell in Peace: An Autobiography* (San Francisco: Harper & Row, 1987), 281.

6. *The Great Berrigan Debate* (New York: Committee on New Alternatives in the Middle East, 1974), 1–8. The balance of the booklet includes reactions by Rabbis Balfour Brickner and Arthur Hertzberg, plus Robert Hoyt, June Stillman, Hans Morgenthau, William Novak, and Allan Solomonow.

7. For a sympathetic account, see *Liberation*'s February 1974 issue devoted to the Middle East.

8. John Deedy, *Apologies, Good Friends: An Interim Biography of Daniel Berrigan, S.J.* (Chicago: Fides/Claretian, 1981), 112.

9. November 12, 1973, Cornell, Box 96.

10. Daniel Berrigan's "My Brother, the Witness," *Commonweal*, April 26, 1968, 181, is but one example of his many sharp critiques of the Roman Catholic Church.

11. Deedy, *Apologies, Good Friends*, 114

12. Arthur Hertzberg, "Response to Dan Berrigan," *American Report*, November 12, 1973, and *The Great Berrigan Debate*, 9–12; Rabbi Balfour Brickner's piece in *American Report*, December 10, 1973, and *The Great Berrigan Debate*, 13–16, was titled "With Friends Like These . . ." Years after the furor died down, Hertzberg was still taking issue with several Israeli policies, especially after the election of Menachem Begin's right-wing government in 1977. He opposed the 1982 invasion of Lebanon by Israel and regularly and rather fearlessly defended the rights of Palestinians. "Palestinians, too, are human beings and if you cannot think that way, you simply aren't a Jew." See, for example, his "Dangerous Delusions," *Present Tense*, September–October 1988, 8.

13. Paul Jacobs, "Some of His Best Friends Were . . . ," *Ramparts*, 12, April 1974, 10–12; Daniel Berrigan, *Liberation*, February 1974; Helen Fein's critical reaction to the notion of "I am a Jew," in "Reading the Second Text: Meanings and Misuses of the Holocaust," in

The Challenge of Shalom: The Jewish Tradition of Peace and Justice,
eds. Murray Polner and Naomi Goodman (Philadelphia: New Society
Publishers, 1994), 71–81, especially 78. In addition, Seymour Cain,
"Berrigan, Buber, and the 'Settler State,'" *Christian Century,* June
26, 1974, 664–68; "Daniel Berrigan and Hans Morgenthau discuss
the moral dilemma in the Middle East," *Progressive,* March 1974,
31–34; "An Open Letter to Father Dan Berrigan," by David Gracie
and Alexander M. Shapiro, two dovish clergymen, January 9, 1974,
Cornell, Box 96. See, too, Robert Alter's "Berrigan's Diatribe,"
Commentary, February 1974, 69–73; and "Discussion," *Commentary,* May 1974, 20.

14. Interview with Arthur Waskow, September 26, 1994; Arthur Waskow,
letter to the *Village Voice,* February 4, 1974.
15. James Munves letter to authors, July 19, 1974.
16. *The Great Berrigan Debate,* 25–26. Jim Forest, Dan Berrigan's close
friend and major defender in the entire furor, thought the extreme
reaction to "Daniel's speech was rooted in the fact that the left in
general still judges nonviolence and pacifism to be thoroughly coun-
terrevolutionary and indeed reactionary," and that "pacifist criticism
of Israel is certainly no more marked than criticism of Arab and
Palestinian groups," though the media emphasized the former and
essentially omitted the latter. See Patricial McNeal, *Harder Than
War: Catholic Peacemaking in Twentieth-Century America* (New
Brunswick, N.J.: Rutgers University Press, 1992), 218. A non-Jewish admirer wrote an open letter to Dan: "What troubles me in your
speech, what pains me really is the apparent absence of love of Jews.
I'm not even certain I really discover a love of Arabs … It is a matter
of tone, over interpretation by you as a … war resister who has 'paid
his dues' over which many of your friends are saddened." Harry J.
Cargas, *St. Louis Jewish Light,* January 16, 1974, 7.
17. Interview with Paul Mayer, August 15, 1994; Daniel Berrigan, *Block
Island* (Greensboro, N.C.: Unicorn, 1985), 103.
18. Interview with Paul Mayer, August 8, 1995, Paul Mayer to Daniel
Berrigan, November 26, 1973.
19. Paul Mayer to Daniel Berrigan, February 26, 1974, Cornell, Box
135.
20. Paul Mayer to Daniel Berrigan, December 25, 1973, Cornell, Box
135. Also, interviews with Paul Mayer, April 22 and August 25,
1994.
21. Interview with Daniel Berrigan, February 19, 1994; interview with
Suzanne Heschel, June 24, 1994.

22. Interview with Suzanne Heschel, March 7, 1994.

23. "A Call to Men of Conscience," *National Catholic Reporter*, September 18, 1968, 2.

24. Daniel Berrigan, "My Friend," in *No Religion Is an Island: Abraham Joshua Heschel and Interreligious Dialogue*, eds. Harold Kasimow and Byron L. Sherwin (Maryknoll, N.Y.: Orbis, 1991), 68–75; Daniel Berrigan, *To Dwell in Peace*, 178–79; and Daniel Berrigan to Freda Berrigan, Cornell, Box 95.

25. Kasimow and Sherwin, *No Religion Is an Island*, 69–70.

26. Daniel Berrigan, *To Dwell in Peace*, 280. The poem was a "Zen poem . . . written for a baptism in an airport," sent to Patrick Henry, a friend.

27. Rabbi Everett Gendler, "Berrigan on the Mid-East," *WIN*, January 24, 1974, 14–15.

28. Interview with David Saperstein, June 30, 1994. FBI files include in its EASTCOM papers, File No. 100–460–493, Jack Anderson's "FBI Erred on Berrigan Musical 'Plot,'" *Washington Post*, August 10, 1972, E7, which, among other items, quotes Harry Kraut, Bernstein's manager, that he and Daniel Berrigan had talked about working together on a production.

29. "Philip Berrigan Raps President, American Jews, 'War Mongers,'" Religious News Service, November 21, 1973.

30. Abraham Joshua Heschel, *The Prophets: An Introduction* (New York: Harper Torchbook, 1962), 4. Forest's correspondence on the speech is in Cornell, Box 96. See, too, Deedy, *Apologies, Good Friends*, 110–16.

31. Daniel Berrigan to Roy Pfaff, late December 1973, Cornell, Box 96. The Gandhi Peace Award papers are also in Box 96.

32. Daniel Berrigan to Roy Pfaff, Cornell, Box 96.

33. Daniel Berrigan, "Dachau I Now Open for Visitors," in *No One Walks Waters* (New York: Macmillan, 1966), 55.

34. Interviews with Paul Mayer, April 22 and August 25, 1994.

35. Daniel Berrigan, May 5, 1974, Carbray Collection, Box 10, Folder 1, General Correspondence, 1974–79.

36. Daniel Berrigan, Cornell, Box 96; interviews with Paul Mayer, March 12, April 22, and August 25, 1994.

37. "Hoover Vacuum Conspiracy," Charles Meconis interview with Paul Mayer, November 1975, 8.

38. Daniel Berrigan correspondence, April 20 and April 23, 1974, Cornell, Box 96.

39. Interviews with Paul Mayer, April 22 and August 25, 1994; interview with Daniel Berrigan, August 11, 1994.

40. Richard Carbray Collection, May 5 (Beirut), May 10 (Cairo), May 20; Daniel Berrigan, letter, May 20, 1974, Cornell, Box 96.

41. Daniel Berrigan, "Dear revolutionary leaders," untitled manuscript, June 21, 1974, Cornell, Box 96; Daniel Berrigan, "Revolution/Retaliation: Or, How We Finally Disposed of the Children," *WIN*, October 3, 1974, 14–16, 18.

42. Daniel Berrigan, "Israel, as Presently Constituted," in *Daniel Berrigan: Poetry, Drama, Prose*, ed. Michael True (Maryknoll, N.Y.: Orbis, 1988), 159–64. First published in *Israel & Palestine*, July 1, 1976.

43. Interview with Daniel Berrigan, January 13, 1994.

Chapter 16: The Rest of Their Lives

1. Philip Berrigan to Father Matthew O'Rourke, *Josephite Archive*, February 25, 1973,

2. Interview with Elizabeth McAlister, January 21, 1995.

3. "We embraced," from Elmer Maas interview, April 7, 1991; interview with Esther Cassidy, May 10, 1994; interview with Barry Cassidy, June 28, 1994.

4. The best source on Jonah House and the hardships of forming their new community is Philip Berrigan and Elizabeth McAlister, *The Time's Discipline: The Beatitudes and Nuclear Resistance* (Baltimore: Fortkamp, 1989); Elizabeth McAlister, "Forming Community: Baltimore's Jonah House," *Fellowship*, February 1974, 5–6; and Philip Berrigan, "Greetings from Jonah House to All Sorts of Our Friends," ca. February 1974, 2, Richard Cusack Collection and letter, 9 pp., Richard Cusack Collection. Also, "I longed for a normal time," Freda Berrigan, "Did I Ever Long for Normalcy . . . " *Year One* (Baltimore), July–August 1993, 7.

5. See, for example, Elizabeth McAlister, "Dear Ones," Carbray Papers, March 2, 1976; Philip Berrigan and Elizabeth McAlister, *Time's Discipline*, 34–35; Liz McAlister, "Raising Children, Resistance Community," *RADIX*, May–June 1977, 3–7; "Dear Dick and Mary [Macek]," Carbray Collection, February 2, 1977; "Dear Dan (Mary et al)[sic]," Dorothy Day–Catholic Worker Collection, Marquette University, Series W–11, Box 5, February 11, 1977; Philip Berrigan, "Dear Dick," Dorothy Day-Catholic Worker Collection, Marquette University, February 10, 1977.

6. Philip Berrigan and Elizabeth McAlister, *Time's Discipline*, 38.

7. Daniel Berrigan "Dear Friends" letter, Carbray Collection, General Correspondence-DB 1968–80, Box 9, Folder 19. Barry Bearak, *Los Angeles Times,* "Berrigan at 71: Still Protesting," April 10, 1993, A–1, mentions the High Point University (as did the interview with Daniel Berrigan, August 11, 1994) and the Gandhi Institute incidents; Earl Crow, letter to High Point Enterprise, January 30, 1991, Cornell, Box B22. On Colorado College, see Jennie Randall, "Daniel Berrigan Turned Down for Honorary Degree; Anti-War Protests Basis of Trustees' Decision," *Colorado College Catalyst,* March 31, 1995, 1, and Faculty Statement, March 17, 1995, objecting to the board of trustees' refusal to present the degree: "We did not think that Daniel Berrigan needed a Colorado College degree; we thought Colorado College needed to offer an honorary degree to Daniel Berrigan."

8. Daniel Berrigan, *A Book of Parables* (New York: Seabury, 1977).

9. On Freda Berrigan, Carbray Collection, General Correspondence-DB-1968-80, Box 9, Folder 19, August 1974; and "a lot of those," Interview with Daniel Berrigan, September 9, 1994.

10. "Whatever Became of Philip Berrigan?" from an unpublished manuscript by Daniel Berrigan, 6 pp., n.d. "We can't save the world," Daniel Berrigan, "The Non-Violent Citizen in the War-Making State" lecture, Cornell University, April 20, 1994; Carole Stone, "Berrigan Urges Integrity in Our Actions," *Cornell Chronicle*, April 21, 1994, 8.

11. Michael Novak, "Blue-Bleak Embers . . . Fall, Gall Themselves . . . Gash Gold-Vermilion," in *Conspiracy: The Implications of the Harrisburg Trial for the Democratic Tradition*, ed. John C. Raines (New York: Harper & Row, 1974), 43, 47.

12. "Dr. Rieux," Jason Berry, "Orleanians Go on a Retreat with Radical-Minded Catholic, Daniel Berrigan," *Figaro* (New Orleans), December 22, 1976, 18–21; interview with Sue Wesselkamper, April 6, 1994. Many others were inspired by the Berrigans. See, for example, Benjamin Spock, M.D., and Mary Morgan, *Spock on Spock: A Memoir of Growing Up with the Century* (New York: Pantheon, 1989), 186: "The example of Daniel and Philip Berrigan was most effective in involving me in civil disobedience. I thought that if priests could bring themselves to break into government offices, steal draft records, and spatter them with duck blood, then I shouldn't be scared of committing milder forms of disobedience."

13. Daniel Berrigan, "sleep tight while your neighbors freeze," *U.S. Catholic*, February 1980, 29–33. See, too, Harry J. Cargas, "The Family: Consumerism Gone Mad?" *Way*, January–February 1974,

15–18. He quotes Daniel Berrigan as saying that the Vietnam War was a consequence of "a consumerism gone mad, making dead meat of men. We have seen human life cheapened to a disposable commodity."

14. Novak, "Blue-Bleak Embers . . . , 43.
15. Robert A. Ludwig's "The Theology of Daniel Berrigan," *Listening*, Spring 1971, 127–37, is an astute discussion.
16. Daniel Berrigan, Cornell, Box 69; final exam questions, Cornell, Box 100.
17. Daniel Berrigan, *The Mission: A Film Journal* (New York: Harper & Row, 1986).
18. Interview with Father John Dear, S.J., January 20, 1995.
19. "He's suffered with the Jesuits," interview with Father John Dear, S.J., ibid.; "He is a terribly sensitive and prickly person," interview with Father David Toolan, S.J., March 11, 1994.
20. Philip and Daniel Berrigan, "Dear Friend," Cornell, April 10, 1973, Box 95; Daniel and Philip Berrigan, "On the Torture of Prisoners," *Fellowship*, September 1973, 4. For the complete text of the Berrigans' letter and North Vietnam's response, see *WIN*, September 1973, 16. In December 1972, on the day Rabbi Abraham Joshua Heschel died, and in commemoration of his life, Daniel wrote Jim Forest, then editor of *Fellowship*, asking if he would suggest that the pope travel to both Vietnams and on behalf of all religious faiths, asking for an end to the war and urging that all political prisoners be treated humanely. Patricia McNeal, *Harder Than War: Catholic Peacemaking in Twentieth-Century America* (New Brunswick, N.J.: Rutgers University Press, 1972), 220.
21. "Too pure," from McNeal, *Harder Than War*, 222; see, too, Guenter Lewy, *Peace & Revolution: The Moral Crisis of American Pacifism* (Grand Rapids, Mich.: Eerdmans, 1988), 73–75; 115–23; interview with Jim Forest, November 6, 1994, Jim Forest review of *Harder Than War*, *Fellowship*, June 1993, 27; David McReynolds, "Pacifists and the Movement," in *Give Peace a Chance: Exploring the Vietnam Antiwar Movement*, eds. Melvin Small and William D. Hoover (Syracuse, N.Y.: Syracuse University Press, 1982), 58. McReynolds of the War Resisters League wrote: "My own position, as someone very anti-Communist, was that we simply had no right to dictate the history of Vietnam, and that whether a left, right, or center government took over should be the decision of the Vietnamese. It became clear that the only aggressor in Vietnam was the United States." David McReynolds later said he was disturbed by reports of human rights

violations in southern Vietnam and sent a letter to Hanoi asking questions. He says his main objections to the proposal was that it had been made public and was too rushed. Interview with David McReynolds, January 13, 1994 and September 17, 1996.

22. Interview with Jim Forest, November 6, 1994; John Maher, "90 Protest Vietnam's 'Repression,'" *National Catholic Reporter*, January 7, 1977, 16; Richard Rashke, "Berrigans Back Vietnam Regime, Call Letter Publicity 'Irresponsible,'" *National Catholic Reporter*, January 14, 1977, 3.

23. Lewy, *Peace & Revolution*, 138–40. The ad appeared in the *Los Angeles Times*, the *New York Times*, the *San Francisco Chronicle*, the *San Francisco Examiner*, and the *Washington Post*. "Phil Berrigan," Joan Baez told the *New York Times*, "signed and then unsigned the letter." Robert Lindsay, "Peace Activists Attack Vietnam on Rights," *New York Times*, June 1, 1979, 8.

24. On Freda Berrigan's death, Daniel Berrigan, "Dearest Friends," January 1977, courtesy of Patrick and Mary Ann Henry; Philip Berrigan, "Dear Sisters and Brothers," Carbray Collection, January 1977.

25. Daniel Berrigan to Richard Cusack, June 9, 1982, Richard Cusack Collection; "Dan Berrigan to Soviet Prisoners: 'The Future Will Be Different Because of You,'" Fellowship of Reconciliation, n.d. The latter was written after a meeting with a delegation of the Soviet Peace Committee in New York. The preface to the FOR release read that Berrigan "agreed to speak in Moscow at an international meeting in Moscow *only* if the Soviet Peace Committee would arrange for him to meet first with various Soviet political prisoners and to report at the Moscow meeting on the content of these discussions. His request met with anger and, finally, shouts from the delegation members." His request was turned down.

26. Daniel Berrigan, *Portraits of Those I Love* (New York: Crossroad, 1982), 133–34.

27. "The obscenity to eclipse all obscenities," Philip Berrigan to Mary and Dick [Carbray], Carbray Collection, General Correspondence–Philip Berrigan, 1977–79, University of Washington, Box 10, Folder 1, October 15, 1978; "you know what they say about liberals," Philip Berrigan to Frank [Cordaro], Dorothy Day–Catholic Worker Collection, Marquette University, Series W–21.1, Box 1, August 1977.

28. "Mother Teresa's influence" from interview with Martin Sheen, April 3, 1991; on Catholic Worker influence, interview with Daniel Berrigan, January 13, 1994; on St. Rose's Home, Daniel Berrigan, *We Die Before*

We Live: Talking with the Very Ill (New York: Seabury, 1980), 137–38. "I don't know" from June Preston, "Berrigan: The Fight Continues," *Sunday Advocate* (Baton Rouge), December 27, 1981, 2G–3G.

29. Interview with Father William Hart McNichols, February 24, 1995; interview with Daniel Berrigan, January 13, 1994; Daniel Berrigan, *Sorrow Built a Bridge: Friendship and AIDS* (Baltimore: Fortkamp, 1989); Daniel Berrigan, *To Dwell in Peace: An Autobiography* (San Francisco: Harper & Row, 1987), 308–30; See, too, Daniel Berrigan, "God Has Chosen the Fools of This World to Confound the Wise," *Catholic Agitator* (Los Angeles), July 1983, 4–6.

30. "We, The Undersigned" advertisement sponsored by the Seamless Garment Network, *Pax Christi USA*, Spring 1994, 22.

31. "Livermore death trap," from Daniel Berrigan to "Phil and Liz," February 6, 1980, Cornell, Box 100. "Notorious Livermore," Daniel Berrigan letter dated March 1980, Cornell, Box 100. Fourteen people were arrested for trespassing, but all charges were later dropped.

32. On Philip Berrigan, interview with Father John Dear, S.J., December 14, 1994.

33. Interview with Father David Toolan, March 11, 1994.

34. "Peace movement," from Patricia McNeal, *Harder Than War*, 170–72, 211, 256–58; Nancy Roberts, *Dorothy Day and the Catholic Worker* (Albany: State University of New York Press, 1984), 172; John J. Conley, "Catholic Pacifism in America," *America*, December 14, 1974, 381–83; see, too, letters in response, *America*, January 18, 1975, 22; Jim Castelli, *The Bishops and the Bomb: Waging Peace in a Nuclear Age* (New York: Doubleday, 1983), 13–25; Richard McSorley, S.J., *It's a Sin to Build a Nuclear Weapon: The Collected Works on War and Christian Peacemaking of Richard McSorley, S.J.*, ed. John Dear, S.J. (Baltimore: Fortkamp, 1991), 223–26, 238–42; Jim Wallis, ed., *Peace-Makers: Christian Voices from the New Abolitionist Movement* (San Francisco: Harper & Row, 1983), 28–40; interview with James O'Gara, February 2, 1994.

35. "Had a strong influence," from interview with Bishop Thomas Gumbleton, August 8, 1994; "modern-day prophets," from Bishop Walter F. Sullivan letter, April 26, 1994; Bishop Charles Buswell comments from letter, May 26, 1994; "Bishops Target Arms," *New York Newsday*, June 16, 1995, A27; Gustav Niebuhr, "U.S. Bishops Attack Arms Trade and Spread of Land Mines," *New York Times*, June 17, 1995, 10. See, too, Gene Burns, *The Frontiers of Catholicism: The Politics of Ideology in a Liberal World* (Berkeley: University of California Press, 1992), 112–24.

36. The debate took place during the spring semester, 1977, and the speech was obviously still on Daniel's mind, as it may have influenced some of the critical questions he was asked, such as whether he still considered himself a good Christian (Dan, testily: "Aw, c'mon!"). Interview with Elliot M. Abramson, April 4, 1994.

37. Daniel Berrigan, *To Dwell in Peace*, 282.

38. Interview with Peter Steinfels, January 17, 1994.

39. Peter Steinfels, "Bearing Moral Witness of a Difficult Kind," a review of Daniel Berrigan's *To Dwell in Peace* in the *Boston Globe*, February 21, 1988, Books, 47. For a favorable review, see Anne Klejment, *Church History*, March 1990, 127–28: "Daniel Berrigan raises a rare prophetic voice, urging Christians to live the gospel and to question complacency within the church as rigorously as they challenge the injustices of the secular order."

40. Interview with Daniel Berrigan, January 13, 1994; Daniel Berrigan to "Dear Pat," May 30, 1988; Patrick Henry interviews, April 25, 1994 and September 16, 1996.

41. "Dan resisted," interview with Father John Dear, S.J., January 20, 1995.

42. Interview with Father John Dear, S.J., January 20, 1995, on Daniel Berrigan's reactions to the reviews. Dear calls Daniel Berrigan his closest friend and Philip Berrigan one who has made "a very deep impact on my life."

43. Remarks, December 10, 1987, Richard Cusack Collection; "not by ideology but by a core of religious beliefs" from Lee Lockwood, "Still Radical After All These Years," *Mother Jones*, September–October 1993, 14.

44. On the General Electric raid, interview with Bob Smith, March 16, 1994 and July 23, 1996; interviews with John Schuchardt, April 1, April 25, 1994, and July 29, 1996; on Philip Berrigan's phone call, the call to the Jesuit provincial in New York, and discussions with the judge, interview with Charles Glackin, May 11, 1994.

45. On the raid, the files of the *Norristown (Pa.) Times Herald* and the *Philadelphia Inquirer* are invaluable. Daniel and Phil Berrigan's remarks after leaving court are from Margaret Gibbons, "Plowshares Eight Granted Parole," *Norristown (Pa.) Times Herald*, April 11, 1990, 1; and "Plowshares Case Ends," *Christian Century*, May 2, 1990, 456–57; see, too, Michael de Courcy Hinds, "Eight Sentenced in 1980 Protest at Nuclear Unit," *New York Times*, April 11, 1990, 10.

46. For sympathetic accounts of Plowshares, see John Schuchardt's "Prisoners of Conscience," August 30, 1986, unpublished, 6 pp.;

"Conscience, Religion and Resistance: Civil Disobedience & The Law in the Nuclear Crisis," n.d., unpublished, 7 pp.; "Public Events & the Peace Movement," *Year One*, May 1982, 7–15, all in John Schuchardt Papers, State Historical Society of Wisconsin. See, too, Philip Berrigan and Elizabeth McAlister, *Time's Discipline*, 226–66; Liane Ellison Norman, *Hammer of Justice: Molly Rush and the Plowshares Movement* (Pittsburgh: PPI, 1987); Arthur J. Laffin and Anne Montgomery, eds., *Swords Into Plowshares* (San Francisco: Harper & Row, 1987); Fred A. Wilcox, *Uncommon Martyrs: The Plowshares Movement and the Catholic Left* (Reading, Mass.: Addison-Wesley, 1991); Daniel Berrigan, ed., *For Swords Into Plowshares: The Hammer Has to Fall: The Griffiss Plowshares Action* (Piscataway, N.J.: Plowshares Press, n.d.), and Karl Welsher, *Violence Ends Where Love Begins* (Piscataway, N.J.: Plowshares Press, n.d.). Among the films produced are Emile DeAntonio's *In the King of Prussia* and *The Trial of the AVCO Plowshares*.

47. Interview with Father John Dear, S.J., January 20, 1995. See, especially, Dear's personal account as a Plowshares prisoner, "Peace Behind Bars: A Peacemaking Priest's Journal from Jail," 9 pp., unpublished, 1994.

48. See Felton Davis, "No to Death & War, Yes to Peace & Life," *Catholic Worker*, March–April 1994, 3.

49. Interview with Father John Dear, S.J., interview, January 20, 1995.

50. Daniel Berrigan, "The Non-Violent Citizen in the War-Making State," lecture, Cornell University, April 14, 1994.

51. Interview with Father Richard McSorley, S.J., June 9, 1994.

52. Joe Lersky, "Differing Legacies: The President & The Protestor; Dick Is Dead, Phil's in Jail," *Commonweal*, June 3, 1994, 4–6.

BIBLIOGRAPHY

In addition to published and unpublished materials listed below, we relied on the following publications: *America, Catholic Worker, Commonweal, National Catholic Reporter,* and *Year One* (Baltimore), the Jonah House publication, and *City Paper* (Baltimore). Among the daily newspapers researched were the *Baltimore Sun, Baltimore Evening Sun, Norristown (Pa.) Times Herald, New York Times, Philadelphia Inquirer, Philadelphia Evening Bulletin,* and *Washington Post*. We would have liked to do more research on the extensive FBI files, but our Freedom of Information requests for files on the Berrigans as well as other main actors in the Catholic resistance movement were unable to be filled because the agency asserted they were several years behind in fulfilling FOI requests. We were able, however, to examine the FBI's vast EASTCOM file, which had earlier been opened to public scrutiny.

Books

Abrams, Ray H. *Preachers Present Arms*. Scottdale, Pa.: Herald, 1969.
Allit, Patrick. *Catholic Intellectuals and Conservative Politics in America, 1950–1985*. Ithaca: Cornell University Press, 1993.
Alter, Norma M. *Vietnam Protest Theatre: The Television War on Stage*. Bloomington: Indiana University Press, 1996.

Bainton, Roland. *Christian Attitudes Toward War and Peace*. Nashville: Abingdon, 1960.

Bannan, John F., and Rosemary S. Bannan. *Law, Morality and Vietnam: The Peace Militants and the Courts*. Bloomington: University of Indiana Press, 1974.

Baranski, Johnny. *Lonesome Journey*. Chicago: Sunburst, 1973.

Barkan, Stephen E. *Protestors on Trial: Criminal Justice in the Southern Civil Rights and Vietnam Antiwar Movements*. New Brunswick, N.J.: Rutgers University Press, 1985.

Baskir, Lawrence M., and William A. Strauss. *Chance and Circumstance: The Draft, the War and the Vietnam Generation*. New York: Vintage, 1978.

Becker, Theodore L., ed. *Political Trials*. New York: Bobbs-Merrill, 1971.

Berrigan, Daniel. *Time Without Number*. New York: Macmillan, 1957.

———. *The Bride: Essays in the Church*. New York: Macmillan, 1959.

———. *The World for Wedding Ring*. New York: Macmillan, 1962.

———. *No One Walks Waters*. New York: Macmillan, 1966.

———. *They Call Us Dead Men: Reflections on Life and Conscience*. New York: Macmillan, 1966.

———. *Consequences: Truth and . . .* New York: Macmillan, 1967.

———. *Night Flight to Hanoi: War Diary with 11 Poems*. New York: Macmillan, 1968.

———. *False Gods, Real Men: New Poems*. New York: Macmillan, 1969.

———. *The Trial of the Catonsville Nine*. Boston: Beacon, 1970.

———. *No Bars to Manhood*. New York: Doubleday, 1970.

———. *The Geography of Faith: Conversations Between Daniel Berrigan, When Underground, and Robert Coles*. Boston: Beacon, 1971.

———. *The Dark Night of Resistance*. New York: Doubleday, 1971.

———. *America Is Hard to Find*. New York: Doubleday, 1972.

———. *Prison Poems*. Greensboro, N.C.: Unicorn, 1973.

———. *Lights On in the House of the Dead: A Prison Diary*. New York: Doubleday, 1974.

———. *A Book of Parables*. New York: Seabury, 1978.

———. *The Discipline of the Mountain: Dante's Purgatories in a Nuclear World*. New York: Seabury, 1979.

———. *We Die Before We Live: Talking with the Very Ill*. New York: Seabury, 1980.

———. *Portraits of Those I Love*. New York: Crossroad, 1982.

———. *Steadfastness of the Saints: A Journal of Peace and War in Central and North America*. Maryknoll, N.Y.: Orbis, 1985.

———. *Block Island*. Greensboro, N.C.: Unicorn, 1985.

————. *The Mission: A Film Journal.* New York: Harper & Row, 1986.

————. *To Dwell in Peace: An Autobiography.* San Francisco: Harper & Row, 1987.

————. *Sorrow Built a Bridge: Friendship and AIDS.* Baltimore: Fortkamp, 1989.

————. *The Nightmare of God.* Baltimore: Fortkamp, 1989.

————. *Tulips in the Prison Yard: Selected Poems of Daniel Berrigan.* Dublin, Ireland: Dedalus, 1992.

————. ed., *For Swords into Plowshares: The Hammer Has to Fall.* Piscataway, N.J.: Plowshares Press, n.d

Berrigan, Daniel, with Thich Nhat Hanh. *The Raft Is Not the Shore: Conversations Towards a Buddhist/Christian Awareness.* Boston: Beacon, 1975.

Berrigan, Daniel, with Tom Lewis. *Trial Poems.* Boston: Beacon, 1970.

Berrigan, Daniel, with Lee Lockwood. *Absurd Convictions, Modest Hopes: Conversations After Prison.* New York: Random House, 1972.

Berrigan, Daniel, with Margaret Parker. *Stations: The Way of the Cross.* San Francisco: Harper & Row, 1989.

Berrigan, Philip. *The Catholic Church and the Negro.* St. Louis: Queen's Work, 1962.

————. *No More Strangers.* New York: Macmillan, 1966.

————. *A Punishment for Peace.* New York: Macmillan, 1969.

————. *Prison Journals of a Priest Revolutionary.* Edited by Vincent McGee. New York: Holt, Rinehart & Winston, 1970.

————. *Widen the Prison Gates: Writing from Jails, April 1970–December 1972.* New York: Simon & Schuster, 1973.

————. *Whereon to Stand: The Acts of the Apostles and Ourselves.* Baltimore: Fortkamp, 1993.

Berrigan, Philip, and Elizabeth McAlister. *The Time's Discipline: The Beatitudes and Nuclear Resistance.* Baltimore: Fortkamp, 1989.

Berrigan, Philip, with Fred A. Wilcox. *Fighting the Lamb's War: Skirmishes with the American Empire.* Monroe, Maine: Common Courage Press, 1996.

Boyle, Francis Anthony., *Defining Civil Resistance Under International Law.* Ardsley-on-Hudson, N.Y.: Transnational, 1987.

Brown, Robert McAfee, Abraham Joshua Heschel, and Michael Novak. *Vietnam: Crisis of Conscience.* New York: Association Press, Behrman House and Herder & Herder, 1967.

Burns, Gene. *The Frontiers of Catholicism: The Politics of Ideology in a Liberal World.* Berkeley: University of California Press, 1992.

Burtschnall, James Tunstead. *A Just War No Longer Exists. The Teaching and Trial of Don Lorenzo Milani.* Notre Dame, Ind.: University of Notre Dame Press, 1988.

Cargas, Harry James. *Daniel Berrigan and Contemporary Protest Poetry.* New Haven: College & University Press, 1972.

Casey, William Van Etten, S.J., and Philip Nobile, eds. *The Berrigans.* New York: Praeger, 1971.

Castelli, Jim. *The Bishops and the Bomb: Waging Peace in a Nuclear Age.* New York: Doubleday, 1983.

Cogley, John. *Catholic America.* New York: Dial, 1973.

Cohen, Carl. *Civil Disobedience: Conscience, Tactics and the Law.* New York: Columbia University Press, 1971.

Colaianni, James. *The Catholic Left: The Crisis of Radicalism Within the Church.* Philadelphia: Chilton, 1968.

Cooney, John. *The American Pope: The Life and Times of Francis Cardinal Spellman.* New York: Times Books, 1984.

Cowan, Paul, Nick Egleson, and Nat Hentoff, with Barbara Herbert and Robert Wall. *State Secrets: Police Surveillance in America.* New York: Holt, Rinehart & Winston, 1974.

Coy, Patrick, ed. *Revolution of the Heart: Essays on the Catholic Worker.* Philadelphia: New Society Publishers, 1988.

Craig, Robert H. *Religion and Radical Politics: An Alternative Christian Tradition in the United States.* Philadelphia: Temple University Press.

Cross, Robert D. *Emergence of Liberal Catholicism in America.* Cambridge, Mass.: Harvard University Press, 1958.

Curtis, Richard. *The Berrigan Brothers: The Story of Daniel and Philip Berrigan.* New York: Hawthorne, 1974.

Day, Dorothy. *On Pilgrimage: The Sixties.* New York: Curtis, 1972.

Dear, John, S.J. *It's a Sin to Build a Nuclear Weapon. The Collected Works on War and Christian Peacemaking of Richard McSorley, S.J.* Baltimore: Fortkamp, 1991.

———. *The God of Peace: Toward a Theology of Nonviolence.* Maryknoll, N.Y.: Orbis, 1994.

———, ed. *Apostle of Peace: Essays in Honor of Daniel Berrigan.* Maryknoll, N.Y.: Orbis, 1996.

———. *Seeds of Nonviolence.* Baltimore: Fortkamp, 1993.

DeBenedetti, Charles, ed. *Peace Heroes in Twentieth-Century America.* Bloomington: Indiana University Press, 1986).

———. DeBenedetti, Charles, and Charles Chatfield. *An American Ordeal.* Syracuse, N.Y.: Syracuse University Press, 1990.

Deedy, John. *Apologies, Good Friends: An Interim Biography of Daniel Berrigan, S.J.* Chicago: Fides/Claretian, 1981.

Demaris, Ovid. *J. Edgar Hoover as They Knew Him: An Oral Biography.* New York: Carroll & Graf/Richard Gallen, 1994.

Donner, Frank. *The Age of Surveillance: The Aims and Methods of America's Political Intelligence System.* New York: Knopf, 1980.

Douglas, R. Bruce, and David Hollenbach, eds. *Catholicism and Liberalism.* New York: Cambridge University Press, 1994.

Douglass, James W. *Resistance and Contemplation. The Way of Liberation. The Yin and Yang of the Non-Violent Life.* New York: Doubleday, 1972.

Ellis, John Tracey. *American Catholicism.* Chicago: University of Chicago Press, 1956.

Epstein, Barbara. *Political Protest and Cultural Revolution: Nonviolent Direct Action in the 1970's and 1980's.* Berkeley: University of California Press, 1991.

Falk, Richard A., and Robert Jay Lifton. *Indefensible Weapons.* New York: Basic Books, 1983.

Feinrider, Martin A., and Arthur S. Miller. *Nuclear Weapons and Law.* Westport, Conn.: Greenwood, 1984.

Finn, James. *Protest: Pacifism and Politics. Some Passionate Views on War and Nonviolence.* New York: Random House, 1967.

Fisher, James Terence. *The Catholic Counterculture in America.* Chapel Hill: University of North Carolina Press, 1989.

Forest, Jim. *Living with Wisdom: A Life of Thomas Merton.* Maryknoll, N.Y.: Orbis, 1991.

———. *Love Is the Measure: A Biography of Dorothy Day.* Maryknoll, N.Y.: Orbis, 1994.

———, ed. *The Great Berrigan Debate.* New York: The Committee on New Alternatives in the Middle East, 1974.

Furlong, Monica. *Merton: A Biography.* San Francisco: Harper & Row, 1986.

Gallagher, Joseph. *The Pain and Privilege: Diary of a City Priest.* New York: Doubleday, 1983.

Gallagher, Michael. *Laws of Heaven: Catholic Activists Today.* New York: Ticknor & Fields, 1992.

Gentry, Curt. *J. Edgar Hoover. The Man and the Secrets.* New York: Norton, 1991.

Gilman, Richard. *Faith, Sex, Mystery.* New York: Penguin, 1988.

Gitlin, Todd. *The Sixties. Years of Hope, Days of Rage.* New York: Bantam, 1987.

Gray, Francine du Plessix. *Divine Disobedience: Profiles in Catholic Radicalism.* New York: Knopf, 1970.

Halpert, Stephen, and Tom Murray, eds. *The Witness of the Berrigans.* New York: Doubleday, 1972.

Hare, A. Paul, and Herbert H. Blumberg, eds. *Nonviolent Direct Action. American Cases: Social-Psychological Analyses.* Washington and Cleveland: Corpus, 1968.

Haring, Bernard. *A Theology of Violence.* New York: Farrar, Straus & Giroux, 1970.

Herngren, Per. *Path of Resistance: The Practice of Civil Disobedience.* Philadelphia: New Society Publishers, 1993.

Hertzberg, Arthur. *The Zionist Idea: A Historical Analysis and Reader.* Westport, Conn.: Greenwood, 1970.

Heschel, Abraham Joshua. *The Prophets.* New York: Harper Torchbooks, 1962.

Hitchcock, James. *The Decline and Fall of Radical Catholicism.* New York: Herder & Herder, 1971.

Hollander, Paul. *The Survival of the Adversary Culture. Social Criticism and Political Escapism in American Society.* New Brunswick, N.J.: Transaction, 1988.

Horn, Zoia. *Zoia! Memoirs of Zoia Horn, Battler for the People's Right to Know.* Jefferson, N.C.: McFarland, 1995.

Ignatiev, Noel. *How the Irish Became White.* New York: Routledge, 1995.

Inglis, Fred. *The Cruel Place: Everyday Life and the Cold War.* New York: Basic Books, 1991.

Isaacson, Walter. *Kissinger.* New York: Simon & Schuster, 1992.

Kaiser, Charles. *1968 in America. Class, Counterculture, and the Shaping of a Generation.* New York: Weidenfeld & Nicolson, 1988.

Karnow, Stanley. *Vietnam: A History.* New York: Viking, 1993.

Kasimow, Harold, and Byron L. Sherwin, eds. *No Religion Is an Island: Abraham Joshua Heschel and Interreligious Dialogue.* Includes Daniel Berrigan's "My Friend," 68–75. Maryknoll, N.Y.: Orbis, 1991.

Kendrick, Alexander. *The Wound Within: America in the Vietnam Years, 1945–1974.* Boston: Little, Brown, 1974.

Klejment, Anne. *The Berrigans: A Bibliography of Published Writings by Daniel, Philip, and Elizabeth McAlister Berrigan.* New York: Garland, 1979. Lists writings through 1977.

Kohn, Stephen. *Jailed for Peace. The History of American Draft Law Violations.* Westport, Conn.: Greenwood, 1986.

Labrie, Ross. *The Writings of Daniel Berrigan.* Latham, Md.: University Press of America, 1989.

Laffin, Arthur J. and Anne Montgomery, eds. *Swords into Plowshares: Nonviolent Direct Action for Disarmament.* San Francisco: Harper & Row, 1987.

Lapomarda, Vincent A. *The Jesuits and the Third Reich*. Lewiston, N.Y.: Mellen, 1989.

Lewy, Guenter. *Peace and Revolution: The Moral Crisis of American Pacifism*. Grand Rapids, Mich.: Eerdmans, 1988.

McDonough, Peter. *Men Astutely Trained. A History of the Jesuits in the American Century*. New York: Free Press, 1992.

McNeal, Patricia F. *The American Catholic Peace Movement 1928–1972*. New York: Arno, 1978.

———. *Harder Than War: Catholic Peacemaking in Twentieth-Century America*. New Brunswick, N.J.: Rutgers University Press, 1992.

McPherson, Myra. *Long Time Passing: Vietnam and the Haunted Generation*. New York: Doubleday, 1984.

Malits, Elena, C.S.C. *The Solitary Explorer: Thomas Merton's Transforming Journey*. San Francisco: Harper & Row, 1980.

May, Rollo. *Power and Innocence: A Search for the Sources of Violence*. New York: Norton, 1972.

Meconis, Charles. *With Clumsy Grace: The American Catholic Left, 1961–1975*. New York: Seabury, 1979.

Melville, Thomas, and Marjorie Melville. *Whose Heaven, Whose Earth?* New York: Knopf, 1971.

Merton, Thomas. *Faith and Violence: Christian Teaching and Christian Practice*. Notre Dame, Ind.: University of Notre Dame Press, 1968.

———. *The Nonviolent Alternative*. Rev. ed. Edited by Gordon Zahn. New York: Farrar, Straus & Giroux, 1980.

———. *The Hidden Ground of Love: The Letters of Thomas Merton on Religious Experience and Social Concerns*. Selected and edited by William H. Shannon. New York: Farrar, Straus & Girous, 1985.

———. *Journals, 1964–1965: A Vow of Conversation*. Edited by Naomi Burton Stone. New York: Farrar, Straus & Giroux, 1988.

———. *The Road to Joy: Letters to New and Old Friends*. Selected and edited by Robert E. Daggy. San Diego: Harcourt Brace Jovanovich, 1989.

———. *The Courage for Truth: Letters to Writers*. Edited by Christine M. Bochen. New York: Farrar, Straus & Giroux, 1993.

———. Witness to Freedom: The Letters of Thomas Merton in Times of Crisis. Selected and edited by William H. Shannon. New York: Farrar, Straus & Giroux, 1994.

Miller, William D. *A Harsh and Dreadful Love: Dorothy Day and the Catholic Worker Movement*. New York: Liveright, 1973.

———. *Dorothy Day: A Biography*. New York: Harper & Row, 1982.

Moorhead, Caroline. *Troublesome People: The Warriors of Pacifism*. Bethesda, Md.: Adler & Adler, 1987.

Morris, Benny. *The Birth of the Palestinian Refugee Problem, 1947–1949.* New York: Cambridge University Press, 1987.

Morrison, Joan, and Robert K. Morrison, eds. *From Camelot to Kent State: The Sixties Experience in the Words of Those Who Lived It.* New York: Times Books, 1987.

Mott, Michael. *The Seven Mountains of Thomas Merton.* Boston: Houghton Mifflin, 1984.

Mueller, John E. *War, Presidents and Public Opinion.* New York: Wiley, 1973.

Murray, John Courtney, S.J. *We Hold These Truths: Catholic Reflections on the American Proposition.* New York: Sheed & Ward, 1960.

Nelson, Jack, and Ronald J. Ostrow. *The FBI and the Berrigans: The Making of a Conspiracy.* New York: Coward, McCann & Geoghegan, 1972.

Nhat Hanh, Thich. *Love in Action: Writings on Nonviolent Social Change.* Berkeley, Cal.: Parallax, 1993. Foreword by Daniel Berrigan.

Norman, Liane Ellison. *Hammer of Justice: Molly Rush and the Plowshares Eight.* Pittsburgh: Pittsburgh Peace Institute, 1989.

Novak, Michael. *The Open Church.* New York: Macmillan, 1964.

———. *Confession of a Catholic.* New York: Harper & Row, 1983.

O'Brien, David J. *American Catholics and Social Reform. The New Deal Years.* New York: Oxford University Press, 1968.

Ochs, Stephen J. *Desegregating the Altar: The Josephites and the Struggle for Black Priests, 1871–1960.* Baton Rouge: Louisiana State University Press, 1990.

O'Dwyer, Paul. *Counsel for the Defense: The Autobiography of Paul O'Dwyer.* New York: Simon & Schuster, 1979.

O'Rourke, William. *The Harrisburg 7 and the New Catholic Left.* New York: Crowell, 1972.

Polner, Murray. *No Victory Parades: The Return of the Vietnam Veteran.* New York: Holt, Rinehart & Winston, 1971.

———, ed. *When Can I Come Home? A Debate on Amnesty for Exiles, Anti-War Prisoners and Others.* New York: Doubleday Anchor, 1972.

Powers, Richard Gird. *Secrecy and Power: The Life of J. Edgar Hoover.* New York: Free Press, 1987.

Quigley, Thomas E., ed. *American Catholics and the Vietnam War.* Grand Rapids, Mich.: Eerdmans, 1968.

Raines, John C., ed. *Conspiracy: The Implications of the Harrisburg Trial for the Democratic Tradition.* New York: Harper & Row, 1974.

Riemer, George. *The New Jesuits.* Boston: Little Brown, 1971.

Roberts, Nancy L. *Dorothy Day and the Catholic Worker.* Albany: State University of New York Press, 1984.

Shannon, Thomas A., ed. *War or Peace? The Search for New Answers.* Maryknoll, N.Y.: Orbis, 1980.

Small, Melvin, and William D. Hoover, eds. *Give Peace a Chance: Exploring the Vietnam Antiwar Movement.* Syracuse, N.Y.: Syracuse University Press, 1992.

Stringfellow, William, and Anthony Towne. *Suspect Tenderness: The Ethics of the Berrigan Witness.* New York: Holt, Rinehart & Winston, 1971.

Strout, Cushing. *The New Heavens and New Earth: Political Religion in America.* New York: Harper & Row, 1974.

Sullivan, William with Bill Brown. *The Bureau: My Thirty Years in Hoover's FBI.* New York: Pinnacle, 1982.

Swomley, John M., Jr. *Liberation Ethics.* New York: Macmillan, 1972.

Tessler, Mark. *A History of the Israeli-Palestinian Conflict.* Bloomington: Indiana University Press, 1994.

Theoharis, Athan, and John Stuart Cox. *The Boss: J. Edgar Hoover and the Great American Inquisition.* Philadelphia: Temple University Press, 1988.

——. *J. Edgar Hoover, Sex and Crime.* Chicago: Dee, 1995.

——, ed. *From the Secret Files of J. Edgar Hoover.* Chicago: Dee, 1991.

Trials of the Resistance. New York: New York Review of Books, 1970.

Troester, Rosalie R., ed. *Voices from the Catholic Worker.* Philadelphia: Temple University Press, 1993.

True, Michael, ed. *Daniel Berrigan: Poetry, Drama, Prose.* Maryknoll, N.Y.: Orbis, 1988.

Twomey, Gerald, ed. *Thomas Merton: Prophet in the Belly of a Paradox.* New York: Paulist Press, 1978.

Useem, Michael. *Conscription, Protest, and Social Conflict. The Life and Death of a Draft Resistance Movement.* New York: Wiley, 1973.

Van Allen, Rodger. *The Commonweal and American Catholicism: The Magazine, the Movement, the Meaning.* Philadelphia: Fortress, 1974.

Walzer, Michael. *Obligations. Essays on Disobedience, War and Citizenship.* Cambridge: Harvard University Press, 1970.

Weigel, George. *Tranquillitas Ordinis: The Present Failure and Future Promise of American Catholic Thought on War and Peace.* New York: Oxford University Press, 1987.

Wells, Tom. *The War Within: America's Battle Over Vietnam.* Berkeley: University of California Press, 1994.

Welsher, Karl, ed. *Violence Ends Where Love Begins.* Piscataway, N.J.: Plowshares Press, 1984.

Wilcox, Fred A. *Uncommon Martyrs: The Plowshares Movement and the Catholic Left.* Reading, Mass.: Addison-Wesley, 1991.

Windass, Stanley, trans. and ed. *Chronicle of the Worker-Priests*. New York: Humanities, 1967).

Wise, David. *The American Police State: The Government Against the People*. New York: Random House, 1976.

Wittner, Lawrence S. *Rebels Against War: The American Peace Movement, 1933–1983*. Philadelphia: Temple University Press, 1984.

Young, Marilyn B. *The Vietnam Years, 1945–1990*. New York: Harper-Collins, 1991.

Zahn, Gordon C. *German Catholics and Hitler's Wars. A Study in Social Control*. New York: Sheed & Ward, 1962.

———. *In Solitary Witness: The Life and Death of Franz Jagerstatter*. Boston: Beacon, 1964.

———. *Vocation of Peace*. Baltimore: Fortkamp, 1992.

Zaroulis, Nancy, and Gerald Sullivan. *Who Spoke Up? American Protest Against the War in Vietnam, 1963–1975*. New York: Doubleday, 1984.

Zinn, Howard. *Vietnam: The Logic of Withdrawal*. Boston: Beacon, 1967.

Articles

Bach, John. "Numbers: A Season's Prison Journal." Unpublished.

——— and Mitchell Snyder. "Danbury: Anatomy of a Prison Strike." *Liberation*, May 1972, 1–11.

Bartelme, Elizabeth. "Visiting Dan." *Critic*, November-December 1971, 66–68.

Bartz, Michael. "An Interview with Daniel Berrigan, S.J." *Round Table*, Winter 1991, 3–5.

Bearak, Barry. "Berrigan at 71: Still Protesting." *Los Angeles Times*, April 10, 1993, 1.

Berns, Walter. "The 'Essential Soul' of Dan Berrigan." *National Review*, November 9, 1973, 1231–41.

Berrigan, Daniel. "Christian Witness." Speech, Rosemont College, Autumn 1964, unpublished.

———. "Selma and Sharpeville." *Commonweal*, April 9, 1965, 71–75.

———. "Berrigan at Cornell." *Jubilee*, February 1968, 28–36.

———. "Father Daniel Berrigan on his trip to Hanoi: Interview." *America*, March 9, 1968, 320–24.

———. "The Best of Times: The Worst of Times." *Continuum*, Summer 1968, 249–53.

———. "Letter to the Weathermen." In *The Eloquence of Protest*, ed. Harrison G. Salisbury. Boston: Houghton Mifflin, 1972, 13–18.

Berrigan, Daniel, and Hans Morgenthau "discuss the moral dilemma in the Middle East," *Progressive*, March 1974, 31-34.

———. "Where Death Abounded—Life: St. Rose's Home." *Catholic Worker*, June 1979, 1;7.

———. "Sleep Tight While Your Neighbors Freeze." *U.S. Catholic*, February 1980, 29–33.

———. "Christian Peacemakers in the Warmaking State." In *Celebrating Peace*, ed. Leroy S. Rouner. Notre Dame, Ind.: University of Notre Dame Press, 1990, 181–91.

———. "O That You Would Return to Me." *Year One*, May 1990, 2–3.

———. "A Liturgy of Grief." *Year One*, March–April 1991, 8–14.

———. "Holy, Healing Spirit, Come!" *The Other Side*, May–June 1991, 16–21.

———. "My Friend" [Abraham Joshua Heschel]. In *No Religion Is an Island,* eds. Harold Kasimow and Byron L. Sherwin. Maryknoll, N.Y.: Orbis, 1991, 68–75.

———. "Their Speech Is All of Forgiveness." Foreword to Thich Nhat Hanh, *Love in Action: Writings on Nonviolent Social Change*. Berkeley, Cal.: Parallax, 1993.

———. "Nonviolent Citizen in the Warmaking State." Speech, Cornell University, April 14, 1994.

———. "Priests, Women, Women Priests and Other Unlikely Recombinants." *Movement* (Bristol, U.K.), n.d., 10–13.

Berrigan, Philip. "Lay Leaders in Action." *Josephite Harvest 1,* Sept.–Oct. 1963: 18–21.

———. "Christianity in Harlem." *Commonweal*, November 27, 1964, 323–25.

———. "Newburgh." *Commonweal*, May 14, 1965, 239.

———. "Witnesses in Selma," *Josephite Harvest*, May–June 1965, 8–9.

———. "The Priest and Society." *Ave Maria*, January 8, 1966, 19.

———. "Resistance & The Warfare State." ASUH Symposia Committee, Honolulu, 1970. Unpublished paper.

———. "Why We Seized the Hammer." *Progressive*, May 1981, 50–51.

———. "What Keeps Me Going." *Progressive*, October 1988, 50.

———. "Lessons Not Too Late for the Learning." *Year One*, September 1991, 2–5.

———. "Creation—Intended as Envelope and Nourishment of Life Recoils in Outrage and Shock." *Year One*, January 1992, 5–6.

———. "The Anointing at Bethany & the Washing of the Disciples' Feet: Preparing One Another for Martyrdom and Mission." *Year One*, December 1994, 4.

Berry, Jason. "Orleanians Go on a Retreat with Radical-Minded Catholic, Daniel Berrigan." *Figaro* (New Orleans), December 22, 1976, 18–21.

Brown, Robert McAfee. "A Symbol Is a Symbol Is a Symbol: A Reply to Michael Novak." *Christian Century*, May 22, 1974, 563–66.

"The Burden of the Berrigans." *Holy Cross Quarterly*, January 1971. Entire issue.

Byrne, Richard Jr., "Revolution 9," *City Paper*, January 29, 1993, 12–21.

Cargas, Harry James. "Daniel Berrigan: The Activist as Poet." *Laurel Review*, Spring 1969, 11–17.

———. "The Path of Greatest Resistance." *U.S. Catholic/Jubilee*, January 1970, 7–11.

———. "The Family: Consumerism Gone Mad?" *Way*, January-February 1974, 15–18.

———. "An Open Letter Written to Daniel Berrigan." *St. Louis Jewish Light*, January 16, 1974, 7.

———. "Interview with David Darst." *Year One*, July-August 1993, 4–5.

Chomsky, Noam. "Daniel in the Lion's Den: Berrigan and His Critics." *Liberation*, February 1974, 15–24.

Coffey, Thomas. "A Talk with Daniel Berrigan." *Catholic Library World*, March 1958, 315–17.

Conley, John J. "Catholic Pacifism in America." *America*, December 14, 1974, 381–83.

Cornell, Tom. "The Catholic Church and Witness Against War." In *War or Peace? The Search for New Answers*, ed. Thomas A. Shannon. Maryknoll, N.Y.: Orbis, 1980, 200–13.

———. "From Protest to Resistance to Jail—a Draft Resister's Story." *New York Times Magazine*, January 19, 1968, 22–80.

———. "Nonviolent Napalm in Catonsville." *Catholic Worker*, June 1968, 1–8.

Cowan, Paul. "The Moral Imperialism of Dan Berrigan." *Village Voice*, January 31, 1974, 22–23.

———. "Boyd Douglas" and "Twelve Anguished Jurors." In *State Secrets: Police Surveillance in America*, eds. Cowan, Egleson, and Hentoff. New York: Holt, Rinehart & Winston, 1974, 236–467; 303–33.

Davidon, Anne Morrissett. "Warheads Into Plowshares: When Is a 'Crime' a Prophetic Act?" *Progressive*, May 1981, 49–51.

———. "Pacifists and Their Shifting Alliances." *Confrontation*, Winter 1981, 141–50.

Davis, Felton. "No to Death & War, Yes to Peace & Life." *Catholic Worker* (March–April 1994), 3. A criticism of the Plowshares movement, it was answered by Philip Berrigan, "From a North Carolina Jail," *Catholic Worker*, March—April 1994, 3, 7.

Day, Dorothy. "The Berrigans and Property Rights." *Fellowship*, May 1971, 25.

Dear, John. "Keep on Resisting Evil: A Conversation with Phil Berrigan." *Fellowship*, September—October 1993, 12–13, 28.

———. "In Jail, Keeping Watch." *Sojourners*, July 1994, 33.

Deedy, John. "A Priest in Hiding Calls for Moral Revolt." *New York Times*, August 9, 1970, E7.

Desbarats, Jacqueline. "Repression in the Socialist Republic of Vietnam: Executions and Population Relocation." In *The Vietnam Debate: A Fresh Look at the Arguments*, ed. John Norton Moore. Lanham, Md.: University Press of America, 1990, 193–202.

Dowd, Douglas. "The Strengths and Limits of Resistance." In *The Witness of the Berrigans*, eds. Stephen Halpert and Tom Murray. New York: Doubleday, 1972, 176–78.

Elmer, Jerry. "Draft Board Rip-Off." *WIN*, August 1970, 19.

Femia, Frank. "Destroying Draft Files Was *My* Duty." *Peacemaker*, October 24, 1970, 3.

Finlay, Dan. "Notes on the Catonsville Trial." Unpublished, 11 pp., Cornell, Box 74.

Finn, James. "Why Did You Sign That Ad?" In *Political Passages: Journeys of Change Through Two Decades, 1968–1988*, ed. John H. Bunzel. New York: Free Press, 1988, 273–301.

Finnegan, Molly, Maggie Geddes, Jill Boskey, and Valentine Green. "Women's Day at the Draft Board." *WIN*, August 1969, 1, 38–39.

Forest, Jim. "Harrisburg Conspiracy: The Berrigans and the Catholic Left." *WIN*, March 15, 1973, 4–31.

———. Harrisburg Memoir, unpublished, Cornell, Box 74.

———. "Daniel Berrigan's Outraged Love." *Fellowship*, February 1974, 2–3.

———. "Daniel Berrigan: The Poet and Prophet as Priest." In *The Witness of the Berrigans*, eds. Stephen Halpert and Tom Murray. New York: Doubleday, 1972, 84–110.

———. "The Roots of Catholic Resistance." *Catholic Herald*, November 1971, 61–65.

Geltman, Max. "The Berrigans vs. the United States." *National Review*, May 4, 1971, 470–74.

Glick, Ted. "Getting at the Truth." Unpublished, 370–441.

———. "Harrisburg: An Insider's View." Unpublished, Cornell, Box 75.

———. "An Open Letter of Resignation from the Catholic Left." *WIN*, October 30, 1974, 17–18.

Grant, Philip A., Jr. "Archbishop Joseph F. Rummel and the 1962 New

Orleans Desegregation Crisis." *Records of the American Catholic Historical Society of Philadelphia*, March-December 1980, 59–66.

Gray, Francine du Plessix. "The Politics of Salvation." Part I, June 1, 1972, 34–40; Part II, June 15, 1972, *New York Review of Books*, 14–21.

Greeley, Andrew. "Phrenetic." *Holy Cross Quarterly*, January 1971, 15–21.

Hogan, Peter E., S.S.J. "The Legend of the New Catholic Left: Rev. Philip Berrigan." Unpublished, June 10, 1972, 15 pp.

Jacobs, Paul. "Daniel Berrigan . . . Some of His Best Friends Were . . .", *Ramparts*, April 1974, 10–12.

Jones, Arthur. "Michael Novak: Acclaim, Disdain and a Big Prize Follow His Pen From Left to Right." *National Catholic Reporter*, January 13, 1994, 8–12.

Klejment, Anne. "The Berrigans." In *Peace Heroes in Twentieth Century America*, ed. Charles DeBenedetti. Bloomington: Indiana University Press, 1986, 228–54.

———. "War Resistance and Property Destruction. The Catonsville Nine Draft Board Raid and Catholic Worker Pacifism." In *Revolution of the Heart: Essays on the Catholic Workers*, ed. Patrick G. Coy, Philadelphia: New Society, 1988, 272–309.

———. "From Holy Homemaker to Madonna of the Movement: Daniel and Philip Berrigan's Ideology of Social Reform and Its Implications for Catholic Women." Unpublished, 22 pp.

———. Review [Daniel Berrigan's autobiography], *Church History*, March 1990, 127–28.

Lejeune, Robert, book review of Robert D. Holsworth, *Let Your Life Speak: A Study of Politics, Religion, and Antinuclear Weapons Activism* in *Peace & Change*, July 1991, 316–19.

Lersky, Joe. "Differing Legacies: The President & the Protestor: Dick Is Dead, Phil's in Jail." *Commonweal*, June 3, 1994, 4–6.

Levin, Hoag. "Sister Elizabeth: A Quiet Nun Becomes a Peace Extremist." *Philadelphia Inquirer*, September 14, 1971, 1; 6–9.

Lockwood, Lee. "Still Radical After All These Years." *Mother Jones*, September-October 1993, 14.

Ludwig, Robert A. "The Theology of Daniel Berrigan." *Listening*, Spring 1971, 127–39.

Mattern, Evelyn J. "Vacation in Harrisburg." *America*, April 22, 1972, 1968, 424–28.

Mayer, Paul. "Diary of a Dissenting Priest." *Commonweal*, April 3, 1970, 78–79.

———. "Voices of the Middle East." *WIN*, December 5, 1974, 12–19.

————. "A Courtroom Outside the World: The Milwaukee Fourteen vs. the State of Wisconsin." In Halpert and Murray, 24–44.

McAlister, Elizabeth. "Letters From Berrigan Case." *New York Times* [Week in Review], May 2, 1972, 10.

————. "Forming Community: Baltimore's Jonah House." *Fellowship*, February 1974, 5–6.

————. "Vietnam: A Case for Remembering." *Harrisburg Independent Press*, May 23–30, 1975, 7.

————. "Proposal for a National Debate on Nuclear Policy." *Year One*, March 2, 1976, 2–3.

————. "A Prison Letter: Raising Children, Resistance Community." *Radix*, May–June 1977, 3–7.

————. "Rachel Weeping for Her Children and She Cannot Be Comforted . . . : A Scripture Reflection." *Year One*, January 1992, 7–8.

————. "Behind U.S. Bars, Brutalities Boggle the Mind and More." *National Catholic Reporter*, October 30, 1992, 24.

McCarthy, Patrick. "Ten Years After the Plowshares Eight," *Christianity and Crisis*, May 28, 1990, 169–70.

Miller, David J. "The Draft Resister in Prison." *Katallagete: Be Reconciled*, 3–4, Winter–Spring 1972: 37–40.

Miller, Loy Jr. "Why Did Mild Phil Berrigan Turn Firebrand?" *Philadelphia Inquirer*, September 13, 1971, 8.

Morrison, John. "The Legality and Morality of Nuclear Weapons." Speech, Veterans for Peace Box 3881, Portland, ME 04104], August 14, 1994.

Moylan, Mary. "Being Underground." *Peace News*, July 3, 1970, 2.

————. "Underground Woman." *Hard Times*, April 20, 1970, 1.

Nobile, Philip. "Senator Goodell and Philip Berrigan: An Untold Story." *New York Review of Books*, November 5, 1970, 38–40.

Novak, Michael. "Draft Board Theology." In *American Catholics and the Vietnam War*, ed. Thomas E. Quigley. Grand Rapids, Mich.: Eerdmans, 1968, 93–96.

————. "The Oranging of the Berrigans: Neither in Their Political nor in Their Moral Judgment Are the Berrigans Suitable Models for Thought and Action." *Christian Century*, April 17, 1974, 417–22.

————. "And Now a Few Words from the Real World." *Notre Dame*, February 1982, 21–23.

Novak, William. "Berrigan: Nine Lies About Israel." *Genesis II*, December 1973, 1;7.

O'Brien, William. "Daniel Berrigan: Portrait of the Peacemaker as a Healer." *Other Side*, July-August 1987, 12–16.

Oddo, Thomas C. "The Monk and the Activist." *Harvard Theological Review*, July-October 1979, 320.

Patton, John H. "Rhetoric at Catonsville: Daniel Berrigan, Conscience, & Image Alteration." *Today's Speech*, Winter 1975, 3–12.

Peattie, Noel. "Passage for Dissent." In *The Best of Sipapu, 1970–1988*. Jefferson, N.C.: McFarland, 1989, 352–57.

Raines, John C. "The Pursuit of Legitimacy." In *Conspiracy: The Implications of the Harrisburg Trial for the Democratic Tradition*, ed. John C. Raines. New York: Harper & Row, 1974, 161–79.

Rasmussen, Larry. "Daniel Berrigan and Dietrich Bonhoeffer: Parallels and Contrasts in Resistance." *Dialogue*, Autumn 1972, 264–72.

Rasmussen, Larry, with Ranat Bethge. "Resistance." In *Dietrich Bonhoeffer: His Significance for North Americans*. Minneapolis: Fortress, 1990, 43–56.

Rosenblum, Constance. "A History of the Vietnam Protest Movement." *Ave Maria*, December 23–30, 1967, 10–14.

Ruether, Rosemary. "The Discussion Continues." *Commonweal*, September 1970, 431.

Ruether, Rosemary and Daniel Berrigan, exchange of open letters, *National Catholic Reporter*, June 5, 19, and 26, 1968.

Sax, Joseph L. "Civil Disobedience. The Law Is Never Blind." *Saturday Review*, September 28, 1968, 22–25, 56.

Schuchardt, John. "Public Events and the Peace Movement." *Year One*, May 1982, 1, 7–15.

———. "Prisoners of Conscience and the Challenge of Non-Violent Direct Action." Speech, Weston Priory, Weston, Vt., August 30, 1986.

———. "What Is a Person of Conscience?" *Peacework* (Cambridge, Mass.) February 1994, 8.

Steinfels, Peter. "Why I Went to Jail." *Commonweal*, April 23, 1971, 158.

True, Michael. "Poetry and the Vietnam Vortex." *Cross Currents*, Summer 1976, 251–56.

———. "En Route with Berrigan." *Cross Currents*, Summer 1988, 250–53.

———. "American Pacifism and Catholic Radicalism." *Confrontation*, Winter 1981, 153–61.

Vree, Dale. "Stripped Clean: The Berrigans and the Politics of Guilt and Martyrdom." *Ethics*, July 1975, 271–87.

Waskow, Arthur. "The Middle East: Two Justices Crossing Each Other, Colliding." *WIN*, September 12, 1974, 4–6.

Weber, Paul, S.J. "Daniel Berrigan: Political Theology in the Post-War Years." *Chicago Studies*, Spring 1973, 77–90.

Weigel, George. "'Vietnam' and the Transformation of the American Catholic Debate on War and Peace." In *The Vietnam Debate. A Fresh Look at the Arguments*, ed. John Norton Moore. Lanham, Md.: University Press of America, 1990, 211–22.

Wilcock, Evelyn. "A Crisis of Conscience. Abraham Joshua Heschel and the War in Vietnam" In Evelyn Wilcock, *Pacifism and the Jews*. Gloucestershire, U.K.: Hawthorn, 1993, 166–91.

Wool, Robert. "The Harboring of Daniel Berrigan: An Exercise in Christian Charity." *Esquire*, November 1971, 156–61, 206.

Zahn, Gordon C. Foreword. In *American Catholics and the Vietnam War*, ed. Thomas E. Quigley. Grand Rapids, Mich.: Eerdmans, 1968, 15–23.

———. "The Berrigans—A Catholic Pacifist's Views." *Dissent*, June 1971, 200–206.

———. "The Great Catholic Upheaval." *Saturday Review*, September 1971, 24–27, 54, 56.

———. "Scandal of Silence." *Commonweal*, October 22, 1971, 79–85.

———. "Catholicism and Peace: A Journey of Rediscovery." *Confrontation*, Winter 1981, 150–53.

Other Sources

Fahey, Sarah A., S.N.D. "The Catonsville Nine Action, A Study of an American Catholic Resistance Position." Ph.D. dissertation, Temple University, 1975.

Gustainis, J. Justin. "Daniel Berrigan and the Catholic Ultra-Resistance: The Roots of a Political Genre." Ph.D. dissertation, Bowling Green State University, 1981.

Klejment, Anne. "In the Lion's Den: The Social Catholicism of Daniel and Philip Berrigan, 1955–1965." Ph.D. dissertation, State University of New York at Binghamton, 1980.

Ludwig, Robert A. "Political Theology in America: Daniel Berrigan as a Contemporary Profile." Ph.D. dissertation, Aquinas Institute, 1972.

McLaughlin, Sara J. "Prison and the Christian Resister: The Letters and Journals from Prison of Daniel and Philip Berrigan." M.A. thesis, State University of New York at Buffalo, 1976.

Meconis, Charles A. Unpublished portions of interviews for his book, *With Clumsy Grace: The American Catholic Left, 1961–1975* (New York: Seabury, 1979), are part of the Charles Meconis Collection.

Roberts, Jonathan. "Voices of an Antiwar Movement: Baltimore During the Vietnam War." Johns Hopkins University History Department, unpublished, 1991, 38 pp. and Roberts, Jonathan. "Voices of an Antiwar Movement: Baltimore During the Vietnam War." M.A. essay, Johns Hopkins University, 1991, 75 pp.

Films

Holy Outlaw, 1970
The Trial of the Catonsville Nine, 1973
In The King of Prussia, 1982
The Trial of the AVCO Plowshares, 1984
The Mission, 1986

Tapes & Records

Berrigan Raps (Caedmon), 1970
America Is Hard to Find, 1972
The Trial of the Catonsville Nine, 1973
Daniel Berrigan speaking at the Catholic Worker, 1981–86, five cassettes, Catholic Worker Collection: Marquette University Archives.
Martin Sheen. *Call to Conscience*. Plowshares Defense Fund, n.d.

INDEX

INDEX   433

against Vietnam War, 122–29,
185. *See also* Baltimore Four;
Demonstrations; Draft
board raids; Sit-ins, Berkeley
(1980)
Punishment for Peace, A (P. Berrigan), 168

Quang Duc, 123
Quayle, Vinnie, 68, 94

Racism, Phil's position, 79–80, 98,
100–104, 112, 114–17. *See also*
Blacks; Civil rights
Raids
  Dow Chemical, 243–45
  General Electric (1980), 345–47.
  See also Draft board raids
Reale, Jim, 230
Resistance and Contemplation (Douglass), 258
Riga, Peter, 105
Riots, Los Angeles, 122
Riverside Research Institute, 2–4,
9–10, 353n1
Roccosalvo, Joe, 95, 162
Rosebaugh, Larry, 235, 238
Ruether, Rosemary, 211
Rusk, Dean, 146

Sachs, Stephen, 187, 201, 205, 207,
372n12
St. George, Jack, 65–66, 70
St. Rose's Home, 336–37
St. Vincent's Hospital, New York
City, 338
Saperstein, David, 154, 259, 315–16
Schaar, Stewart, 291
Schuchardt, John, 344–46
Schulder, Diane, 294
Schulman, Jay, 294
Scoblick, Anthony, 273–74, 276
Scoblick, Mary Cain, 273, 274, 276
Seeds of Contemplation for America
(Merton), 107
Segregation, 114–16
Seven Storey Mountain, The (Merton),
101, 107

Seymour Johnson Air Force Base, 7,
339
Shapiro, Barbara, 240–42
  See also Dougherty, Barbara
  Shapiro
Shehan, Lawrence (cardinal)
  on actions of Baltimore Four,
  189–90
  as custodian of indicted priests,
  276
Shriver, Sargent, 143–44, 150
Silberman, Charles, 242
Sit-ins, Berkeley (1980), 338–39
Smith, Bob, 344–45
Smith, John Lee, 149, 152
Snyder, Mitch, 258, 261
Society of Jesus. *See* Jesuits
Society of St. Joseph. *See* Josephites
Solitary Witness (Zahn), 108
Spellman, Francis (cardinal)
  Dan's opinion of, 142–43
  financial contributions to Society
  of Jesus, 127–28
  influence of, 136
  on Laporte self-immolation,
  128–29
  position on Vietnam War, 118–19
  role in Dan's exile to Latin America, 128–32
  with troops in Vietnam, 137
Stevenson, Alden, 130, 134, 137–38
Stringfellow, William, 204, 227–30
Students for a Democratic Society
(SDS)
  Cornell chapter, 150–51
  Dancis as chair of Cornell chapter,
  154–56
  Dan's conflicts with, 160
Suhard, Emmanuel (cardinal), 85,
102
Sullivan, Walter F. (bishop), 341
Sullivan, William (FBI agent), 269
Sullivan, William (U.S. ambassador),
183–84, 371n7
Susman, Sue, 291

Teilhard de Chardin, Pierre, 84,
113–14